Randall J. Brewer

THE SHEPHERD KING
LESSONS FROM THE LIFE OF DAVID

RANDALL J. BREWER

"The Lord has sought for Himself a man after His own heart"
1 Samuel 13:14

PUBLISHED by PARABLES
Earthly Stories with a Heavenly Meaning

Randall J. Brewer

The Shepherd King
Randall J. Brewer

Published By Parables
June, 2020

All Rights Reserved. No part of this book may be reproduced or utilized in any form or by any means, electronic or mechanical, including photocopying, recording, or by any information storage and retrieval system, without permission in writing from the author.

    ISBN 978-1-951497-72-9
    Printed in the United States of America

Readers should be aware that Internet Web sites offered as citations and/or sources for further information may have been changed or disappeared between the time this was written and the time it is read.

THE SHEPHERD KING
LESSONS FROM THE LIFE OF DAVID

RANDALL J. BREWER

""The Lord has sought for Himself a man after His own heart"
1 Samuel 13:14

Randall J. Brewer

"INTRODUCTION"

Next to Jesus, there is more written about David than any other person in the Bible. Abraham and Joseph each had fourteen chapters devoted to their individual lives and Elijah had ten chapters. As great as these men were, the number of chapters telling of their lives does not compare to what was written about David. In the Bible there are sixty-six chapters that chronicle the life of David from his youth to his forty-year reign as king and finally his death. Not only that, his name is mentioned fifty-nine times in the New Testament. The reason for all this is that God wants you to know about David and the lessons you can learn from the life he lived. God said in Is. 55:4, "Indeed I have given him as a witness to the people, a leader and a commander for the people."

God chose David to be a model of how people are to respond to life's circumstances. What makes David so special was that he was a man after God's own heart (1 Sam. 13:14). This was said about nobody else in the Bible. This is important because what's in the heart is what determines if a person is qualified for leadership and other important tasks in the kingdom of God. David was called and commanded to be king over Israel but the dream of his heart was to be a lover of God in a way that deeply moved Him. Throughout history God has sought for people who would love and respond to Him in such a way. 2 Chron. 16:9 says, "For the eyes of the Lord run to and fro throughout the whole earth, to show Himself strong on behalf of those whose heart is loyal to Him."

Even as a youth David1determined in his heart to receive the love of God and to return that same love back to Him. He diligently pursued the Lord throughout every season of his life. Above all, David was a student of the beauty of God. He wrote in Ps. 27:4, "One thing I have desired of the Lord, that I will seek: That I may dwell in the house of the Lord all the days of my life, to behold the beauty of the Lord, and to inquire in His temple." David gazed upon the Lord and asked Him many questions. The Message Bible says, "I'll contemplate His beauty; I'll study at His feet." David saw the beauty of the heart of God, the way He thinks and feels, the way He responded when David called upon Him. David saw himself through the lens of God's grace just like you're to see yourself in the plan of redemption.

David lived a thousand years after Abraham and a thousand years before Christ. His life was a foreshadow of what was to come for it contains many pictures of the ministry of Jesus. As a teenager David was chosen to be king proving that God can use anybody, at any time, if their heart is right toward Him. You can see the heart of David in many of the psalms he wrote. Consider Ps. 25:4,5, "Show me Your ways, O Lord; Teach me your paths. Lead me in Your truth and teach me, for You are the God of my salvation; On You I wait all the day." You can't be a great leader if God is not your leader. David was radical in his quest to obey God. He failed many times but always resolved to get himself back into the graces of God.

People are drawn to the story of David because he lived a very exciting life. As a teenager he killed a lion and a bear and his encounter with Goliath is probably the best-known Bible story of all time. His faith in God that gave him the courage to face the giant and kill him is legendary. His story is inspirational for he knew how to trust God in the depths of depression and in the midst of great danger. He continually offered high praises to God as he saw Him in all His glory. The songs he wrote are still read today as they point you to the same God he knew. David was a mighty warrior and a leader of men but he always allowed his faith in God to direct the course of his career. Acts 13:36 (NIV) says David "served God's purpose in his own generation."

David was a great king and he was also a prophet and judge, and the priest of his people (1 Sam. 30:7). He was also a great sinner. When he sinned he took hold of God's grace and forgiveness, teaching you to also hope in God's mercy for yourself. People can see themselves in the life of David and this is why they can relate to him and the events that took place in his life. Yes, David was a flawed man and made many mistakes but he was still chosen by God to be king over Israel. It is also important to note that it was through the bloodline of David that God would send His only begotten Son into the world, the King of kings and Lord of lords. In Matt. 1:1 Jesus is called the Son of David, the man whose life this book is about.

Randall J. Brewer

-1-

"PRAYER FOR A KING"

The story of David began many years before he was born. It began in the life of a barren woman named Hannah. The name "Hannah" means "grace" and she needed it because of the hardship she would go through. At this time in history, Israel was in a state of transition. It was going from the time of the judges to the time when kings would rule and reign over the land. As strange as it may sound, many times in the Bible when God was about to do a great and mighty work, He began with a barren woman. God told Abraham that he would one day be the father of many nations. This promise was made at a time when Abraham's wife was barren and could not have children. Years of pain and frustration went by when ultimately God moved and did something great. Sarah was in her nineties when she gave birth to Isaac. From Sarah's barrenness all the nations of the world would be blessed. Isaac would later go through the same trial. After twenty years of marriage, his wife Rebekah had still not given birth to a child and was believed to be barren. Isaac prayed for her and she conceived giving birth to twin boys, Esau and Jacob.

The mindset of the day is if you were childless, you were actually cursed by God. When Jacob's wife Leah conceived and bore a son she said, "The Lord has surely taken away my affliction" (Gen. 29:32). Back then, not having children was seen as an affliction. Some rabbis went so far as to say you couldn't go to heaven if you had no children. And, in some cases, barrenness was a grounds for divorce. Jacob had a second wife, the beautiful Rachel, who could not have children. One day she said to her husband, "Give me children, or else I die!" (Gen. 30:1). Rachel would later become the mother of Joseph and, sad to say, would die giving birth to Benjamin. Another woman in scripture who was childless was Samson's mother, the wife of Manoah of the tribe of Dan. She was miraculously healed and bore a son who would save God's people from forty years of bondage to the Philistines. In the New Testament, Elizabeth was also barren but God touched her life in her old age and she conceived and gave birth to John the Baptist.

Hannah was an incredible woman who was in deep emotional pain. She couldn't have children and was scorned and ridiculed by her husband's second wife who could. 1 Sam. 1:6,7 (MSG) says, "But her rival wife taunted her cruelly, rubbing it in and never letting her forget that God had never given her children. This went on year after year. Every time she went to the sanctuary of God she could expect to be taunted. Hannah was reduced to tears and had no appetite." It takes little imagination to feel the pain Hannah must be in, the deep anguish in her soul. There are many stories in the Bible where a man had more than one wife. It needs to be pointed out that God never once said this was acceptable. He gave Adam one wife, not two. The Bible records history as it happened but that doesn't mean everything was the will of God. Eph. 5:31 says, "For this reason a man shall leave his father and mother and be joined to his wife, and the two shall become one flesh." Not three, not four. Two! One man, one woman. In the Bible, whenever a man had two or more wives, all you read about is pain, heartache, and frustration.

There is confusion and turmoil in the household of Elkanah. His wife Peninnah provoked his other wife Hannah and tried to make her miserable. The word "provoke" means 'to stir up.' Day after day, year after year, Hannah would suffer the ridicule of this evil woman. There is conflict between these two women who had the same husband who was caught in the middle of it all. This family was a reflection of what the nation of Israel was like at that particular time in history. There are problems in the nation both physically and spiritually. They were at war with the Philistines and Judges 21:25 says, "In those days there was no king in Israel; everyone did what was right in his own eyes." There is no leadership in Israel and the priests are corrupt (1 Sam. 2:12). The nation had turned away from God and didn't realize that He was about to raise up a man to bring the people back. Unknown to Hannah, God was about to touch her life and allow her to give birth to the first prophet to bring revival to a nation, the same prophet who would one day anoint a teenager named David to be king over Israel.

Deep in her heart, all Hannah wanted was to be equal to her rival and have children like everyone else. Having children was a sign of God's blessing. Ps. 127:3-5 says, "Behold, children are a heritage from the Lord, the fruit of the womb is His reward. Like arrows in the hand of a warrior, so are the children of one's youth. Happy is the man who has his quiver full of them." In the culture of that time, having children was everything. People lived in a society where everybody contributed to the community and the welfare of everyone else. It was the responsibility of the children to take care of their parents in old age. Also, the more children you had, the more workers you had on your farm which gave you a greater chance for success and prosperity. Sons were especially important because they'd be able to protect the family from rival tribes and clans and help maintain a place of peace and security. Women at that time who gave birth to many children, especially sons, were looked upon as heroes. That was their role, that was how they contributed to the welfare of the family and the community they lived in.

Hannah was in pain because barrenness meant there was no hope for the future. Her soul is in turmoil and her heart is ripped in two. What good was her life if she couldn't have children? She was accepting what society was offering to her but she was giving nothing back. This caused people to avoid her and talk about her behind her back. If she was going to matter, if her life was to have purpose, then she was going to have to have children. If not, then she really wasn't worth anything. To her credit, not one time does scripture say she responded to those who criticized her. She did, however, find a way to deal with her pain. 1 Sam. 1:9 says, "So Hannah arose after they had finished eating and drinking in Shiloh." This verse is saying she did more than just stand up. This is a Hebrew phrase saying she decided to take action. After years and years of scorn and ridicule, Hannah arose and decided to do something about the pain she is in. No longer is she going to feel sorry for herself and no longer is she going to continue on the same path she's been on for many, many years.

What is so remarkable about Hannah is she is going to show you the means in which to process whatever pain you may be in. The truth is, most people don't know what to do with their pain. They go to God and say, "Why me, Lord?" They ask, "What should I do? Where should I go? How can I make the pain go away?" Hannah knew the answer to these questions. She rose up, she said enough is enough, and she went straight to the Lord in prayer where ultimately she arrived at a place of great peace. Vs. 10 says, "And she was in bitterness of soul, and prayed to the Lord and wept in anguish." No matter what you're going through, God wants your eyes to be on Him because many great works of redemption are birthed in a time of hopelessness and despair. You must process your pain through prayer for it is only through prayer that you'll ever arrive at a place of peace. Jesus is called the Wonderful Counselor (Is. 9:6) and the Holy Spirit is called the Comforter (John 14:16). Is. 11:2

says about Jesus, "The Spirit of the Lord shall rest upon Him, the Spirit of wisdom and understanding, the Spirit of counsel and might, the Spirit of knowledge and of the fear of the Lord."

Concerning prayer, Heb. 4:16 says, "Let us therefore come boldly to the throne of grace, that we may obtain mercy and find grace to help in time of need." The word "boldly" comes from a Greek word that depicts a person who speaks his mind in an unconcealed and forthright manner and does it with great confidence. It depicts a frankness that is so bold it is often met with resistance, hostility, and opposition. You don't have to worry about that happening with the Lord. The Message Bible says, "So let's walk right up to Him and get what He is ready to give. Take the mercy, accept the help." When you go to the Lord in prayer, never fear that you are being too bold or too blunt with Him. Take comfort knowing He wants to hear exactly what you have to say. Be respectful when you pray, but never be ashamed to speak exactly what's on your heart. Don't act like some "holy roller" who never has a problem. God knows what you're going through and He's waiting for you to talk to Him about it. Like Hannah, pour your soul out to Him and lay all your problems at His feet.

More than anything, Hannah wanted to identify herself with the children she so desperately wanted. She saw children not as an inconvenience, not as a burden financially, but as a blessing from God. She also knew that good parents are those who would rely upon God's strength and be committed to each other and their children no matter what. So, in her brokenness and pain, Hannah trusted in God's power and ability to work on her behalf. This was a holy moment as she poured out her soul to the Lord. She was humbled, broken, and knew the only way to find relief was in God alone. She begins her prayer by saying, "O Lord of hosts..." (vs. 11). This term is found throughout the Bible. Indeed, God is the

Lord of angelic hosts. Hannah is saying her God is the Lord of the biggest army in all the universe. All the heavenly angels are at His sovereign command for He is the universal ruler over every force whether in heaven or on earth. When you pray, do so with the right perspective. Know who you're talking to. Hannah did for she knew God is the Commander of the armies of heaven.

Hannah prayed to God and made a vow to Him. She said if He would give her a male child "then I will give him to the Lord all the days of his life, and no razor shall come upon his head" (1 Sam. 1:11). This was the vow of a Nazirite, the same vow received by Samson (Judges 13:5) and John the Baptist (Luke 1:13-17). Num. 6:2-8 says a person who has taken this vow couldn't eat grapes or drink wine, they couldn't touch any dead thing, and they could never cut their hair. These are all symbols of dedication and consecration to God. It was a picture of being set apart for holy service unto the Lord. Hannah vowed to make her son a Nazirite for his entire life. She was saying, "Give me a son, and I'll give him back to You." Under the Mosaic law, if you made a vow, you were obligated to keep that vow (Num. 30:2; Deut. 23:21). Eccl. 5:4,5 (NLT) says, "When you make a promise to God, don't delay in following through, for God takes no pleasure in fools. Keep all the promises you make to Him. It is better to say nothing than to make a promise and not keep it."

Num. 30:12 says a husband can make void any vow his wife makes. This Elkanah did not do and Hannah's vow to the Lord remained as she had spoken it. Her husband was from the priestly tribe of Levi (1 Chron. 6:16-30) which meant their son could begin serving in the tabernacle at age twenty-five until the age of fifty (Num. 8:24-26). Hannah, however, wasn't going to wait that long. She vowed to give her son to the Lord at the earliest possible age and he would serve God all the days of his life. Unknown to Hannah as she prayed, she was being watched by Eli the high priest. He is not used to seeing emotional prayers such as this and wrongly assumes that Hannah is drunk (vs. 13). She answers him and says, "No, my lord, I am a woman of sorrowful spirit. I have drunk neither wine nor intoxicating drink, but have poured out my soul before the Lord" (vs. 15). Notice how Hannah described her prayer. It was a heartfelt, and spontaneous expression of what she was feeling on the inside. Ps. 55:22 says, "Cast your burden on the Lord, and He shall sustain you; He shall never permit the righteous to be moved."

Eli heard what Hannah said and answered her, "Go in peace, and the God of Israel grant your petition which you have asked of Him" (vs. 17). Hannah now believed her prayer would be answered so she "went her way and ate, and her face was no longer sad." When you pour out your heart honestly to God, there is a lifting of the countenance for fervent prayer brings feelings of peace. Phil. 4:6,7 (NLT) says, "Don't worry about anything; instead, pray about everything. Tell God what you need, and thank Him for all He has done. Then you will experience God's peace, which exceeds anything we can understand. His peace will guard your hearts and minds as you live in Christ Jesus." The Message Bible says, "It's wonderful what happens when Christ displaces worry at the center of your life." The cure for worry is prayer. Some people may think their trial is too small to bring before God. They only bring the big problems to Him. The problem with that is there is nothing in life that would be considered big to God. He spins the universe, after all. Your problem may be big to you but it's not big to Him.

1 Sam. 1:19 says, "Then they rose early in the morning and worshiped before the Lord, and returned and came to their house at Ramah. And Elkanah knew Hannah his wife, and the Lord remembered her." Notice that Hannah and her husband worshiped God before she became pregnant, not afterward. They worshiped not because the Lord blessed

them in a certain way, but because of who He is. That is true worship. It's a response to God from the heart for who He is and not for what He does. Ps. 145:3 says, "Great is the Lord, and greatly to be praised." When Hannah prayed she said to the Lord, "Remember me, and forget not Your maidservant" (vs. 11). God did remember her and vs. 20 says, "So it came to pass in the process of time that Hannah conceived and bore a son, and called his name Samuel, saying, 'Because I have asked for him from the Lord.'" God is a good God, a faithful God. He hears prayers and He answers them. The name "Samuel" means "God heard." Hannah prayer and God answered. He heard her prayer so she named her son "God heard."

God is a sovereign God "who works all things according to the counsel of His will" (Eph. 1:11). This is why you need to seek after His will and not your own. God used Hannah's barrenness to get her in line with His purposes. If God answered her the first time she prayed, then Samuel would have been raised as any other normal child. This means God wouldn't have had the man He had in Samuel who would bring revival to the nation at a time when people weren't listening to Him and doing what was right in their own eyes. Hannah would give her son to the Lord but not until she had weaned him first (vs. 22). This process took three to five years, probably closer to five. In Hebrew the word "wean" means 'to deal fully with a child' and has the idea of instruction as well. Hannah was instructing her son from an early age to follow the Lord. The Hebrews were serious about weaning, training, and preparing a child for life. Paul wrote in 2 Tim. 3:15 (GWT), "From infancy you have known the Holy Scriptures. They have the power to give you wisdom so that you can be saved through faith in Christ Jesus."

Children need to be nurtured because most of a person's character is developed during the first five years of their life.

They need to have concentrated time spent with them and they need to be trained in the things of God. This is so important because a parent's window of opportunity to have an input in a child's life is very limited. There's a period where a child will let you into their world so wisely take advantage of this opportunity that's been given to you. The sad truth is, some parents spend more time training their dog to fetch a stick than they do molding their children and training them in the ways of the Lord. Children quickly grow up and before long their peers will have a greater influence on their lives than the parents. And remember, it's not the job of the Sunday school to give your children spiritual training, it's your job. A truth in life is it's easier to build up a child than it is to repair an adult who is broken. Elkanak said to Hannah, "Do what seems best to you; wait until you have weaned him. Only let the Lord establish His word" (vs. 23).

Elkanah was telling Hannah that she made a vow to God, now she must keep that vow. The Message Bible says, "Yes! Let God complete what He has begun!" Vs. 23 goes on to say, "So the woman stayed and nursed her son until she had weaned him." You also must be a person who keeps their word. Be a person of character and do what you say you're going to do. If you make a promise, keep it! Let your "Yes" be "Yes" and your "No" be "No" (Matt. 5:37). Once the child was weaned, Hannah was faithful and strong to keep her vow to the Lord. She knew that God's purposes for the child were greater than her own. She brought the young child to Eli the high priest and from that day forward Samuel served the Lord for the rest of his life. She said to Eli, "Therefore I also have lent him to the Lord; as long as he lives he shall be lent to the Lord" (vs. 28). The word "lent" means 'an irrevocable giving to the Lord.' From an early age, Samuel would be loving God and bringing revival to a wayward nation. And because of her faithfulness, God honored Hannah and gave her five more children (1 Sam. 2:21).

Through all the pain and suffering, and ultimately joy and peace, Hannah saw how God works but also saw who He is. 1 Sam. 2:1-10 records a prophetic prayer spoken by Hannah to the Lord. The language of this prayer is woven beautifully into a hymn of praise as she considers those who mocked her and how the Lord has treated her. What a contrast this prayer is from the weeping prayer of anguish before the Lord in the previous chapter. She begins by saying, "My heart rejoices in the Lord; My horn is exalted in the Lord. I smile at my enemies, because I rejoice in Your salvation" (vs. 1). To Hannah, God is a God who brings salvation. This is not referring to eternal life. The word "salvation" used here means 'deliverance from harm, ruin, or loss.' Hannah is rejoicing because the Lord has made her strong and saved her from being barren. Vs. 2 says, "There is none holy like the Lord, for there is none besides You, nor is there any rock like our God." In other words, God is in a class all by Himself. He is a God of absolute perfection. He is high above all others and no one can compare to Him.

The love of God is a holy love as is His mercy and compassion. To have a relationship with a holy God, you also must be holy. Set yourself apart from the world and live by God's standards. 1 Peter 2:9 describes believers as "a holy nation." Holiness comes from having a right relationship with God by believing in Jesus Christ as your Lord and Savior (John 3:16). God is unchanging so allow Him to be your Rock, the foundation on which you stand. God is also a God of knowledge. Vs. 3 says, "Talk no more so very proudly; Let no arrogance come from your mouth. for the Lord is the God of knowledge; And by Him actions are weighed." The NLT says, "Stop acting so proudly and haughty! Don't speak with such arrogance! For the Lord is a God who knows what you have done; He will judge your actions." God knows everything (1 John 3:20). He knows when the sparrow falls to the ground (Matt. 10:29) and He knows the number of hairs on your head (vs. 30). He knows your thoughts before you speak them out (Ps. 139:4) and Solomon said in 1 Kings 8:39, "For You, only You, know the hearts of all the sons of men."

Hannah learned what to remember in your pain as you go to God in prayer, that He humbles those who are proud, and exalts those who are humble. She prayed in vs. 4,5, "The bows of the mighty men are broken, and those who stumbled are girded with strength. Those who were full have hired themselves out for bread, and those who were hungry have ceased to hunger. Even the barren has borne seven, and she who has many children has become feeble." Hannah is saying that God is sovereign and has the absolute right to do all things according to His own good pleasure. Vs. 8 says, "He raises the poor from the dust and lifts the beggar from the ash heap, to set them among princes and make them inherit the thrones of glory." This is the pattern of how God does things. He gives strength to those who are weak. To those who have no ability, God's ability shows up. Hannah saw her own inability to bring a child into this world and threw herself completely on the ability of God. She summarizes what she's learned in vs. 9 where she said, "For by strength no man shall prevail." The NLT says, "No one will succeed by strength alone."

Hannah saw that God's strength always works through human weakness. Paul had a problem, a thorn in the flesh, and he wrote in 2 Cor. 12:8-10 (NLT), "Three different times I begged the Lord to take it away. Each time He said, 'My grace is all you need. My power works best in weakness.' So now I am glad to boast about my weaknesses, so that the power of Christ can work through me. That's why I take pleasure in my weaknesses, and in the insults, hardships, persecutions, and troubles that I suffer for Christ. For when I am weak, then I am strong." The Message Bible says, "I just let Christ take over! And so the weaker I get, the stronger I become." Hannah knew what God had to remind Paul of a thousand years later. She knew what Jesus said in Luke 18:27, "The things which are impossible with men are possible with God." She also knew that "the Lord is near to those who have a broken heart, and saves such as have a contrite spirit" (Ps. 34:18). The Message Bible says, "If your heart is broken, you'll find God right there; if you're kicked in the gut, He'll help you catch your breath."

Those who God uses over and over again are people like Hannah, those who say, "God, I can't but You can. Your grace is sufficient for me." When you say, "God, I am weak," God says, "That's okay, I am strong." Your inability is always the place where God's ability will work. Vs. 10 (MSG) says, "God's enemies will be blasted out of the sky, crashed in a heap and burned. God will set things right all over the earth, He'll give strength to His king, He'll set His anointed on top of the world!" Inspired by the Holy Spirit, Hannah is writing about two people in this verse. The book of 1 Samuel is about the search for a true king. Ultimately, Jesus will be the true King who rules over all the earth and this verse is prophetic of His dominion and reign. Here in 1 Samuel, however, the true king to come will be David. The people would later choose Saul to be their first king but this wasn't God's choice. Hannah said God would give strength to His king, a king after His own heart, a king who will act and lead in a manner worthy of the throne.

There was no king in Israel at the time Hannah's prayer for a king was spoken but here she is talking about one who will be anointed. The Hebrew word for "anointed" is "Messiah" and David was a type and shadow of the true King who was to come. This is why Jesus is called the Son of David. Mary, the Lord's mother, after she conceived also wrote a poetic song in Luke 1:46-55 that is based on what Hannah said centuries before. In vs. 46,47 she says, "My soul magnifies the Lord, and my spirit has rejoiced in God my Savior." Vs. 52,53 says, "He has put down the mighty from their thrones, and exalted the lowly. He has filled the hungry with good things, and the rich He has sent away empty." Mary is the ultimate Hannah, the one God used to bring the true King into the world. Matt. 5:3 says, "Blessed are the poor in spirit." Blessed are people like Hannah and Mary because they're the ones God can and will use in a mighty way. This happens when people submit to the plan of God. Hannah gave her son to the work of God, and Mary did also.

-2-

"PROPHET OF THE LORD"

Samuel ministered to the Lord before Eli the priest (1 Sam. 2:11) at a time when Israel was in a darkened spiritual environment. There were no rules to follow so the people made up their own rules and did what was right in their own eyes. Corruption was everywhere. The leadership was corrupt as was all the nation and the religious community. In the midst of all this, the child Samuel served the Lord and performed priestly, Levitical duties. If your heart is right, never think you're too young to be used in service to the Lord. God called Jeremiah when he was young (Jer. 1:6,7) and Daniel served in Babylon as a young man (Dan. 1:10). Timothy was also a young man and Paul wrote to him and said, "Let no one despise your youth, but be an example to the believers in word, in conduct, in love, in spirit, in faith, in purity" (1 Tim. 4:12). The Message Bible says, "Teach believers with your life." God can use anybody at any age. Abraham and Moses were both old men when God called them. All God wants is people to say to Him, "Lord, use me. I want to be involved in Your plan for this world. Not my will, but Yours be done."

It is during a person's early years when they start seeking answers to the big questions in life. They ask, "Why am I here? What is the meaning of life? What happens when I die?" Young people are more open to the gospel message at an early age for people become more calloused as they get older. This is why more conversions happen at a very young age. The majority of people who get saved do so before the age of thirty. Why is that? Because the older a person gets, the more set in their ways they become. They're not as open-minded as they were in their younger days. Studies have shown that odds diminish with age that a person will give their life to Jesus. It truly is a genuine miracle when an older person gets born again. As a youngster Samuel served under Eli the high priest but 1 Sam. 2:12 says, "Now the sons of Eli were corrupt; they did not know the Lord." A lot of people have religion but they don't have a personal relationship with God. The word "corrupt" literally means they were the sons of Belial.

In scripture, the name "Belial" was used to personify wickedness and worthlessness. The only time the word is used to identify a person is 2 Cor. 6:15 where the name is applied to Satan. The Old Testament uses this name as a personification of evil and not as an actual entity. There is no indication in scripture that Belial is the name of a specific demon. The sons of Eli, Hophni and Phinehas, were working in the house of the Lord but they were wicked and worthless. They did not know God which means they were children of the devil. Jesus said in Matt. 23:27, "Woe to you, scribes and Pharisees, hypocrites! For you are like whitewashed tombs which indeed appear beautiful outwardly, but inside are full of dead men's bones and all uncleanness." Vs. 28 (MSG) says, "People look at you and think you're saints, but beneath the skin you're total frauds." It's true, there are people who go to church who are not what they seem to be. Jesus said, "Not everyone who says to Me, 'Lord, Lord,' shall enter the kingdom of heaven, but he who does the will of My Father in heaven" (Matt. 7:21).

The problem with not having a relationship with God is people won't have a fear of God. It doesn't bother them when they sin so they go about doing what is right in their own eyes. People who fear the Lord have respect and honor for Him and want to obey Him because of how much they love Him. People who don't fear God only go through the motions. They're not what they seem. They talk the talk but don't walk the walk. The sons of Eli were corrupt in the way they handled the people's sacrifices to the Lord (vs. 13-16). The law said the priest was to take the animal sacrifice, offer it to God, then cook it. The priest would then take some of the meat for himself for this was his portion. The sons of Eli, however, did not follow the proper order of how God wanted things done. Instead, they wanted their portion first before the animal was offered to God. This was not right and was considered a great sin before the Lord. Vs. 17 says, "Therefore the sin of the young men was very great before the Lord, for men abhorred the offering of the Lord."

Here is the power of a bad example. The true worshipers of God began to despise worship because of the corruption of Eli's sons. This proves that a person will follow the footsteps of a leader faster than they'll follow their advice. Eli would later confront his sons and say, "No, my sons! For it is not a good report that I hear. You make the Lord's people transgress" (1 Sam. 2:24). People are watching you and not living a godly life can cause them to sin against God. When David sinned with Bathsheba the prophet Nathan told him, "By this deed you have given great occasion to the enemies of the Lord to blaspheme" (2 Sam. 12:14). In contrast to the sons of Eli, vs. 18 says, "But Samuel ministered before the Lord, even as a child, wearing a linen ephod." This was a priestly garment for Samuel was being groomed for the priesthood. Prov. 22:6 says, "Train up a child in the way he should go, and when he is old he will not depart from it." The Message Bible says, "Point your kids in the right direction." Apparently, the sons of Eli were not trained in a proper, godly manner.

The Hebrew word for "train" means 'to put something into the mouth or to create a taste for.' It means to stimulate a godly taste for something. You do that by setting a godly example for your children to follow. Abraham Lincoln once said, "For a man to train up a child in the way he should go has to walk that way himself." If you live a godly life in this dark world, your children and those around you will notice it. You are the light of the world and God will use you to make a difference in their lives. 1 Sam. 2:21 says "the child Samuel grew before the Lord." No matter how bad the world gets, there will always be people on fire for God. These are the ones He will raise up and use in a powerful way. Just like in the days of old, the world today needs spiritual leaders who will stand up and live godly lives and walk in the truth of God's Word. It goes without saying how bad it was in the land of Israel during the early days of Samuel. The sons of Eli had sexual relations with the women who served at the tabernacle and all their father did was give them a slap on the wrist (vs. 22-25).

When leaders close their eyes to sin and look the other way, it causes people to turn their backs on God and the Christian lifestyle. As dark as the nation was, there was a light at the end of the tunnel. Vs. 26 says, "And the child Samuel grew in stature, and in favor both with the Lord and men." Light shines in the darkest places. The spiritual darkness that the nation of Israel was in was the best time to turn on a spiritual light. When people willfully sin, when they openly rebel against God, it is a sure thing that God will deal with them. An unnamed man of God came to Eli and condemned him for honoring his sons more than God (vs. 29). Never should a parent allow their children to get away with wrongdoing. Loving your children does not mean you let them do wrong without any consequences for doing so. Sin needs to be dealt with then and there. Eli knew his sons were doing wrong and he let them get away with it. The man of God then said God was going to remove Eli and his sons from the priesthood and every person in their family would die young (vs. 31,32).

What's more, this man of God told Eli that his two sons would both die on the same day (vs. 34). He then painted a picture of what the future would look like. Speaking for the

Lord, he said in vs. 35, "Then I will raise up for Myself a faithful priest who shall do according to what is in My heart and in My mind. I will build him a sure house, and he shall walk before My anointed forever." Just like Hannah's prayer for a king, this verse also has a double reference. Samuel is going to take over as priest at that time but a thousand years later Jesus will come as the great High Priest who will offer up His life as a sacrifice for all sin. Vs. 36 says the offspring of Eli will come and bow down before this priest wanting to be made priests as well but will not be allowed to do so. When you openly disobey God, you can expect Him to discipline you. Gal. 6:7,8 says, "Do not be deceived, God is not mocked; for whatever a man sows, that he will also reap. For he who sows to the flesh will of the flesh reap corruption, but he who sows to the Spirit will of the Spirit reap everlasting life."

In the Bible, God would often speak to the people through the voice of the prophet of whom Samuel was the first. 1 Sam. 3:1 says, "Then the boy Samuel ministered to the Lord before Eli. And the word of the Lord was rare in those days; there was no widespread revelation." God wasn't speaking because the people weren't listening. They were too busy doing what was right in their own eyes. They didn't understand that hearing from God is a privilege, a treasure never to be taken for granted. The truth be told, because of their sinful lifestyle, most of the people didn't want to hear what God had to say anyway. Many had the attitude of Pharaoh who said to Moses. "Who is the Lord, that I should obey His voice to let Israel go? I do not know the Lord, nor will I let Israel go" (Ex. 5:2). God had spoken to the nation several times in the past but the people weren't obeying what He had already said. When people don't obey God, rarely will He speak to them, if at all. It also doesn't help when the spiritual leaders are more corrupt than the people they've been sent to minister to.

The Shepherd King

Darkness was covering the land of Israel, both morally and spiritually. Vs. 2 says the lamp of God was about to go out in the tabernacle. God said in Ex. 27:20 that this lamp should burn continually and the priest's job was to never let it run out of oil. Nobody filled the lamp this day and the flame was dying out. This is a picture of the priesthood at this time and the nation of Israel as a whole. In the midst of this darkness, there was a young lad named Samuel who was about to hear God speak to him. He is going to be called upon to rekindle the flame of God in the hearts of the people. You are called to do the same thing. Let your light shine and don't be afraid to be bold for Jesus. While Samuel was lying down to sleep the Lord called to him and the boy said, "Here I am!" (vs. 4). That is always a good thing to say when God calls your name. Samuel didn't know this was God speaking so he ran to Eli thinking it was him. The high priest said, "I did not call; lie down again" (vs. 5). And Samuel did as he was told.

Here was a young boy with a heart to serve God and his whole life was in front of him. The great evangelist Dwight L. Moody once had a meeting where he said two and a half people got saved. His wife asked, "Do you mean two adults and one child?" He said back to her, "No, two children, one adult. The adult has already wasted half of his life. The children have their whole life to live for God." Think about that. Twice more God called to Samuel with the lad thinking it was the high priest calling him. Then Eli perceived that the Lord had called the boy. He told Samuel to lie down and if it happens again say, "Speak, Lord, for Your servant hears" (Vs. 8,9). Samuel is called a servant of God revealing that hearing from God requires availability and an active involvement in the things of God. Samuel lived in the tabernacle and he was a servant of the high priest. He worked and did whatever needed to be done. He is ministering to the Lord and here God is speaking to him. People who don't hear from God are probably spiritually inactive.

1 Sam. 3:10 says, "Then the Lord came and stood and called as at other times, 'Samuel! Samuel!' And Samuel answered, 'Speak, for Your servant hears.'" The word "hears" means 'to pay heed to.' It means to be actively listening in order to obey. Samuel was saying, "Speak, Lord, for I am listening to You in order that I might obey what You say." You should be telling God the same thing because a willingness to obey is required if you are to hear the voice of God when He speaks. Notice that God called Samuel all these times but didn't reveal His will to him until the boy said he would obey Him. Hearing from God requires a willingness to obey Him no matter what it is He wants you to do. Become a living sacrifice for God (Rom. 12:1) and be willing to endure whatever He calls you to do for His name's sake. Place God's eternal plan and purpose above your own. If you'll do that, you'll hear from God. Samuel had a heart that was willing and obedient and God said to him in vs. 11, "Behold, I will do something in Israel at which both ears of everyone who hears it will tingle."

The Message Bible says, "Listen carefully. I'm getting ready to do something in Israel that is going to shake everyone up and get their attention." God proceeded to tell Samuel that His judgment against Eli and his house would be fulfilled. God calls those in ministry to a higher standard, to live head and shoulders above all others. This Eli and his sons did not do. The sons did wrong and Eli did not refrain them from doing so (vs. 13). Prov. 19:18 says to discipline your children while there is hope because, if you don't, you'll ruin their lives. Every child needs a father's firm, fair, and consistent discipline as well as a mother's supervision and companionship during the day. This did not happen in the household of Eli. There was no repentance from Eli or his sons and they were now going to be held accountable for the notorious sins that plagued their lives. Vs. 14 (NLT) says, "So I have vowed that the sins of Eli and his sons will never be forgiven by sacrifices of offerings." Hearing from God may not always be pleasant. Be aware of that. Be willing to obey anyway.

1 Sam. 3:15 says, "So Samuel lay down until morning, and opened the doors of the house of the Lord. And Samuel was afraid to tell Eli the vision." Here is a lad called to be a prophet of God and he's afraid to say the truth. Speaking on God's behalf is not always easy. One is reminded of when the prophet Nathan was called upon by God to confront David with his sin of adultery and murder. The next morning Eli called to Samuel and asked what the Lord said to him. He said, "Please do not hide it from me. God do so to you, and more also, if you hide anything from me of all the things that He said to you" (vs. 17). Samuel then told Eli everything and hid nothing from him. Eli then said, "It is the Lord. Let Him do what seems good to Him" (vs. 18). Hearing from God brings with it the responsibility to tell the truth, the whole truth, and nothing but the truth. You must be willing to say what God tells you to say no matter how unpleasant it may be. Speak the truth in love (Eph. 4:15) in a gentle, kind, and inoffensive manner. Doing this causes hard truths to be more readily received.

Vs. 19-21 says, "So Samuel grew, and the Lord was with him and let none of his words fall to the ground. And all Israel from Dan to Beersheba knew that Samuel had been established as a prophet of the Lord. Then the Lord appeared again in Shiloh. For the Lord revealed Himself to Samuel in Shiloh by the word of the Lord." Hearing from God will be evident to others that you heard from Him. Everything Samuel said proved to be reliable. None of his words failed or fell to the ground. Samuel spoke to Eli who said, "It is the Lord." You don't have to manipulate people or prove yourself to anybody. Just do what God tells you to do and say what God tells you to say. Obey God and leave the results to Him. 1 Sam. 4:1 says, "And the word of Samuel came to all

Israel." God spoke to Samuel for a purpose. Not only did God speak to Samuel, He also wanted to speak through Samuel. 1 Thess. 1:8 says, "For from you the word of the Lord has sounded forth." God still speaks today and He wants to speak to you and through you to other people. Are you available? Are you listening?

The "word of the Lord" (1 Sam. 3:21) has now become equivalent to the "word of Samuel" (1 Sam. 4:1) for he is going to speak a message from God in a day when there was no widespread revelation. The problem in the nation is that God wanted to speak but the people weren't listening. So what did God do? He raised up Samuel to be His spokesman and his word is the same as if God were speaking Himself. Eli knows that judgment is coming because he failed to deal with the sins of his two sons. God told him what was coming through the words of the unnamed man of God and Samuel. Scripture next says Israel went out to battle against the Philistines (1 Sam. 4:1). These were aggressive warriors who migrated from the northern shores of Asia Minor and now occupied territory southwest of Israel between the Mediterranean Sea and the Jordan River. At first they were peaceful but eventually became unsatisfied with the portion of land they had. They then went to war with Israel in an effort to gain control and take over all the land. Israel was defeated in this battle and four thousand soldiers were killed in the field (vs. 2).

This battle is the judgment of God on the house of Eli and the nation of Israel. You win if you obey God, you lose if you don't. Remember that. The elders of Israel then asked an interesting question, "Why has the Lord defeated us today before the Philistines?" (vs. 3). They recognized that God somehow allowed this defeat to happen. Perhaps they remembered one of the curses for disobedience recorded in Deut. 28:25, "The Lord will cause you to be defeated before your enemies; you shall go out one way against them and flee seven ways before them." The problem this day is the elders didn't wait for an answer to the question they asked. Instead of praying about the situation and waiting on God, they took matters into their own hands and came up with a plan of their own making. They decided to bring the ark of the covenant from the tabernacle in Shiloh believing "that when it comes among us it may save us from the hand of our enemies" (vs. 3). They were trying to gain the victory without confessing their sin and getting right with God. As they're about to find out, you can't sneak in the back door where sin is concerned.

In times past God had promised to take care of the people if they would obey Him. As a sign of His covenant, He had the Israelites make a box according to His own design. This box was called an "ark" and it was made of acacia wood overlaid with gold. Once a year the high priest would go before the ark and offer sacrifices for the sins of the people (Lev. 16). Remember, the people were living in a time when they made up their own rules as they went along. Since the ark represented the presence of God, they reasoned having it in their midst would save them from their enemies. Doing religious things doesn't mean you have a close relationship with God. The people didn't seek God, they sought the symbol of God. They thought of the ark as a divine good luck charm. In the box God would be containable, controllable, and usable for their purposes instead of them being used for His. They were trying to manipulate God and that you cannot do. The problem with this is they are not trusting in God but in a gold-plated box. Their trust was in the ark and not God Himself.

The bottom line is God doesn't want a religion where He's not in it. Wearing a cross around your neck or hanging one on the wall doesn't mean you have a deep, personal relationship with God. Problems happen when you substitute that relationship for an image made with human hands. The elders were saying, "Bring in the box, and the box will save us." They forgot God is omnipresent. He is everywhere. David wrote in Ps. 139:7,8, "Where can I go from Your Spirit? Or where can I flee from Your presence? If I ascend into heaven, You are there; If I make my bed in hell, behold, You are there." The elders thought the presence of God was restricted to a specific place and this is why they wanted the ark brought to the battle. The wicked sons of Eli were with the ark (vs. 4) and they shouldn't have allowed it to leave the tabernacle. It was before the ark where people came to worship and where sacrifices were made. For sure, the ark should have stayed right there. Because they were already corrupt, they didn't make any kind of spiritual stand and gave in to the will of the people.

1 Sam. 4:5 says, "And when the ark of the covenant came into the camp, all Israel shouted so loudly that the earth shook." The people got very excited and emotional. Beware of this because enthusiasm doesn't mean you're in the will of God. In the parable of the sower Jesus said, "The seeds on the rocky soil represent those who hear the message and receive it with joy. But since they don't have deep roots, they believe for a while, then they fall away when they face temptation" (Luke 8:13 NLT). Some people get excited very quickly but fizzle out just as fast. God doesn't care how high you can jump, but how straight you can walk when you hit the ground. The Philistines heard all the commotion that was going on two miles away and when told the ark was in the camp they were greatly afraid (vs. 6-8). They are in fear but got encouraged to stand up and fight like men (vs. 9). "So the Philistines fought, and Israel was defeated, and every man fled to his tent. There was a very great slaughter, and there fell of Israel thirty thousand foot soldiers" (vs. 10).

The ark of the covenant didn't help the Israelites win the battle. The box didn't save them because it couldn't save them. The faith of the people was based on superstition and not on the saving power of God. The ark of God was captured and both the sons of Eli died on the same day just like the man of God said they would. A messenger went and told Eli what happened and when he heard about the ark he fell off his seat backwards, broke his neck, and died (vs. 11-18). This was one of the worst days in the history of Israel. In one day a great slaughter happened, the people scattered, the priests are dead, and the ark of the covenant was taken in battle. How worse could it get? Judgment had come to the land of Israel. The flame had gone out. Jer. 7:12-14 indicates the ark was never returned to Shiloh because God destroyed the city because of the wickedness of the people. The pregnant wife of one of Eli's sons went into labor when she heard the ark had been captured. Before dying giving birth she named her son "Ichabod" which means, "The glory has departed from Israel" (vs. 19-22).

The word "departed" means 'to go into exile.' The ark of God went into exile. Since the people regarded the ark as the symbol of God's presence and His glory, it was as if God Himself had gone into exile. He wasn't helping them anymore nor was He coming to their aid. Unknown to the people at this time, God is going to use these challenging circumstances to bring in a time of refreshing to the land of Israel. Before spiritual renewal can take place, there needed to be a cleansing and a clearing away of the old so God could begin the work of the new. This is called "pruning" in the New Testament. Jesus said in John 15:2, "Every branch in Me that does not bear fruit He takes, and every branch that bears fruit He prunes, that it may bear more fruit." He cuts away the old branches to make room for the new branches that will grow and bear fruit. A pruned tree is a scary thing to look at. It looks dead and lifeless. However, the next year that same tree will be in full bloom producing fruit like it's supposed to. Under the leadership of Samuel, the prophet of the Lord, Israel is about to become better than it was before.

-3-

"BATTLE OF THE GODS"

The children of Israel were living in an era where there was no king in power and every person did what was right in their own eyes (Judges 21:25). They had symbols of God but not the substance of a personal relationship with Him. They were like those living today who have a Christless Christianity, people who are "lovers of pleasure rather than lovers of God, having a form of godliness but denying its power" (2 Tim. 3:4,5). The result of all this is they were acting just like their pagan neighbors. The one symbol they clung to the most was the ark of the covenant which was now in the hands of their enemy. Since the ark was made it was always associated with the presence of God. Lev. 16:2 says the cloud that appeared over the ark was a sign of God's presence and blessing. Also, 1 Sam. 4:4 says that God "dwells between the cherubim" referring to the two winged angelic beings on the ark's cover. It was at the ark where atonement was made for the forgiveness of sin through sacrifice and the shedding of blood. With the ark now in the hands of the Philistines, there is no forgiveness of sins for the people of Israel.

The Philistines believed that going to war was not one army going against another army. They believed it was one god going against another god. Every war they were in was looked upon as a battle of the gods. There is no doubt that the Philistines were jubilant because of their victory over Israel. They were overflowing with confidence in the superiority of their god over the God of Israel. The battle of the gods had been fought and their god had won. Or so they thought. The ark was taken to the city of Ashdod, one of five such Philistine cities that existed (1 Sam. 5:1). It was placed in the house of Dagon, the chief deity of the Philistines. So committed were they to this false god that they offered up a great sacrifice to him believing their idol had delivered Samson into their hands (Judges 16:23). In Hebrew the word "dag" means 'fish' and Dagon, who was said to be the father of Baal, was represented as a half-man, half-fish creature. He looked like a male mermaid and this image solidified their evolutionary belief that both man and fish evolved together from the same primal waters.

Images reveal people have a problem with an invisible God. Is. 45:15 says, "Truly You are God, who hide Yourself, O God of Israel, the Savior!" The Philistines had visible representations of their gods all over the place. The Israelites, on the other hand, had no image of their God. Ex. 20:4 says, "You shall not make for yourself any carved image, or any likeness of anything that is in heaven above, or that is in the earth beneath, or that is in the water under the earth." The reason God said this is because a statue can never express to those who gaze upon them who God is or what He is like. God doesn't want people to focus on an isolated concept of His character represented by some statue and be misled by what they see. No statue can capture His essence so He said don't make one. Why do people still make statues of God when He told them not to? People make images because they've lost a consciousness of God and need a reminder that He is there. If you're in a close relationship with God, you don't need a reminder. You talk to Him every day and His presence is real to you.

Another problem some people have is they believe God literally inhabits the images they have made. By praying to a statue, they believe they're praying to God. They relate to God by the way they relate to the statue. The truth is, you don't need a statue to see God. All you have to do is look to Jesus who said, "He who has seen Me has seen the Father" (John 14:9). The Philistines had many gods with Dagon being the primary one, later to be replaced by Baal. The Israelites, however, had only one God. By putting the ark of the covenant in the temple of Dagon, the Philistines were saying, "We won the battle. Our god is better than your God. Yahweh is inferior to Dagon." The Israelites were defeated because of their disobedience but, as the Philistines were about to find out, that doesn't mean their God was defeated. As the Philistines slept that night, in the house of Dagon another battle of the gods was taking place. It's not hard to imagine who won. The people of Ashdod arose early in the morning and found the statue of Dagon fallen on its face to the earth before the ark of the Lord (1 Sam. 5:3).

God made this statue bow down in worship before Him. When people don't glorify God, God will glorify Himself (Is. 48:9-11). Never will God go without glory. He created all people for His glory. Is. 43:7 says, "Everyone who is called by My name, whom I have created for My glory." Jesus sought the glory of the Father in all He did (John 7:18) and He told you to do good works so that the Father gets the glory (Matt. 5:16). Jesus also said He would answer your prayers so that the Father would be glorified (John 14:13). When believers have fellowship with one another, God is glorified. Rom. 15:7 says, "Therefore receive one another, just as Christ also received us, to the glory of God." 1 Cor. 10:31 says, "Therefore, whether you eat or drink, or whatever you do, do all to the glory of God." There is a penalty to pay when God is not glorified. Herod blasphemed God and Acts 12:23 says, "Then immediately an angel of the Lord struck him, because he did not give glory to God. And he was eaten by worms and died."

What did the Philistines do? "So they took Dagon and set it in its place again" (vs. 3). You don't want to serve a god you have to pick up, you want to serve a God who picks you up. Is. 41:10 says, "Fear not, for I am with you; Be not dismayed, for I am your God. I will strengthen you, yes, I will help you. I will uphold you with My righteous right hand." They put their idol back in its place and the next morning they saw that the same thing occurred. This time, however, his head and hands had been broken off and only his body remained (vs. 4). God is revealing Himself in a way these pagans will understand. In ancient times, when one people subdued another people, their heads or their hands were cut off as a token of total subjection. David cut off Goliath's head and the Philistines cut off the head of King Saul. God is making a profound statement. He's the true God and Dagon isn't. Ps. 115:5,6 says false gods have mouths but do not speak, eyes but do not see, and ears but do not hear. Everything their god isn't, God is. He speaks, He sees, He hears. And He needs no human help to stand upright.

Concerning false gods, Ps. 115:8 says, "Those who make them are like them; So is everyone who trusts in them." The psalmist is saying you'll become like the gods you worship. You can become like the false gods who are dead and lifeless, or you can become like the one, true God who is alive and well. The Philistine priests rejected God in spite of what happened and chose to believe this was all an accident. They made up a religious tradition out of it by refusing from that day forward to tread on the threshold of Dagon where his head and hands were fallen (vs. 5). They reasoned it was easier to do this than to change their thinking and the way they lived. 1 Sam. 5:6 says, "But the hand of the Lord was heavy on the people of Ashdod, and He ravaged them and struck them with tumors, both Ashdod and its territory." God isn't playing games and people are falling over dead left and right. When people close their hearts and minds to God, He often finds another way to get their attention. The people got tumors and rats ravaged the land (1 Sam. 6:5) producing panic among the affected population.

It was made clear who the true God was but the Philistines chose not to make Him their God. Jesus said in Matt. 13:14,15 (MSG), "Your ears are open but you don't hear a thing. Your eyes are awake but you don't see a thing. The people are blockheads! They stick their fingers in their ears so they won't have to listen; They screw their eyes shut so they won't have to look, so they won't have to deal with Me face-to-face." Instead of submitting to the God of Israel, they decided to get rid of Him so they carried the ark to Gath which was twelve miles to the east. The Philistines were very territorial. They weren't trying to pass their problems on to the city of Gath. No, they reasoned the God of Israel wouldn't be as strong over there as He was here. They were in for a rude awakening. The judgment of God followed them to Gath for "the hand of the Lord was against the city with a very great destruction; and He struck the men of the city, both small and great, and tumors broke out on them" (vs. 9). They then sent the ark six miles north to Ekron. The people there heard what had happened and they wanted nothing to do with the God of Israel.

The city of Ekron also suffered a deadly destruction and all the men who did not die were stricken with tumors. The people cried out telling the lords of the Philistines to send the ark back to Israel where it came from. If the people would have repented and turned toward God, the ark would have been a blessing to them. Instead, it became a curse against them and judgment fell. Even today the presence of God can be a fragrance of life to some and the aroma of death to others (2 Cor. 2:15,16). 1 Sam. 6:1 says the Philistines had the ark seven months. Why so long? They didn't want to give up their victory trophy, the symbol of their victory in the battle of the gods. Sometimes it takes a while before people realize the futility of resisting God. They now realize that the true God is in control and the ark has now become a burden to them and not a trophy. They now decide to send it back to the people of Israel. They didn't know how to do it so they called upon their priests and fortune tellers seeking their advice. They were told to return the ark with a trespass offering and hopefully they'll be healed of their tumors (vs. 3).

The people didn't know what the trespass offering should be so they were told to make five golden tumors and five golden rats, one for each of the five Philistine cities (vs. 4). Some commentators think the tumors were the result of bubonic plague carried by rats. If not stopped, the infestation of these rats were capable of destroying the entire population. They are making a weak effort to say they're sorry for what they did. They're trying to gain God's favor by performing a series of good works. This is religion and not faith. People are always trying to please God by the things they do. They think they can earn their way to heaven by doing more good things than bad. Is. 64:6 says, "And all our righteousness are like filthy rags." 1 Sam. 6:5 says, "And you shall give glory to the God of Israel. Perhaps He will lighten His hand from you, from your gods, and from your land." They are admitting that the God of Israel is judging their gods yet they refuse to worship Him as the one true God. They remembered what happened in Egypt, that no good comes when anyone hardens their heart against the Lord (vs. 6).

Hos. 10:12 (NLT) speaks to those with hardened hearts, "Plant the good seeds of righteousness, and you will harvest a crop of love. Plow up the hard ground of your hearts, for now is the time to seek the Lord, that He may come and shower righteousness upon you." The Philistines did not seek the Lord, they sought to get rid of Him. They then came up with a plan to return the ark which included a test to see if the judgment was from God or if it happened by chance. They're going to conduct an experiment. They think the calamity of the plagues came from God but they're not totally sure. They devise a way to find out, a test that will force God to do something miraculous to demonstrate that it was He who has been the cause of the plagues that came upon them. They're going to make it almost impossible for the ark to get back home naturally. 1 Sam. 6:7 says, "Now therefore, make a new cart, take two milk cows which have never been yoked, and hitch the cows to the cart; and take their calves home, away from them."

Cows that have never been yoked have never pulled anything before. They don't know how to work in unison with the other animal to pull the cart. The result of this is that these cows will fight against each other and they'll try to break free from the yoke around their neck. Also, the people decided to take their calves away from them. The maternal instinct of the mother cows would have drawn them not toward Israel but back home to search for their calves. In other words, there is no way naturally that this cart is going to make it to Israel. It will have to get there supernaturally, through the intervention of a supreme God. The people were told to put the ark on the cart with the trespass offering in a chest by its side. "Then send it away, and let it go" (vs. 8). God never wanted the ark to be transported on a cart. He wanted it to be carried by gold-plated wooden poles that were inserted into gold rings at each corner of the ark (Ex. 25:12-15). What the Philistines were doing was wrong but God excused them because of their ignorance of the law.

The cows were sent on their way. If they made it to Israel, then it was by the hand of God this judgment came. If not, then "it was by chance it happened to us" (vs. 9). Many people think things happen by chance. Some even say the world was created by chance. People who think this way are extremely ignorant and superstitious. Chance has no power and can make nothing happen. All chance can do is describe a probability, giving people an ungrounded explanation as to why something happened or didn't happen. Nothing happens by chance but everything happens by choice. The freedom of choice is the foundation that allows life to manifest itself.

What you sow is what you will reap. The Philistines followed the cows as they headed straight for the road to Beth Shemesh, the city where Samson was born. Against all expectations, the cows made it to the land of Israel. They had no driver to lead them but still they marched ten miles to a city they had never been to. This shouldn't have happened but God wasn't leaving this up to chance.

1 Sam. 6:12 says the cows were "lowing as they went." They were making a deep, grunting sound and this means the cows were not happy. They were longing for their calves back home but still they did the will of God who was able to overpower the instinctive nature of the cows. The cows indeed made it to the land of Israel and the people who were working in the fields saw it and rejoiced (vs. 13). They must have felt like the disciples did on the day they saw the resurrected Jesus. When the ark was captured the glory of God departed from Israel. The people were desperate, discouraged, and overcome with a sense of despair and hopelessness. Now, in their eyes, the Lord God of Israel has risen from the dead. The people split the wood of the cart and offered the cows as a burnt offering to the Lord. It seems as if this offering was accepted by God even though the Mosaic law said only male animals could be offered to the Lord (Lev. 1:3). The Levite priests took the ark down from the cart and made offerings up to the Lord (vs. 15).

The people of Israel then made a grave mistake. They got curious and looked inside the ark. By doing this they profaned the holiness of God. The ark of the covenant was a box containing sacred things and was only to be touched and handled by specific Levites from the family of Kohath. Even they were commanded not to touch the ark itself lest they die (Num. 4:15). Not only did the men of Beth Shemesh touch the ark, but they looked inside of it inappropriately. They were an unholy people coming into the presence of a holy God. 1 Sam. 6:19 says, "Then He struck the men of

Beth Shemesh, because they had looked into the ark of the Lord. He struck fifty thousand and seventy men of the people, and the people lamented because the Lord had struck the people with a great slaughter." God is dealing with the Israelites more strictly than He did with the Philistines. 1 Peter 4:17 says judgment begins at the house of God. He did this because the Israelites had His law and knew what they did was forbidden.

The men of Beth Shemesh asked, "Who is able to stand before this holy Lord God?" (vs. 20). These men should not have asked this question for it makes God seem too harsh instead of showing themselves to be too disobedient. They're blaming God for being overly strict while saying nothing of their disobedience. Yes, God is a holy God. The angelic creatures before the throne of God cry out continually, "Holy, holy, holy is the Lord Almighty" (Rev. 4:8). God's holiness is what separates Him from all other beings. It's what makes Him separate and distinct from everything else, both in His nature and in the perfection of His ways. When people encounter the holiness of God, many want to run away from it. When Peter saw the holy power of Jesus he said, "Depart from me, for I am a sinful man, O Lord!" (Luke 5:8). Light and darkness don't mix and it can be frightening for some when they see how different God is from themselves. Ps. 96:9 says, "Oh, worship the Lord in the beauty of holiness! Tremble before Him, all the earth." Holiness is a beautiful thing and the psalmist is saying you are to be excited and have reverential fear both at the same time.

God doesn't want you to run from His holiness, He wants you to partake of it (Heb. 12:10). God is different from the world and He wants you to be different also. 1 Peter 1:15,16 says, "But as He who called you is holy, you also be holy in all your conduct, because it is written, 'Be holy, for I am holy.'" The Message Bible says, "As obedient children, let yourselves be pulled into a way of life shaped by God's life, a life energetic and blazing with holiness." Holiness is not achieved through your own efforts but is received when you ask Jesus into your heart. Eph. 4:24 says to "put on the new man which was created according to God, in righteousness and true holiness." The men of Beth Shemesh knew God is holy but it didn't make them want to be closer to God, it made them want to distance themselves from Him. They then asked, "And to whom shall it go up from us?" (vs. 20). Like the Philistines, they wanted the ark as far away from them as possible. They weren't seeking how to make things right with God but instead asked the inhabitants of Kirjath Jearim to come and take the ark of the covenant away (vs. 21).

The men of Kirjath Jearim treated the ark of the covenant with honor and respect. They put it in a house on a hill instead of in a tabernacle where it belonged (1 Sam. 7:1). Still, they showed a desire to do the right thing which was more than the men of Beth Shemech did. The ark stayed in the home of Abinadab for twenty years and his son Eleazar was charged to look after it. Israel had the ark back but things were still not right between them and God. Instead of rejoicing, vs. 2 says "all the house of Israel lamented before the Lord." They had good reason to do this. Their cities were in ruins, their armies were defeated, and they were under the dominion of the Philistines. The word "lament" means to 'be sad, to have no joy.' They've been out of fellowship with God and sin always brings sadness. After sinning, David prayed, "Restore to me the joy of Your salvation" (Ps. 51:12). The Greek translation says, "They looked back after the Lord." They remembered the way things used to be. To have revival there must be a restlessness for God. You look back and remember how it once was, how at one time your heart was on fire for God.

The ark has been returned but it's in some obscure place nobody ever heard of. Worshiping God before the ark is no longer taking place and the people are longing for the way it once was. Without God, your soul becomes weary and all the people are feeling the effects of their wayward lifestyle. Unfortunately, it takes a catastrophe to bring some people back to the Lord. C.S. Lewis once said, "God whispers to us in our pleasures but shouts to us in our pain." He also said, "Pain is God's megaphone to rouse a deaf world." God now has their attention. When you're restless, your heart is open and receptive to the truth of God's Word. The people are ready to hear what God, speaking through Samuel, has to say to them. They'd been worshiping the same false gods as the pagans. Samuel said if they would put away these gods and serve God only, then the Lord would deliver them from the Philistines (vs. 3). With revival comes removal. Heb. 12:1 says, "Let us lay aside every weight, and the sin which so easily ensnares us." Repentance goes beyond saying you're sorry for what you did. It means to walk away from sin and start living a holy life.

1 Sam. 7:4 says, "So the children of Israel put away the Baals and the Ashtoreths, and served the Lord only." Baal was said to be the god of weather and could bring good crops and financial success. Ashtoreth was attractive to the people because she was thought to be the goddess of love and sex. Not only did the people stop doing bad things, they started doing good things. They gathered at Mizpah which was the city where Jacob separated from Laban (Gen. 31:49). Mizpah was a place remembered for separation and repentance. 2 Cor. 6:17 says, "Come out from among them and be separate, says the Lord." The people drew water and poured it out before the Lord (vs. 6). They poured out their life in submission to God. They were expressing what was said in Lam. 2:19, "Arise, cry out in the night, at the beginning of the watches; pour out your heart like water before the face of the Lord." This is what humility is all about.

The people prayed and they fasted. They took their eyes off the things of the world so they could focus completely on God. They were saying by their actions that nothing else mattered except getting right with the Lord God of Israel.

As this revival was taking place the Philistines drew near to go to battle against Israel (vs. 7). The idea was to catch the people praying, hoping they would be caught off guard. This threat of attack caused the people to be greatly afraid. They should have been more confident than they were. Still, they were humble and repentant before the Lord and will soon see a great victory. Instead of trusting in the ark to save them, they did the right thing and asked Samuel "to cry out to the Lord our God for us" (vs. 8). Samuel offered up a burnt offering and the Lord answered him. Vs. 10 says, "But the Lord thundered with a loud thunder upon the Philistines that day, and so confused them that they were overcome before Israel." In Hannah's prayer for a king she said in 1 Sam. 2:10, "The adversaries of the Lord shall be broken in pieces; From heaven He will thunder against them." She probably said that poetically but God did it literally. It is interesting to note that Baal was thought to be the god of weather and was sometimes pictured with a thunderbolt in his hand. This day God showed the Philistines who the real God of thunder was.

Samuel wanted the people to remember the victory God gave them so he set up a memorial and called it the Stone of Help (vs. 12). God is a good God and He doesn't want you to forget the good things He does for you. Ps. 78:7 says to "not forget the works of God." Your memory of the goodness of God can inspire you. He saved you before, He'll save you again. Ps. 46:1 says, "God is our refuge and strength, a very present help in trouble." Vs. 13 says, "And the hand of the Lord was against the Philistines all the days of Samuel." Vs. 14 then says that all the cities the Philistines took from Israel were restored back to the people. There was now peace in the land and Samuel judged Israel all the days of his life. He was a faithful man and worked hard in his service to the Lord. Every year he went all about Israel to help settle disputes and promote righteousness. He always returned to his home in Ramah and there he built an altar to the Lord. An altar was a place of sacrifice and worship. Samuel knew how good God is and worship is a response to Him for all the good He has done.

-4-

"LONG LIVE THE KING"

A change is happening in the land of Israel. Up until this point in time, God had always been in charge of the nation. He ruled through mediators who were divinely guided, people like Moses who raised up seventy elders to help him. Then came Joshua who brought the people into the land of Canaan, the Promised Land. After Joshua came the judges, people like Samson, Deborah, and Gideon. These God-appointed judges were given to rule, lead, and guide the people. It seems as if Samuel is going to be the last judge because the people will soon be crying out for a change. They no longer want a theocracy, a system of government in which a deity is the supreme ruler. The people of Israel are going to reject the rulership of God as they crave and desire the rulership of a king. This is not to say that having a king is a bad thing. It was predicted in Gen. 49:10 that a king would one day rule over the land, "The scepter shall not leave Judah; He'll keep a firm grip on the command staff until the ultimate ruler comes and the nations obey Him" (MSG).

The term "scepter" refers to a ruler's staff which served as a symbol of a king's honor, authority, and right to administer justice. It was the plan of God to have a king of His choosing to rule over the nation of Israel. In fact, He gives detailed instructions in Deut. 17:14-20 on how a king should act along with directions for picking a king. The people, however, refused to wait on the timing of the Lord. They wanted a king right here, right now. They pushed for it and wouldn't take no for an answer. People need to be careful what they wish for because they wanted a king at the wrong time and for the wrong reason. Biblical history records this was not the first time the children of Israel asked for a king. After Gideon defeated the Midianites the people wanted him to be their king (Judges 8:22,23). Gideon said, "I shall not be king over you. The Lord shall be your king." It wasn't God's timing then and it's not His timing now. 1 Sam. 8:1 says, "Now it came to pass when Samuel was old that he made his sons judges over Israel."

Samuel was one of the most godly men in all the Bible but it was wrong for him to make his sons judges over Israel. Judges were appointed by God and there is no pattern in the Word of the office of judge being passed from father to son. These sons, Joel and Abijah, were judges in name only. They did not walk in their father's footsteps but did evil just like the sons of Eli did. They were greedy for money and "turned aside after dishonest gain, took bribes, and perverted justice" (vs. 3). This is why Samuel was wrong to appoint his sons as judges over Israel. Showing favoritism based on kinship is a common but harmful mistake that many leaders in ministry make, especially as they grow older. Sins are excused in loved ones that are seen more clearly in others. How could these sons be so corrupt with them having a father like Samuel? Perhaps the answer is found in the fact that Samuel was a circuit preacher and he was away from home for long periods of time. He was doing the work of the Lord while his loved ones were getting left behind.

What is the answer to all this? Seek God and He will give you balance between your commitment to Him and your responsibilities toward your family. Sometimes people fall off the deep end of both sides of the equation. You can't ignore God for the sake of your family while at the same time you can't be so consumed with your work for the Lord that your family is ignored. God does not expect you to fulfill your obligation to Him at the expense of not fulfilling your God-given responsibilities toward your family. You can't obey Him in one area if it causes you to sin in another. Trust God and He will give you a plan and a schedule to do both. 1 Sam. 8:4,5 says, "Then all the elders of Israel gathered together and came to Samuel at Ramah, and said to him, 'Look, you are old, and your sons do not walk in your ways. Now make for us a king to judge us like all the nations!'" The sons of Samuel are corrupt and the people don't want them in charge once Samuel is gone. It was wise for the elders to not want leaders who were ungodly and unfit to lead.

The elders were correct in their assessment of Samuel's sons but they asked for a king for the wrong reason. They wanted a king not according to the will of God but because the other nations around them had one. In other words, they wanted to be like everybody else. In truth, some things in the world are very attractive. Even the devil comes as an angel of light (2 Cor. 11:14). Sin is pleasing to the flesh as it tries to entice you and pull you into a web of deceit, decay, and death. Nothing but trouble comes when believers want to be like the world. This is why 2 Cor. 6:17 says, "Come out from among them and be separate, says the Lord." The Message Bible says, "Don't link up with those who will pollute you. I want you all for Myself." God calls His people to be unlike the nations, to be a people governed by Him and not a king. 1 Peter 2:9 says, "But you are a chosen generation, a royal priesthood, a holy nation, His own special people, that you may proclaim the praises of Him who called you out of darkness into His marvelous light."

What is the difference between a judge and a king? A judge was a leader raised up by God to meet a specific need in a time of crisis. When the crisis passed, the judge usually went back to what he was doing before. A king, on the other hand, would establish a standing government and would reign for as long as he lived. When he died his throne would be passed down to his descendants. The people wanted a king, a visible monarch who would lead them in military battles and who would set up a national governmental structure. Forget the fact that God had fought all their battles in the past. What made Israel so unique as a nation is that they had this invisible, all-powerful God who they trusted to do everything for them. Sad to say, things are not like they once were. No longer do the people want to trust a God they cannot see, they want a king they can see, a king like the other nations have. Rom. 12:2 (Philips) says, "Don't let the world squeeze you into its mold." This is what the people are doing and Samuel was displeased in what they asked (vs. 6).

Samuel was bothered by the people's request because he saw the ungodly motive behind their desire to have a king rule over them. They were like the Jewish mob who would later cry out when Jesus stood before Pilate, "We have no king but Caesar" (John 19:15). In spite of how he felt, Samuel did not rebuke the people nor did he lash out at them. Instead, he brought it to the Lord in prayer who said, "Heed the voice of the people in all that they say to you; for they have not rejected you, but they have rejected Me, that I should not reign over them" (vs. 7). God is giving comfort to Samuel. He's saying to not take this personally. Jesus said in Luke 10:16, "He who rejects you rejects Me." God is saying the same thing to Samuel. The problem is the people wanted independence from God and that is the root of all sin. People complain and have no contentment in life because they don't want God to control their lives. They want to be in charge, not God. They wanted a king and that's how it was going to be.

Sometimes, when people insist on having something bad, God will let them have what they want in hopes they'll learn a valuable lesson through the trying consequences that follow. There's an old proverb that says you can learn the easy way or you can learn the hard way. Because the people didn't want to wait on God's timing but instead wanted a king now and for the wrong reasons, they're about to get what they want and learn a hard, valuable lesson. God told Samuel in vs. 9, "Now therefore, heed their voice. However, you shall solemnly forewarn them, and show them the behavior of the king who will reign over them." You want a king, fine, but know there will be dreadful consequences for having one. God wants the people to know the answer they're seeking will bring worse problems than they had before. With information comes responsibility and by forewarning the people Samuel is holding them accountable for the choices they're about to make. Afterward, when great harm has been done, the people will be unable to say they didn't know what was going to happen.

Thomas Jefferson once said, "Whenever a man casts a longing eye on a political office, a rottenness begins in his conduct." Without divine influence, people have a tendency to let power corrupt them. This is what will happen to the man about to become their king. Samuel then tells the people in vs. 11-18 what life will be like under this new king. Their daughters will work in the palace and cook the king's food and bake his bread. A king needs an army so their sons will be drafted into military service. He'll take their livestock and fields for his own purposes. The best of the vineyards and olive groves are going to go to the government. The people will have to plow the king's fields and a form of slavery like the people have never known since Egypt is about to develop. It's expensive to run a government so, for the first time ever, the people will have to pay taxes. This new king is going to take a tenth of their grain and a tenth of their sheep, and he'll rob them of their best harvest. Be careful and learn from this. What you wish for can be costly.

Most kings are takers, not givers. They come to be served, not to serve. Samuel attempts to tell the people that a king will only turn them into slaves instead of uniting them together as a nation. "And you will cry out in that day because of your king whom you have chosen for yourselves, and the Lord will not hear you in that day" (vs. 18). People get into bondage when they look to the government to solve their problems. Samuel is telling the people that having a king at this time isn't going to be as good a thing as they think it will be. "Nevertheless the people refused to obey the voice of Samuel; and they said, 'No, but we will have a king over us, that we also may be like all the nations'" (vs. 19,20). The Hebrew word for "refused" means 'to refuse utterly; to dig your heels in.' They're saying, "No way will we listen to you." There is none so blind as those who refuse to see. They are looking to the government to be their master, not God. When they do get their new king, they will learn the hard way what a cruel master the government really is.

Israel demands a king despite God's warning and Samuel went and told the Lord what the people said (vs. 21). God already knew what was said but He loves it when His people talk to Him. He loves the fellowship, the intimacy. This is why prayer is so important. There is a bond between God and Samuel that got stronger each time they talked to one another. The Lord said, "Heed their voice, and make them a king" (vs. 22). Samuel then told every man to go home to his own city. You asked for a king, now you'll get one. The people are about to get enrolled in the school of hard knocks. They're about to learn that rebellion and stubbornness have lasting consequences. There is an ancient Chinese proverb that says, "Outside noisy, inside empty." These words describe the man who is about to be made king over Israel, a king God gave in His anger (Hosea

13:11). He will be a noisy man, very self-centered, and he will make many bad choices during his reign as king. He started out well, as many people do, but his ending is nothing to write home about.

Time will tell that this new king will not finish the work he was called upon to do. In his own words he will one day say, "Indeed, I have played the fool and erred exceedingly" (1 Sam. 26:21). On the other hand, Jesus said in John 4:34, "My food is to do the will of Him who sent Me, and to finish His work." Another time He said, "The Father has not left Me alone, for I always do those things that please Him" (John 8:29). The last thing Jesus said on the cross before He died was, "It is finished!" (John 19:30). The ultimate goal of every believer is to finish the work God gives them to do. Paul said in Acts 20:24 (NLT), "But my life is worth nothing to me unless I use it for finishing the work assigned me by the Lord Jesus." Starting out well doesn't mean much if you don't finish well. Never talk about the "good old days" as if the past is as good as your life is ever going to get, as if your beginning is better than your ending. No, today should be better than yesterday and tomorrow should be better than today. This is how you run the race and finish the course.

The story of the first king of Israel begins in 1 Sam. 9:1 with the introduction of a very wealthy and influential man, "There was a man of Benjamin whose name was Kish the son of Abiel." Benjamin was the youngest son of Jacob and Paul would later say he was from the tribe of Benjamin (Phil. 3:5). Before he died, Jacob spoke over his son these words, "Benjamin is a ravenous wolf; In the morning he shall devour the prey, and at night he shall divide the spoil" (Gen. 49:27). The tribe of Benjamin became known for its ferocity in battle. They would be fierce warriors and the tribe's existence would be one of continual violence day and night. This is why vs. 1 also says Kish was "a mighty man of power." Vs. 2 says, "And he had a son whose name was Saul, a choice and handsome young man. There was not a more handsome person than he among the children of Israel. From his shoulders upward he was taller than any of the people." Very rarely does scripture go to such great lengths to describe a person's physical appearance. As the people of Israel will one day find out, looks can be deceiving.

Saul came from a prestigious family and was a man who stood out in a crowd. In Hebrew the name "Saul" means 'asked of God,' an appropriate name since the people were asking for a king. It needs to be pointed out that nothing is said here about this family's relationship with the Lord God of Israel. Could it be that there is nothing to say, that Saul is a reflection of the spiritual state of Israel as a whole? There may have been some images or symbolism present but their hearts were far from where God wanted it to be. The Bible does say that Kish had many donkeys and they had run away and were lost. In ancient times, donkeys were a symbol of industry and hard work while horses were the sign of war, power, and the strength of a military force. Donkeys were considered to be reliable helpers, surefooted on mountain terrain, capable of enduring difficult conditions and harsh environments, and very strong burden carriers. Donkeys were very valuable animals and Kish told his son to take a servant and go look for the animals (vs. 3). It was a journey that would change Saul and the nation of Israel forever.

It is amazing to see how God is about to open up one of the most important chapters in the history of Israel. A king will be led to the throne as the result of a man and his servant looking for donkeys. Saul honored his father's request and searched throughout the land for the donkeys to no avail. This must have been frustrating to Saul not realizing that God was working out His plan in a way he couldn't imagine. Those donkeys could have gone anywhere but they went exactly where God wanted them to go. They submitted themselves to what God wanted them to do just like those female cows who pulled the ark to the land of Israel. If animals are smart enough to submit to the will of God, shouldn't believers do the same? Several days passed and Saul thought his father might be worried about them so he suggested to his servant that they return home. Just as he was about to leave for home, his servant tells him there is a man of God here in the city they're now at, "an honorable man; all that he says comes to pass. So let us go there; perhaps he can show us the way that we should go" (vs. 6).

The reputation of Samuel was well known. He was a man of God, an honorable man, a man whose words came to pass. What is your reputation like among those who know you? When they are looking for a man or woman of God, will they come looking for you? Think about it. The suggestion of Saul's servant reveals that they were not men of spiritual character. They didn't want to go to the prophet for spiritual guidance, they wanted him to help them find their donkeys. Saul agreed with his servant that this was a good idea and together they set off to find the man of God. As they approached the city they asked some young women if the prophet was here. They said yes, indeed, the man of God was here. They said, "Hurry now; for today he came to this city" (vs. 12). It is no coincidence that Saul and his servant came looking for their donkeys on the same day Samuel was in town. God is directing their steps all the way. Unknown to them, God had spoken to Samuel the day before and told him a man from the land of Benjamin was coming to see him. God also said this man was the one chosen to be king over Israel (vs. 16).

Notice in 1 Sam. 8:21 that Samuel spoke to the Lord and here God is speaking to him. God wants to hear from you and He wants you to hear from Him. Go to God and pour out your heart to Him. Tell Him what your day has been like and all the things you have on your mind. God speaks to those who open the doors of communication. Do you want to hear from God? Talk to Him first. Draw near to God and He will draw near to you (James 4:8). "And when Samuel saw Saul, the Lord said to him, 'There he is, the man of whom I spoke to you. This one shall reign over My people'" (vs. 17). God specifically identifies the man to Samuel. What God says one day will be confirmed by Him speaking another day. He is telling Samuel that He is giving the people what they asked for. He is giving them a flawed king because they are a flawed people. Saul drew near to Samuel and asked where the prophet's house was. Samuel then told Saul he was the man of God he'd been looking for. This is so amazing. Saul is looking for a noted prophet and the first person he talks to is the man of God he came to see.

Saul is invited to dinner and then hears words most people would be afraid to hear from a man of God, "Tomorrow I will let you go and will tell you all that is in your heart" (vs. 19). Samuel then tells Saul not to be anxious for the donkeys for they have been found. This must have shocked Saul because he had not mentioned to Samuel that this was the reason he was seeking him out. Samuel is proving that he is a true prophet of God by telling of things he could not have known unless it was revealed to him supernaturally. Samuel then hints at Saul's destiny by asking a couple of interesting questions, "And on whom is all the desires of Israel? Is it not on you and on all your father's house?" (vs. 20). All of Israel desired a king, and Saul would be the answer to that desire. The Message Bible says, "At this moment, Israel's future is in your hands." Saul was not prepared to hear this and was blindsided by the words of the prophet. After all, he only came here because he wanted to find his father's donkeys. It seems as if God had other plans.

Immediately Saul responded, "Am I not a Benjamite, of the smallest of the tribes of Israel, and my family the least of all the families of the tribe of Benjamin? Why then do you speak like this to me?" (vs. 21). Why would Saul say such a thing since his father and family were actually prominent men in a tribe known for producing fierce warriors? What appears to be humility is actually a display of false humility for Saul was a man of low self-esteem. Samuel will later say to him, "I remember when you were little in your own eyes" (1 Sam. 15:17). Samuel took Saul and his servant into the hall to eat and sat them in the place of honor among thirty other people. A special meal was prepared and "the cook took up the thigh and its upper part and set it before Saul" (vs. 24). The upper part was the shoulder of the animal and was symbolic of the position he was being called upon to fulfill. Is. 9:6 says, "And the government shall be upon His shoulders." Samuel spent some time talking with Saul and the next day it was time to send him home.

On the outskirts of the city, Samuel told Saul to send the servant ahead. When they were alone he said, "But you stand here awhile, that I may announce to you the word of God" (vs. 27). Without warning, Samuel pours olive oil over Saul's head for God was anointing him to be king of Israel (1 Sam. 10:1). The anointing is God on flesh doing only what God can do. The Holy Spirit was being poured out on him, equipping him for the job of being commander over God's people. Through the anointing, God is giving Saul everything he needs to succeed. He is giving him His power and His presence. Samuel then kissed Saul on the forehead. This was a kiss of allegiance, a sign of respect and Samuel's personal support of Saul. It was important that the first king of Israel feel the support of the man of God. Saul is now king whether he likes it or not. Samuel and Saul were alone when this anointing took place. There was no flashy, public ceremony announcing the significance of the moment for now was not the time to reveal Saul as king to the nation. First, confirmation must be given to Saul to prove this was the will of God.

2 Cor. 13:1 says, "By the mouth of two or three witnesses every word shall be established." Saul is told that God has anointed him and Samuel then tells him there will be a series of signs to confirm that what just happened was of God. When Saul departs to go home, he will meet two men by Rachel's tomb who will tell him that his father's donkeys are safe. He will then meet three men carrying various items and one of them will give him two loaves of bread. Saul will then come near a place where the Philistine troops are stationed and there he'll meet a group of prophets who are playing various instruments as they prophesied. 1 Sam. 10:6,7 says, "Then the Spirit of the Lord will come upon you, and you will prophesy with them and be turned into another man. And let it be, when these signs come to you, that you do as the occasion demands; for God is with you." In Hebrew the words "will come upon you" means 'to leap or rush upon thee.' Before this time, Saul never seems to have been a particularly spiritual man. For him to prophesy, to speak as one inspired of the Lord, was the evidence that he was turned into another man.

All the things Samuel said would happen came to pass. Still, one more confirmation would be given. Samuel called the people together and scolded them for rejecting God and for their insistence on having a king rule over them. He then told the people to present themselves before the Lord and proceeded to cast lots to see who would be king. The Bible contains several examples of the casting of lots as a means of determining God's will for a given situation (Joshua 18:6-10). The closest modern practice to casting lots is flipping a coin, an Old Testament procedure God instructed the people to do several times (Num. 26:55). In order to find the right person to be king, they must determine by lot the tribe, the family, and then the individual. This would show to the whole nation who had been chosen by God to be king over Israel. After whittling down all the options by casting lots, Saul is eventually chosen. The people sought him out but he could not be found for he was hiding among the equipment (vs. 22). Hidden behind his handsome physique, Saul was a man of low self-esteem. He was a weakling and a coward, and yet he was the new anointed king of Israel.

The people ran and found Saul and had him stand in front of the huge crowd where he stood taller than any person who was there. Samuel said to the people, "Do you see him whom the Lord has chosen, that there is no one like him among all the people?" (vs. 24). So all the people shouted and said, "Long live the king!" They had been waiting a long time to shout these words. This day their ungodly desire had been fulfilled for a monarchy has now been established. Samuel explained to the people the behavior of royalty. He taught them God's guidelines, probably using Deut. 17:14-20 as his text. Afterward Saul went home to Gibeah and many valiant men went with him. Others despised him probably because they never had a king before. Still, Saul kept his peace (vs. 27). He started his reign with so much promise. He was chosen and anointed by God. The Spirit of God was upon him and he had the support of Samuel. He also had the support of most of the nation and valiant men stood by his side. In spite of all these advantages, Saul's life would still end up as a great tragedy. Long live the king? Yeah, right.

-5-

"CHANGING OF THE GUARD"

Saul has been made king of all Israel. There is no palace for him to live in so he returns to his homeland of Gibeah, a city in the hill country north of Jerusalem. Instead of organizing a government and a military, he instead goes back to work in the fields of his father. There he stays until one day a group of weeping messengers comes and tells him of a battle that is about to take place in a northern city isolated east of the Jordan River. The Ammonites, led by Nahash, came against the city of Jabesh Gilead and the people there offered no resistance at all. They've got a king but not everybody knows it. There's been no military presence in the area, no strategy, and no organization of any kind. Not knowing what to do, the people of the city immediately go out to surrender in hopes of bringing peace to the situation. The men of Jabesh said to Nahash, "Make a covenant with us, and we will serve you." Nahash responded back, "On this condition I will make a covenant with you, that I may put out your right eyes and bring reproach to all Israel" (1 Sam. 11:1,2).

The Ammonites were ruthless barbarians who would stop at nothing in their savage and merciless quest for more land. So brutal were these people that Amos 1:13 says "they ripped open the woman with child in Gilead, that they might enlarge their territory." It stands to reason that these city dwellers would make quick haste to surrender to this invading army. Nahash was an evil man and he wanted no part of a peaceful surrender. He wants to brutalize these people by gouging out their right eyes first. Mutilation in ancient times was quite common. The idea was to take away depth perception and a soldier's peripheral vision thus making him useless on the battlefield. The people of Jabesh Gilead certainly didn't want their eyes gouged out so the elders made what seemed like a strange request. They asked Nahash to hold off for seven days so they could go seek for help. If they could find no one to save them, they would surrender without resistance. The Ammonites were always looking for a good fight so they said, "Go ahead, see what you can do."

"So the messengers came to Gibeah of Saul and told the news in the hearing of the people. And all the people lifted up their voices and wept" (vs. 4). The people are in despair. The Philistines are at their southern border and now the Ammonites are attacking them from the north. What are they going to do? They have a king but there is no army to defend them. There was nothing they could do so they wept. It was at this time that Saul came in from the field. He asked why the people were weeping and was told what the messengers from Jabesh had said. "Then the Spirit of God came upon Saul when he heard this news, and his anger was greatly aroused" (vs. 6). Saul was filled with a divine indignation because of the unfair treatment that came upon these people. Martin Luther called this "the anger of love." It is not wrong to have a righteous anger when it is aimed at immorality, injustice, and sin. Jesus got angry at the money changers in the temple. He overturned their tables and with a whip drove them and the animals out of the holy place of prayer and worship.

The Spirit of God is upon Saul and he is mad. He takes a yoke of oxen, cuts them in pieces, and sends them by messenger throughout all the territory of Israel. He is doing this to rouse the people into action. He is saying if the people don't join him and Samuel in battle, then the enemy will come in and cut their oxen into pieces. He is saying, "You have a king and now we need a military. You're it." Vs. 7 says, "And the fear of the Lord fell on the people, and they came out with one consent." More than three hundred thousand men came forward and Saul sent the messengers back to Jabesh to tell the people help was on the way and would be there the next day. To lower the guard of the enemy, the men of Jabesh told the Ammonites that they would surrender tomorrow. "So it was, on the next day, that Saul put the people in three companies; and they came into the midst of the camp in the morning watch, and killed Ammonites until the heat of the day. And it happened that those who survived were scattered, so that no two of them were left together" (vs. 11).

War is an ugly thing. In modern warfare the enemy is killed from a distance. In ancient warfare the enemy was killed at arm's length. You looked into the eyes of your enemy and you smelled their breath. The odds of walking away from hand-to-hand combat unscratched was very low. You didn't know if the blood covering you was your own or that of the enemy. If you died, you wouldn't receive a proper burial because the birds of the air and the beasts of the field would come and prey on your lifeless body. Thankfully, the Spirit of God was with the people of Israel this day and a great victory was won. As long as people live in a fallen world, good men and women will have to stand up and fight against evil. One is reminded of Eccl. 3:8 that says there is "a time to love, and a time to hate; a time of war, and a time of peace." Edmund Burke, an eighteenth-century philosopher, once said, "The only thing that is needed for evil to overwhelm us is for good people to do nothing." Do people love peace enough to fight for it? They did this day.

Filled with adrenaline, the fighting men of Israel now want to kill those who despised Saul and resisted him when he was announced as their king. Saul stepped in and said, "Not a man shall be put to death this day, for today the Lord has accomplished salvation in Israel" (vs. 13). He knew when to attack, he knew when to stop. Samuel called all the people to Gilgal and once more proclaimed that Saul was their king. "So all the people went to Gilgal, and there they made Saul king before the Lord in Gilgal. There they made sacrifices of peace offerings before the Lord, and there Saul and all the men of Israel rejoiced greatly" (vs. 15). Samuel now has the people's attention and he takes this opportunity to talk about what's coming next. This is going to be his last message to the people. After Saul's victory over the Ammonites, Samuel knows the nation will now begin to look to their new king for leadership and guidance. He now speaks to the people to help them make the transition from prophet to king. His days are over and the reign of the new king has begun.

Samuel said in 1 Sam. 12:2, "And now here is the king, walking before you; and I am old and gray headed." Samuel judged Israel all the days of his life but now that a king has been raised up, his role will change and come to an end. He is saying the same thing John the Baptist said about Jesus, "He must increase, but I must decrease" (John 3:30). He makes it clear that it wasn't his idea to appoint a king over Israel, and it certainly wasn't God's timing for this to happen. It was the people who wanted a king and God allowed it and directed its execution. Samuel then asks the people if he ever did anything wrong to them and if they have a witness who can prove he did. The people respond and say they have no proof that Samuel has committed any wrongdoing and no one claims he has. This is a witness of the godly character of Samuel, a man who walked before the Lord and served the people all the days of his life. All parties agree that he has led Israel well. If the people later try to blame Saul's problems on Samuel, what they say this day would be a witness against them (vs. 5).

Samuel then goes back into their history and reminds the people of all the things God has done on their behalf. He told them to never forget that they were slaves in Egypt and God delivered them by sending Moses and Aaron to help them escape the tyranny of their oppressors. The people later forgot the Lord their God and soon came under the dominion of their enemies. As soon as the people repented of their ways, the Lord brought them once again to freedom. Samuel then mentions that when the people asked for a king, they were insulting the Lord for it is He who is their true king (vs. 12). The Lord has been a good king for all of Israel but now thy wanted a human king for carnal, fleshly reasons. Samuel says, "Here is the king whom you have chosen and whom you have desired. And take note, the Lord has set a king over you" (vs. 13). He then presents the people with an important choice. They had been disobedient in their desire for a king, yet God gave them a king anyway. Even so, if they will fear the Lord and serve Him, God will bless them. If not, judgment will fall (vs. 13,14).

Samuel wants the people to know he's speaking on the Lord's behalf so he prays and asks God to send a sign to confirm his words. He tells the people, "Now therefore, stand and see this great thing which the Lord will do before your eyes" (vs. 16). It was the season of the wheat harvest and it was unusual for it to rain during this time of the year. Samuel said, "Is today not the wheat harvest? I will call to the Lord, and He will send thunder and rain, that you may perceive and see that your wickedness is great, which you have done in the sight of the Lord, in asking a king for yourselves" (vs. 17). It happened just as Samuel said "and all the people greatly feared the Lord and Samuel" (vs. 18). This sign not only displayed God's power but also His judgment. Prov. 26:1 says it is not fitting for it to rain during harvest because heavy rain could destroy all the crops. So unexpected was this rain and thunder that it could only be interpreted as a sign of God's displeasure. Israel now sees their sin of desiring a king and they ask Samuel to pray for them so they won't die because of the evil they have done (vs. 19).

Israel finally sees their sin of wanting a king but he is here and he's not going away. Like it or not, there is now a king in Israel. Still, there is hope. Samuel says to the people, "No not fear. You have done all this wickedness; yet do not turn aside from following the Lord, but serve the Lord with all your heart" (vs. 20). He is saying you can't change the past but you can determine your future by the things you do today. In spite of all the wrong the people have done, Samuel then makes a startling statement in vs. 22, "For the Lord will not forsake His people, for His great name's sake, because it has pleased the Lord to make you His people." Samuel wants Israel to know that God loves them. He then said, "Far be it for me that I should sin against the Lord in ceasing to pray for you; but I will teach you the good and right way" (vs. 23). Samuel wants the people to know that as he steps back and allows Saul to emerge as their leader, he will still serve them through prayer and teaching. His final remarks to the people is to fear the Lord and serve Him with all their heart. "But if you do wickedly, you shall be swept away, both you and your king" (vs. 25).

The changing of the guard is now complete and the people have been warned. Set before them is life and death, good and evil. British theologian Adam Clarke once said, "Never was a people more fully warned; and never did a people profit less by the warning." Israel now has a king but, in truth, he is not the man he appears to be. He sometimes said the right words and sometimes did the right things. However, it is quite evident that his heart is far from God. One is reminded of the words of English philosopher Francis Bacon who said, "A bad man is a worse man when he pretends to be a saint." This is a good description of the type of man Saul was. He was a hypocrite who acted spiritual and always sought to justify himself when he did wrong. The problem with denial is it always leads to arrogance. Two years after Saul became king he put together a small army to fight the Philistines who were camped nearby. For the first time, Israel now has a professional army. Saul has two thousand soldiers with him in one city while his son Jonathan has a thousand men in another city. On this day, Jonathan was the warrior and not Saul.

1 Sam. 13:3 says Jonathan attacked the garrison of the Philistines, proving what a remarkable military leader he was. After the battle Saul had trumpets blown throughout all the land saying, "Let the Hebrews hear!" Arrogance loves attention. Vs. 4 then says, "Now all Israel heard it said that Saul had attacked a garrison of the Philistines." Saul didn't attack the enemy, Jonathan did. He's taking credit for something his son did. This shows the heart and character of Saul. His insecurity stops him from giving credit where it is due. Instead, he drinks in the praise of the people like a thirsty man drinks water. He had twice as many men but still did nothing as his son risked his life in battle. He was a king in name only while Jonathan was the true warrior in the family. The Philistines didn't take this defeat sitting down. Angered by the Israelites, they gathered together a huge army to oppose them. This army consisted of "thirty thousand chariots and six thousand horsemen, and people as the sand which is on the seashore in multitude" (vs. 5). This army is enormous and the men of Israel are terrified.

Jonathan had been bold enough to launch the initial attack against the Philistines but the men of Israel refuse to likewise stand against the enemy. They recognize they're greatly outnumbered so in fear they run away and hide in thickets, rocks, holes, and pits. Some of them even flee all the way across the Jordan River. These are the same people who thought having a king would solve all their problems. Where was their king anyway? "As for Saul, he was still in Gilgal, and all the people followed him trembling" (vs. 7). He probably reasoned it was better to have scared followers than no followers at all. Word had gotten to Samuel what had happened and he sent word back to Saul telling him to wait for him and he would be there in seven days. At that time Samuel would make sacrifices to the Lord and Israel would then be spiritually prepared for battle. The seventh day came and still Samuel had not arrived. The people with Saul were frightened so they scattered away from him. Desperate, Saul decides to take matters into his own hands.

Instead of waiting for Samuel, Saul offered up a burnt offering to God himself. This he should not have done. After all, it was still the seventh day. That, plus the fact he was a king and not a priest. Only priests were allowed to offer sacrifices. He thinks he's something more than what God called him to be. Suddenly, Samuel arrives just as the flaming embers are dying down and he asks Saul, "What have you done?" Saul told Samuel of the situation at hand and said, "Therefore, I felt compelled and offered a burnt offering" (vs. 12). He tried to justify the wrong he had done. He said, "The people are scattered, the Philistines are coming, and you're late." He didn't confess his sin but made excuses as he tried to justify his behavior. What's more, he tries to place the blame of his actions on the prophet of God. Samuel's piercing eyes looked at Saul as he said, "You have done foolishly. You have not kept the commandment of the Lord your God, which He commanded you" (vs. 13). All Saul had to do was trust God and wait one more hour. The final moments of waiting are usually the most difficult. It is at this time when people are tempted to do what is right in their own eyes.

Samuel tells Saul that his kingdom will not continue even though he will reign for another twenty years. The whole point of being a king is to set up a dynasty where their own son would sit on the throne once they've passed away. Samuel is telling Saul that his descendants will not reign after him. "The Lord has sought for Himself a man after His own heart, and the Lord has commanded him to be commander over His people, because you have not kept what the Lord commanded you" (vs. 14). A man after God's own heart is a man who loves God and has a deep desire to do what God wants him to do. Ps. 119:2,3 (NLT) says, "Joyful are those who obey His laws and search for Him with all their hearts. They do not compromise with evil, and they walk only in His paths." Samuel is telling Saul that another man will rise up and become king in his place. Another changing of the guard will one day take place. God is going to select someone of His own choosing, someone according to His own will and purpose, a man after His own heart. Samuel then turns and walks away.

Saul returns to his hometown of Gibeah and he only has six hundred men with him. The Philistines then send out three raiding companies of soldiers. They are unopposed because the Hebrews have no blacksmiths, thus they have no weapons. On the day of battle the only people with weapons are Saul and his son Jonathan. The rest of Israel fought with whatever they could find. The enemy is coming but what is Saul doing at this time? 1 Sam. 4:2 says he is sitting under a pomegranate tree. He has no concern for the needs of his people. He's eating and watching and thinking only of himself. When you're self-focused, you don't have time to think about what others need. Thankfully, Jonathan did not come from the same mold as his father. Without telling his father, Jonathan said to the young man who bore his armor, "Come, let us go over to the garrison of these uncircumcised; it may be that the Lord will work for us. For nothing restrains the Lord from saving by many or by few" (vs. 6). Jonathan knew Israel was hopelessly outnumbered and something had to be done. He was willing to be used by God to do it.

The armorbearer pledges his allegiance to Jonathan and together the two of them head toward the camp of the Philistines. They knew they were outnumbered but they also knew God was on their side. He doesn't need six hundred scared men sitting under trees eating pomegranates. All He needs is a few good men with a "let's go for it" attitude, men who will trust Him even when the odds are not in their favor. There is a huge difference between Jonathan and Saul. Jonathan has a proper concept of God, Saul does not. Jonathan is focused on God while his father is focused on himself. Jonathan recognized that God is not limited by human resources or capabilities. God has no limitations at all. He is a God who can do the impossible. Jonathan had this kind of perspective and he and his armorbearer defeated the enemy that day. At the conclusion of the battle the earth quaked and there was great trembling (vs. 15). Jonathan did his part, now God was doing His part. This earthquake caused the remaining enemy soldiers to also tremble and they scrambled away in every direction.

There were watchmen sent to keep an eye on the Philistines and they are shocked as they see the enemy melt away before their eyes. They report this to Saul who should have rose up and gone after the fleeing troops then and there. Instead, he takes a roll call because he's probably concerned about who's going to get the credit for the victory that just happened. This roll call revealed that Jonathan and his armorbearer were no where to be found in the camp. Wanting to get in on the action, Saul tries to look spiritual by having the ark brought into the camp. He then talks to a priest because he wants to know what the will of God is. He's the king and he should already know what to do but his insecurity and fear have paralyzed him. As the priest was about to speak, the noise from the Philistines camp continued to increase. Saul then said to the priest, "Withdraw your hand" (vs. 19). He withdraws his desire to hear from God. He tells the priest to stop seeking an answer from God as to what He wants Saul to do. Once again, he takes matters into his own hands.

Saul gathered all the people together and went to the battle. It says something about the man who wants to fight a war that has already been won. Anybody can do that. "Likewise all the men of Israel who had hidden in the mountains of Ephraim, when they heard that the Philistines fled, they also followed hard after them in battle" (vs. 22). These runaways were afraid when things looked bad but now that victory is assured, they join in the battle. The first century historian Josephus said six thousand Philistines were killed this day and there is no doubt that it was Jonathan who was at the forefront of this battle. He struck a mighty blow against the enemy and it is now King Saul's responsibility to finish the job by striking down the fleeing Philistine army. His men are tired, distressed, and in need of energy. Saul then gives an order that is lame and foolish. He said, "Cursed is the man who eats any food until evening, before I have taken vengeance on my enemies" (vs. 24). He's trying to act spiritual, and he will enforce this command with a curse.

The true character of Saul is revealed even in the midst of doing something spiritual like fasting. He says these are his enemies and not the enemy of the people. He also says he will take vengeance on them with no mention of God. His focus is only on himself. He's not seeking God's glory, he's seeking his own. Also, what right did he have to proclaim such a curse? If a fast was to be declared with a curse attached to it, it was Samuel who had the authority to do this, not Saul. The king is trying to act spiritual but he's being very irrational. The fighting potential of his men will be hindered if they don't have any energy. As they continued their pursuit of the enemy they came to a forest and there was honey on the ground. This was the provision of God. The men were tired and hungry and they needed energy to continue the pursuit and finish the battle. Still, no man ate of the honey. Jonathan was there but he had not heard the command his father had given. He knew he needed energy to fight and here the honey was. He ate some of it "and his countenance brightened" (vs. 27).

Right away one of the men told Jonathan the command his father had given. Jonathan had little or no regard to what was told him and openly declared that his father had troubled the land (vs. 29). The people were weak and distracted on a day when they should have been strong. Jonathan points out how well he looks after tasting the honey and he says the victory could have been greater if the people could have eaten (vs. 30). The people then drove the Philistine army back eighteen miles and they were very faint. They needed food so they rushed on the spoil and didn't drain the blood from the animals before they were butchered. Their obedience to Saul's foolish command led them to disobey God's command to first drain the blood (Deut. 12:23-25). Saul then blames the people for something that is his own fault. It was his command that provoked the people into this sin. He made the people butcher the animals the right way and he then built an altar to the Lord. Again he was trying to act spiritual. He soon came up with a plan to plunder the enemy and he asked counsel of God. "But He did not answer him that day" (vs. 37).

God has nothing to say to those who are repeatedly disobedient. Instead of looking at himself, Saul is convinced God's silence is because someone else has sinned in the camp. He vowed to have the culprit put to death, even if it turns out to be his son Jonathan (vs. 39). The people loved and respected Jonathan so nobody told Saul that his son had eaten some honey. Saul then cast lots to find the wrong doer and the lots fell on his son. Jonathan told Saul what he had done and, instead of admitting his command was foolish, Saul said, "God do so and more also; for you shall surely die, Jonathan" (vs. 44). He was willing to kill his own son rather than humbly admitting he was at fault. Thankfully, the people talked him out of it. They would not allow

Jonathan to be executed for they knew he was working for the Lord and not against Him. "Then Saul returned from pursuing the Philistines, and the Philistines went to their own place" (vs. 46). The enemy lived to fight another day because of Saul's foolish command. 1 Sam. 14:52 says, "Now there was fierce war with the Philistines all the days of Saul."

-6-

"THIS IS THE ONE"

All during his reign as king, Saul was a man who played the fool and erred exceedingly. He was a giant among men, at times a hero, but inside he was a coward and a slave to his insecurities. He became a victim of himself because he was full of impatience, pride, rebellion, and jealousy. He played the fool many ways but mainly by arrogance, indifference, and disobedience. He was a king destined for greatness until he decided to do things his own way instead of God's way. His life stands as a warning that you cannot rebel against God and get away with it. Sooner or later your wrong choices and actions will catch up to you. They always do. For sure, your sin will find you out (Num. 32:23). In spite of all his flaws and weaknesses, Saul was still the king of Israel and God had a job for him to do. Before telling him what his new assignment was, God sent Samuel to him who said, "The Lord sent me to anoint you king over His people, over Israel. Now therefore, heed the voice of the words of the Lord" (1 Sam. 15:1). In other words, "Listen carefully to what you're about to be told."

Centuries before, a tribe of nomads living in the area south of Canaan attacked the children of Israel after their escape from Egypt. The Amalekites were a brutal people and they committed a terrible sin against Israel. The people were tired and weary from their journey and thus were very vulnerable. The Amalekites attacked them from the rear ranks where the older people were lagging behind, along with the women and children. They destroyed those who were helpless and unguarded for no reason except violence and greed. God hates it when the strong take advantage of the weak and He promised to bring judgment upon these people and "utterly blot out the remembrance of Amalek from under heaven" (Ex. 17:14). Many of their descendants were still alive and God said to Saul through Samuel, "I will punish what Amalek did to Israel, how he laid wait for him on the way when he came up from Egypt. Now go and attack Amalek, and utterly destroy all that they have, and do not spare them. But kill both man and woman, infant and nursing child, ox and sheep, camel and donkey" (1 Sam. 15:2,3).

What God told Saul to do may seem a bit extreme but God doesn't play games where sin is concerned. He knew that the Amalekites would always oppose Israel (Ex. 17:16). Their children would do it when they grew up and so would all their descendants. Their actions for hundreds of years had been on stopping God's plan to bless the world. He knew if they weren't utterly destroyed, they would continue to oppose His plan and His people. God remembered what happened to Israel when they came out of Egypt. This shows that time does not erase sin before God. Only the blood of Jesus can erase sin, not time. The Amalekites were given the opportunity to repent just like everyone else but their hardened, unrepentant hearts stopped them from doing so. The question also needs to be asked, why didn't God do it Himself? He destroyed Sodom and Gomorrah without any help from man. Why not do the same here? The reason is that God had a purpose for His command to Saul. He wanted it to be a test of obedience for him and all Israel.

Saul gathered together two hundred thousand foot-soldiers and attacked the Amalekites. They killed everybody with the edge of the sword but foolishly spared the life of the king. Perhaps Saul wanted to keep King Agag as a living testimony of the glory of his triumph in battle. Whatever the reason, Saul disobeyed the word of God who commanded him to bring judgment on all the people, including the king. What's more, the people also spared the best of the animals. 1 Sam. 15:9 says, "But Saul and the people spared Agag and the best of the sheep, the oxen, the fatlings, the lambs, and all that was good, and were unwilling to utterly destroy them. But everything despised and worthless, that they utterly destroyed." The people wanted the best animals for themselves and this made them unwilling to obey the command from God. Saul and his men obeyed God as long as it suited their needs, not realizing that partial obedience is the same as complete disobedience. God's heart was broken over Saul's sin and He told Samuel He regretted setting up Saul as king. This grieved Samuel also and he cried out to the Lord all night (vs. 11).

Saul had to be confronted for what he did so Samuel rose early the next morning to go discipline the disobedient king. He was told that Saul went to Carmel where "he set up a monument for himself" (vs. 12). Here is a man fervent in his passion for honor and fame. Gone is the man who once hid among the equipment because of his fear of being made king. Saul was pleased with himself and believed he was justified in what he had done. There is no shame and guilt in Saul, only pride. Prov. 16:18 says, "Pride goes before destruction, and a haughty spirit before a fall." Pride is a sin that hardens the heart and causes a person to be so consumed with themselves that their thoughts are far from God (Ps. 10:4). His heart was dead to shame because his heart was dead to God. He sees Samuel coming and he boldly proclaims, "Blessed are you of the Lord! I have performed the commandment of the Lord" (vs. 13). Pride always leads to self-deception for it makes you blind to sin. Don't let this happen to you. Say to God, "Search me, O God, and see if there is any wicked way in me, and lead me in the way everlasting" (Ps. 139:23,24).

As Saul was boasting of his accomplishments to the man of God, the sound of the livestock could be heard in the background. Samuel asked, "What then is this bleating of the sheep in my ears, and the lowing of the oxen which I hear?"

(vs. 14). Weren't all the animals supposed to be killed? It is obvious to Samuel that they weren't. Apparently, Saul wasn't listening. Jesus said in Matt. 11:15, "He who has ears to hear, let him hear!" This is God's way of saying, "Listen up! Pay close attention!" Samuel had already told Saul to heed the voice of the Lord but the seduction of worldly pleasures and comfort prevented God's command from taking root in his heart. Saul has always been a man full of excuses for his sinful behavior and they are not lacking here. He blames the people for sparing the best of the sheep and oxen but makes a point of saying he helped kill the worthless animals. They sinned and he didn't, or so he said. He then makes the lamest excuse of all. He tells Samuel, "The people spared the best of the sheep and the oxen, to sacrifice to the Lord your God" (vs. 15). He claims to have done what he did for spiritual reasons.

Unknown to Saul, his words to the prophet revealed what the real problem was. He told Samuel that he was going to sacrifice not to his God but to Samuel's God. Saul had no relationship with God because he removed Him from the throne of his heart. Samuel had heard enough and will listen to Saul no more. With a loud voice he says, "Be quiet!" (vs. 16). Saul has talked long enough and it's now time for him to listen to what the Lord has to say through Samuel. The man of God reminded Saul that when he was little in his own eyes, God still anointed him to be king over Israel. He asks, "Why then did you not obey the voice of the Lord?" (vs. 19). The answer is obvious. Because of pride he is now big in his own eyes and this makes God small in his eyes. He is so deceived that he insists he is innocent of any wrong doing even though he admits to sparing the life of Agag, king of Amalek. He again blames the people for taking the best of the livestock although he did nothing to stop or discourage them. He consented to what they did and this makes him just as guilty as they are.

Samuel tells Saul that obeying the voice of the Lord is more important to Him than any sacrifice. 1 Sam. 15:22 says, "Behold, to obey is better than sacrifice, and to heed than the fat of rams." So many people are generic when it comes to their relationship with God. They say they love God all the while sin runs rampant in their lives. All the confessions they make mean nothing if they don't have a heart that is surrendered to God. Martin Luther once said, "I had rather be obedient, than able to work miracles." Samuel then says, "For rebellion is as the sin of witchcraft, and stubbornness is as iniquity and idolatry. Because you have rejected the word of the Lord, He also has rejected you from being king" (vs. 23). Reprimanded for his actions, Saul makes a weak attempt to repent for what he did. He admits that he sinned but why did he disobey God? "Because I feared the people and obeyed their voice" (vs. 24). Once again Saul refuses to own up to his sin. Instead, he blames the people who made him do it. Saul said the right words at first but clearly his heart was not in what he said. He feared the people when he should have feared God (Matt. 10:28).

Saul can no longer escape the fact that he did wrong. His sin has found him out so he makes a desperate plea to Samuel for a quick fix to his problem. He says, "Now therefore, please pardon my sin, and return with me, that I may worship the Lord" (vs. 25). Samuel knows that a word from him would not change the rebellious nature of Saul's heart so he refuses to go anywhere with Saul. As Samuel turned around to go away Saul seized the edge of his robe and it tore. Samuel looked at him and said, "The Lord has torn the kingdom of Israel from you today, and has given it to a neighbor of yours, who is better than you" (vs. 28). Saul replied, "I have sinned, yet honor me now, please, before the elders of my people and before Israel" (vs. 30). Saul's desperate plea shows the depth of his pride. He is far more concerned with his image than his soul. There is still unfinished business at hand. Samuel had Agag brought before him and without hesitation takes a sword and hacks the king in pieces. Samuel then returned home and "went no more to see Saul until the day of his death. Nevertheless Samuel mourned for Saul" (vs. 35).

God has rejected Saul and the substance of his kingdom is gone. He is king in name only for he is only a shell of what he was called to be. He was like the religious leaders Jesus spoke to in Matt. 23:27, "For you are like whitewashed tombs which indeed appear beautiful outwardly, but inside are full of dead man's bones and all uncleanness." Samuel is grieving over the king he once anointed but whom God has now rejected. The word "mourn" in Hebrew means 'to grieve as if someone had died.' Godly people are sensitive to sin and they grieve when the potential in a person's life has been wasted. Samuel is weeping and is broken-hearted because of the man Saul has become. He was the people's king and on the outside he looked like the right man for the job. But on the inside, his heart and his life was in total opposition to the things God stood for. He did not use his role as king as a means to promote the lives of those under him. He hoarded the power and authority that came with being king and he was overcome with arrogance and self-interest. He didn't come to serve but to be served.

The problem with Saul is he was more concerned with what he wanted than what God wanted. One of the keys to living a good life, a life pleasing to God, is to learn what's important and what's not important. Too many people waste their lives focusing on the wrong things just like Saul did. They'd rather have fortune and fame instead of a close relationship with God. They allow the world to tell them how to live and because of that they never focus on that which is most important, on the things that matter most. Then, as their life draws to a close, they realize they've played the fool and now it's too late to get back the years that have been wasted. The bottom line is you can't chase after what the world says is important. You must look at life through the eyes of God. You must see things the way God sees them. God doesn't look at the external, He looks at the internal. He looks at the heart for in the heart is the real you. On the outside you can pretend to be somebody else, but the inside reveals who you really are. It's where true character is found and developed.

God spoke to Samuel and said, "How long will you mourn for Saul, seeing I have rejected him from reigning over Israel?" (1 Sam. 16:1). There is a time to mourn but there is also a time to move on and do what God wants you to do. God's work goes beyond the failures of any man. God told Moses at the Red Sea, "Why do you cry to Me? Tell the children of Israel to go forward" (Ex. 14:15). One thing to learn in the midst of trial and hardship is life goes on. The clock is always ticking and you must put the past behind you. Keep going forward for you are about to enter a new chapter in your life. God's breakthrough for your life is in front of you, not behind you. Old things have passed away, behold, all things become new (2 Cor. 5:17). God tells Samuel to stop mourning. Enough is enough. There is a new king, the one chosen by God, ready to be anointed. He tells Samuel, "Fill your horn with oil, and go; I am sending you to Jesse the Bethlehemite. For I have provided Myself a king among his sons" (vs. 11). He is saying to get ready because something great is about to happen.

In Hebrew this verse says, "Among the sons of Jesse I have seen a king." People look but do they really see? Do they see as God sees? You must have the right vision in order to run your race and finish your course. Saul was a king who ran his race but he crossed the wrong finish line. He missed the mark of the high calling of God. Why? He didn't see things through the eyes of God and this is why his life and reign as king was a total disaster. He didn't see as God sees. Know also that God is looking at your life and He sees what nobody else sees. He sees your full potential. He sees what you can become in Him as you submit your will to His will. Even if setbacks happen, you can take comfort knowing that things are never out of His control. God is never without a plan. His new plan for Israel is about to unfold as He sends Samuel to the home of Jesse, the grandson of Ruth and Boaz (Ruth 4:17,22). Samuel appears to be a little hesitant, fearing that Saul might kill him. He had just publicly embarrassed the king so he's got every right to be concerned for his life.

God, in His infinite mercy, meets Samuel where he's at and tells him to take a heifer with him and say he's come to sacrifice to the Lord. "Then invite Jesse to the sacrifice, and I will show you what you shall do; you shall anoint for Me the one I name to you" (vs. 3). Samuel did what the Lord said and went to Bethlehem, a small town not far from Jerusalem. It was a hilly region with many grain fields carved into the hillsides. The elders of the city trembled when they saw him coming. Considering what Samuel had just done to King Agag, it is no wonder they were afraid. They should have been excited that the man of God was coming to their town. Still, it was a dark period in history at that time so the people trembled at his coming. When a man of God like Samuel comes into your presence, it typically means you're going to be judged for some wrong behavior. The elders ask Samuel if he comes in peace and he responds that he indeed has come in peace. He told them to get ready to take part in the sacrifice to the Lord. He then invited Jesse and his sons to the same sacrifice.

It is now time to do what Samuel came here for. It is time to anoint the next king of Israel. Jesse's oldest son Eliab came and stood before the prophet and Samuel must have thought to himself, "Now there's a king if I ever saw one." He's tall and handsome and looks the part of a king, just like Saul. To be big and tall in those days meant you were probably the head of your clan or tribe. It also meant you were typically a better fighter than those around you. Scottish knight William Wallace was a foot taller than his fellow patriarchs and his sword was five and a half feet long. He was unstoppable in battle and everybody rallied around him. Samuel was certain Eliab was the one so he proclaimed out loud, "Surely the Lord's anointed is before you" (vs. 6). Samuel didn't seem to remember that God said He would point out the son to be anointed. Here, Samuel is making the choice himself. God rebukes him for this and says, "Do not look at his appearance or at the height of his stature, because I have rejected him. For the Lord does not see as man sees; for man looks at the outward appearance, but the Lord looks at the heart" (vs. 7).

God sees everything. Heb. 4:13 (NLT) says, "Nothing in all creation is hidden from God. Everything is naked and exposed before His eyes, and He is the one to whom we are accountable." All doors to your life are open to Him and there are no rugs under which things get swept. God sees it all and He's looking for a heart that is open and loyal to Him. Ps. 4:3 says, "But know that the Lord has set apart for Himself him who is godly." God wants Samuel to see what He sees, to see that the character of a person's heart is far more important than one's physical appearance. God is saying looks can be deceiving. You can't tell a book by its cover. People crave to be like the best known Hollywood actors not realizing their lives are drenched in sex, drugs, and every evil known under the sun. These people have fortune and fame but don't have character and they're on their way to eternal judgment. What does it mean to be a person after God's own heart? It's when your heart is in perfect alignment with His heart. Rom. 8:5 says, "For those who live according to the flesh set their minds on the things of the flesh, but those who live according to the Spirit, the things of the Spirit."

The Lord now has Samuel's attention. Eliab was not the one chosen to be king so six other sons pass before the prophet. To each one Samuel says, "Neither has the Lord chosen this one." He then asks Jesse, "Are all the young men here?" Jesse responds, "There remains yet the youngest, and there he is, keeping the sheep." Samuel then says to Jesse, "Send and bring him. For we will not sit down till he comes here" (vs. 11). So small was David in the eyes of his family that his father doesn't even mention him by name. He wasn't invited to the sacrificial feast and would not have been brought in from the fields had Samuel not insisted on it. Why was David considered the outcast of the family? Perhaps the answer is found in Ps. 51:5 where he wrote, "Behold, I was brought forth in iniquity, and in sin my mother conceived me." The event spoken of here is the conception of David and not his birth. He is not saying he was born a sinner but that his mother was in sin when she got pregnant. Either Jesse's wife had an affair with another man or Jesse had an affair with another woman. Either way, David was the byproduct of this infidelity.

One thing that is known is that David had a sister named Abigail (1 Chron. 2:16) whose father was not Jesse (2 Sam. 17:25). As a result of his mother's sin, David grew up in a family where he was despised, rejected, and shunned. He was treated with scorn and ridicule and was considered the outcast of the family. Perhaps this is why he was forced to be a shepherd alone in the fields. His family was hoping a lion or a bear would kill him. Psalm 69 addresses the misery David endured growing up. His childhood was full of loneliness and he speaks of hours crying because of the rejection (vs. 3). He explains his frustration of being punished for a sin he did not commit (vs. 4). He writes in vs. 7,8, "Because for Your sake I have borne reproach; Shame has covered my face. I have become a stranger to my brothers, and an alien to my mother's children." The Hebrew word for "stranger" is "muzar" which means 'bastard; an illegitimate child.' When David was born his family greeted his birth with scorn and contempt. He became the object of mockery as the drunkards sang about his plight (vs. 12). He adds that he carried the personal shame of his mother's sin (vs. 19,20).

It is interesting to note that nowhere in scripture is David's mother mentioned by name. In the Bible many of the mothers of the prophets and founding fathers are written about because they often played a significant role in their upbringing. Not so with David's mother. She was a woman who brought shame upon Jesse and his family and it is no surprise that her name is not mentioned in scripture. David was viewed as an illegitimate child and this explains why he was not initially included in the meeting with Samuel. While everybody waited, David was out in some field performing the lowest, least honorable position of service in the land. He was relegated to the task of looking after his father's sheep in a lonely, miserable place. Just because you're not visible doesn't mean you're not valuable. It's in the daily grind of everyday life where hearts are molded and prepared to be used by God. Nobody sees you changing those messy diapers or cleaning that dirty toilet but God sees it. Never put yourself in a box, never paint yourself into a corner. Don't let your current position determine what your future will look like.

Sheep are some of the hardest animals on the planet to take care of. They're stubborn, they smell, and they're stupid. Taking care of them is a very humiliating thing to do but it was in the role of a shepherd that God was training David to be a king. Pastor Paul Daugherty once said, "What looks like humiliation is actually preparation for an acceleration toward your destiny." David was out of the limelight in an obscure place unseen and unappreciated by others but God was molding and preparing him to fulfill his destiny. While his family saw a runt, the lowest of the low, a mere shepherd boy, God saw a king. David would one day become the shepherd king of all Israel. No matter what you look like, no matter what your position is, no matter what other people think about you, always remember that God sees your heart. David was brought in from the field and 1 Sam. 16:12 (NLT) says, "He was dark and handsome, with beautiful eyes." And the Lord said, "Arise, anoint him; for this is the one!" You need to say the same thing about yourself. Say out loud, "I am the one!" You are the one God has chosen. Rejoice over that and be glad.

David was a young man, a teenager really, whose own heart beat after the heart of God. He was a man of "character", a word that means 'to cut; to engrave.' Character is developed through an engraving process where the ways of God cut into you and mark your heart and soul. It's a process that causes you to love and serve God with all your heart, and to joyfully serve others with all that is in you. If you want to develop kingly character, then you must know the King. Saul knew about God but never knew Him in a personal way. This is why his character was never developed and why he failed as king. David wrote in Ps. 27:4, "One thing I have desired of the Lord, that I will seek: That I may dwell in the house of the Lord all the days of my life, to behold the beauty of the Lord and to inquire in His temple." These are the words of a man after God's own heart. Some people spend more time in the gym developing their muscles than they do in the Bible developing the character of their heart. Paul reminds everybody in 2 Cor. 4:16 that the "outward man is perishing, yet the inward man is being renewed day by day."

1 Sam. 16:13 says, "Then Samuel took the horn of oil and anointed him in the midst of his brothers." God will cause you to shine in front of those who hate you the most. If they didn't make you, they can't break you. They can't disqualify you in the race of life. "And the Spirit of the Lord came upon David from that day forward." This is the first mention of

David's name in scripture. The name "David" means 'beloved' or 'the loved one' and is mentioned over a thousand times in the Bible. He was an outstanding young man who was worthy of his name. Powerfully the Spirit of God came upon David. In Hebrew it says the Spirit literally "rushed upon him." This was not a one time event but a continuous action. For the rest of his life, the Spirit of God would be rushing and flooding into the life of David, empowering him to fulfill his calling. He wrote in Ps. 27:10, "When my father and my mother forsake me, then the Lord will take care of me." Paul would later write in Phil. 1:6, "He who has begun a good work in you will complete it until the day of Jesus Christ." So begins the story of David, the shepherd king.

The Shepherd King

-7-

"A MAN OF WAR"

The life of David is praised in the New Testament. Acts 13:21,22 says, "And afterward they asked for a king; so God gave them Saul the son of Kish, a man of the tribe of Benjamin, for forty years. And when He removed him, He raised up for them David as king, to whom also He gave testimony and said, 'I have found David the son of Jesse, a man after My own heart, who will do all My will.'" God did not see David like his siblings saw him. He looked into David's heart and saw a man to whom He could show Himself strong on his behalf. In David he saw the heart of a servant. Godly character is in the heart and is revealed when it works its way out of you and into the lives of others. It's shown when you put the needs of others above your own. Phil. 2:3,4 says, "Let nothing be done through selfish ambition or conceit, but in lowliness of mind let each esteem others better than himself. Let each of you look out not only for his own interests, but also for the interests of others." The Message Bible says, "Don't be obsessed with getting your own advantage. Forget yourselves long enough to lend a helping hand."

Dietrich Bonhoeffer once said, "When Christ calls a man, He bids him come and die." God is looking for people who have the heart of a servant, a heart He can mold and shape into one like His own. He found such a man in David. Ps. 78:70,71 (CEV) says, "The Lord God chose David to be His servant and took him from tending sheep and from caring for lambs. Then God made him the leader of Israel, His own nation." God is also looking for a heart of integrity. Vs. 72 says, "So he shepherded them according to the integrity of his heart, and guided them by the skillfulness of his hands." The GNT says, "David took care of them with unselfish devotion and led them with skill." The Hebrew word for "integrity" means 'complete, wholesome, sound, and unimpaired.' It's having a godly character and doing the right thing when nobody is looking. It's the things you do that only God can see. He looks beyond those things which are superficial and looks directly into a person's heart. Samuel anoints David and what does David do next? He goes back to the sheep. He was first and foremost a shepherd and he did it faithfully with all his heart.

As the Spirit of the Lord comes upon David, a distressing spirit came to Saul and it troubled him (1 Sam. 16:14). The same Holy Spirit that is empowering David has now departed from Saul. He lost his spiritual covering and protection and an evil spirit came in to fill the void. The word "troubled" means 'tormented; terrorized.' There are severe consequences to rebellion and disobedience, especially among those called to be leaders in the kingdom of God. This distressing spirit fell upon Saul and overwhelmed him. He now has to do everything in the energy of the flesh and that is the prescription for a miserable life. So many people try to do a spiritual work with their own energy. This means the anointing is not there so they try to make up for it with hard work and perspiration. The anointing only flows when a person is doing what God assigned them to do. The Holy Spirit brings inspiration to go along with the perspiration and this is how destinies get fulfilled. Saul's servants recognize the problem and make a suggestion to him. Here is a sign that Saul's kingdom has begun to crumble. Servants don't talk to kings; kings talk to servants.

The servants said to Saul, "Let our master now command your servants, who are before you, to seek out a man who is a skillful player on the harp; and it shall be that he will play it with his hand when the distressing spirit from God is upon you, and you shall be well" (vs. 16). The harp was a portable instrument that could be easily carried around wherever a person went. This wasn't one of the big harps found in an orchestra. The Greek word for this instrument is where the English word "guitar" comes from. Music has a powerful impact on the human soul and the servants of Saul knew this. They knew that a well-played harp could calm the savage beast that was tormenting their king. The problem is they're trying to use music to cover up the real issue. They were trying to deal with the symptoms rather than the cause. Saul is distressed and they think he'll feel better if some soft music is played. Yes, he'll get a little peace from the music but it will be a false peace. It won't change who he is on the inside so in the long run the music doesn't do him any good.

Saul does not reprimand or chastise his servants for speaking out of place but instead says to them, "Provide me now a man who can play well, and bring him to me" (vs. 17). Here is where God steps in. One of the servants answers Saul, "Look, I have seen a son of Jesse the Bethlehemite, who is skillful in playing, a mighty man of valor, a man of war, prudent in speech, and a handsome person; and the Lord is with him" (vs. 18). This description of David is mind-boggling considering the fact he is only a teenager. The Lord was with him and this will cause anybody to stand out in a crowd. Saul sent messengers to Jesse and said to him, "Send me your son David, who is with the sheep" (vs. 19). After being anointed, David returned to the sheep. He understood that it was God's job to bring him to the throne. He didn't have to manipulate his way to the palace. He allowed God to open the doors for him. He's still out in the field attending to his father's sheep while behind the scenes God is setting in motion a plan that will eventually cause David to be crowned king of Israel.

"So David came to Saul and stood before him. And he loved him greatly, and he became his armorbearer" (vs. 21). The word "stood" means 'to remain; to stay; to endure.' David came and stayed with Saul and ministered to him with the music he played. He was skillful with the harp and this reflects an attitude as much as it tells of his ability to play. God uses the evil that was going on in the life of Saul to bring David to the throne room of the king. Saul loved David and took to him immediately. He made David his chief assistant in battle by giving him the important and trusted position of armorbearer. God was showing Himself strong on David's behalf because he was a person with a loyal heart. He used David to minister to Saul where for the first time he was in the royal court where he began to learn the customs and manners that he would need to be a good king later in his life. David poured his life out to a man who didn't deserve it, just like Jesus poured His life out to a sinful world who also didn't deserve it. Unwittingly, Saul became dependent on the one designated to succeed him.

The story of David and Saul takes place in the Promised Land, the land flowing with milk and honey. There were battles to be fought when Joshua first led the people across the Jordan River, and there are battles to be fought now. All during his reign as king, Saul and the people of Israel were plagued with battle after battle, enemy after enemy. Being anointed doesn't mean you'll have an easy life, that you'll travel down a smooth road with no obstacles on it. No, being anointed puts you into an arena where you'll be used and empowered by God and this makes you a target of the devil. It's when the hard battles of life take place day after day after day. David has just been anointed to be the next king of Israel and almost immediately his battles begin. 1 Sam. 17:1-3 tells how the Philistines gathered their armies together to once again go to war against the people of Israel. They were in Sochoh which belongs to Judah, the land God had given to His people. Saul responded to this challenge and the men of Israel gathered together and encamped in the Valley of Elah where they lined up in battle formation to face the enemy.

The Valley of Elah is a wide valley about a mile across that runs mostly east and west and is located about fifteen miles southwest of Bethlehem. Vs. 3 says, "The Philistines stood on a mountain on one side, and Israel stood on a mountain on the other side, with a valley between them." There was a champion in the Philistine army who stood over nine and a half feet tall. His name was Goliath and he was big, obnoxious, and loud. The word "champion" comes from a Hebrew word that means 'a middle man; a man between two.' The idea is that this man stood between the two armies and fought as a representative of his army. Goliath was a mountain of a man, a fearsome gladiator, a wrecking ball, a weapon of mass destruction. So huge was this giant that his armor weighed over two hundred pounds. For forty days he openly defied the armies of Israel, challenging them to send a man out to fight him. He said in vs. 9, "If he is able to fight with me and kill me, then we will be your servants. But if I prevail against him and kill him, then you shall be our servants and serve us."

Where did this monster of a man come from? Giants are first mentioned in the Bible in Gen. 6:4, "There were giants on the earth in those days, and also afterward, when the sons of God came in to the daughters of men and they bore children to them. These were the mighty men who were of old, men of renown." There has been much debate to who these "sons of God" were and one must always allow the Bible to interpret itself. In the Old Testament, the phrase "sons of God" always refers to angels (Job 1:6, 2:1, 38:7). That being established, this verse is saying that fallen angels took on human form and mated with human females. Don't be in denial thinking this couldn't happen. While angels are spiritual beings, they can still appear in human form (Mark 16:5). The men of Sodom and Gomorrah wanted to have sex with the two angels who were with Lot (Gen. 19:1-5). Abraham had three heavenly messengers who came in human form and ate a meal with him. Let's also not forget Heb. 13:2 (NLT), "Don't forget to show hospitality to strangers, for some who have done this have entertained angels without realizing it!"

Yes, angels can take on the form of humans and it was these fallen "sons of God" who produced a race of giants. The Message Bible says, "The giants came from the union of the sons of God and the daughters of men. These were the mighty men of ancient lore, the famous ones." The "sons of God" were supernatural beings who produced men of supernatural strength and stature. There are many giants in the Bible besides Goliath and none of them were godly men. Og, king of Bashan, was a man so big his bed was made of iron and was over thirteen feet long and six feet wide (Deut. 3:11). 2 Sam. 21:20 goes on to say that in Gath "there was a man of great stature, who had six fingers on each hand and six toes on each foot, twenty-four in number, and he was also born to the giant." Why would these fallen angels mate with human women? Scripture does not say but it is plausible they were attempting to pollute the human bloodline in order to prevent the future birth of the Messiah. God did say in Gen. 3:5 that the Seed of the woman, meaning Jesus, would one day bruise the head of the serpent, meaning the devil.

So deplorable was what these angels did that immediately after giants are first mentioned in Gen. 6:4, God decides to destroy the whole world with a great flood. All the giants at that time were killed along with everyone else. However, Gen. 6:4 says the giants were on the earth after the flood took place. It stands to reason that the fallen angels repeated their sin with the descendants of Noah. More giants were born and they were in the Promised Land when Moses sent twelve men to spy it out. Ten of the spies came back with a bad report saying, "The land through which we have gone as spies is a land that devours its inhabitants, and all the people whom we saw in it are men of great stature. There we saw giants and we were like grasshoppers in our own sight, and so we were in their sight" (Num. 13:32,33). Years later, when Joshua and Caleb invaded the land of Canaan, the giants were killed off although a few scattered to Gaza, Gath, and Ashdod (Joshua 11:21,22). Goliath was from Gath and at the time he lived only a handful of giants remained.

Why are there no giants alive today? It seems that God put an end to demons mating with humans by placing all the fallen angels who did in isolation. Jude 6 says, "And the angels who did not keep their proper domain, but left their own habitation, He has reserved in everlasting chains under darkness for the judgment of the great day." Clearly not all demons are in a spiritual prison today so there must have been a group of them that sinned beyond the original fall. It can be presumed that the demons who mated with human females are the ones who are bound with everlasting chains. This would prevent any more giants from being born. There may be no giants alive today, but there was a huge one in the Valley of Elah challenging the army of the living God. Goliath is a symbol of what seems to be an insurmountable problem in your life. It's an obstacle that you've tried to bring down but in the end it grows bigger and stronger with the passing of time. Instead of fighting army against army, the giant proposed they fight one-on-one, him against a person of Israel's choosing.

Goliath said, "I defy the armies of Israel this day; give me a man, that we may fight together" (vs. 10). The giant's deep voice vibrated against the tall hills surrounding the Valley of Elah. The sound struck fear into the hearts of every Israelite soldier. This was the giant's exact intention in issuing the challenge. He did this to intimidate the children of Israel, to erode their morale. He wanted to win the battle before it even began by striking fear into those who heard him. Vs. 11 says, "When Saul and all Israel heard these words of the Philistine, they were dismayed and greatly afraid." The Message Bible says "they were terrified and lost all hope." Saul, the once anointed king, is paralyzed by fear from what he heard the giant say. When the Spirit of God left him, so did his courage. This is sad because the people initially wanted a king who would "go out before us and fight our battles" (1 Sam. 8:20). The people placed their hope in their king and they wanted him to come out of his tent and accept the challenge of Goliath. Sad to say, Saul is nowhere to be found.

The credibility of Saul is slipping away as each minute passes and the challenge is not accepted. This, in turn, causes the hope of his army to wither up and die. Prov. 13:12 says, "Hope deferred makes the heart sick." The Message Bible says, "Unrelenting disappointment leaves you heartsick." A fact of life is people place their hope in what they depend on. When the person you place your hope in disappoints you, oftentimes the measure of your hope becomes the measure of your disappointment and anger. This is why many people resent their parents and their spouses. Their hope is in them and they feel they've been let down. Successful people also struggle because now they're sitting on the throne of their lives. They place their hope in themselves because of the success they've achieved. This is called pride which means they're in imminent danger of ruin and destruction. Prov. 16:18 (MSG) says, "The bigger the ego, the harder the fall." God didn't want the people to put their hope in their king, their family, or themselves. He is the God of hope (Rom. 15:13) and He wants the people to put their hope in Him.

Goliath is relentless in his challenge. By defying the armies of Israel, he is in fact defying God. To him, this is another battle of the gods, a battle to see whose god is more supreme. 1 Sam. 17:16 says, "And the Philistine drew near and presented himself forty days, morning and evening." In the Bible, the number "forty" appears 146 times and symbolizes a period of testing, trial, or probation. At the time of the great flood, it rained for forty days and forty nights. Abraham tried to bargain with God to not destroy Sodom and Gomorrah if forty righteous people could be found. Both Isaac and Esau were forty years old when they got married. Moses lived for forty years in Egypt, forty years on the back side of the desert, and forty years wandering in the wilderness. The prophet Ezekiel laid on his right side for forty days to symbolize Judah's sin. Jesus was tempted in the wilderness forty days. After He was raised from the dead, He walked on the earth for forty days. It was forty years after the death of Christ when the Roman Empire burned Jerusalem to the ground.

Goliath is not going away until somebody accepts his challenge. Until then, he'll be back every day relentlessly taunting the people of God. Little did he know what was taking place fifteen miles away in the little town of Bethlehem. David has been anointed by Samuel and God is preparing him to become king of Israel. He was the youngest of Jesse's eight sons but God said in Ps. 89:27, "Also I will make him My firstborn, the highest of the kings of the earth." God wasn't using the term "firstborn" as a description of David's birth order but was pointing to his preeminence as king. Paul uses this term in Col. 1:15 when he called Jesus "the firstborn over all creation." David was Saul's armorbearer but occasionally he would return home to Bethlehem to feed his father's sheep (vs. 15). It seems David was only called to the palace when he was needed, when Saul was tormented by the distressing spirit. David was at home serving his father while his three oldest brothers followed Saul to the battle. Jesse then told David to take some food to his brothers and bring back word of how things were going.

Here's the future king of Israel being a servant to his father and three brothers, those who despise him the most. No matter what ministry God has called you to, know for certain you will be called upon to serve others. Even Jesus said in Matt. 20:27,28, "And whoever desires to be first among you, let him be your slave. Just as the Son of Man did not come to be served, but to serve, and to give His life a ransom for many." Jesus served people and this is what David is doing here. He's anointed to be king but he's still willing to serve. He's a shepherd boy at heart being prepared to lead people. A king serves by leading and leads by serving. All this is preparing David for the role of being a public servant as king of Israel. Vs. 20 says, "So David rose early in the morning, left the sheep with a keeper, and took the things and went as Jesse had commanded him." This shows the heart of David. He didn't sleep in but rose early so that he may obey his father. He also made sure the sheep were well cared for while he was away. He was faithful in the little things and this caused him to be faithful in the big things.

The requirement of having authority is you must first learn to be under authority. According to the Bible, authority ought to be submitted to and respected (Rom. 13:1-7). The way you submit to those over you now, determines whether or not God can give you a leadership position later on. Don't expect to get promoted in life if you rebel against those in positions of authority over you now. You can't murmur and complain to your boss at work and expect God to use you to work in His kingdom. You can't work hard when your boss is watching you and slack off when he's not. Eccl. 9:10 says, "Whatever your hand finds to do, do it with all your might." Paul wrote in Col. 3:23, "And whatever you do, do it heartily, as to the Lord and not to men." How you respond and perform at your job shows God how you'll work for Him in whatever assignment

He gives you. If you don't think God is using you in a meaningful way, check up on yourself and see how you're handling your responsibilities at home and at the workplace. It does make a difference.

David was no doubt praising his God as he made the long, hot fifteen mile journey to the Valley of Elah. When he reached the army camp, he left his supplies in the hand of the supply keeper and ran to the front line to greet his brothers. It was here that David heard for the first time the defying challenge coming from the mouth of Goliath. He saw with his own eyes the men of Israel as they ran in fear from the giant because they were dreadfully afraid (vs. 23,24). The soldiers said, "Have you seen this man who has come up? Surely he has come up to defy Israel" (vs. 25). Goliath is aggressive in his challenge. In vs. 8 he leaves his line and calls out to the army of Israel from the middle of the valley. He advances forward and here he is coming up the mountain on the Israeli side of the valley. He's getting closer and closer to the frightened men of Israel. He's acting just like the devil. He's unceasing in his intimidation and is very aggressive. The longer it takes him to be confronted, the closer he gets and his attacks will become stronger than ever.

If you allow the enemy to go unchallenged, he will always advance in your life. Remember, all it takes for evil to triumph is for good men to do nothing. Thankfully, David was a good man and he's about to do something. He hears the men talking about the situation at hand and he asks an interesting question to the men who stood by him, "What shall be done for the man who kills this Philistine and takes away the reproach from Israel?" (vs. 26). There is a reward for killing giants and it is not wrong to expect rewards from God. He said in Rev. 22:12, "And behold, I am coming quickly, and My reward is with Me, to give to every one according to his work." David then asks, "For who is this uncircumcised Philistine, that he should defy the armies of the living God?" These are the first words recorded in scripture that David spoke. He knows there is a living God, a God who lives, who thinks, who feels, who creates, who acts. He also knew that God was taking this defiance personally. He said in Zech. 2:8 (CSB), "For whoever touches you touches the apple of My eye."

What made David different from everybody else is he saw things from God's perspective while the men of Israel saw things from man's perspective. They called Goliath "this man" (vs. 25) but David called him "this uncircumcised Philistine." He knew that circumcision was required of Abraham and all his descendants as a sign of the covenant God made with him (Gen. 17:9-14). David asked, "Who is this giant who's not part of Israel's covenant with God? Who does he think he is trying to take land promised to the people by the God of Israel? What shall be done to the man who kills him?" David was not terrified of the giant but he was offended at his defiance of God. The men answer him and said what they talked about in vs. 25, "It shall be that the man who kills him the king will enrich with great riches, will give him his daughter, and give his father's house exemption in Israel." Rewards give people the motivation to do the right thing. Jesus talked about rewards given as a motivation for righteousness, for things such as persecution (Matt. 5:12), love (Matt. 5:46), giving (Matt. 6:4), prayer (Matt. 6:6), and fasting (Matt. 6:18).

David's oldest brother Eliab heard this conversation and his anger is greatly aroused. He asks David, "Why did you come down here? And with whom have you left those few sheep in the wilderness? I know your pride and the insolence of your heart, for you have come down to see the battle" (vs. 28). David's motive and character is attacked by Eliab. Sometimes the greatest insults you'll ever hear come from those closest to you. The greater the vision, the greater the opposition. Eliab knew about David's past but he didn't know about his brother's destiny. People see who you are now but they don't see who you'll become. They don't see the plans and destiny God has for your life. They don't see your potential but you do. You know who you are and what your future holds because you belong to the King of kings and Lord of lords. You know who you are by knowing whose you are. You are a child of the living God. Your identity is not in your ability, it's in Christ. Don't allow the condemnation from others rob you of God's plan for your life.

The Shepherd King

-8-

"RUN TO THE ROAR"

Don't allow yourself to be held back from fulfilling your destiny because of what other people say. David is being scorned by his brothers just like Jesus was scorned by His. As long as there are people, there will be slander. It is a dark sin and can do great damage to the victims of such evil speaking. It can unravel families, break up marriages, and cause division in the local church. This happens because the devil wants you to take your eyes off of him and focus on those attacking you. Eph. 6:12 (NLT) says, "For we are not fighting against flesh-and-blood enemies, but against evil rulers and authorities of the unseen world, against mighty powers in the dark world, and against evil spirits in the heavenly places." You can't turn your eyes off the real enemy in order to defend these unwarranted attacks on your character. Turn the situation over to God and let Him be your vindicator. Ps. 4:2 (CJB) says, "O God, my vindicator! Answer me when I call! When I was distressed, You set me free; now have mercy on me, and hear my prayer."

David's visit should have pleased Eliab considering all the things he brought from home. So why was Eliab angry? Did

David's courage magnify his cowardice? He was a tall man of good appearance and he may have felt David was trying to push him into battle. When you are dismayed and dreadfully afraid, the last thing you want is someone telling you to be courageous. Or maybe he's angry because he remembers he was the first son to stand before Samuel and the first to be rejected. He's angry and jealous over David being anointed as king. He accuses David of being lazy and coming to the battle just to observe and see what happens. He is also jealous because he saw in David a level of trust and confidence in God that nobody else had. The giant was intimidating but people of intense faith can be intimidating as well. David said to his brother, "What have I done now? Is there not a cause?" (vs. 29). He then turned away and asked another person what shall be done to the person who kills the giant. He was given the same answer he was told the first time he asked.

Charles Spurgeon wrote, "The word-battle in which he had to engage with his brother and with King Saul was a more trying ordeal to him than going forth in the strength of the Lord to smite the uncircumcised boaster. Many a man meets with more trouble from his friends than from his enemies." David was publicly rebuked by his own brother, probably amid the laughter of other soldiers. What Eliab said no doubt hurt David but he would not let it hinder him. He was more concerned with God's cause than his own feelings. Don't let the negative words of others slow you down but keep pressing forward. The dog barks but the train keeps rolling. If Eliab's words can get David to respond in the flesh, then he would be out of step with the Spirit of God. You don't have to respond to every critical word said against you. It's a waste of your time and energy. It's not worth the hassle. Don't fight battles that are unnecessary. David wasn't going to argue with his brother. Prov. 15:1 says, "A soft answer turns away wrath but a fool will stir up strife and anger."

Many of God's people are so busy fighting each other they don't have enough energy to fight the real enemy. A story is told that tells of two deer who got in a fight with one another. They rammed each other so hard they couldn't break loose from the grip their antlers had on one another. Eventually the two deer starved to death. The moral of the story is believers will starve themselves from a relationship with God if they fight each other rather than fighting the real enemy. Choose your battles wisely. When Christians fight among themselves, it gives the devil free reign to gain ground. David knew Eliab was not the real enemy so he did the right thing. He turned away from his brother and talked with somebody else. David showed more courage than anyone there so his words were reported to Saul who then sent for him. When he arrived before the king, David said, "Let no man's heart fail because of him; your servant will go and fight with this Philistine" (vs. 32). David is absolutely fearless. This sounds like youthful pride but it's not. It's faith in the living God.

Saul waited forty days to hear someone say these words and it seemed ridiculous coming from this teenage boy. David could have said, "You should fight this giant" but instead he said, "I'll do it." In the Bible, when the Spirit of God comes upon a person, boldness and courage comes with it. This boldness causes you to rise up in the midst of extreme hostilities and persecution. Faith makes you unafraid of the enemy. With faith you don't have to fear sickness, poverty, or what people say about you. It is God's will for you to live a bold, courageous life. This boldness doesn't stop problems from coming your way but it does give you the confidence to face what's in front of you. In life, all people deal with fear in one form or another but real courage is facing your fear and doing the right thing anyway. Don't retreat in battle when things are coming against you. Paul wrote in Rom. 8:31, "If God is for us, who can be against us?" Martin Luther King Jr. once defined courage as "being dangerously unselfish." Selfish people run away, those with courage don't.

As David stood before the king, he was obeying the command Jesus gave in Mark 11:22 when He said, "Have faith in God." Faith is a lifestyle, a way of living. Heb. 10:38 says, "The just shall live by faith." David knew he could defeat the giant because he knew God was with him. He didn't look at the size of Goliath, he looked at the size of his God. He walked by faith and not by sight (2 Cor. 5:7). He also knew that the spirit of faith is the spirit of victory. 2 Cor. 2:14 (GWT) says, "But I thank God, who always leads us in victory because of Christ." God wants you to walk in victory in every area of your life. He wants you to get out of your comfort zone and walk on the water, to step into the plan He has for your life. He wants you to do things that others say are impossible. The people thought Goliath couldn't be defeated but nobody told David that. To fight giants you've got to leave fear behind and live a life fueled by faith. You must step beyond the shores of complacency and raise the level of your expectation. If you'll do that, you will experience extraordinary manifestations of the greatness of God.

You have a biblical right to expect good things to happen in your life when your expectancy level is high. Prov. 23:18 says, "For surely there is a future hope; and your expectation shall not be cut off." The Message Bible says, "You won't be left with an armload of nothing." The key to David's confidence is he was aware of God's presence in his life. He wrote in Ps. 27:1, "The Lord is my light and my salvation; Whom shall I fear? The Lord is the strength of my life; Of whom shall I be afraid?" You can step out on the water if you know Jesus is in front of you calling you to come to Him. When hard times come, be aware of His presence as He says to you, "Be of good cheer! It is I; do not be afraid" (Mark 6:50). There were many struggles in David's life but he found a guiding principle that allowed him to thrive in life and overcome that which would try to hinder him. With laser-like precision there is one thing he chose to focus on more than anything else. That one thing was the presence of God in his life. What David desired most was continual, unbroken fellowship with the living God.

David wrote in Ps. 27:4, "One thing I have desired of the Lord, that will I seek; That I may dwell in the house of the Lord all the days of my life, to behold the beauty of the Lord, and to inquire in His temple." The Message Bible says, "I'm asking God for one thing, only one thing; To live with Him in His house my whole life long. I'll contemplate His beauty; I'll study at His feet." Vs. 8 says, "When You said, 'Seek My face,' my heart said to You, 'Your face, Lord, I will seek.'" He wrote in Ps. 63:1, "O God, You are my God; Early will I seek You; My soul thirsts for You; My flesh longs for You in a dry and thirsty land where there is no water." David was disciplined. He got up early and sought the Lord. Lazy people don't get used by God. Getting up early puts you in good company. Referring to Jesus, Mark 1:35 says, "Rising very early before dawn, He left and went off to a deserted place, where He prayed." Start your day with the Word of God and prayer. Prayer changes everything. As you pray, you'll be reminded of the greatness of God and the smallness of your enemy.

David knew that life is a battle, a place of conflict. Enemies come and enemies go. 1 Peter 4:12 says, "Behold, think it not strange concerning the fiery trial which is to try you, as though some strange thing happened to you." David also knew that life must be faced head-on. You can't escape from your problems by turning to drugs and alcohol. Becoming a workaholic won't help either. David didn't run away from the challenge because he had faith and confidence in the goodness of God. He wrote in Ps. 27:13, "I would have lost heart, unless I had believed that I would see the goodness of the Lord in the land of the living." Vs. 14 (MSG) says, "Stay with God! Take heart. Don't quit. I'll say it again! Stay with God." Standing before Saul was a little shepherd boy just come in from the field who has more faith and courage than the king and all the men of Israel. Was Saul impressed? Hardly. He looks at David and says, "You are not able to go against this Philistine to fight with him; for you are but a youth, and he a man of war from his youth" (vs. 33).

The first words out of Saul's mouth are words of unbelief. People love to discourage those who walk by faith. He thought David was disqualified because of his age, size, and inexperience. He thought there was no way David could win, David thought there was no way he could lose. People may say you don't stand a chance against the giants in your life but Phil. 4:13 says, "I can do all things through Christ who strengthens me." It's not what other people say that matters, it's what you say about yourself on the inside. It's knowing how big your God is and who you are in Christ. In David's eyes, God was a lot bigger than the overgrown Goliath. He wrote in Ps. 18:2,3, "The Lord is my rock and my fortress and my deliverer; My God, my strength, in whom I will trust; My shield and the strength of my salvation, my stronghold. I will call upon the Lord, who is worthy to be praised; So shall I be saved from my enemies." Who could lose having a God like that? All people have giants in their life, hardships and trials that must be dealt with. Thankfully, David knew every giant can be defeated.

David is not about to let Saul weaken his faith. He talks back to him like the man of war he is. "Your servant used to keep his father's sheep, and when a lion or a bear came and took a lamb out of the flock, I went out after it and struck it, and delivered the lamb from its mouth; and when it rose against me, I caught it by its beard, and struck and killed it" (vs. 34,35). David didn't run from the lion, he ran to the lion. When trials come your way, run to the roar. In the jungle, female lions do most of the work hunting prey. While the female stalks their prey from behind, the male lion will come from the front and let loose a roar that is so powerful it can be heard up to five miles away. The hunted animal is so frightened by this roar that they turn around and run right into the path of the female lion. You need to realize that the devil's roar is more bark than bite. When you run away from things that scare you, you run into that which can destroy your life. If you fail to face your fears, they will always be right there behind you.

It will not take long for a person who has made the commitment to walk by faith to realize there is a demonic host arrayed against the body of Christ. James 1:2,3 says your faith will be tested by various trials hurled at you by the evil one. There is a curse on the earth and your adversary the devil is a thief who comes to steal, kill, and destroy (John 10:10). What should you do when the storm clouds of life cast their dark shadows over your head? Fear not! Run to the roar! Most shepherds would have stayed with the flock where it was most safe. Not David. He went after the one sheep that was taken. Jesus said in the parable of the lost sheep, "What man of you, having a hundred sheep, if he loses one of them, does not leave the ninety-nine in the wilderness, and go after the one which is lost until he finds it" (Luke 15:4). David was not afraid of any lion and he's not afraid of this giant. Is. 54:14 says, "In righteousness you shall be established; you shall be far from oppression and you shall not fear; and from terror, for it shall not come near you."

Giants are not a cause for fear or panic for the born again believer. All you have to do is run to the roar and face your storm. A cattle rancher in Montana made a discovery that taught him a lesson for living life. The winters in Montana are brutal and only the strong cattle survive. This rancher observed that the cattle who marched headfirst into the blizzard always survived while the cattle who turned their tails to the storm died. The rancher found these cows frozen against a barbed-wire fence with their heads down whereas he found the other cattle who faced the storm alive and well, strong survivors. With God on your side, you can face your storm and fear not. Ps. 118:6 says, "The Lord is on my side; I will not fear. What can man do to me?" Phil. 1:28 (AMP) says, "And do not for a moment be frightened or intimidated in anything by your opponents and adversaries, for such constancy and fearlessness will be a clear sign to them of their impending destruction; but a sure token and evidence of your deliverance and salvation, and that from God."

The storms of life come to prevent the forward progress of the work of God being done in and through the lives of all willing believers. There is never any forward motion without resistance and, if you are to continue to be a vessel of honor for the Lord, you must never let some giant delay your plans and interfere with the call on your life. Don't be terrified when the odds seem to be against you and don't give up the first time a door is slammed in your face. Be like David who with bold confidence ran to the roar. He killed the lion and the bear and this giant would be no different (vs. 36). Goliath has taunted the living God and he's not going to get away with it. Notice also the humility of David. Three times during this conversation with Saul he refers to himself as "your servant." This humble shepherd boy was between a man of low self-esteem and a man of pride. That's precisely where humility should be. Unworthiness is wrong and so is arrogance. Humility takes no credit for what one does but gives all the glory to God. This David does continually.

David has no confusion about what's going on. With extraordinary clarity he knows that an enemy of the people of God is an enemy of God. He wrapped his faith around the fact that the man or woman whose hope is in the Lord need not fear. He wrote in Ps. 23:4, "Yea, though I walk through the valley of the shadow of death, I will fear no evil; For You are with me." He also wrote in Ps. 25:1,2 (NIV), "In You, Lord my God, I put my trust." This trust in Him is what God wanted from the entire nation but they wanted to trust in a human king instead. Vs. 3 (NIV) says, "No one who hopes in You will ever be put to shame." Vs. 5 (NIV), "Guide me in Your truth and teach me, for You are God my Savior, and my hope is in You all day long." Those whose hope is in the Lord see clearly, act confidently, and walk humbly. They realize they can't control some of the things that happen to them so they trust in the one who has the whole world in His hands. They say to Him, "In You, Lord my God, I put my trust. My hope is in You all day long."

David increases in boldness as the story progresses. First he says he will fight Goliath, now he says he will kill him. He says to Saul, "The Lord, who delivered me from the paw of the lion and from the paw of the bear, He will deliver me from the hand of this Philistine" (vs. 37). This is one of the strongest statements of faith in all the Bible. David knew what was going to happen before it did. He knew that God's help in times past is a prophecy of His help in the future. This is what faith is all about. Keep your focus on God and not your circumstances. Don't look at the problem but at the God who solves your problems. David believed in God and trusted Him with all his heart and soul. He said, "I can defeat this giant because of my background. God delivered me before, He'll do it again." Don't run away from the trials you're facing today because they're preparing you for the bigger battles you'll fight in the years ahead. Fighting the lions and the bears prepare you for the giants of tomorrow. It was David's past that prepared him for this battle and those which were to come.

Saul beheld the confidence of David and said to him, "Go, and the Lord be with you!" He then did what can be considered highly unusual. He put his armor on David. Why would Saul do this? He's over seven feet tall and surely he knows his armor wouldn't fit this teenager. Was he scheming a way to take credit if David somehow won the battle? If David won, he reasoned, it would be because he was wearing the king's armor. This sounds like something Saul would do. David puts the armor on, it doesn't fit, so he takes it off. Good armor will not win this battle, the God of Israel will win it. David said, "I will not fight with man's armor, I will trust in the Lord and His armor instead." David wasn't going to fight dressed up like Saul, he was going to fight like the shepherd boy he was. He was going to use the same weapons he used to kill the lion and the bear. What God used before, He will use again. The anointing doesn't flow when you're trying to be somebody you're not. Why be a copy when God made you an original?

Do the world a favor and be the person God created you to be. The world needs you, otherwise God wouldn't have made you. If God wanted you to be somebody else, you'd be them and not you. Ps. 139:14 says, "I will praise You, for I am fearfully and wonderfully made; Marvelous are Your works, and that my soul knows very well." God made you and you are beautiful and marvelous in His eyes. Trust Him and He'll change you into the image of Jesus, making you more and more like Him. 2 Cor. 3:18 says you are changed "from glory to glory." You have to learn to enjoy and appreciate the glory you're in right now. Accept yourself where you're at today knowing that God is the potter and you are the clay. He's the one making you and molding you. He's turning you into His personal masterpiece. When you like the person you are, you're in agreement with God. After all, He made you that way. He's saying to you what He said to Jesus, "This is My beloved Son, in whom I am well pleased" (Matt. 3;17). Each morning put on the breastplate of God's approval. Do that and you'll become everything God created you to be.

David's assets are his youth and mobility. He has speed and agility. Goliath was big but all that armor he carried slowed him down. David had God on his side, Goliath didn't. Was this going to be a fair fight? There's no way it could be. "Then he took his staff in his hand; and he chose for himself five smooth stones from the brook, and put them in a shepherd's bag, in a pouch which he had, and his sling was in his hand. And he drew near to the Philistine" (vs. 40). The stones in this creek were very dense because they were made of an earth metal called barium sulfate. This gave the stones a mass density almost double that of normal stones. Goliath began drawing near to David and he disdained him because of his youth (vs. 42). Notice that everybody is judging David based on his age. His father did, Saul did, and now his arch enemy is doing the same. Goliath has size and strength and the people saw him in comparison to their own size. David saw him in comparison to the size of God. The people said, "He's too big to hit." David said, "He's too big to miss."

David drew near to the giant. That's real faith. Not only did David talk the talk, he walked the walk. He's doing what he said he was going to do. The Philistine looked about and saw David. He was so small compared to this giant that Goliath had to look around to find him. He took one look down and sneered at David. There was nothing in David that struck fear in him. Goliath felt insulted that they sent a boy to fight him. "So the Philistine said to David, 'Am I a dog that you come to me with a stick?' And the Philistine cursed David by his gods" (vs. 43). The Hebrew word for "dog" is "kaleb" and is used to describe male homosexual prostitutes (Deut. 23:18). Goliath felt that sending David to fight him was an insult to his manhood. Goliath had no fear and it was based on his size, his equipment, and the fact that his enemies feared him. Goliath had courage but it was a false courage. It was based on who he was and not on who God is. Unknown to him at the time, he was the underdog in the battle that was about to take place.

Goliath said, "Come to me, and I will give your flesh to the birds of the air and the beasts of the field" (vs. 44). Bring it on, little boy! David was more than happy to oblige Goliath's request. Full of faith, David replies to Goliath, "You come to me with a sword, with a spear, and with a javelin. But I come to you in the name of the Lord of hosts, the God of the armies of Israel, whom you have defied" (vs. 45). Talk back to your giant. Don't let him do all the talking. When the devil tempted Jesus in the wilderness, the Lord talked back to him quoting the Word of God. Over and over again He said, "It is written..." That's how you talk to giants. Turn the volume up. Speak out loud that which God put in your heart. David gets bolder and bolder. It's one thing to tell Saul he will kill Goliath, it's entirely different to tell the giant the same thing. David said, "This day the Lord will deliver you into my hand, and I will strike you and take your head from you. And this day I will give the carcasses of the camp of the Philistines to the birds of the air and the wild beasts of the earth, that all the earth may know that there is a God of Israel" (vs. 46).

Martin Luther once said, "With God, one is always a majority." David had true courage because he knew God was on his side. True courage comes when your thoughts are fixed on God. David thought about God all the time. He was David's champion and he wrote in Ps. 27:13 (NIV), "I remain confident of this: I will see the goodness of God in the land of the living." Goliath told David he was going to feed him to the birds of the air. "No," David said, "I'm going to feed you to the birds of the air." The Bible says in the great judgment of the wicked there will be a feast of the birds. Rev. 19:17,18 says, "Then I saw an angel standing in the sun; and he cried with a loud voice, saying to all the birds that fly in the midst of heaven, 'Come and gather together for the supper of the great God, that you may eat the flesh of kings, the flesh of captains, the flesh of the mighty men, the flesh of horses and of those who sit on them, and the flesh of all people, free and slave, both small and great.'" David hastened and ran toward the giant all the while thinking to himself, "It's supper time!"

-9-

"THE HARDER THEY FALL"

When the time came to anoint David to be king, God sent Samuel to the house of Jesse. David, however, wasn't there. He was out in the field tending to his father's sheep. Why, then, didn't God send Samuel out to the field? Why send him to the house if David wasn't there? The answer is quite simple. Although David was in the field, God saw him in the house. God sees what you'll be like in the future. Not only does He see what you're like today, He sees the person you will become. He sees you fulfilling your destiny. God doesn't see the bad report the doctor gave you, He sees your healing and your miracle. In David, God didn't see a shepherd boy, He saw a king. God also sent Samuel to the house because He wanted Jesse and his sons to see it was David who was anointed to be king. If David had been anointed in the field, his family wouldn't have seen it, thus they wouldn't have believed it happened. Sometimes God's greatest work in your life will be in front of those who despise you the most. The same thing is about to happen here in the Valley of Elah.

Goliath disdained David and considered him unworthy of consideration and respect. He despised this young shepherd boy and treated him with contempt and scorn. One thing all giants have in common is they're big and they're intimidating. They also come in all shapes and sizes and they won't leave you alone. They'll hinder you day after day after day. They come to rob you of all hope for a better future. Life can't be great if there are giants in your life. There are sickness giants and poverty giants and relationship giants. A giant in your life can be overwhelming. It can be a problem or a pain that looms large and doesn't go away. It intimidates you and produces emotional insecurity. It can cause you to tremble in fear which leads to instability in life's situations. Twice David called Goliath "this uncircumcised Philistine" and that fact alone changes the nature of the battle. Every giant you face must begin with a spiritual perspective of the problem. You must look beyond the size of your giant because what you look at will affect what you see.

Paul said in 2 Cor. 4:18, "While we do not look at the things which are seen, but at the things which are not seen." Circumcision was a sign of the covenant between God and the children of Israel. A covenant is a divinely ordained relational bond. It is the official channel through which God works to render His judgment on those who oppose Him. It is also the mechanism by which His Spirit flows to accomplish His works. The purpose of the covenant is to cover you from the fiery darts the enemy shoots your way. David had this covering and he knew Goliath did not. When you change what you see, it will change what you do. No longer are you in a defensive mode, you now go on the offensive. You run to the roar when everyone else runs away. Never run away from your fears. Anything you can't confront in life, you'll not be able to conquer. When you have the courage to confront the giant that stands before you, God gives you the power to overcome him. Like David, you've been anointed for the battle. You carry inside of you the solution to any problem you have.

Jesus said, "Whatever you bind on earth will be bound in heaven, and whatever you loose on earth will be loosed in heaven" (Matt. 16:19). In other words, when you move, heaven will back you up. Understand that you must move first. You must take an offensive posture before the supernatural shows up. God only responds to motion. His supernatural engagement in your life requires motion on your part. It's what activates the power that is already in your life. Ps. 25:14 says, "The secret of the Lord is with those who fear Him, and He will show them His covenant." God has secrets that are not shared with everybody. The Word of God is shared with everybody but His personal guidance is not. It's shared with those who fear Him, those who don't run away when the giants show up, those who put one foot in front of the other, those who take one step forward. Trust God and He'll give you divine thoughts telling you what to do in the situation you are in. Remember, humble people fear God, those in pride do not and this leads to their destruction.

On a recent adventure a rock climber saw something that taught him a valuable lesson on the subject of humility. Two mountain goats stood facing each other on a narrow ledge, one going up the mountain, the other coming down. There was not enough room for both of them to pass each other at the same time so there they stood, facing each other in a silent confrontational showdown. Moments later the lesson was learned. The climber watched in utter amazement as the goat going up the mountain lowered itself down onto its knees and then laid down further onto its stomach. It became perfectly still as it allowed the other goat to walk over him on its way down the mountain. Once passed over, the goat got to its feet and continued its journey up the mountain. The lesson here is that when you humble yourself in the sight of the Lord you may sometimes be walked over and downtrodden but ultimately the Lord will lift you up to success and victory. On the other hand, prideful people who walk over others are all heading downhill on the path to defeat and destruction.

Goliath was full of pride and he thought it was an insult to his dignity to have a mere teenager with no armor to come challenge him. He railed against David and cursed him by his gods. No longer was this a battle between a giant and a shepherd boy. Now it was a battle between the God of Israel and the gods of the Philistines. David said, "I come to you in the name of the Lord of hosts, the God of the armies of Israel." He calls upon the name of God that applies to the situation he is in. God said, "I am who I am" (Ex. 3:14) because He is whatever the situation calls for. God's name is tied to the covenant connection He has with His people. David did not become irritated because he was looked upon as being inferior to the giant nor did he tremble at the threats made by Goliath. David had a big God and he told the giant he came in the name of the Lord. He picked up five smooth stones representing the five letters J-E-S-U-S. Phil. 2:10 says, "That at the name of Jesus every knee shall bow, of those in heaven, and of those on earth, and of those under the earth."

David said, "I come as a representative of the Lord of hosts, the God who has heavenly armies at His command. I am a sent man, a man on a mission from God." The devil is like a roaring lion (1 Peter 5:8) but Jesus is the real thing. He's the Lion of the tribe of Judah. The giant you're facing has no power to defeat you. This is why you can rise up, look the giant in the eye and say, "Enough is enough. No more will you intimidate me." Never run from your enemy but rise up and prepare for war. The anointing is a force that cannot be overcome by the enemy. It can only be responded to. The first step in having breakthrough in your life and defeating the enemy is to once and for all get fed up with his efforts to bring you down. Things happen when a holy fervor rises up inside of you. Your countenance will change, you'll speak with authority, and you'll walk in dominion. You're not here to survive the assaults of the enemy, you're here to start them. Jesus said in Matt. 11:12, "The kingdom of God suffers violence, and the violent take it by force."

War has been declared and you can't have a lukewarm attitude when it comes to fighting the enemy. Don't be a weak-kneed nobody but rise up and go to war for the glory of

God. Don't be afraid of the enemy, make him be afraid of you. Also, you must attack the giant quickly. The longer you wait, the bigger he gets. The day David heard the giant talking is the day he did something about it. He was a humble shepherd boy who was bold in God and not in himself. He knew the battle belonged to the Lord. He told the giant, "The battle is the Lord's, and He will give you into our hands." There is no shame in acknowledging the fact that you are powerless to carry out God's will on your own. Even Jesus said in John 5:19, "Most assuredly, I say to you, the Son can do nothing of Himself, but what He sees the Father do; for whatever He does, the Son also does in like manner." Notice also David's humility. He didn't say God would give Goliath into his hands but into the hands of all Israel. He was fighting for them. If they weren't trusting in the Lord, David would trust for them.

To defeat the giants in your life, you must lay pride aside and admit you can't win the battle in your own strength. Jesus said in John 15:5, "Apart from Me you can do nothing." Ignore the modern day culture of this world that promotes individualism and personal achievement. Instead, "be strong in the Lord and in the power of His might" (Eph. 6:10). By now Goliath has reached the peak of his wrath as he arose and drew near to meet David. In turn, David ran toward the giant just like he ran after the lion who took one of his father's sheep. This is a picture of courage and trust. This is how the work of God gets done. A man of war runs to the roar, not away from it. You attack your giants. You don't tolerate them and you don't negotiate with them. No, you kill them. It's the same thing you do to a rattlesnake. You kill it by cutting its head off. "Then David put his hand in his bag and took out a stone; and he slung it and struck the Philistine in the forehead, so that the stone sank into his forehead, and he fell on his face to the earth" (vs. 49).

David had the calm hand and careful aim of someone who trusted God. With skilled precision he slung a smooth stone at his adversary. The stone sank into his forehead and cracked his skull. His legs began to tremble, he stumbled, and he fell on his face. The bigger the giants are in your life, the harder they fall. Just as the Philistine god Dagon fell on his face before the Lord (1 Sam. 5:2-5), so now the worshiper of Dagon falls on his face. Goliath was bowing down to the name of the Lord. In an instant moment of time, the pride of the Philistine army lay motionless on the ground. "Therefore David ran and stood over the Philistine, took his sword and drew it out of its sheath and killed him, and cut off his head with it. And when the Philistines saw that their champion was dead, they fled" (vs. 51). David made certain the enemy was dead. You can't mess around with your spiritual enemies. If you don't finish your giants off, they'll come back to haunt you and they'll be stronger next time (Matt. 12:45). It's kill or be killed.

If you don't kill your giant, your giant will kill you. 1 Peter says the devil is "seeking whom he can devour." The word "devour" is the Greek word "katapiein" and means to 'swallow' or 'drown.' The devil wants to swallow you up. This is why you need to put the Word of God in the sling of your mouth and throw it at your adversary. When he's down, take the sword of the Spirit and cut his head off. Notice also that David used Goliath's own sword to cut his head off. What was meant to kill David is now used to kill the enemy. David would later write in Ps. 57:6, "They have dug a pit before me; Into the midst of it they themselves have fallen." With their champion now dead, the Philistine army fled when at first they agreed to surrender to Israel if Goliath lost. Never expect the enemy to live up to their promises. David's victory suddenly becomes the victory of Israel's army. Their courage miraculously returns and they pursued the fleeing Philistine army and plundered their tents.

David's example gave the army of Israel great courage and faith in the Lord. Paul said to Timothy, "Let no one despise your youth, but be an example to the believers in word, in conduct, in love, in spirit, in faith, in purity" (1 Tim. 4:12). Good leaders always lead by example. 1 Sam. 17:54 says David took Goliath's head to Jerusalem. He lived in Bethlehem and Saul lived in Gibeah so why would he go to Jerusalem? The Jebusites lived there and had not yet been conquered by Israel. They were one of the Amorite tribes who were placed under judgment by God for their wickedness (Deut. 20:17). The Jebusites were the original inhabitants of Jerusalem and was mentioned frequently as one of the seven nations doomed to destruction when the children of Israel came into the promised land (Ex. 3:8;13:5). They were defeated by Joshua but were not entirely driven out of Jerusalem. Not until David became king were they conquered. He brought the head of Goliath to Jerusalem to show the Jebusites what one day will happen to them. He was saying to leave now while you still have the chance to do so.

With the defeat of Goliath and the Philistine army, Israel is once again rising in prominence as a nation. The armies are successful in their military quests and Israel is gaining back land that was lost. There is peace and prosperity among the people and excitement is in the land. Songs are being written and sung for they believe the favor of God is upon Israel. As all this is going on, Saul is sitting back looking over his kingdom thinking that everything happening is because of him. A haughty spirit consumes him as he arrogantly believes he is superior to all others. Long live the king! A person like this craves honor and recognition from their peers. They want to be praised and acknowledged for things they have done. So compulsive is this craving that they go so far as to take credit for things someone else has done. They think they're better than they actually are and this leads to the destruction of their soul. This downward spiral then leads to hate and bitterness which, in turn, leads them to do dastardly acts, up to and including murder. Saul was such a man.

When David returned from his adventures he was brought before Saul with the head of Goliath in his hand. "So Saul took him that day, and would not let him go home to his father's house anymore" (1 Sam. 18:2). This was a red flag moment, the beginning of the control Saul tried to bring upon David. Within Saul was a manipulating, dominating spirit that gave him an obsessive passion to control David. This in turn hurled David into the deepest, darkest, most difficult valley he had ever walked through. But first, God would give him an incredible blessing by giving him one of the greatest friends the world has ever known. He knew that in order for David to thrive and survive, he would need a close friend to stand by his side. Jonathan heard David talking to his father as he told the king what was in his heart and the faith he had in the living God. It was then that Jonathan knew he and David had the same heart. It was probably at this time that God revealed to Jonathan that David would be the next king of Israel.

1 Sam. 18:1 says, "And it was so, when he had finished speaking to Saul, that the soul of Jonathan was knit to the soul of David, and Jonathan loved him as his own soul." An immediate bond was forged between the two of them and Jonathan became totally committed to David. He so identified himself with David that he joined his life together with him. Their lives were bound up and knit together as one. Jonathan became an intimate friend to David, a constant source of encouragement. He gave David permission to be himself and that is one of the best traits in a friend there is. The need is great for somebody to encourage you and stand by your side in good times and bad. Prov. 18:24 (NIV) says, "One who has unreliable friends soon comes to ruin, but there is a friend who sticks closer than a brother." The

Message Bible says, "Friends come and friends go, but a true friend sticks by you like family." God never intended for you to face the challenges of life alone. This is why you need to make, keep, grow, and cultivate good friendships.

Deep, meaningful friendships are essential in life but, sad to say, most people will say they don't have such a friend. They want a friend who will never leave them or forsake them but they soon realize there is a famine of good friendships in the land. A problem people have is they are reckless in the way they select their friends. Jonathan wanted to be friends with David because he knew his heart was full of love, joy, and trust in God. He knew David had a heart like his own. True friendships are built upon a common passion. C.S. Lewis wrote, "Friendship is born at the moment when one man says to another, 'What? You, too?'" Something awakens inside of you when you find someone who likes what you like, someone going in the same direction you are. This allows the two of you to walk side by side with one another because you're both on the same path heading toward the same horizon. Amos 3:3 asks the question, "Can two walk together, unless they are agreed?" Jonathan saw the same spirit in David that was in himself.

The name "Jonathan" means 'gift of God' and he is the son of the king. This makes him a type and shadow of Jesus, also a gift from God and the Son of the King. 1 Sam. 18:3 says, "Then Jonathan and David made a covenant, because he loved him as his own soul." Jonathan vowed to David that he would be his friend for the rest of his life. Friendship is the most important foundation that relationships are built on. Marriages crumble when the husband and wife are not best friends with one another. Passion in a marriage is good and wonderful but it won't get you through the dark times like friendship will. Passion is a temporary emotion that flees when the dark clouds of despair form over your home. Nothing binds two people together more stronger than friendship. Prov. 17:17 says, "A friend loves at all times, and a brother is born for a time of adversity." The Message Bible says, "Friends love through all kinds of weather." You need friends to get through the storms of life. God brought Jonathan into David's life because He knew hard times were coming.

In the beginning God said, "It is not good that man should be alone; I will make him a helper comparable to him" (Gen. 2:18). God put within Adam, and you too, the need for someone other than Himself. He put in people the need for relationships, the need for a friend. So what makes a true friend? First of all, true friendships are built on commitment, not convenience. That's what a covenant is, a commitment to stand by another person's side no matter what hardships life may bring. People will say they're your friend as long as things are easy and convenient for them, when something is not required of them to make the relationship work. That's not a friend. That's a selfish person trying to take advantage of you. Good friendships won't happen if a person is more concerned with what they can get out of a relationship than with what they can put into it. If a favor is asked of them, they get offended and say, "You're just using me!" not realizing that's what a covenant is. A covenant is friends using one another all for the glory of God.

It is God's plan for a friend to oftentimes be the means to an end. God will often meet your needs through the actions of a friend responding to your time of turmoil. That's what friends are for. They're with you in the good times but even more so in the bad times. Jonathan knew that God had a plan for David's life and he wanted to be a part of that plan. That's what a friend is and that's what a friend does. Friends help one another fulfill their destiny. They help each other do what God has called them to do. A friendship can never merely be about itself. It must be two friends committed and passionate about something beside who they are as individuals. Friends who talk about themselves all the time will have a boring friendship. Talk like that grows old and stale after awhile. C.S. Lewis wrote, "This is why those pathetic people who simply want friends can never find any. The very condition of having friends is we should want something else beside friends. Those going nowhere can have no fellow travelers."

The focus of your life should always be on Jesus and your friends should have the same vision. If they don't, then they shouldn't be your friend. Light and darkness don't mix. All of life should be about Him and so should your friendships. Having the same love for God caused Jonathan to love David as his own soul. This was a deep friendship that went below the surface of some superficial relationship. They shared the same hopes and dreams and their friendship was deeply emotional and pure in its truest form. These were manly men who weren't afraid to share their emotions with one another. When Paul left Ephesus, Acts 20:37 says, "Then they all wept freely, and fell on Paul's neck and kissed him." They were honest and transparent in how they felt. Real friends don't wear masks. They're able to reveal themselves to one another as the person they truly are. That's what intimacy is. It's when you let another person see the real you. It's when you have the freedom to be yourself.

Jonathan was probably a few years older than David but they had a lot in common. They were bold, men of action, and both trusted God. Jonathan was the oldest son of the king while David was the youngest son of a farmer. Jonathan was the crown prince, the heir apparent to the throne, but he and David knew God had other plans. "And Jonathan took off the robe that was on him and gave it to David, with his armor, even to his sword and his bow and his belt" (vs. 4). This robe is a symbol of royalty and Jonathan was accepting the fact that David would be the next king of Israel. He set aside his right and ambition to be the next king in order to honor God's choice. If this had not been settled in their hearts, they never could have had a deep, close friendship. They loved God and each other more than the throne of Israel. David received the armor of Jonathan whereas he took off the armor of Saul. He and the king lived for different things but he and Jonathan shared the same soul. They both loved God and lived for Him more than they lived for themselves.

David knew what God's plans were for his future but destinies don't get fulfilled overnight. Trials will come along with years of aimless wandering in the wilderness. You need to understand there is a three step process that God takes you through to get you to your destiny. First, He'll give you a glimpse of where He's taking you. Samuel anointed David to one day be king. Not now, but later on he would sit on the throne. So first there's the promise, then comes the process. The process is your wilderness experience, the time when God refines you so you'll have the character to handle the promise. 1 Peter 1:6 (NLT) says, "So be truly glad. There is wonderful joy ahead, even though you have to endure many trials for a little while." That's the process. Know this for certain, no man and no devil can keep your destiny from being fulfilled if you refuse to give up. When you successfully go through the process, then comes the promotion which is the fulfillment of the promise. The process David will go through is about to begin.

-10-

"THE JUST AND UNJUST"

Nothing will hinder your destiny from being fulfilled more than stepping out of the timing of God. Rushing things along with selfish efforts will stop God's perfect will from taking place in your life. You must go through the process of allowing God to take you from where you are now to where He wants you to be. Understand that "to everything there is a season, a time for every purpose under heaven" (Eccl. 3:1). The best thing you can do is leave the future in God's hands and focus all your time and attention on what He wants you to do today. Yes, David would one day be king but today he was the servant of King Saul. He would not dishonor Saul's position as king or his authority in any way. David was in total and complete submission to a man he knew he had been called to replace. He is supporting his greatest enemy. He never challenged Saul, never questioned him, and never turned against him. In fact, he did everything he could to make Saul successful. Because of David's loyalty and past success, Saul made him a general in the army of Israel.

"So David went out wherever Saul sent him, and behaved wisely. And Saul set him over the men of war, and he was accepted in the sight of all the people and also in the sight of Saul's servants" (1 Sam. 18:5). The word "wisely" means 'to prosper; to be prudent; to be wise.' David quickly became more popular than Saul because the people saw in him the love, peace, and wisdom of God. He was no doubt happy about this but at no time did he become proud and arrogant. Pride comes before a fall, as Goliath well knew, but David behaved wisely in all his ways. He never received praise when he killed the lion and the bear and this is what kept him humble when praise and popularity came his way. Most people are corrupted by being praised to the same degree they are crushed by scorn and criticism. David didn't let the rebuke of Eliab bring him down and neither would he let his popularity fill him with pride and arrogance. He cared more about what God thought and this is how he was able to put the opinions of others in their proper perspective.

David was a man of war and Saul sent him to fight the Philistines. A great victory had been won and when he returned home "the women had come out of all the cities of Israel, singing and dancing, to meet King Saul, with tambourines, with joy, and with musical instruments" (vs. 6). This is a victory parade for Saul and he loved it. He was the man of the hour. There's shouting and singing, and music is playing. Saul is riding high on the praises of his people until he heard what the women were actually singing. The women sang as they danced, saying "Saul has slain his thousands..." (vs. 7). Surely this fed the arrogance of Saul. He thinks he's awesome. He thinks this song is all about him, at least until he hears the next verse of the song, "...and David his ten thousands." At that moment, darkness invades the heart of Saul. The seed of envy is planted and the slow burn of anger grips his soul. His bitterness waters this seed and it grows very quickly, growing to the point that it will destroy his life.

This song the women were singing was different than the one sang by Miriam and all the women after the people crossed through the Red Sea on dry ground. They sang with timbrels and dances, "Sing to the Lord, for He has triumphed gloriously! The horse and its rider He has thrown into the sea!" (Ex. 15:21). God was the subject of that song but here the women are singing about Saul and David. Not once did Saul say that all the glory belongs to God, and God alone. Saul had one thing on his mind and one thing only. Himself. He was very angry because David was getting more recognition than he was. The word "angry" in Hebrew means 'to kindle; to burn.' It refers to a slow, simmering fire. Saul was in a slow burn as he becomes a demon-possessed, murderous madman. Envy is one of the seven deadly sins listed in the Bible that are fatal to spiritual progress. The other deadly sins are lust, gluttony, greed, sloth, wrath, and pride. Because of the turmoil going on inside of him, Saul is going to be tormented until the day of his death.

It is a sign of weakness in a leader when they resent or feel threatened by the success of one of their subordinates. Some people are just not happy with what they have or if someone else has more than they do. Millionaires are happy until they meet a billionaire. Nelson Rockefeller was asked how much money does it take to make a person happy. He replied, "A little more." A person who does not have the Spirit of God is never satisfied. In truth, Saul should have been grateful that he was being praised for killing his thousands because he was being treated better than he deserved. He had no right to be angry. Jesus said in Matt. 5:22, "But I say to you that whoever is angry with his brother without a cause shall be in danger of the judgment." Anger is sinful when it is motivated by pride (James 1:20), when it is unproductive (1 Cor. 10:31), and when it is allowed to linger (Eph. 4:26). The poisonous words of uncontrolled anger is a common trait of fallen man. Rom. 3:14 (MSG) says, "They open their mouths and pollute the air."

An insecure person is one who is threatened by the success and ability of another person. Martin Luther once said, "Many are not happy unless they see their neighbor doing poorly." Saul couldn't accept the fact that God was with David and the people loved him. David had everything that Saul wanted. The people praised David and this is what Saul wanted most. He craved the allegiance of all men but they freely and willingly gave it to David. These women and everyone else knew he was using David's victory over the enemy to make himself look good. The women weren't fooled and this caused a jealous anger to rise up in Saul. What people thought was important to him. Many times in the past he heeded their voice above the voice of God and Samuel. He couldn't grasp the reality that the people liked David more than him. Envy grows in the soil of discontentment and is fertilized when comparison is made with another person. Envy eats at you like a cancer and stops you from enjoying anything in life.

Don't be surprised when the world compares you to others. Don't allow comparison to cloud the clarity of your calling. As long as you're comparing yourself to someone else, you won't be able to see clearly the path God wants you to travel on. When you run a race, you've got to stay in the lane you've been assigned. If you'll do that, you'll be able to celebrate the success of others. You'll recognize that you're all on the same team. Their success is your success and your success is their's. Saul got out of his lane and this turned him into a very evil man. Indeed, the road of comparison is a road of destruction. It leads to envy and jealousy, bitterness and hatred. 1 Sam. 18:9 says, "So Saul eyed David with suspicion from that day forward." The king of Israel is no longer concerned with God's purposes and His people. His all-consuming focus was the destruction of David's life. This young shepherd boy had killed the giant, he ministered to Saul, and he behaved wisely. Still, David must die and Saul will do everything in his power to make it happen.

Envy created a fire in the bosom of Saul and he lost his grip on all things spiritual. From this conflict in his flesh he never recovered. Vs. 10 says, "And it happened on the next day that the distressing spirit from God came upon Saul, and he prophesied inside the house." The word "prophesied" is a bad translation here. The Hebrew word used in this verse means 'idle ravings; wild, irrational, and incoherent talk.'

What's happening here is Saul is babbling senseless words like a man not in his right mind. "So David played music with his hand, as at other times; but there was a spear in Saul's hand." The same hands that carried the severed head of Goliath is now playing comforting music, ministering to a deeply troubled king. As long as it was possible, David ministered to Saul. This was the position God put him in and he did it faithfully. He knew he was anointed to one day be king and that God would protect him. He wrote in Ps. 7:1, "O Lord my God, in You I put my trust; Save me from all those who persecute me; and deliver me."

David is a worshiper of God and there's a harp in his hand. He's playing his healing music in front of a jealous ruler who happens to have a spear in his hand. At one time this sweet music caused the distressing spirit to leave Saul. Now, it has no effect at all. There is too much jealousy and rage inside of Saul for it to do any good. Saul's life is overcome with extreme anxiety and paranoia. The more you give in to anger and envy, and any other sin, the more you put yourself in touch with supernatural forces of evil until you come under their control. God said to Cain in Gen. 4:7, "If you do well, will you not be accepted? And if you do not do well, sin lies at the door. And it's desire is for you, but you should rule over it." Know with certainty that sin is forever crouching at your door, waiting to destroy your life. If left unchecked, envy will consume you. It leads to fear, fear leads to anger and, if not dealt with, anger can lead to murder. Overcome with jealousy and rage, Saul hurls the spear at David saying, "I will pin David to the wall with it" (vs. 11).

Twice Saul threw his spear at David and twice he missed. This means that after the first miss, David came back and played again. He knew what was in Saul's heart and the danger that represented. Still, he trusted God and played anyway. Thankfully, David escaped both times. It is a testimony to David's character that he refused to throw the spear back at Saul. He was forever determined to leave the matter in God's hands. He placed Saul on the throne, who was David to take him off? He also knew that God doesn't bless hate, evil, and dishonor. Jesus said those who live by the sword will die by the sword (Matt. 26:52). A person who lives violently will probably die in a violent manner. Violence begets violence. When verbal spears are thrown at you, continue to trust God and walk in love at all times. Give honor to whom honor is due, even if that person is throwing a spear at you. And most of all, stay focused and don't quit. David was going through the process of becoming the man God wanted him to be. Through it all, David grew continually in humility and grace.

David was a good man, a man after God's own heart. This being true, why was he destined to go through the process? Why did he have to go through a season of great hardship and turmoil? Persecution comes because the devil wants you to lose your confidence in God. David would not let this happen in spite of the extreme adversity that plagued his life. He stayed humble even though he knew he didn't deserve what was happening to him. By killing Goliath, he had saved the nation from a military disaster that would have resulted in many people getting killed and many more put into slavery. This victory caused David to be celebrated and promoted and all was well, at least for the moment. It's easy to have confidence in God at times like this, but what about the hard times? Saul would try to kill David twenty-one times. Would David have the same confidence in God when he was being attacked by Saul and made to be a wandering fugitive for many years? As long as David stayed focused and not quit, Saul can not overthrow what God has ordained.

Matt.5:45 says God "sends rain on the just and on the unjust." Tough times not only come to people who do wrong, but even on those who are doing everything right. It's a fact of life. It can be a struggle trying to figure out why you're going through hard trials in the rain when your evil neighbor is enjoying bright sunshine. Just make sure you never complain when things don't go the way you think they should. Why? Because it's an attack on the character of God. It's the same as telling Him He doesn't know what He's doing and that your way is better than His way. The Greek word translated "complainer" means literally 'one who is discontented with his lot in life.' It describes the low, threatening, discontented muttering of a mob who distrusts their leader and are on the verge of an uprising. A complaining spirit leads to fighting and quarreling because complaints come from unfulfilled desires which lead to envy and strife. The reason people complain is because they don't believe God is working all things out for their good (Rom. 8:28).

It's easy to see Jesus in the sunshine but do you see Him in the rain? He never promised you an easy life but He did promise to be your shelter in the storm. Remember, you're in the process of having your life molded and shaped by God. It's in the rain where decisions are made. You decide to either get bitter or better. It's in the rain where you find where your joy is at and what your foundation is. It's rain that causes crops to grow and it's rain that brings forth the harvest. No rain, no grain. If it didn't rain in your life, you also wouldn't grow. No pain, no gain. No matter what you're going through, God will use it for your good and spiritual growth. James 1:2 (NLT) says, "When trouble comes your way, consider it an opportunity for great joy." God wants you to sing and dance in the rain and to consider your trial as an opportunity to grow in Him. Vs. 3 (NLT) says, "For you know when your faith is tested, your endurance has a chance to grow." Don't quit in difficult times. People who run from adversity forfeit their spiritual growth.

If there was one thing David needed at this time in his life, it was endurance. Over and over again Saul tried to kill him and David continually had to flee for his life. He knew he would one day be king and he wasn't going to quit now. Instead, he would embrace the season he was now in and the process he was going through. Like David, you also are anointed to succeed even when the spears of life are being thrown at you. Just keep on running your race and by doing so you'll be heaping coals of fire on the heads of those who try to stop you. Heb. 12:1,2 says, "And let us run with endurance the race that is set before us, looking unto Jesus, the author and finisher of our faith, who for the joy that was set before Him, endured the cross, despising the shame, and has sat down at the right hand of the throne of God." The key is to not look at what you're going through but look to where you're going to. The Message Bible says, "Because He never lost sight of where He was headed - that exhilarating finish in and with God - He could put up with anything along the way."

Bumblebees were once brought into outer space to see how they would handle the weightless environment. They floated with ease for three days without flapping their wings. Then, on the fourth day, they all died. Why? Because they were not created to live without resistance. It was the fuel that kept them alive. When they stopped working, when they stopped flapping their wings against the resistance, they died. God will use the pain and tension in your life to not only keep you alive, but to keep your purpose and reason for living alive inside of you. Heb. 6:7 says, "For the earth which drinks in the rain that often comes upon it, and bears herbs useful for those by whom it is cultivated, receives blessing from God." God wants you to drink in the rain, to make the most of the difficult times, to come out stronger than you were before. Use your pain as a steppingstone on the path to fulfilling your destiny. Trust God and He'll give you the direction you need. David wrote in Ps. 37:23, "The steps of a good man are ordered by the Lord, and He delights in his way."

Paul was in a great struggle and God said to him, "My grace is sufficient for you, for My strength is made perfect in weakness" (2 Cor. 12:9). There is power in the midst of your storm. David knew the more tension on a slingshot, the farther the stone will go. Likewise, the more resistance that comes against you, the farther God will launch you. This is why you must embrace the rain and count it all joy when trials come your way. Take your eyes off yourself and look for ways to help other people. Walk in compassion toward those who are also in the rain. Be there for them and tell them how good God is. Comfort them and pray with them. Ps. 126:5 says, "Those who sow in tears shall reap in joy." It's true, April showers bring May flowers. There's always a rainbow on the other side of your storm, a reward on the other side of your trial. Run to it and it will be there waiting for you. Ask God to give you eyes to see His plan for your life, ears to hear, and a heart to understand. He is a good God and you can have the confident assurance that your best days are ahead of you.

1 Sam. 18:12 says, "Now Saul was afraid of David, because the Lord was with him, but had departed from Saul." God is a gentleman. If you don't want Him in your life, He won't hang around. This is what happened with Saul. He shut God out of his life and God's presence is no longer there. This made Saul very bitter and angry and the last thing he wants is to have spiritual people around him. He knew he was outmatched. He was the one throwing the spear but he was afraid of the one he threw the spear at. All the spears in the world couldn't defeat David. The Lord was with him and this made Saul all the more afraid. "Therefore Saul removed him from his presence, and made him his captain over a thousand; and he went out and came in before the people" (vs. 13). Here is a humble shepherd boy leading a thousand trained soldiers. Saul promoted David in order to set him up for harm. It appears as if he was honoring David but behind

this dark cloud of deceit is the hidden agenda of getting David killed in battle.

"And David behaved wisely in all his ways, and the Lord was with him" (vs. 14). There is no change in David's behavior. It was because of his humility that God was able to pour into him godly wisdom. No where in scripture does it say David ever lost a military battle. He was very wise, very brave, and very successful. The more victories David won and the more kingly he appears, the more it bothered Saul. He wants to be lifted up whereas David remains forever humble. The truth be told, popularity and promotion comes from God (Ps. 75:6,7). Promotion is not always easy to handle. The higher up on a pedestal you're put, either by people or yourself, the farther you're going to fall. There are many actors and musicians who can't handle the pressure of being famous. They become secluded from the rest of the world, they take drugs, and many commit suicide. John Oswald Sanders, one time director of Overseas Missionary Fellowship, once said, "Not every man can carry a full cup." Saul certainly couldn't.

David's wisdom seemed like foolishness to Saul. Even so, something told him this wisdom was from God and he was afraid of David because of it. The people, however, had a different opinion of David. Because he was a man after God's own heart, he had a positive influence on others and became even more popular. "But all Israel and Judah loved David, because he went out and came in before them" (vs. 16). In Hebrew, this means David conducted several successful military operations. In turn, this inflamed the ever-present jealousy in the heart of the king. Saul's resentment of David is so great that he uses his oldest daughter Merab as a dawn to get David killed. It had been promised to the man who killed Goliath that his family wouldn't have to pay taxes and he'd be given the king's daughter as a wife. Saul said David could marry Merab if he'd be more valiant for him and fight more battles (vs. 17). Saul is trying to manipulate the situation. He wants to take advantage of David's loyalty and patriotism. In Saul's heart, his only motive is he wants to see David dead.

David's humility rises up and catches Saul by surprise. David said to him, "Who am I, and what is my life or my father's family in Israel, that I should be son-in-law to the king?" (vs. 18). David had no idea what evil plot was stirring in Saul's heart. He was only responding like the humble person he was. He was famous and all Israel loved him. Women sang and danced in his honor. Still, he remains humble and says he's not worthy to marry the king's daughter. Because David was hesitant, Saul suddenly reneges and gives Merab to a man named Adriel in hopes of making David jealous and angry. Perhaps David would retaliate thus making him guilty of treason. Saul was doing everything he could to provoke David, all to no avail. David remained humble and continually trusted God to work everything out in his life. Saul, however, had another daughter named Michal who loved David very much. This is very ironic. Saul hated David but his son Jonathan and daughter Michal loved him. Saul's manipulative plan didn't work with Merab so he tries again with Michal.

Saul wants to use Michal as a pawn against David just like he did with Merab. He wants David to be snared by the dowry. In that day, a dowry was required whenever a man got married. The more important and prestigious the bride and her family, the higher the dowry would be. The family would be losing a worker so the groom had to pay a sum of money to compensate for the family's loss. There was no way David could afford the expensive dowry for the daughter of the king. Saul knew this so he instead demanded that David bring to him one hundred foreskins of the Philistines as a dowry (vs. 25). Saul reasoned in his evil heart that David would be killed doing this. Manipulation is evil, sneaky, and secret. It uses concealed motives to accomplish hidden agendas. Saul wants David dead so he puts his life in great jeopardy. David has such a pure heart that he is blind to Saul's cunning ploy. Neither did he ask why a dowry was needed. The king's daughter was promised to the man who killed Goliath. The head of the giant should be the only dowry the king needed.

No Philistine soldier would ever volunteer to be circumcised so David is going to have to kill them first. Saul is hoping as this battle is taking place that David would be killed in the process. So what does David do? He goes out and kills two hundred Philistine soldiers, twice as many as Saul asked for (vs. 27). Jesus said in Matt. 5:40,41, "If anyone wants to sue you and take away your tunic, let him have your cloak also. And whoever compels you to go one mile, go with him two." David wasn't killed in this battle and he comes back a hero. Saul then gives Michal to him as a wife. Saul knew the Lord was with David and this made him still more afraid. "So Saul became David's enemy continually" (vs. 29). Because Saul was the enemy of the Lord, he also was the enemy of David. The Philistines retaliated for what David had done but lost every battle against the future king of Israel. The name of David was precious and honored among all. God was with him and everybody knew it. There is only one thing left to do. Assassinate him.

-11-

"PUBLIC ENEMY NUMBER ONE"

Saul is a bitter man because all of Israel loved David. He had position, prominence, and popularity. He was on his way to the throne and everything seemed to be working out in his favor. This angered Saul and he is offended by the military success of David and his popularity among the people. Heb. 12:15 (NLT) warns, "Watch out that no poisonous root of bitterness grows up to trouble you, corrupting many." The Message Bible says, "Keep a sharp eye out for weeds of bitter discontent. A thistle or two gone to seed can ruin a whole garden in no time." No longer does Saul try to hide his feelings. No longer does he try to act like all is well. He's openly hostile toward David and his bitterness of heart is open for all to see. David is about to learn that life is not always lived on a playground. More times than not, it is lived on a battleground. There is a storm gathering in David's life. It is a fierce and dark storm that David did nothing to cause. This storm will not relent until every earthly foundation in David's life is gone, swept away by this violent tempest.

None of Saul's past attempts to have David killed worked but this did not dwindle his determination to see his evil desire come to pass. Continually he persists in his efforts to eliminate David. 1 Sam. 19:1 says, "Now Saul spoke to Jonathan his son and to all his servants, that they should kill David, but Jonathan, Saul's son, delighted much in David." This puts Jonathan in a difficult position. He knows David is destined to one day be king and here his father is telling him to kill him. Saul wants Jonathan to submit to him both as father and king. What was Jonathan to do? One of the Ten Commandments says to honor your father and mother (Ex.

20:12). The one after that, however, says, "You shall not murder" (vs. 13). Jonathan knew what his father is asking of him is not a righteous judgment against David but is instead the result of a jealous heart that is angry and bitter. Jonathan knows that if he were to obey his father, he'd be committing murder. What does Jonathan do? He sides with David. He goes and tells him what his father plans to do (vs. 2).

Jonathan's loyalty to David remains strong as he tells his friend of Saul's evil intent. "My father Saul seeks to kill you. Therefore please be on your guard until morning, and stay in a secret place and hide" (vs. 2). This would surely make Saul furious if he found out what his son had done but Jonathan did it anyway. Yes, people are told in scripture to be in submission to those in authority over them. Even so, a person is never excused from sin even if someone in authority commanded it. When told to stop preaching the gospel, the disciples said in Acts 5:29, "We ought to obey God rather than men." It took courage for Jonathan to take David's side in this matter. His life was in danger but he warned David anyway. Why? Because he "delighted much in David." The word "friend" is not a term to be taken lightly. A true friend takes risks on behalf of another. They become vulnerable and oftentimes get hurt somewhere along the way. Anytime there is love, there will be risks involved that can bring about hurt and pain. This is why a true friend is hard to find.

Most people run away from the thought of being hurt and this is why finding a true friend is a rare occurrence. There is a price to pay to be a friend, a price most people don't want to pay. Jonathan had taken the initiative to be a friend to David. He did not choose to have a friend but rather to be a friend. Ruth did the same thing to Naomi when she said, "For wherever you go, I will go; And wherever you lodge, I will lodge; Your people shall be my people, and your God, my God. Where you die, I will die, and there I will be buried. The

Lord do so to me, and more also, if anything but death parts you and me" (Ruth 1:16,17). It is not uncommon for people to want others to be a friend to them. This is based on need and not supply. It causes you to be demanding as you ask, "Where were you when I needed you?" Those who don't take the initiative will probably never have a good friend. Why? Because they're selfish and self-seeking. Prov. 18:1 says, "A man who isolates himself seeks his own desire." The Message Bible says, "Loners who care only for themselves spit on the common good."

Relationships have to be well-oiled and maintained. It goes beyond a quick shaking of the hands and a short greeting as you nonchalantly pass them by in the hallway at church. Friendships are maintained with the oil of encouragement. People are lifted up and inspired when you give them your time, your resources, and words that lift them up during times of trial. Your actions of giving into the lives of others is a reflection of who God is. Encouragement is vitally needed in the body of Christ but is lacking in so many lives. Scottish evangelist Henry Drummond once asked, "How many prodigals are kept out of the kingdom of God by all of those unlovely characters who profess to be inside?" Heb. 3:13 (NIV) says to "encourage one another daily." This is what you've been called by God to do. A pat on the back goes a lot farther than a kick in the pants. People need your support in hard times. Jonathan gives David his support as he says in vs. 3, "And I will go out and stand before my father in the field where you are, and I will speak to my father about you. Then what I observe, I will tell you."

In loyalty to David, Jonathan goes and intercedes on David's behalf to his father. Reconciliation is a powerful ministry for "blessed are the peacemakers" (Matt. 5:9). Jonathan prized David immensely and he spoke well of him to his father. He could not do this without putting his life in danger. He supported David in front of a madman who wanted to kill him. By doing this he performed the duty of a true friend and of a man with great courage. Preserving his friend's life gave Jonathan a cause to be brave. It takes courage to do what God has called you to do. Esther was asked to approach her husband the king to request his intervention in a plot to kill all the Jews. It was prohibited at that time to do this and the person who violated this law could be put to death. But Esther did it anyway. She said, "And so I will go to the king, which is against the law; and if I perish, I perish!" (Esther 4:16). There is no room in the kingdom of God for complacency. The road that is easy leads to a life of insignificance, a life where no one will notice when you're gone.

It is a sad but undeniable truth that some people reach a point in their lives where they stop doing things that require courage. They stop taking risks that require them to use their faith and be brave. They're afraid to confront situations that may be difficult. They don't realize that how they handle things that are not easy is what determines the degree to which God can use them. Know this, you were created by God to be brave. Acts 1:8 says, "But you shall receive power when the Holy Spirit has come upon you." This power gives you the ability to be brave. 1 Tim. 1:7 says, "For God has not given us a spirit of fear, but of power and of love and of a sound mind." Once filled with the Holy Spirit, the disciples "spoke the word of God with boldness" (Acts 4:31). Boldness is the courage to act or speak fearlessly despite real or imagined danger. It is the assertiveness to do or speak what is necessary in spite of the possibility of a negative outcome. Boldness comes from a determination to do what is right, motivated by a passion for God and His divine truth.

Real bravery performs selfless acts of sacrifice. It's having the strength of character to face and endure any challenge. Heb. 10:39 (GWT) says, "We don't belong with those who turn back and are destroyed. Instead, we belong with those who have faith and are saved." You must have the backbone to stand up for what you believe in. J.B. Phillips says, "Surely we are not going to be men who cower back and are lost, but men who maintain their faith until the salvation of their souls is complete!" Jonathan had this courage and boldness as he talks to his father on David's behalf. Twice he tells Saul that what he wants to do is sin. He's pulling no punches here in his attempt to bring his father back to reality. He is boldly declaring that Saul's attitude and behavior is wrong. He's calling sin for what it is as he gives his father a much needed word of correction. Saul is judging David in an inappropriate way and has forgotten all the good that David did. Jonathan reminds Saul how David took his life in his hands and killed Goliath. He also reminded his father that he saw what David did and rejoiced.

After pleading his case, Jonathan asks his father, "Why then will you sin against innocent blood, to kill David without a cause?" (vs. 5). David has done nothing wrong, only good. This is reality but Saul is not dealing with reality. In his mind, there is a reason to kill David. That's what bitterness does to you. It gives you justification to commit a dreadful wrong. The twisted eyes of bitterness will cause you to see things through the prism of darkness and not light. It appears as if Saul is listening to reason as he vows to Jonathan, "As the Lord lives, he shall not be killed" (vs. 6). Beware when bad people make vows of goodness. They're almost always controlled by their moods and thoughts. If a good thought happens to come, they'll speak it out. However, the good things they say are hollow and short-lived. Before long a negative thought will come and replace the good one and with it evil words and actions will surely follow. This is not Saul's last vow to spare David. He later vows twice more to not kill him and reneges on his promise both times.

For the moment things are back to normal, or so it seems. The command to kill David is revoked "so Jonathan brought

David to Saul, and he was in his presence as in times past" (vs. 7). Not long after this there was another war with the Philistines. David went out and won a great victory against them and the enemy fled from his presence. This battle brought with it the warning clouds of a coming storm. David was becoming more and more popular and his success once again aroused the jealousy of Saul. The evil, distressing spirit returned and attacked Saul where he was the most vulnerable. He never dealt with the root of the problem and this brought torment to his soul. History repeats itself as David is called upon to play his music for Saul who sat and listened while holding a spear in his hand. Like before, the harmful spirit did not leave and once again he tries "to pin David to the wall with the spear" (vs. 10). Thankfully, the Lord was with David as he fled and escaped the presence of Saul.

One of the character flaws that makes Saul unworthy to be king is his unwillingness to honor his own solemn promise. Did he not vow that David would not be killed? All that was thrown away as easily as the spear was thrown. You can never trust a person who can't keep their word. This is why you need to get to know people before you give them your trust. It is foolish to carelessly give somebody your trust when you know nothing about them or their background. The truth of the matter is that all believers should be known for their trust and honesty (Prov. 12:22) and for a willingness to suffer with a friend (Prov. 17:17). They should strive to "walk in a manner worthy of the calling to which you have been called, with all humility and gentleness, with patience, bearing with one another in love" (Eph. 4:1,2). The first and foremost thing you can ever do is put your total and complete trust in the living God (Ps. 118:8). That way, if people fail you, God will always be there keeping you safe from all harm (Ps. 118:6).

Saul was not prepared to handle temptation and the spiritual attacks of the enemy. The opportunity to kill David was there and he took it. This time David realizes that Saul will not be deterred from killing him so he flees from the palace. Never again will he play music in the king's court and his position in the kingdom is washed away by the storm. From this day forward, David will be a wandering fugitive for many years to come. He becomes public enemy number one in the eyes of Saul and will be hunted like a wild animal. Assassins are sent to look for him and to kill him, making this one of the lowest moments in David's life. "Saul also sent messengers to David's house to watch him and to kill him in the morning. And Michal, David's wife, told him, saying, 'If you do not save your life tonight, tomorrow you will be killed.'" (vs. 11). Michal may have seen the hit men outside and at that moment decided her obligation to her husband took precedence over her loyalty to her father. She knew the type of man Saul was so she let David down through a window.

David fled and that night he wrote Psalm 59, a song where he pleads his case before God. Vs. 1 says, "Deliver me from my enemies; O my God; defend me from those who rise up against me." He describes his attackers in vs. 3,6,7, "They lie in wait for my life. They growl like a dog. They belch out with their mouth. Swords are in their lips." David knows he has done nothing wrong as he declares his innocence, "Not for my transgression nor for my sin, O Lord. They run and prepare themselves through no fault of mine" (vs. 3,4). Through all this, David is still a man after God's own heart and he expresses his total and complete trust in the living God, "But You, O Lord, shall laugh at them. For God is my defense; My merciful God shall come to meet me; God shall let me see my desire on my enemies" (vs. 8-10). David ends his song by declaring his triumphant confidence in God. "But I will sing of Your power; Yes, I will sing aloud of Your mercy in the morning; For You have been my defense and refuge in the day of my troubles" (vs. 16).

Saul's henchmen are at David's house to take him away but Michal devices a plan to deter their evil intentions. "And Michal took an image and laid it in the bed, put a cover of goat's hair for his head, and covered it with clothes" (vs. 13). This image was a "teraphim," a Hebrew word that refers to household idols or family gods. Throughout the Bible this word is used in conjunction with idolatry and pagan worship. Rachel, the wife of Jacob, stole her father's household idols as she fled with her husband back to his homeland (Gen. 31:19). In Judges 17:5, Micah used household idols in his corrupt worship of God. Before the temple was built by Solomon and after it was destroyed, the people of Israel often resorted to bringing teraphim into their homes, pretending these idols represented God. Later, in the godly reforms of Josiah, he prohibited the use of household idols (2 Kings 23:24). People would bow down and worship these idols. Having one in her home shows that Michal was an idol worshiper.

God's people have no business having idols like this in their home. This shows that Michal did not have the kind of relationship with God she should have. This will show up in her life as the story of David unfolds. Saul knew his daughter was void of godly character and this is why he hoped she would be a snare to David. On this day Michal appears to be on David's side because her future in the royal kingdom is tied up with David. She tells the assassins that David is sick and they go and report this to Saul. He doesn't want to hear any excuses. He doesn't care if David is sick or not. He tells the men to bring the whole bed to him with David in it and he'll personally kill him then. They go back to David's house, uncover the sheets, and find that David isn't there. This makes Saul very angry at his daughter. He asks her, "Why have you deceived me like this, and sent my enemy away, so that he has escaped?" (vs. 17). Michal answered, "He said to me, 'Let me go! Why should I kill you?'"

Michal was faithful to David with her actions but not her words. To protect herself, she told her father that David threatened to kill her and this is why she helped him escape. She painted herself as the victim of a man who would murder his own wife in cold blood. Clearly, her loyalty is not to David but to her own selfish interests. This fed the rage of Saul thinking David threatened his daughter. Michal's foundation of loyalty to David is washed away with this lie. Never again will David have a close relationship with her. For the third time, David fled and escaped (vs. 18). He went to Ramah where the elderly Samuel lived and presided over a center where prophets engaged in worship. David did the right thing considering the predicament he was in. He went and spent some time with a godly man where he told Samuel all that Saul had done to him. The prophet of God listened intently as David poured his heart out to him. Afterward they both went and stayed in Naioth, the city where the school of the prophets was located.

Life is not always fair but God is. This is why you need to believe the disappointments in life is often the platform God uses to launch you into the fulfillment of your destiny. You can't always control what comes against you, but you can control what happens inside of you. Disappointment is unavoidable but misery is optional. Ps. 105:4 (MSG) says, "Live a happy life! Keep your eyes open for God, watch for His works; be alert for signs of His presence." Happiness does not come from having more money, a bigger house, or a newer car. It's all based on where your eyes are at. You must keep your eyes on God for He has so much more for you than what you're seeing right now. People have a tendency to compare themselves with others when their eyes are closed to God. Open those eyes and be alert for signs of His presence. Surely those signs are there. You'll see them once you realize there's more in life to be thankful for than there is to complain about. Ps. 16:11 says, "In Your presence is fullness of joy; At your right hand are pleasures forevermore."

To live a good life you've got to go beyond the surface of Christianity, beyond the normal church service on Sunday morning. Paul wrote in Col. 2:2,3 (NLT), "I want them to have complete confidence that they understand God's mysterious plan, which is Christ Himself. In Him lie hidden all the treasures of wisdom and knowledge." In his writings, Paul used the word "mystery" twenty-one times. He's saying that God is trying to get your attention just like He used a burning bush to get the attention of Moses. "This is amazing," Moses said to himself. "Why isn't that bush burning up? I must go see it" (Ex. 3:3 NLT). There's more to God than what you know right now. You can't do the same thing year after year after year and call that a life. Go beyond the rim of mediocrity and step into God's plan for your life. There are mysteries waiting to be discovered and you must be willing to go find them. Don't let fear hold you back. Go beyond the surface and dig deeper into the things of God.

You're not here to survive this world, you're here to change the world. God wants you to rise up and dream big dreams. He said in Is. 43:18,19, "Do not remember the former things, nor consider the things of old. Behold, I will do a new thing, now it shall spring forth, shall you not know it?" The Message Bible says, "It's bursting out! Don't you see it? There it is!" God is saying to you personally, "You think you've seen Me move before? You haven't seen anything yet!" To see what God has for you, you've got to step out of your comfort zone and step into a life of obedience. Be committed and loyal to God and to that which He would have you do with your life. Sure, you'll have setbacks but who doesn't? This was the central theme of David's early life but he would go on to persevere anyway. What is so amazing about God is the devotion He has for you. As you take the necessary steps that lead to the fulfillment of your destiny, you can have the total and complete confidence that God is forever on your side. He'll be there through the good, the bad, and the ugly.

Rom. 8:31 says, "If God is for us, who can be against us?" Fear is driven out when you believe that God is on your side. David didn't run from the giant, he ran toward him. He was a warrior, not a worrier. He had the boldness to do what God wanted him to do because he knew God was on his side. He's on your side, too. Yes, His stamp of approval is on your life. You must believe that because what you believe about God's feelings toward you will have a direct effect on how you live the rest of your life. God loves you and He created you to do great and mighty things for His glory. Stop saying negative things about yourself. God made you to be great and your best days are in front of you. The only reason you think your neighbor's grass is greener is because you're not watering your own grass. If you don't like where you're at today, do something about it. Lay your own personal plans aside and grab onto God's plan. Own it, make it your own. Say to Him, "Not my will, but Your will be done." If something needs to be done, say to Him, "Here I am! Send me."

Don't run from who you're supposed to be. Don't run from the destiny God called you to fulfill. 1 Cor. 7:17 (MSG) says, "And don't be wishing you were someplace else or with someone else. Where you are right now is God's plan for you. Live and obey and love and believe right there." God wants you here, not there. Where you're at right now is where God wants you to be. If you'll get that truth settled in your heart, you'll then be able to maximize your potential and fulfill your destiny. You're here on purpose because you're here for a purpose. Don't be complacent and coast through life. Become all that you were called by God to become. It is God who defines your life and purpose and how worthy you are. You truly are special and God wants you to see yourself through His eyes. He didn't want David to see himself as a wandering fugitive but as the next king of Israel. You have inside of you the gifts and personality to fulfill the dream God put in your heart. Believe you can change the world. Believe you can make a positive difference in the life of another. Then go out and do it.

The Shepherd King

-12-

"FLIGHT OF AN ARROW"

Your purpose in life, no matter what it is you do, is to bring glory to God. That's what you're here for. Believe it and act on it. Col. 3:17 (NIV) says, "And whatever you do or say, do it as representatives of the Lord Jesus, giving thanks through Him to God the Father." When hard times come, if you feel like you're down to nothing, believe that God is up to something. Phil. 1:6 says, "He who has begun a good work in you will complete it until the day of Jesus Christ." The Message Bible says God will bring the great work in you "to a flourishing finish on the very day Christ Jesus appears." This is a truth you can put your confidence in. As David sought solitude and comfort in the presence of Samuel, behind the scenes God was working on his behalf. Saul is very persistent in his effort to have David killed. He is told where David is at so he sends more assassins to find him and kill him (1 Sam. 19:20). Sad to say, nothing is sacred to Saul. His root of bitterness is so deep that he seeks to kill David in the very sanctuary of Israel's prophet, Samuel.

The hit men sent to kill David arrive in the middle of a worship service and something strange happens. "And when they saw the group of prophets prophesying, and Samuel standing as a leader over them, the Spirit of God came upon the messengers of Saul, and they also prophesied" (vs. 20). These were not godly men who diligently sought after God. Why, then, did the Holy Spirit come upon them? First and foremost, God was protecting David. The Holy Spirit came upon these men to remove their intent to kill David. As the Spirit came upon them, they lost their connection to the evil purpose for which they had come to this place. This was God's way of disarming those who sought to do David harm.

This was indeed a very unusual thing that happened. In John 3:8, Jesus described the activity of the Holy Spirit as being very mysterious, "The wind blows wherever it pleases. You hear its sound, but you cannot tell where it comes from or where it is going." The Holy Spirit was not under the control of these messengers, they were under His.

God has plans for David and this is His way of sending a message to Saul that He does not want David to be killed. These deadly assassins had a strange conversion experience and returned not to King Saul. They stayed there with the other prophets for they no longer sought to kill David. Vs. 21 says, "And when Saul was told, he sent other messengers, and they prophesied likewise. Then Saul sent messengers again the third time, and they prophesied also." Saul didn't get the message God was trying to send him. He then decides to pursue David himself. He reasoned there are some things you must do yourself. He took matters into his own hands and went to Ramah. Surprisingly, the same thing happened to him. "And he also stripped off his clothes and prophesied before Samuel in like manner, and lay down naked all that day and all that night" (vs. 24). Saul was stripped of his royal clothing and pride and became like any other man. God was showing him who the true King really is. He's saying, "I'm in charge!"

God, in His infinite mercy, is reaching out to Saul. He wants to bring him to repentance. Of course, this doesn't happen for he will once again harden his heart to the things of God. A person can be affected by the power of God but that does not guarantee they'll surrender their life to Him. Saul was an nonspiritual man who for a moment became spiritual when the Spirit of God came upon him. David knew Saul's heart was still hardened and, as the king lay naked on the ground, he was given the opportunity to once again flee from the presence of Saul. As he left, he was leaving behind Samuel and the influence he had on his life. One is made to wonder why David did leave. The Spirit of God had protected him in a powerful way so why not stay there until it was time to be made king? Being the person that he was, David left because he wanted to make one final attempt to reconcile with Saul. He arranged a secret meeting with Jonathan and asked, "What have I done? What is my iniquity, and what is my sin before your father, that he seeks my life?" (1 Sam. 20:1).

Jonathan responds, "By no means! You shall not die!" Jonathan doesn't believe his father still wants to kill David, especially not after hearing his oath that David shall not be killed. "Indeed, my father will do nothing either great or small without first telling me. And why should my father hide this thing from me? It is not so!" (vs. 2). Jonathan expresses astonishment that his father did not tell him about the attempt to kill David at Naioth. David says it's because the king knew they were close friends that Jonathan wasn't told what his father wanted to do. He then said, "But truly as the Lord lives and as your soul lives, there is but a step between me and death" (vs. 3). These are the words of a man under the tremendous pressure of a mounting storm, a man who has lost everything. The events surrounding his life appear to be in direct conflict to God's promises. All trials will try to throw you and your faith in God off balance, where your eyes are no longer on God but on the hardships surrounding you. David thinks Saul will not stop pursuing him until he is killed.

David thinks any day now could be his last. "There is but a step between me and death." The same thing can be said about you. You need to live with this in mind. You need a new perspective. You need to see things in a different light. People would live so much differently if they lived as if today would be the day they took their last breath. What's so deceiving about death is everybody knows they're going to die one day, they just don't think it will be today. They then live life recklessly saying they've got plenty of time to make things right between them and God. They'll change tomorrow not realizing that tomorrow never gets here. People who wait until tomorrow to get saved usually die today. Jonathan hears what's in the heart of David and he says to him, "Whatever you yourself desire, I will do it for you" (vs. 4). This is the mark of a true friend. Jonathan assures David of his continual loyalty. He is giving encouragement to a discouraged man by offering to help anyway he can. David then proposes a plan to test Saul's intentions toward him.

The next day would be the festival of the New Moon. In Bible times, the new moon marked the beginning of a new month. The Hebrew word for "month" is "kodesh" which literally means 'new moon.' It was a time when the people of Israel were to bring an offering to God (Num. 28:11). The New Moon festival was a feast where the people dedicated to God each new month in the year. It was marked by sacrifices, the blowing of trumpets (Num. 10:10), the suspension of all labor and trade (Neh. 10:31), and social and family feasts (1 Sam. 20:5). David chose not to go to the monthly festival where it was a custom for him to dine at the king's table. Jonathan would make an excuse for David's absence and Saul's reaction would reveal the condition of his heart. "If he says thus: 'It is well,' your servant will be safe. But if he is very angry, then be sure that evil is determined by him" (vs. 7). David is anointed to be king but here he calls himself Jonathan's servant. He said the same thing to Saul just before he killed Goliath.

David then says something highly unusual, "Therefore you shall deal kindly with your servant, for you have brought your servant into a covenant of the Lord with you. Nevertheless, if there is iniquity in me, kill me yourself, for why should you bring me to your father?" (vs. 8). David is still shaken by the fact that Jonathan did not tell him about the attempted arrest at Naioth. When pressure mounts, people and relationships can change. Good relationships can go bad or they can go deeper. If Jonathan has switched sides and is now working for his father, then he should go ahead and kill David right now. Jonathan didn't take this very well as he answers in a loud voice, "Far be it from you! For if I knew certainly that evil was determined by my father to come upon you, then would I not tell you?" (vs. 9). Jonathan's response is the same as in vs. 2. He didn't know Saul set out to kill David at Naioth. He is still shocked this happened because previously his father would tell him everything. He tells David to set aside any doubts about his loyalty. They are friends for life.

David then wants to know how Jonathan will get the message to him if Saul still wants him dead. Jonathan has a plan but first a matter of great importance must be settled between them. Jonathan agrees to find out the state of his father's heart and will report it to David. In return, he wants David to promise that kindness will be shown to his family once he is gone. "And Jonathan again caused David to vow, because he loved him; for he loved him as he loved his own soul" (vs. 17). David and Jonathan have to trust one another. David must trust that Jonathan won't betray him to Saul and Jonathan must trust David to not kill his family once he becomes king. Upon ascending the throne, a king would usually kill all his potential rivals in order to secure his kingship. David promises not to do this with regard to Jonathan and his descendants. With this now settled, Jonathan reveals to David his plan of letting him know the reaction of Saul to David's absence at the festival of the New Moon.

First of all, Jonathan wants David to wait three days and then go to a field and remain by a stone called Ezel (vs. 19). In Hebrew, the word "Ezel" means 'shows the way.' Jonathan wants David to wait by the rock that shows the way. In your personal life, let Jesus be your Rock of direction. In 1 Peter 2:4 He is called the "living stone." Is. 28:16 says, "Behold, I lay in Zion a stone for a foundation, a tried stone, a precious cornerstone, a sure foundation; Whoever believes will not act hastily." A cornerstone is the stone that gives direction to the entire building. The Message Bible says, "A trusting life won't topple." Jonathan proposes a signal to inform David of Saul's reaction. He'll go out to practice with his bow and arrow. Where he shoots the arrows will tell David the answer he's looking for. If the arrows are shot close to the rock, all is well. If they're shot beyond the rock, then Saul's intentions are evil and David must then flee (vs. 20-22). David's future was going to be revealed to him by the flight of an arrow.

If you need godly direction in your life, more than likely it won't come from a flying arrow. It will, however, come from the throne room of God if you'll be still long enough to hear what He has to say. Rev. 2:29 says, "He who has an ear, let him hear what the Spirit says to the churches." It is so important in this day and age that you pay attention to what you're listening to. The words you hear is what determines how you'll live your life. They have the power to dictate what you say and what you do. It is interesting how people can be listening to the same thing yet hear something different. Experiments were made where a certain word was spoken to a group of people and half of them said they heard a different word. It's true, you can hear something contrary to what is actually being said. This is why Jesus said seven times, "He who has ears to hear, let him hear!" (Matt. 11:15). In other words, it's possible to have ears but not have ears to hear. Your ears can be clogged up with the garbage of the world that you miss what God is saying.

God is calling His people to listen up and pay close attention to what He has to say to them. When was the last time you heard God's voice? Do you hear God for yourself or do you expect your pastor to do all the hearing for you? God wants to speak to you on a daily basis but do you have the ears to hear Him? People who don't hear God think He's not speaking when the truth is they're not listening. They don't have ears to hear. The parable of the sower (Mark 4:13-20) tells how some hear the Word yet don't allow it to take root because of the seduction of worldly pleasures and sensual comforts. Others reject what's being said because of persecution and trials. Then there are those who hear God and open themselves up to godly direction as they allow what He says to transform their lives. Those who have ears to hear will bear fruit all to the glory of God. Matt. 13:12 can be translated, "He who has ears to hear, to him will be given, and he will have abundance; but whoever does not have ears to hear, even what he has will be taken away from him."

Some people have never learned to hear from God because they're unwilling to hear what they need to hear. Quoting Isaiah, Jesus said in Matt. 13:14,15 (MSG), "Your ears are open but you don't hear a thing. Your eyes are awake but you don't see a thing. The people are blockheads! They stick their fingers in their ears so they won't have to listen; They screw their eyes shut so they won't have to look." These are the people who only listen to those who tell them what they want to hear. 2 Tim. 4:3,4 (NLT) says, "For a time is coming when people will no longer listen to sound and wholesome teaching. They will follow their own desires and will look for teachers who will tell them whatever their itching ears want to hear. They will reject the truth and chase after myths." So many people make decisions without inclining their ears to hear what God has to say about it. If you're a follower of God, then you should be hearing the voice of God. God is speaking. Are you surrendered to Him so that you can hear what He's saying? Do you have ears to hear?

If God sent His Son to die for you, why wouldn't He send His Son to talk to you? What's relationship without fellowship, and what's fellowship without communication? Jesus said in John 10:27, "My sheep hear My voice, and I know them, and they follow Me." In other words, the person who hears God, obeys God. God stops speaking to you when you stop obeying what He last said. God spoke about the people of Israel in Jer. 7:24, "Yet they did not obey or incline their ear, but walked in the counsels and in the imagination of their evil heart, and went backward and not forward." How well you hear what God has to say is what determines the direction your life will take. If you want to hear what God has to say about your future, obey what He said in your past. The Message Bible says, "But do you think they listened? Not a word of it. They did just what they wanted to do, indulged any and every evil whim and got worse day by day." People want God to speak to them about specific things but they're not doing what He already said.

God is speaking and there are ways to know if what you're hearing is from Him. First of all, what God says will never contradict His Word. Gal. 1:8 (NLT) says, "Let God's curse fall on anyone, including us or even an angel from heaven, who preaches a different king of Good News than the one we preached to you." The words God speaks to you will always line up and agree with the Bible. Second, does what you're hearing make you more like Christ? You're made in the image of Jesus and what you hear should cause you to think of yourself the way Christ Jesus thought of himself (Phil. 2:5). Is what you're hearing consistent with how God made you? Rom. 12:6 (NLT) says, "In His grace, God has given us different gifts for doing certain things well." Is what you're hearing harmful to someone else? Rom. 13:10 says, "Love does no harm to a neighbor." Is it convicting or condemning? God convicts, the devil condemns (Rom. 8:1). Does it concern your responsibility in the kingdom of God? Stop trying to hear God's voice for others. Finally, is there peace in your heart (Col. 3:15)?

As David hid in the field, Jonathan went to eat at the king's table in celebration of the new month that had just begun. Saul noticed that David was not there but said nothing. He thought to himself, "Something has happened to him; he is unclean, surely he is unclean" (vs. 26). Under the Mosaic Law, there were certain things that could make a person unclean and unable to participate in spiritual events. Touching a dead body, whether human or animal, was one thing they could not do. Certain foods were unclean for Jews and forbidden for them to eat, such as pork, certain fish, and certain birds. A skin infection could make a person unclean (Lev. 13:3). A house with certain kinds of mold was unclean. A woman was unclean during her monthly cycle and for a certain period of time following childbirth. On holy days couples were restricted from engaging in sexual activity as the release of body fluids made them unclean until evening (Lev. 15:18). This state of being unclean would only last a day (Lev. 22:3-7) so when David was absent the next day also, Saul demanded an explanation.

Saul asked Jonathan, "Why has the son of Jesse not come to eat, either yesterday or today?" (vs. 27). He doesn't even call David by name. He calls him the son of Jesse to draw attention to David's lowly position of being the son of a farmer. Jonathan covers for David by telling his father he gave David permission to spend the New Moon festival with his family in Bethlehem. This was a believable explanation but still the anger of Saul was greatly aroused. He's a man out of control as he shouts to his son, "You son of a perverse, rebellious woman! Do I not know that you have chosen the son of Jesse to your own shame and to the shame of your mother's nakedness?" (vs. 30). These words reveal the extreme depth of Saul's jealousy and hatred of David. He is full of bitterness and frustration as he hurls coarse and emotionally charged words at his son. He is saying Jonathan is the "bastard son of a wayward woman" and has no royal blood in his veins. Why else would he be willing to give up his right to the throne to a shepherd boy from the fields of Bethlehem?

Saul was not attacking his wife but is trying to bring shame upon his son. Spoken in public, these words were a bitter insult to Jonathan. Saul is saying Jonathan's mother will feel ashamed at having brought such a son into the world. He then offers to help Jonathan redeem himself as he tries to entice his help in killing David. "For as long as the son of Jesse lives on the earth, you shall not be established, nor your kingdom. Now therefore, send and bring him to me, for he shall surely die" (vs. 31). Jonathan responds by defending David, "Why should he be killed? What has he done?" (vs. 32). This question was previously asked, after which Saul vowed that David would not be killed. Jonathan is once again supporting his friend based on what was right in the eyes of the Lord. This enraged Saul and he cast a spear at Jonathan in an effort to kill him. This shows how deep Saul's hatred for David is. Jonathan now knew his father was determined to kill David at all costs. This made him very angry and he refused to continue participating in the feast.

Jonathan's heart is broken as he grieves for his friend because his father has treated him with scorn and contempt. The only thing left for him to do is tell David about Saul's state of mind through the prearranged signal of the arrows. As the bow arches and the arrow flies, David soon learns what his immediate future looks like. He knew through the flight of an arrow that his whole life had just changed, that God was sending him to the rugged mountains and the dark valleys of the Judean wilderness. No longer would he be welcome at the palace, a place where his enemy rules unjustly. No longer would he lead the king's army in battle against the enemies of the land. He couldn't go home to his wife for now he would have to live as a fugitive on the run from an angry, jealous king who wanted him dead. Still, there was hope. Somehow, someway, the will of God would be fulfilled. David believed this with all his heart. Smith Wigglesworth once said, "I am not moved by what I see or feel. I am only moved by what I believe."

Are arrows flying in your life? If so, are you going in the direction they're telling you to go? If those arrows send you to the valley of the shadow of death, then so be it. God has a path He wants you to walk on, a path that leads to His perfect will and purpose. If that path leads you to a storm, have no fear for God will be by your side every step of the way. Trust God and good will come out of the situation you are in. Remember, no pain, no gain. You would be weak if there were no struggles in your life. You cannot grow without pain for strength is only developed through resistance. If you never failed, you'd never develop the courage and the strength to keep pressing forward. To become the person God wants you to be, you must allow pain to become your friend. The truth is, you're stronger than you think. You were given pain because you're strong enough to handle it, strong enough to snatch victory out of defeat. Without pain, you would be weak your entire life. Your pain, your struggle, is what made you the person you are today. Don't ever forget that.

Jonathan brought a lad with him to retrieve the arrows. When he did, he was sent back to the city. It was then that David came out of hiding. He honors Jonathan as he "fell on his face to the ground, and bowed down three times. And they kissed one another, and they wept together, but David more so" (vs. 41). David and Jonathan loved each other and between them was a strong bond of friendship. There can be deep, tender feelings between men without a hint of sexual attraction. This is a lesson the world needs to hear today. Real men don't need to be afraid or apologetic for their godly love for other men. Talking to men, Jesus said in John 15:12, "This is My commandment, that you love one another as I have loved you." The time has come for them to part. David can't stay with Jonathan and Jonathan can't go with David. In times past they probably envisioned themselves working together for the glory of the Lord but now those plans are all but gone. This being so, they wept together with David weeping especially hard.

It is almost too much to bear. One chapter of David's life is closing while a dark, dreary chapter is opening. David is leaving the honor of being in the king's palace and the stability of having his own military command. David will now spend the next several years of his life as a fugitive, always looking over his shoulder. The most powerful man in the kingdom will be pursuing him relentlessly, intent on his demise. David is leaving behind his closest, dearest friend. Jonathan risked his life being loyal to David and there is no better friend than that. Jonathan tells David to go in peace as they make an enduring covenant between themselves and their descendants that will last forever (vs. 42). David is weeping as Jonathan turns to go back to the city while he walks into exile alone. This is a bleak and desolate road David must walk on but it's the road God chose for him. It's on this road that David will learn to depend on God, and God alone. The throne is God's ultimate purpose for David and this bare, windswept road is the path that will take him there.

-13-

"LIFE ON THE RUN"

There comes a time when a season of darkness falls upon the person whose heart is being shaped and molded by God. This is where David finds himself at this point in his life. What was true and sure is behind him and a cloud of uncertainty is before him. He is alone and confused. His soul is dried up of all emotion and the blue sky over his head has turned a dark gray. Things aren't the way they used to be. Not long before this he was on the fast track to the throne when suddenly a dark storm formed over his life. He had everything going for him but the jealous wrath of Saul caused him to flee for his life. David is now living a life on the run, a life of isolation and great loneliness. He is a fugitive, removed from the royal court of Israel, separated from his wife and his good friend Jonathan. This is a miserable, wretched experience that leads to exhaustion and hopeless despair. There seems to be no where to turn and there's nothing he can do to escape what he is now feeling. Nothing, that is, except to cling to the Lord with all his heart and soul.

After bidding farewell to Jonathan, David begins his days as a fugitive by fleeing three miles to Nob, a priestly city near the Mount of Olives (1 Sam. 21:1). The tabernacle had been at Shiloh and this is where Samuel was raised under Eli the high priest. When the ark was lost and Eli's sons were killed, Shiloh was abandoned and destroyed. The tabernacle was then moved to Nob even though the ark is no longer within it. The word "Nob" means 'high place' and the word "tabernacle" means 'dwelling place.' David went to the house of the Lord to be in the company of godly people. In a similar story, Psalm 73 tells how Asaph is troubled by the injustice in the land and the prosperity of the wicked. He wrote in vs. 16,17, "When I thought how to understand this, it was painful for me, until I went into the sanctuary of God; then I understood their end." Nothing made sense to Asaph until he went to the house of the Lord. Perhaps David will have clarity about his dilemma if he does the same thing.

Nob was about twelve miles from Jerusalem and the tabernacle was presided over by Ahimelech the high priest. When he saw David he immediately thought something was wrong. He asked, "Why are you alone, and no one is with you?" (vs. 1). It seemed unusual that a prominent man like David would be wandering around all by himself. He is the commander of thousands of soldiers and there is no royal guard with him. This suspicion caused Ahimelech to be afraid as he asked David why no one is with him. At this point David should have been honest with the priest and together they could have believed God to deliver him out of this ordeal. People spend their entire lives learning to trust in the Lord but it's hard to do when fear grips your heart. It drives you to depend on your own schemes and wit instead of depending on God. David is afraid and he doesn't know Ahimelech well enough to fully trust him. With fear driving his actions, David makes up a story about a secret mission the king has sent him on.

David said to Ahimelech, "The king has ordered me on some business, and said to me, 'Do not let anyone know anything about the business on which I send you, or what I have commanded you.' And I have directed my young men to such and such a place" (vs. 2). When you're led by fear, you make really bad decisions. This is a new experience for David. He didn't fear the lion and the bear and he didn't fear Goliath. Here is a mighty man of war, a man anointed to be king, struggling with fear. Some people may sympathize with David and understand why he lied. Even so, David would later regret this lie and his soul would melt for the destruction this lie would cause. Ps. 119:28,29 says, "My soul melts from heaviness; Strengthen me according to Your word. Remove from me the way of lying, and grant me Your law graciously." David then asks, "Now therefore, what have you on hand? Give me five loaves of bread in my hand, or whatever can be found" (vs. 3). He didn't come to the tabernacle to worship the Lord, he came to get something to eat.

David's request should have told the priest something was not right. Five loaves of bread wouldn't feed that many people. Why only five loaves if he's got a lot of soldiers to feed? The truth is, there are no men with David. He's telling one lie after another. Here is a man after God's own heart lying to a priest at the tabernacle. This is a horrible moment in his life. He's at the right place with the right people but his heart is not where it should be. He's replaced his faith with fear and the cost of this deception will be quite high. David asked the priest for food and all that was available was the sacred showbread (vs. 4). In the tabernacle there was a table which held twelve loaves of bread, one loaf for each of the twelve tribes of Israel. This bread was a symbol of intimate fellowship (Acts 2:46). It was God's way of telling the people He wanted to fellowship with them. In that culture, eating together formed a bond of friendship that was permanent and sacred. The word "showbread" means 'bread of faces' and is called "the bread of the Presence" in Ex. 25:30.

The bread that was put in the tabernacle was always to be fresh. God wants your fellowship with Him to be fresh, not stale and moldy. Jesus said to pray, "Give us this day our daily bread" (Luke 11:3). Just as bread is necessary for survival, so is fellowship with God a necessity in your life. It is also a picture of God's provision. It reminded one of the manna that fell from heaven when the children of Israel wandered aimlessly in the wilderness. Jesus said in John

6:35 (NLT), "I am the bread of life. Whoever comes to Me will never be hungry again. Whoever believes in me will never be thirsty." The showbread was not to be taken casually for it was to be regarded as being holy in the eyes of the Lord. Once a week this bread would be replaced and the priests would eat the old bread (Lev. 24:5-9), especially those on duty at the time. David was not a priest so it was technically unlawful for him to eat this bread. Jesus later refers to this event, using it as proof that the Law was designed for man's benefit, and that He is Lord of the Sabbath (Luke 6:3-5).

David was hungry and the only thing to eat was the bread that had been before the Lord in the tabernacle the previous week. Ahimelech knew the Law was given to further life, that human need supersedes the ceremonial obligation of the tabernacle. He also knew that the spirit of the Law demanded that feeding the needy must be put ahead of ritual if the two seem to be in conflict (Deut. 15:7,8). Prov. 10:3 (GNT) says, "The Lord will not let good people go hungry, but He will keep the wicked from getting what they want." Ahimelech does his due diligence to protect the holiness of the bread by asking David if his men were ritually clean (vs. 4). If they have had sex, they would be considered unclean until evening. David answered, "Truly, women have been kept from us about three days since I came out. And the vessels of the young men are holy, and the bread is in effect common, even though it was sanctified in the vessel this day" (vs. 5). Here is another lie! He has no men with him. When you lie one time, you've got to tell another lie to support the first lie you told.

David assures the priest that he and his men are ritually clean and Ahimelech gives him the bread to eat. The cost of David's deception will be quite high. A death blow will come upon the city of Nob, delivered by a man who was in the tabernacle that day. Vs. 7 says, "Now a certain man of the servants of Saul was there that day, detained before the Lord. And his name was Doeg, an Edomite, the chief of the herdsmen who belonged to Saul." Doeg is a servant of Saul and he sees what's going on with David and Ahimelech. The word "chief" means 'mighty; violent; stubborn; headstrong; unyielding; iron-willed.' Doeg was an Edomite and not a Hebrew. Israel had been at war with Edom (1 Sam. 14:47) so Doeg was either a captive or a traitor to his people. He was not a spiritual man and he was probably at Nob fulfilling some ceremonial requirement related to his employment for the king of Israel. He was an evil man and although he pretended to serve Israel, he served only himself and would later report David's location to King Saul.

David saw Doeg lurking in the shadows and this should have caused him to get his heart right with God. It didn't. Instead, he makes a second request of the priest, asking for a weapon with which to defend himself. "Is there not here on hand a spear or a sword? For I have brought neither my sword nor my weapons with me, because the king's business required haste" (vs. 8). Won't David stop lying? He's digging a hole he won't be able to climb out of. Once again the priest should have suspected that something was wrong. David is the commander of the king's army and he shows up without a weapon. It is sad to see David, a man who soared to such great heights in his encounter with Goliath, now resorting to lies and self-preservation. He's trying to protect himself instead of trusting God to protect him. Didn't he remember that his weapons of faith wasn't a spear and a sword but his sling and five smooth stones? Where's the faith that brought him such a great victory on that glorious day? Better than a spear and a sword would be his sling and the faith to use it.

Ahimelech tells David that the only weapon there is the sword of Goliath, kept at Nob as a memorial to what David had done. David said, "There is none like it; give it to me" (vs. 9). Sad to say, he is now trusting in the sword of the enemy, a sword that couldn't protect Goliath, more than in the things that helped him kill the lion, the bear, and the giant. This sword should have reminded him how God intervened on his behalf when he fought Goliath. It should have driven him to once again trust God instead of his own schemes and this weapon of warfare. It didn't, proving that your view of life often gets distorted when you're in fear. "Then David arose and fled that day from before Saul, and went to Achish the king of Gath" (vs. 10). Gath is twenty-five miles west of Nob and is the home town of Goliath. It wasn't uncommon for a fugitive to seek refuge with his pursuer's enemy. David flees the tabernacle, the dwelling place of the King of kings and Lord of lords, and goes to the city of the enemy where Achish is king.

David went to God's house seeking refuge and comfort but still he ends up running for his life. He believes accurately that Saul has spies looking for him so he goes to the least likely place Saul would look for him. He flees one enemy and goes to another. It's sad but true, oftentimes a persecuted Christian can find more comfort and support in the world than they do in the church. Many Christians tell sinners about the unconditional love and mercy of the Lord but refuse to offer a crumb of forgiveness to a fellow believer who has missed the mark. By going to Gath, David is basically jumping out of the frying pan into the fire. It is ironic that he would go to the home town of Goliath while having on his person the sword of the giant he had slain. Indeed, he was throwing caution to the wind. He's hoping he won't be recognized but right away that hope is shattered when the servants of Achish the king recognize who he is. They even went so far as to call him "the king of the land" (vs. 11). The ungodly understood David's destiny better than Saul did.

David knew he had been discovered and that the king would not let him go free. The Philistines did capture David and who knows what vicious plans they had for the man who brought dishonor to their nation? Vs. 12 says David "was very much afraid of Achish the king of Gath." The faith David had when he ran toward Goliath has now been turned to fear, causing him to reach the lowest point of his life up to that time. Things aren't happening the way he thought they should. Prov. 13:12 says, "Hope deferred makes the heart sick." The trials of life can sometimes feel overwhelming. The Message Bible says, "Unrelenting disappointment leaves you heartsick." Paul wrote in 2 Cor. 11:26,27 (MSG), "I've been at risk in the city, at risk in the country, endangered by desert sun and sea storm, and betrayed by those I thought were my brothers. I've known drudgery and hard labor, many a long and lonely night without sleep, many a missed meal, blasted by the cold, naked to the weather." In other words, when it rains, it pours.

In the eyes of David, the world is crashing in around him. He's falling deeper and deeper into isolation, loneliness, and despair. Have you ever stumbled on the path God told you to walk on? Have you ever felt like God has abandoned you? Has fear and doubt ever overcome your faith? Have you made wrong choices that took you into the camp of the enemy? All these things happened to David and fear grips his heart. It was at this time that he wrote Psalm 56. He knows it was his fear and wrong choices that got him in this predicament so he begins by wisely asking for God's mercy. "Be merciful to me, O God, for man would swallow me up; Fighting all day he oppresses me" (vs. 1). David is crying out to God in the midst of this dark valley. Suddenly, he has a change of heart. Instead of trusting in himself and in his enemies to find refuge, he writes, "Whenever I am afraid, I will trust in You. In God (I will praise His word), in God I have put my trust; I will not fear. What can flesh do to me?" (vs. 3,4). It sounds as if he's ready to take on the entire enemy camp.

The Message Bible says, "I'm proud to praise God; fearless now, I trust in God." These words weren't written after a great victory but in the midst of horrendous failure. David then renews his confidence in God. He writes in vs. 9, "When I cry out to You, then my enemies will turn back; This I know, because God is for me." He also says in vs. 11, "In God I have put my trust; I will not be afraid. What can man do to me?" What David is writing is in direct contrast to what he's doing at this time in his life but that's the point. That's what you should do. Joel 3:10 says, "Let the weak say, 'I am strong.'" This is what pulls you out of the pit in which you have fallen. David is showing you the method and source of recovery from such a low point in your life. Vs. 10 says, "In God (I will praise His word), in the Lord (I will praise His word)." Three times in this psalm David praises the Word of God. When he had trusted in himself, he distanced himself from God's Word. He's now praising the things God has to say.

David ends this psalm by praising the Lord once again. "I will render praises to You, for You have delivered my soul from death. Have You not delivered my feet from falling, that I may walk before God in the light of the living?" (vs. 12,13). David stumbled severely but God kept his feet from falling. All he had to do is reach back and cling to the relationship he once had with God. He now believes that God is again with him just like He was on the day he fought Goliath. He's now ready to rise up and boldly confront the evil Achish, king of Gath. Right? Wrong! 1 Sam. 21:13 says, "So he changed his behavior before them, feigned madness in their hands, scratched on the doors of the gate, and let his saliva fall down on his beard." The man who would be the greatest king in the history of Israel is acting like a madman, scratching on doors and foaming at the mouth. In that culture, it was intolerable to drool on one's beard. Only a man out of his mind would allow such an unbearable thing to happen.

David humiliated himself and acted like a madman. This he did by design so he might be able to escape from Gath and all the evil there. The question to be asked is was David walking in the Spirit or in the flesh when he did this? Some say he was in the flesh and trusting in his own methods to get him out of this predicament. They say he refused to stand up for God and neither did he have the confidence that God would protect him. Instead of trusting God, he changed his behavior and acted like a raving lunatic. However, Psalm 56 was written before this happened and shows David had a change of heart and once again was trusting in the Lord. He would later write in Ps. 37:23, "The steps of a good man are ordered by the Lord." Achish decided that David wasn't the man he thought he was or else he had indeed gone insane. Either way, he released David and let him go. God got David out of a mess that he himself had made. God's amazing grace and boundless love is shown when He delivers His people when they don't deserve it (Rom. 5:8).

1 Sam. 22:1 says, "David therefore departed from there and escaped to the cave of Adullam." Somewhere between Gath and the city of Adullam David found the time to write Psalm 34, one of the most popular psalms in all the Bible. He doesn't mention what he just went through, only the fact that God heard him in his hour of peril. When some people give their testimony they spend too much time exploiting their own past behavior and the work the devil did in their life. Don't do that! Don't glamorize sin by talking about it in abundant detail. No, focus on what God did and His heavenly goodness toward you. Vs. 1 begins, "I will bless the Lord at all times; His praise shall continually be in my mouth." When the goodness of God is revealed in your life, you'll be driven to praise Him continually. To God alone is praise due and David will not rob Him of the honor He so richly deserves. You need to praise Him in every situation and under every circumstance. Praise Him in good times

and bad, in the sunshine and in the rain, on the mountaintop and in the valley.

The sincere lover of God will bless Him at all times. Vs. 2 says, "My soul shall make its boast in the Lord; The humble shall hear of it and be glad." Love and gratitude for God is felt in the heart before it is expressed (Matt. 12:34). This feeling of praise is so great and so powerful that it is impossible to keep silent about it. Don't praise Him only in your heart. Verbalize your praise! Allow your tongue to reveal the glory of God. When the humble in heart hear your praises to God, they'll be encouraged and in turn will give confirmation of their trust in Him. He is a faithful God and worthy to be praised. "Oh, magnify the Lord with me, and let us exalt His name together" (vs. 3). David is inviting the lowly person, those humble in heart, to join him in magnifying the name of the Lord. There is humility when one says, "I can do all things through Christ who strengthens me" (Phil. 4:13). It is those who feel small who are able to make God look big. David wants them to help make God known among the sons of men, to make His fame grow throughout all the land.

"I sought the Lord, and He heard me, and delivered me from all my fears" (vs. 4). God expects to hear from you before you can expect to hear from Him. David sought the Lord while being held captive by the enemy and God heard him. It is a great blessing to be delivered from all your troubles, an even greater blessing to be delivered from all your fears. Security and tranquility are blessings reserved only for the godly. The wicked can be free from trouble but can never be free from fear. Never do they have the security a believer has. "They look to Him and were radiant, and their faces were not ashamed" (vs. 5). All people who look to God will have faces that shine as a result of their spirits being lifted up. One look at the Lord brings life and liberty, love and joy. "This poor man cried out, and the Lord heard him, and saved him out of all his troubles" (vs. 6). Being in need is no time for modesty. David's plea for help was a poor man's cry. Job wrote, "I go about mourning, but not in the sun; I stand up in the congregation and cry out for help."

"The Angel of the Lord encamps all around those who fear Him, and delivers them" (vs. 7). This is Jesus and He is keeping watch over you. He is the Good Shepherd taking care of His flock. He is there to serve and defend those who are His. "Oh, taste and see that the Lord is good; Blessed is the man who trusts in Him" (vs. 8). Make the blessings of God's grace your very own. Be a partaker of all He has for you. Trust in Him and you'll taste His goodness. You'll say, "His fruit was sweet to my taste." Vs. 9 says, "Oh, fear the Lord, you His saints! There is no want to those who fear Him." Never fear what man can do to you but tremble at the thought of offending God. Humble yourself like a child and give Him reverence and respect. Do what He tells you to do and hasten to serve Him at all times. Fear God and nothing else. If you'll do that, you will lack no good thing. Vs. 10 says, "The young lions lack and suffer hunger; But those who seek the Lord shall not lack any good thing." Make seeking God your top priority in life.

The Roman philosopher Seneca said in the first century, "The benefit of life is not in the length, but in the use of it. He sometimes lives the least who lives the longest." David wants you to live a good life so he writes in vs. 11, "Come, you children, listen to me; I will teach you the fear of the Lord." Step away from things that will occupy your mind and listen to what David has to say. The fear of the Lord should be the uppermost thing you learn in life. With godly wisdom, he will teach you how to do that. "Who is the man who desires life, and loves many days, that he may see good?" (vs. 12). A life of happiness is a desire all people have. Billions of people exist on this planet but very few live life as God intended. "Keep your tongue from evil, and your lips from speaking guile. Depart from evil, and do good; Seek peace, and pursue it" (vs. 13,14). The fear of the Lord shows itself in the hatred of all evil and a departure from it (Prov. 8:13; 16:6). Run from sin the way you would run from a pit of poisonous snakes.

"The eyes of the Lord are on the righteous, and His ears are open to their cry" (vs. 15). When the world ignores you, have the assurance that you have God's undivided attention. Both His eyes and ears are on the righteous. He hears their cry and immediately His whole mind is occupied with their well-being. For sure, help is on the way. "The face of the Lord is against those who do evil, to cut off the remembrance of them from the earth" (vs. 16). Light and darkness don't mix and utter destruction comes to the ungodly. Their honor will be turned to shame and their names will be forgotten. Not so for the righteous. Vs. 17,18 says, "The righteous cry out, and the Lord hears, and delivers them out of all their troubles. The Lord is near to those who have a broken heart, and saves such as have a contrite spirit." If you're hurting, never think God is far away. It's in your pain that God is most near. When you believe that with a simple act of faith, His goodness will be revealed to you.

"Many are the afflictions of the righteous, but the Lord delivers him out of them all. He guards all his bones; Not one of them is broken" (vs. 19,20). There is a joyous end to the believer's affliction. 2 Cor. 2:14 (MSG) says, "God leads us from place to place in one perpetual victory parade." Charles Spurgeon wrote, "No substantial injury occurs to the saints. Eternity will heal all their wounds. They'll be presented after life's trials are over without spot or wrinkle or any such thing." Vs. 21 says, "Evil shall slay the wicked, and those who hate the righteous shall be condemned." The sins of the wicked will be the rope that hangs them. Those in hell will be forsaken forever. It is there that evil is fully developed, tormenting those who have willfully forsaken the salvation of God. "The Lord redeems the soul of His servants, and none of those who trust in Him shall be condemned" (vs. 22). Those who come to Jesus are graciously purchased with His blood and delivered by His power. Joyfully will all believers rule and reign with Him forevermore.

-14-

"KING OF THE CAVE"

David is at a turning point in his life. A lot has happened to him in just a short period of time. He gained instant fame as a giant-killer, he was recently married, he faced danger from the Philistines and several attempts on his life from King Saul. On top of all that, he had a tearful farewell from Jonathan and everyday life and is now living as a fugitive on the run. After a brief but intense period of backsliding, he left Gath after acting like a madman and once again begins to praise God with great exaltation. His circumstances haven't changed but his response to them has. God brought confidence, restoration, and revival into David's life through his relationship with Him. Even so, David still needed a place to go. He couldn't go home to his wife, he couldn't go to the palace, and he couldn't go see Samuel or Jonathan. What's more, he couldn't even go back to the city of the ungodly Philistines. What does David do now? Where does he go? 1 Sam. 22:1 says, "David therefore departed from there and escaped to the cave of Adullam."

Adullam, which means "place of refuge," was a Canaanite city east of Gath near the border of the land occupied by the Philistines. Going there would have provided some protection from Saul because he couldn't mount a military attack against David without risking a war with the Philistines. Adullam was located two miles south of the Valley of Elah where David killed Goliath, fourteen miles west-southwest of Bethlehem, and eighteen miles southwest of Jerusalem. Close by was a hill that was fortified and known for its caves, some of them quite large. Many of the caves in that area are not in the classic form on the side of a rock wall. Most of the caves were holes in the ground with small, well-concealed openings that lead to expansive rooms. The cave of Adullam was one such cave, a dwelling place that could hold up to forty people. This underground asylum was a place of refuge for David. It was far from civilization and David was all by himself. Yes, he was anointed to be king but had not yet been appointed king. At least here he could say he was the king of the cave.

Scholars believe David spent three to six months living in this muddy, dark, lonely cave. Like David, are you having a cave experience? Do you feel all alone with shattered dreams, unbearable pain, and grief that won't go away? If so, you can learn from David's experience in the cave how to handle life at its darkest and most difficult hour. It's at this time in David's life that God is preparing him for the throne. You need to understand that whatever it is God calls you to do, He first prepares you to do it. Before God can use you, He must first make you usable. Before He does something through you, He first does something to you. It's in the cave of Adullam where God shaped young David into the man who would one day be king, a role he could not fulfill had he not had his cave experience. When people join the military, they first go to boot camp where they are trained in a specific kind of warfare. They learn how to use weapons and how to follow orders. Unknown to David at this time, the cave of Adullam would become his spiritual boot camp.

Fear makes people do strange things. It causes you to lean on your own understanding as you lose sight of God and step out of fellowship with Him. Fear turns people into cowards. When Jesus was arrested, Peter followed Him from afar off and then began to warm his hands at the enemy's fire. It was not long after this that he denied Jesus three times. David just went through a season of great fear but now, in the cave of Adullam, God is going to do something that will change the direction of David's life forever. It was in this dark cave that David, like the prodigal son, "came to his senses" (Luke 15:17). He still had hope even though his situation seemed hopeless. He had lost everything that had any value to him but still he chose to once again trust God. He chose to turn this cave into a place of worship, a place were he could give glory to God. He chose to allow the season he was in to become a training ground in his life that will lead to something greater. He trusted in the Lord with all his heart and, by faith, he knew his best days were ahead of him.

All the great heroes of faith had a cave experience. Joseph spent years in Pharaoh's dungeon before he became second-in-command. Moses spent forty years on the back side of the desert before he was sent by God to Egypt. Daniel spent time in the lion's den before he became a leader in the Persian empire. Jonah was in the belly of a whale before he experienced victory in Ninevah. Paul was adrift at sea for a day and a half before he reached his destination. There is no shame or dishonor in being in a cave, whatever your cave may be. What matters is what you do in your cave, how you use what you're going through to better your life. There are some things that can only be learned in a cave experience. It's in a cave where the training school of God is located. In order to get out of the cave, you must learn what God is trying to teach you. For sure, it is His will that you graduate at the top of your class in the school of hard knocks. What did David do? He turned his cave into a prayer closet. It was in the cave of Adullam where he wrote Psalm 142.

People everywhere want to read books about prayer. The problem is, that's all they do. They read about prayer but seldom do they pray. Instead of drawing closer to God, a lot of people make excuses as to why they're in the cave. They blame others for putting them there when in truth it was their own actions that put them in the cave. They throw a big pity party and cry out, "Woe is me!" They get angry and turn their cave into a den of despair. They give up and go deeper and deeper into the cave. There is no light in the back side of the cave and darkness is everywhere. This is when most people turn to God. When life knocks you down and puts you flat on your back, there is only one direction to look. Up! David turned the silence of the cave into the altar of the sacrifice of praise, the darkness into a tabernacle of worship. He turned his bitterness into the sweet incense of praising God, his loneliness into a time of close fellowship. It was in the cave where David learned the importance of being honest with God and telling Him how you feel.

When you're in your cave, pray like David prayed. Ps. 142:1,2 says, "I cry out to the Lord with my voice; With my voice to the Lord I make my supplication. I pour out my complaint before Him; I declare before Him my trouble." The disciples once said to Jesus, "Lord, teach us to pray" (Luke 11:1). Here, in the cave of Adullam, David is doing just that. In this psalm he is teaching you how to pray in times of distress. He begins by pouring his heart out to God believing He is listening to him. Others may listen to you for a short while but they'll quickly grow tired of hearing about all your problems. Before long they'll run away when they see you coming. Not so with God. Ps. 46:1 says, "God is our refuge and strength, a very present help in trouble." David is teaching you to never complain before people, but before God alone. What human wants to be around a person who complains all the time? Even if they did listen to you, you'd only get contempt from those who are proud or showered with false sympathy from those who are not who they say they are.

David says in vs. 4 (NIV), "Look and see, there is no one at my right hand; no one is concerned for me. I have no refuge; no one cares for my life." Back then, in a court of law, the defense lawyer always stood at the right hand of the accused. David looks to the right and sees that nobody is defending him. There is nobody to speak on his behalf. He is all alone. Have you ever been in a position like this? Have you ever felt so low that it seemed like no one cared what was happening to you? Have you felt like the tentacles of despair have you wrapped in its deadly grasp? If so, don't be afraid to tell God how you feel. David then did the right thing. "I cried out to You, O Lord" (vs. 5). Anything that causes you to cry out unto God can be considered a blessing in disguise. With raw honesty, David tells God how he felt and the overwhelming emotions he's experienced since arriving in the cave. This, in turn, opened the door that allowed David to experience God in a powerful way right in the midst of a cold and lonely cave.

David said, "You are my refuge, my portion in the land of the living" (vs. 5). What a great confession of faith this is. At first David cried out bitterly but here the tone of his voice is sweet, fresh, and full of life. The greatest lessons of life are learned by trusting God in difficult times. It is during the hard times where you learn that if you have God, you have all you need. He is your portion, a word that means "allotment, inheritance, or part." David knows he has God's attention, that it's in your cave that God is closest to you (Ps. 34:18). He also knows that if God doesn't rescue him, his destiny will not be fulfilled. "Attend to my cry, for I am brought very low; Deliver me from my persecutors, for they are stronger than I" (vs. 6). Saul is crazy with rage and is seeking the help of all those who sought royal favor. Saul was the king and David was a fugitive, an outlaw hiding in a cave. He prays, "Bring my soul out of prison, that I may praise Your name; The righteous shall surround me, for You shall deal bountifully with me" (vs. 7).

David ends this psalm on a positive note. Yes, before long others would join him in the cave, warriors who will faithfully stand by his side during his reign as king. But first, another psalm would be written. Psalm 142 was a description of David's discouraged heart but was also where his confession of faith and confidence in God started to spring forth and emerge. Psalm 57 was then written as David began to focus on his restoration. It describes David as the Lord strengthened him in the cave and prepared him for what was to come. He begins in prayer but concludes with a jubilant song of praise pouring out of his inner man. Written from the bowels of the earth much like Jonah's prayer from the belly of a whale, David begins in vs. 1, "Be merciful to me, O God, be merciful to me!" The urgency of his need is the reason for his repetition of the cry for mercy. He needs help and he needs it now. "For my soul trusts in You; And in the shadow of Your wings I will make my refuge, until these calamities have passed by" (vs. 1).

Not only does David take refuge in the cave of Adullam, he also finds safety under the parental wing of Almighty God. He places himself under the protection of a heavenly power, a place he will abide "until the hurricane blows over" (MSG). Charles Spurgeon once wrote, "Blessed be God, our calamities are matters of time, but our safety is a matter of eternity." David is quite safe but still he prays, "I will cry out to God Most High, to God who performs all things for me" (vs. 2). Faith is never silent. You pray because you believe. David confesses that help will come from heaven and God will humiliate those who wish to do him harm. He says, "God shall send forth His mercy and His truth" (vs. 3). David got more than what he asked for. He cried out for mercy and truth came with it. Indeed, God is a God "who is able to do exceedingly abundantly above all that we ask or think" (Eph. 3:20). The cave may have reminded David of a lion's den as he says, "My soul is among lions" (vs. 4). Saul and his men are like lions, howling and hunting David. Even so, God saved David just like He saved Daniel many years later.

"I lie among the sons of men who are set on fire, whose teeth are spears and arrows, and their tongue a sharp sword" (vs. 4). David is in the midst of the flames but he is not consumed, much like the burning bush at the time of Moses. Beneath the divine shelter of God he is safe. For this reason he praises God, "Be exalted, O God, above the heavens; Let Your glory be above all the earth" (vs. 5). Praise should always come from the midst of burning flames and in the lion's den. This is what you do in your cave experience. Let your praises rise higher than the heavens to the throne room of God. If you'll do that, your enemies will fall into the same pit they dug for you (vs. 6). David's song of praise now springs forth with radiance and glory, "My heart is steadfast; I will sing and give praise" (vs. 7). Yes, yes, David has found his Savior in a cave. His heart is established and a calm delight fills his soul. He is determined to fill this cave with praises unto God, to have its deep caverns echo the joyous sound flowing out of his heart.

"Awake, my glory! Awake, lute and harp! I will awaken the dawn" (vs. 8). Three times David tells himself to awake. There is no sleeping on the job when it comes to praising God. Indeed, praise is not silent. "I will praise You, O Lord, among the peoples; I will sing to You among the nations" (vs. 10). No matter where you're at or what you're going through, always sing praises to God. "For Your mercy reaches unto the heavens, and Your truth unto the clouds" (vs. 10). David is probably at the mouth of the cave looking up into the sky as he contemplates the loftiness of God's mercy, the vastness of His goodness. He concludes this psalm by saying, "Be exalted, O God, above the heavens; Let Your glory be above all the earth" (vs. 11). David said in the last verse that God's mercy reaches into the heavens. Here he says God is to be exalted above the heavens. There are no boundaries or limits to how high the praises of God can go. Don't think you have to get out of your cave before you can have the heart David had in this psalm. No, you can have it now no matter what situation you may be in.

David's heart is now where God wants it to be. He is standing on the solid rock of revival and confidence in the Lord. Many people tell God how they feel in the caves of life, as well they should, but how many continue on and praise Him while they're in the midst of difficulty and hardship? When you choose to praise God for who He is, in spite of your circumstances, good things will happen. God did a powerful work in David's heart at one of the lowest points in his life. He listened as David told Him how he felt. He then changes the focus of David's heart. He has David take his eyes off his own problems and turns his focus to helping others in need. His family somehow found out where he was hiding and 1 Sam. 22:1 says, "And when his brothers and all his father's house heard it, they went down there to him." This was the hand of God. It seems as if their harsh feelings toward David have vanished and are no longer there. They now join him at the cave for support and safety. What once was lost has now been found.

Not only did Saul want to kill David, he wanted to kill his family as well. When they heard David found a safe place to hide, they go join him. Since some of his brothers were in Saul's army, they had to run away from their duties in order to join David, and desertion meant death. One is made to wonder how David felt as his family approached the opening of the cave. Most people don't want those with problems showing up on their doorstep when they're dealing with their own struggles. But God knew what David needed most. He knows that the most practical way to serve Him is to help others in need. God expects you to use your difficult cave experience as a platform to help others who are going through the same season of hurt and pain. Things don't have to be perfect in your life in order for God to use you. Take your eyes off yourself and look to see if there are hurting people near the entrance to your cave. Surely they are there waiting for you to give them a helping hand. Surprisingly, David's family members are not alone in seeking refuge with him in this cave.

"And everyone who was in distress, everyone who was in debt, and everyone who was discontented gathered to him. So he became captain over them. And there were about four hundred men with him" (vs. 2). These were the malcontents of Israel, the dread of society. Like David's family, these renegades, these bohemian vagabonds, found out where David was hiding and gradually made their way to the cave. These nomads were probably wondering if their dreams would ever come to pass, if they'd ever escape their own cave experience. Many of these misfits have a price on their head. There are those who owe money and are being pursued for repayment. There are also rebels here who want to overthrow Saul, and probably a few bandits wanted for various crimes. Some will say that the tale of Robin Hood and his merry men was taken from this time in the life of David. These were military men with diverse backgrounds. They were all considered a threat to Saul's reign and were fugitives for one reason or another. They joined David in the cave of Adullam and forged a strong bond with him. He became their leader and they were his mighty men.

1 Chron. 12:22 says, "Day after day men came to help David, until he had a great army, like the army of God." Remember, God is preparing David for the throne. As he leads these men, he will learn how to rule over the twelve tribes of Israel. He'll learn how to train an army. These men will later become the best army in the history of Israel. They know David is their anointed king, the one chosen by God to rule over all Israel. They're willing to stay with him during times of persecution and suffering until the time comes when he rightfully takes the throne. What was it that caused these outsiders, this band of misfits, to pledge their allegiance to

David? What drove them to the cave of Adullam where the true king of Israel was hiding in exile? It was distress, being in debt, and discontentment. The Message Bible says, "All who were down on their luck came around - losers and vagrants and misfits of all sorts. David became their leader." They didn't come to David because they were living the high life. No, they were hurting, every one of them. This is also why people come to Jesus.

Wrapped up in this story is a portrayal of the entire gospel message. There is a king on the throne who has been rejected by God and here in a cave is an anointed king ruling over society's rejects. Today there is a rejected king on the throne of this world system. Jesus called him "the ruler of this world" (John 12:31). He appears to be in charge but he's not (Is. 14:12-15). Satan chose his will over God's will, as did Saul who did the same thing that got Lucifer thrown out of heaven. Judgment comes when you put your will above God's will. Col. 2:15 (NLT) says Jesus "disarmed the spiritual rulers and authorities. He shamed them publicly by His victory over them on the cross." The Message Bible says, "He stripped all the spiritual tyrants in the universe of their sham authority at the cross and marched them naked through the streets." The judgment over the devil and his kingdom has already happened, it's already been executed. Those demonic forces that appear to be in control in the world today have already been judged in God's eyes. It's finished, a done deal. His days of controlling your life are over.

These mighty men needed a savior and so do you. They were in distress and this is what drove them to the side of the rightful king. They were under great pressure and stress and had troubles of one kind or another. This is what compelled them to search for a savior in a cave. No self-satisfied person will ever run into the arms of Jesus. People who seem to be living a perfect life don't feel the need for a risen Savior. Jesus said to the church of Laodicea in Rev. 3:17 (NLT), "You say, 'I am rich. I have everything I want. I don't need a thing!' And you don't realize that you are wretched and miserable and poor and blind and naked." You need to see your need for Jesus before you go to Him. It's when you see the hopelessness of worldly satisfaction that you'll run to the true King and the true kingdom. It was distress that caused the prodigal son to return home. He didn't return to his father when he had money, wine, and women. No, he returned home when he was in the pig pen. Ps. 34:6 says, "This poor man cried out, and the Lord heard him, and saved him out of all his troubles."

These societal outcasts were in distress so they fled the temporary pleasures of this world to take hold of the persecution and suffering of God's chosen king. They were also deeply in debt. Saul was probably lending them money with high interest rates even though it was forbidden by Jewish law for a Jew to charge another Jew interest. Back then, if you couldn't pay back the money you borrowed, you would be kept or sold as a slave. In truth, many of these men were runaway slaves. They were an oppressed people who had the overwhelming need to pay a debt that could not be paid. People who find themselves in a situation like this have almost no hope for the future. There are other debts also besides what one owes financially. As people recklessly consume the pleasures of this sinful world they don't realize it's all borrowed pleasure. It's pleasure that comes with a price tag. Heb. 9:27 says, "And as it is appointed for men to die once, but after this the judgment." The Message Bible says, "Everyone has to die once, then face the consequences."

Rom. 6:23 says, "For the wages of sin is death." That's the payment for the borrowed pleasures of sin. Nobody escapes those wages and it's a debt that must be paid. You need to realize that all unpaid debts get paid when one stands before

God on the day of judgment. You can give your life to Jesus and let Him pay your debt now, or you can reject Him and pay the debt yourself after this life is over. The choice is yours. Pay now or pay later. Thankfully, Rom. 6:23 goes on to say "but the gift of God is eternal life in Christ Jesus our Lord." The Message Bible says, "Work hard for sin your whole life and your pension is death. But God's gift is real life, eternal life, delivered by Jesus, our Master." Remember, sin always puts you in spiritual debt. You are bankrupt without Jesus and His shed blood. Being in distress and in debt caused these men to be discontented with life. They know there is something missing in their life. There's a void not yet filled. They want something different, something better, so God led them to David at the cave of Adullam.

The discontented are those who dig deep into the pleasures of the world but still don't find the satisfaction they're looking for. They're restless and disappointed and have no contentment in life. This is why Jesus said in John 7:37, "If anyone thirsts, let him come to Me and drink." Being thirsty is a sign of discontentment. It's what leads to the distress that drives you into the arms of the Savior. These men who came to David acted in faith and left the dark kingdom of this world. They turned away from their current lifestyle and fled to a savior in a cave. They came to David in distress but they didn't stay that way. David turned them into the kind of men described in 1 Chron. 12:8. They became "mighty men of valor, men trained for battle, who could handle the shield and spear, whose faces were like the faces of lions, and were swift as gazelles on the mountains." This describes those who flee the kingdom of the world to join forces with Jesus. Being with David transformed these nobodies into mighty warriors on the front line of battle doing the Lord's work.

-15-

"THY WILL BE DONE"

Speaking of the faithful, Heb. 11:38 (NLT) says, "They were too good for this world, wandering over deserts and mountains, hiding in caves and holes in the ground." These renegades, this band of misfits, came to David when the world turned its back on them. Don't stay isolated if you're having a cave experience. Allow godly people into your life during those moments of dread and despair. Prov. 17:17 (MSG) says, "Friends love through all kinds of weather, and families stick together in all kinds of trouble." The devil wants you to be alone, going here and there, not knowing who your true friends really are. Get planted in a good local church, sign up for home Bible studies. Let people who know God personally into your life. David managed to weld this disorganized group of rebels together and they would later become the leaders in the greatest kingdom in the world. Allow your cave to be a place of restoration and reconciliation, a place where family members can get connected together again, a place where people who have fallen can stand up and be strong.

Security and protection were found in the cave of Adullam but it was now time to move on. David knew his elderly parents couldn't hold up well in the rugged wilderness so he took them to Mizpah of Moab (1 Sam. 22:3). He also wants his parents protected. If Saul is after him, he'll surely go after his parents also. David cared for his parents at a time when he had plenty of problems of his own. Some people think going through trials gives them a license to be unloving and selfish. David shows you must care for others instead of becoming self-absorbed in your own problems. Also, 1 Tim. 5:8 says if one does not provide for his own house, he has denied the faith and is worse than an infidel. David takes his parents to Moab located on the south-eastern corner of the Dead Sea. The city was named after Moab, a son of Lot born of an incestuous relationship he had with his oldest daughter (Gen. 19:37). Ruth was from Moab and she was the grandmother of David's father, Jesse. There were strong family ties there and David got the king of Moab to personally take care of his parents "till I know what God will do for me" (vs. 3).

David knew he was called and anointed to be the next king but he had no idea how God would get him to the throne. God leads one step at a time and David had a prophet with him named Gad who told him what to do next, "Do not stay in the stronghold; depart and go to the land of Judah" (vs. 5). David may have thought he could wait in the cave until Saul died but God had other plans. He wanted David to be active, to "run with patience the race that is set before us" (Heb. 12:1). Gad tells David to leave the stronghold of the cave and go back to Judah, the very place where Saul is waiting. Why did the prophet tell David to do this? How will David learn to trust God with all his heart if he is safe in his cave? God is calling David to be a man of faith. He had to learn to trust God in the midst of danger and not just when he was in a safe place. He probably didn't want to hear this but he obeyed anyway and went to the forest of Hereth. By leaving the cave, David would be able to exercise his faith and walk in godly wisdom and courage, the very things he'll need to be king.

Back in Gibeah, Saul is getting more and more paranoid as the days go by. His informants quickly discover where David is at for it's hard to hide four hundred men. Saul knows where David is but still he can't capture him. This pushes Saul over the edge and he begins to accuse his tribesmen of treason and conspiracy. He is talking to the Benjamites (vs. 7) for he also is from the tribe of Benjamin. Not only were these men his servants, they were also his relatives. They represented his inner circle, those he put in top positions in his kingdom. It goes without saying that this show of favoritism did not create unity among the eleven other tribes. There was no evidence of any disloyalty among his servants but bitterness and envy will blind your eyes to the truth. His deranged and delusional thinking causes him to pour guilt and accusation on those in his presence. He thinks everybody is against him, including his own son Jonathan who he believes is conspiring with David to have him killed. Finally he says, "There is not one of you who is sorry for me" (vs. 8).

Saul is having one major pity party as he pouts before his soldiers. To bring comfort to the king in his outrage, Doeg the Edomite steps forward and says he saw David at Nob with the priest Ahimelech (vs. 9). He incriminates the priest as being David's accomplice in a plot to overthrow the king. In the New Testament, King Herod was also an Edomite. When Jesus was born he ordered the massacre of all male children two years old and younger in hopes of killing the new born Messiah. Doeg was just as evil as he looks for an opportunity to promote himself in the eyes of the king. One way to do that was to divert Saul's anger and suspicions from his own staff to the priests of God. By sharing this information while Saul was in this foul mood, he is placing all the Lord's priests in peril. Saul is outraged at this news of betrayal and he calls Ahimelech, his family, and all the other priests to come to him. When they arrive, Saul calls out to the high priest who answers, "Here I am, my lord" (vs. 12). Ahimelech answers Saul with the honesty of a man with a clear conscience.

Saul said to Ahimelech, "Why have you conspired against me, you and the son of Jesse, in that you have given him bread and a sword, and have inquired of God for him, that he should rise against me, to lie in wait, as it is this day?" (vs. 13). In his reckless paranoia, Saul thinks of himself as the victim. In his twisted mind, David and Ahimelech are out to get him. He even thinks all the other priests are part of the conspiracy as well. Ahimelech is unaware of Saul's hatred for David so he inadvertently praises him before the jealous king. After all, David did tell him that he was on a secret mission for Saul when in truth he was running for his life. Even so, the priest questioned David carefully when he came to him. Instead of telling Ahimelech the truth, David lied to him and this put the priest in a very vulnerable position. He claims his innocence as he says to Saul, "Let not the king impute anything to his servant, or to any in the house of my father. For your servant knew nothing of all this, little or much" (vs. 15). Saul didn't believe him and commands the execution of the priests and their families.

Saul has turned his back on God and he has no regard for the sanctity of the priesthood or the things of the Lord. This is truly the worst thing Saul ever did. His rage was so cruel and unforgiving there is no way this act of barbarism could ever be justified. He was reluctant to kill the enemies of God when he was commanded to (1 Sam. 15:9) but here he doesn't hesitate to murder the priests of God in cold blood. This death sentence was pronounced without any pause or deliberation, without any remorse or regret. Saul has the heart of a monster and is clearly out of his mind. The wretchedness of Saul's hatred, the insanity of his heart and soul, causes him to be filled with raw, uncensored evil. He turns to the guards and tells them to kill all the priests. Something unexpected then happens, "But the servants of the king would not lift their hands to strike the priests of the Lord" (vs. 17). It is unheard of to hear of soldiers disobeying a direct order, especially an order coming from the king. To their credit, they stood there and did nothing.

Rage must have filled Saul because of the rebellion and insubordination among his soldiers. He probably repeated his command with loud shouting but not one man moved. Why did they disobey? It could be they secretly admired David and all he stood for. They also feared God's wrath on anybody who harmed His priests. They may have realized that Saul was not only insane but very evil and this is why they refused the command given to them. If only one soldier had refused the king's order he would have been slain immediately. There is strength in unity and this is what saved their lives. Saul then turned to Doeg and told him to kill the priests. He was a foreigner and didn't care about the priesthood. He was also a descendant of Esau who always hated the descendants of Jacob. Doeg saw this as an opportunity to win the favor of the king so he murdered that day eighty-five priests. Not only that, he continued his slaughter by wiping out the entire population of Nob, "both men and women, children and nursing infants, oxen and donkeys and sheep" (vs. 19).

Doeg was an evil, self-seeking, bloodthirsty man and an enemy of God. He was a terrorist, a man filled with contempt and malignant hostility. He is the worst a person could ever be. He killed everybody even though Saul told him to only kill the priests. David writes about Doeg in Psalm 52 as he shows his outrage against this evil man. "Why do you boast in evil, O mighty man? Your tongue devises destruction, like a sharp razor, working deceitfully. You love evil more than good, and lying rather than speaking righteousness. You love all devouring words, you deceitful tongue" (vs. 1-4). Destruction is promised for what Doeg has done. "God shall likewise destroy you forever; He shall take you away, and pluck you out of your dwelling place, and uproot you from the land of the living" (vs. 5). In contrast to this, the person who follows the Lord has hope for the future. "But I am like a green olive tree in the house of God; I trust in the mercy of God forever and ever. I will praise You forever, because You have done it; And in the presence of Your saints I will wait on Your name, for it is good" (vs. 8,9).

1 Sam. 22:20,21 says, "Now one of the sons of Ahimelech the son of Ahitub, named Abiathar, escaped and fled after David. And Abiathar told David that Saul had killed the Lord's priests." David now has in his company a prophet, a priest, and a small army of men. A kingdom is slowly coming together. After hearing this sad news brought to him by Abiathar, David becomes heartsick and admits what he did was wrong and takes the blame for what happened. He's saying, "It's my fault" and he's absolutely right. No one gets away from sin. All wrong doing is in the clear view of the face of God and it is His moral law that all sin is eventually punished (Num. 32:23). David told a little white lie to Ahimelech and hundreds of innocent people were slaughtered at the command of Saul. From the smallest transgression to the greatest crime, sin must be taken seriously. A proverb from long ago says, "Sin will carry you farther than you want to go, will keep you longer than you want to stay, will cost you more than you want to pay." David then invites the high priest's son to stay with him for his own safety (vs. 23).

Through all of this, David is being trained to be the next king of Israel. It is so important to know that before your destiny can be fulfilled, you must be trained how to handle adversity. David wasn't broken by bitterness because of the unfairness that was taking place in his life. He didn't allow resentment to cloud his vision for the future. He had turned the cave of Adullam into his own personal prayer closet through which he developed a high level of trust in the living God. His brokenness taught him that God was in control. He learned the lesson of looking up when life gets you down. He's now running for his life and he's in a rugged and barren place. As he's running, he gets a chance to come out of his wilderness experience and do something great for God. Some people came to him and said, "Look, the Philistines are fighting against Keilah, and they are robbing the threshing floors" (1 Sam. 23:1). The city of Keilah was an important walled city on the open plains in the southern territory of Judah. This news gives David the chance to once again minister before the Lord.

The Philistines were scavengers as they attacked the people of Keilah at harvest time, a time when they built up their food supply for the months ahead. The threshing floor was where all the grain was brought, processed, and stored. It held a year's supply of food, enough to last until the next harvest. Instead of planting their own food, the Philistines came and stole the food that was being gathered at the threshing floor. Robbing this grain meant death by starvation for many of the people who lived there. David hears about this and now knows why he was told to leave the stronghold of the cave of Adullam. He was safe there but wouldn't have been reached in time to help God's people. While Saul is slaughtering the people of Nob, David is being called upon to save the people of Keilah. He's being given the opportunity to act like a king even though he's not yet the king. In truth, Saul is the king and this is his job. The problem is he's too busy running roughshod over everything and everyone. David, on the other hand, sees God's people in stress and prays about it.

In order to experience victory, you must first engage the enemy. You must be willing to take a risk on God's behalf and pour yourself into the lives of other people. David, however, presumes nothing and doesn't act spontaneously or in disregard of what the will of the Lord may be. "Therefore David inquired of the Lord, saying, 'Shall I go and attack these Philistines?'" (vs. 2). Meditate on that! If you don't learn to inquire of the Lord, to seek His will in whatever it is you do, you will not grow in your walk with God. You'll continually be spinning your wheels in the mud and won't be able to move forward in life. A day should never go by when you don't go to God in prayer and seek His will for your life. The words "Thy will be done" should be the foremost thing you say, whether you're talking about your ministry, your family, your job, your finances, or your play time. Prov. 3:6 (NLT) says, "Seek His will in all you do, and He will show you which path to take." Never jump ahead of God. You need to seek His will every day and then submit to that will no matter what happens.

The people of Keilah were in trouble and reaching out for help. Why did David take it upon himself to help these people? Because that's who David was. He was a warrior and defeating the enemy in battle is what he was called to do. However, he didn't let his instincts take over. He first went to the Lord in prayer to seek out His will in the matter. David inquired of the Lord with a willingness to do what was commanded. He was willing to put himself in further danger in order to obey God and meet the needs of the people. He prayed because he learned the hard way not to act in his own wisdom and strength. He went to Nob without seeking direction from the Lord and the whole town got wiped out by Doeg. He then went to Gath and almost got himself killed there. He eventually came to his senses and now sees the need to consult with God about everything. He doesn't run headlong into battle but stops to see what the will of the Lord is. He's saying, "Not my will, but Thy will be done." He's putting his dependence on the Lord and not on himself.

When you are in the hands of God, gloom disappears in the light of His glory. Fear runs away when faith springs forth. David learned that the most important thing in life is to give each day to God, to seek His will, and then do what He tells you to do. Once you know what the will of God is, you must obey Him unconditionally. Don't allow yourself to be distracted by the distractions of life. In other words, you must be willing to pay the price that comes with obeying God. David inquired of the Lord and He answered him and said,

"Go and attack the Philistines, and save Keilah" (vs. 2). David now knew what he was supposed to do. His men, however, had their own opinion about all this. They said to him, "Look, we are afraid here in Judah. How much more, then, if we go to Keilah against the armies of the Philistines?" (vs. 3). David didn't ask his men what they thought about it but they told him anyway. Judah was the place the prophet Gad told David and his men to go. They were where God wanted them to be but still they were afraid. They tell David he's putting them in harm's way.

David's men were honest and up front with him. They aren't too happy about going into battle. They've got problems of their own so why go help somebody else in need? They were happy to receive David's comfort and encouragement in the cave at a time when they had no contentment in life. They wanted all they could get from the Lord but had second thoughts about going into battle for Him. This is a description of many Christians today. They're happy to receive salvation and all the blessings that come with being a child of God. They all want love, joy, and peace but turn their backs on what Jesus said in Matt. 16:24, "If anyone desires to come after Me, let him deny himself and take up his cross, and follow Me." The Message Bible says, "Don't run from suffering; embrace it. Follow Me and I'll show you how." The call to take up your cross is a call to die to your own selfish desires, a call to absolute surrender to the will of God. It's saying, "Not my will, but Thy will be done." As you pray to the Father, Jesus taught you to say, "Thy kingdom come, Thy will be done on earth as it is in heaven" (Matt. 6:10).

Concerning Keilah, God said, "Go and attack!" and David's men said, "No way!" David doesn't condemn his men but goes to the Lord in prayer a second time. God doesn't mind if you do this and it probably created in David's men a greater confidence in their leader. As David again inquires of the Lord, he's asking, "Lord, did I hear You right the first time?" Don't be presumptuous and don't be afraid to get confirmation from the Lord. If it's God's will to do something, He'll gladly confirm it to you. Gideon asked for confirmation and God gave it to him (Judges 6:36-40). God answered David, "Arise, go down to Keilah. For I will deliver the Philistines into your hand" (vs 4). God's answer didn't change but He did sweeten the pot by adding a promise to it. He gave David a prophetic word to share with his men. He said, "Go fight, for I have ordered the victory." He knows that those who run from the battle never experience the thrill of victory. Once His will is known, it must be obeyed at all costs. A soldier must learn to obey the orders given to him. Trust and obey, for there's no other way.

The more you inquire of the Lord, the more clearer His voice becomes. When you commit to obeying the will of God in your life, when you refuse to be distracted, you will experience victory. David is determined to obey God when it was unpopular with his men to do so. It's not enough to know God's will, you must also be willing to obey His will even when it's difficult. David followed God and, thankfully, his men followed him. Paul said in 1 Cor. 11:1, "Imitate me, just as I also imitate Christ." 1 Sam. 23:5 says, "And David and his men went to Keilah and fought with the Philistines, struck them with a mighty blow, and took away their livestock. So David saved the inhabitants of Keilah." In the midst of his distress and adversity, David inquired of the Lord and put his trust in Him. God said "Go" and David went. He's now back in the game. He's doing what he's been called to do. He's in the battle and God immediately gives him the victory plus the livestock as a bonus. The Philistines were taking the food supply of the people of Keilah and here David takes their food supply.

Yes, David won a great victory but his adversity is far from over. Saul is still after David and he's on a downward spiral toward self-destruction. When told that David is in Keilah he said, "God has delivered him into my hand, for he has shut himself in by entering a town that has gates and bars" (vs. 7). Saul is in no place to discern the will of God. He cares nothing about God and his service to Him. Foolishly he thinks God is working for him and had delivered David into his hand. He mistook his own evil desires for the will of God. He believed what he greedily desires. He looked at what was happening based on what he wanted and not on what God wanted. Saul is totally motivated by self-interest. He wouldn't go to Keilah to defend the city against the Philistines but he'll go there to kill David. "Then Saul called all the people together for war, to go down to Keilah to besiege David and his men" (vs. 8). Saul, the reigning king, is planning to attack a city of his own people and, if necessary, kill everybody in his attempt to get David.

Disobedient believers and even some nonbelievers can misinterpret things that happen as being of God. Saul reasons that because David is in Keilah, a town that has gates and bars, this is proof that God wants him to attack the city and kill David there. He is going to surround Keilah with soldiers and back David and his men into the city until their food and water supply run out. They'll either surrender or die of starvation. Not only would David and his men die, so would all the occupants of Keilah also die. Saul was willing to let all these people perish just so he could carry out his devilish plan. David heard what Saul was planning to do so he said to Abiathar the priest, "Bring the ephod here" (vs. 9). The ephod was the breastplate of the high priest and on it were two gemstones, the Urim meaning "lights" and the Thummin meaning "perfection" (Ex. 28:30). These stones were used by the high priest to determine God's will in certain situations. When Joshua succeeded Moses he received answers from God by means of the Urim through Eleazar the high priest (Num. 27:21).

References to the Urim and Thummin are rare in the Bible and no one knows the precise nature of these gemstones or exactly how they were used. Supposedly, when the high priest wanted to know the will of God, he would go to Him in prayer. If His answer was yes, the Urim and Thummin would begin to shine very brightly. If the answer was no, these two gemstones would become very dull and dim. This wasn't magic or superstition. It was one of the ways God chose to reveal His will in those days. The ephod is no longer used or needed today because people have the Bible and the indwelling Holy Spirit to give them the direction they need. David wants answers and, through the ephod, he once again seeks the Lord. When adversity is on the horizon, go to God and seek His will. David wants to know if Saul will come down to get him and God said, "He will come down" (vs. 11). David then asks if the men of Keilah will deliver him into the hands of Saul. God answers and said, "They will deliver you" (vs. 12).

God knows everything (1 John 3:20). He is omniscient which is "the state of having total knowledge, the quality of knowing everything." He knows reality before it is real, all things and events before they happen, and all people before they exist. Nothing is hidden from the eyes of God and with divine foreknowledge He tells David what Saul and the people of Keilah plan to do. David and his men just rescued these people from the Philistines and now they're going to turn them over to Saul. One is reminded of when the people of Israel praised Jesus on His triumphant entry into Jerusalem only to cry out "Crucify Him!" a short time later. Why would these people betray David? Apparently, they heard what happened at Nob so they were afraid knowing Saul would stop at nothing to kill David. It's one thing to fight an enemy who's standing in front of you, it's another to deal with the treachery of those you've laid down your life for on God's behalf. "So David and his men, about six hundred, arose and departed from Keilah and went wherever they could go" (vs. 13). Once again David is fleeing for his life.

-16-

"BACK TO THE STRONGHOLD"

David flees from Keilah with six hundred men. In the cave of Adullam he had four hundred followers so his small army is rapidly growing. David was a great warrior and he could have stayed and fought with Saul. Instead of letting pride get the best of him, he humbled himself and departed from Keilah. "Then it was told Saul that David has escaped from Keilah; so he halted the expedition" (1 Sam. 23:13). David's humble heart saved the city from Saul's plan to kill them all if he didn't get what he wanted. "And David stayed in strongholds in the wilderness, and remained in the mountains in the Wilderness of Ziph" (vs. 14). Ziph was a town below the southern tip of the Dead Sea. Strongholds are designed to be a safe place, a place that has been fortified so as to protect it against attack. As a believer in Christ, you need to make the Lord your stronghold. No longer do you need to fear people or circumstances that threaten your well-being. Prov. 18:10 says, "The name of the Lord is a strong tower; The righteous run to it and are safe."

Like a roaring lion, Saul is unrelenting in his pursuit of David. Vs. 14 says, "Saul sought him every day." Wherever David went, Saul was close behind. David goes from one place to another trying to hide. He goes to one cave and then another cave. He then goes to a forest and then a desert. He's moving from place to place every single day. He's now in a barren wasteland with six hundred men to feed. He is their captain and this makes him responsible for their needs and welfare. This is a picture of adversity, a picture of how God is training David to be king. It's not hard to imagine David's mental and emotional state of mind at this time in his life. He has done nothing but good to Saul and the nation of Israel but things keep getting worse and worse. Many psalms were written during this period of his life and he speaks of his loneliness, his fear of his enemies, his sense of discouragement, and his desire for God to vindicate him. Thankfully, God is still in charge. Day after day Saul searched for David "but God did not deliver him into his hand" (vs. 14).

Give glory to God for those "but God" moments in your life. Man cannot stop what God has ordained, those things He puts into motion in your life. God will see you through to the end and the devil can't stop you. For this to happen, you must keep going forward no matter how dark the season you may now be in. Make what you're going through a time of worship, a time of preparation for what God is calling you to do. Always remember that God specializes in hopeless and desperate situations. He opened up the Red Sea when the Egyptians were closing in on the children of Israel. He walked with the three Hebrew children who were thrown into the fiery furnace. He even closed the mouths of lions so Daniel could get a good night's sleep. It's true, God always shows up just in time. David is close to the breaking point and God sends to him the one man most able to give him the support and encouragement he needs. "Then Jonathan, Saul's son, arose and went to David in the woods, and strengthened his hand in God" (vs. 16).

It is interesting to note that Saul was always trying to find David and couldn't but yet Jonathan found him anytime he went looking for him. He shows up in the forest where David is hiding and gives him some much needed support and positive encouragement. What a precious gift Jonathan gives David. He couldn't rescue David and he certainly didn't have all the answers to what was going on. What he could do is comfort and support his best friend in time of need. He looks David in the eye and points his thoughts back to God. He said to him, "Do not fear, for the hand of Saul my father shall not find you. You shall be king over Israel, and I shall be next to you. Even my father Saul knows that" (vs. 17). He told David not to fear and then told him why. With words that were uplifting, Jonathan said that God would protect David from his father and that God's promise would come to pass. God always keeps His promises. You defeat fear by hearing and believing the promises of God. Jonathan tells David to remember what God has planned for his life, to believe that the plan and purpose of God will be fulfilled.

Everybody needs a friend like Jonathan in their life, someone who will say, "Do not be afraid. Stand still, and see the salvation of the Lord" (Ex. 14:13). Words like this are always spoken in terrifying circumstances, when fear is the natural and reasonable thing to do. Why shouldn't David fear? Every day he's being hunted like an animal and he knows Saul's intentions are to kill him. Jonathan knows how David feels and tells him to trust God anyway and don't consider the circumstances that surround him. It is the habit of God to encourage His people when they're going through hard times. He comforts those who are downcast and encourages those who are discouraged (2 Cor. 7:6). He is always there when you need Him most. This is why He sent Jonathan to David. Prov. 27:17 says, "As iron sharpens iron, so a man sharpens the countenance of his friend." In your darkest valley, God will send a Jonathan into your life, a person to help you get through the low point you find yourself in, a friend to remind you of God's promises and His provision.

International speaker Stuart Briscoe once wrote, "The secret of lasting friendships isn't simply to find someone like yourself, it's to develop a heart for God and seek others who love Him too." If you're going through a trial, find somebody who loves the Lord and allow them to point your thoughts back to God. A good friend will tell you what you need to hear, not always what you want to hear. They'll speak the truth in love as they point you to the Lord who is able to give you the help you need. Jonathan's words are direct and to the point. He's saying to David, "God is your strength, your stronghold, and His destiny for your life will be fulfilled. Trust Him and be confident. Don't stumble. Don't fall. Don't fail." Jonathan wants to support and serve side by side with David and promises to do so by saying, "You shall be king and I shall be next to you." Sadly, this will never happen and this is the last time these two friends will see each other alive. "So the two of them made a covenant before the Lord. And David stayed in the woods, and Jonathan went to his own house" (vs. 18).

Not long after this, another blow of treachery comes against David. Once again he is betrayed by God's people who are looking for personal gain. The mountain men of Ziph who live on the hills going down to the Dead Sea go to Saul and tell him that David is living among them (Vs. 19,20). The Ziphites were descendants of Caleb, one of only two men who brought back a good report after spying out the Promised Land. The village of Ziph was in the territory of the tribe of Judah, the same tribe David was from. He had every reason to expect his kinsmen to protect him but instead they sold him out to King Saul. They sold their honor in order to gain material rewards and promotions from Saul, much like Doeg did. Saul says to these men, "Blessed are you of the Lord, for you have compassion on me" (vs. 21). He then sends the Ziphites back to pinpoint David's location "for I am told that he is very crafty" (vs. 22). It wasn't David's craftiness that helped him escape from Saul, it was the goodness and faithfulness of the Lord.

The Ziphites didn't care if innocent blood was shed as long as they could gain the graceless favor of the king. David was living quietly in the forest seeking rest from all the fleeing he's been forced to do. He did nothing to hinder the lifestyle of the Ziphites but they betrayed him anyway and reported him to the king. As they tried to pinpoint his exact location, David and his men flee to the Wilderness of Maon which is south and east of Jerusalem and goes to the edge of the Dead Sea. It was at this time that David wrote Psalm 54 as he turns to God in prayer and sings himself into a calm delight. He begins by pleading with God for help after which he lays aside all doubt and sings a song of joyful triumph. "Save me, O God, by Your name, and vindicate me by Your strength. Hear my prayer, O God; Give ear to the words of my mouth" (vs. 1,2). David is asking God to render justice to him for no one else can or will. "For strangers have risen up against me, and oppressors have sought after my life; They have not set God before them" (vs. 3).

These Ziphites were strangers to David and had no reason to have any ill will toward him. The problem is they were also strangers to God and sought only after their own well-being. They have no regard for God and didn't care if what they were doing was right or wrong. So cruel and heartless were these men that they were more than willing to crush the life out of this godly man. David then says "Selah" as if to say, "Enough of this. Let's stop and pause for a moment." Stop being in such a hurry when you pray. Take time for some holy meditation for this will surely improve your times of devotion with the Lord. David then says, "Behold, God is my helper; The Lord is with those who uphold my life" (vs. 4). David had enemies wherever he went but still he gives recognition that God is on his side. He asked for deliverance in the first verse and here he has the confidence God will give it to him. "He will repay my enemies for their evil. Cut them off in Your truth" (vs. 5). The Message Bible says, "Don't let up! Finish them off!" Surely, what a man sows, he will reap (Gal. 6:7).

Charles Spurgeon wrote, "It is appointed, and so it must ever be, that those who shoot upward the arrows of malice shall find them fall upon themselves. The recoil of their own gun has often killed oppressors." So sure is David of his deliverance that he lets go of bitterness and fear and magnifies the name of the Lord in holy praise. "I will freely sacrifice to You; I will praise Your name, O Lord, for it is good" (vs. 6). The more you receive from God, the more you ought to praise Him. God is good and so should your praise be to Him. Your inner man is blessed exceedingly when your love and adoration of God abounds. "For He has delivered me out of all trouble; And my eye has seen its desire upon my enemies" (vs. 7). David was always in danger but still God kept him safe. 2 Chron. 16:9 says God will "show Himself strong on behalf of those whose heart is loyal to Him." David's faith and confidence in God is about to pay off for he is about to have another "but God" moment in his life all to the chagrin of King Saul.

Saul has followed David to the Wilderness of Maon thinking there is no way his rival can escape him now. "Then Saul went on one side of the mountain and David and his men on the other side of the mountain. So David made haste to get away from Saul, for Saul and his men were encircling David and his men to take them" (vs. 26). Saul is doing his best to trap David and it looks like he might succeed. They're on opposite sides of the same mountain and Saul is encircling David, closing him off so there is no way of escape. Many scholars think this mountain is Masada, an ancient fortification situated on top of an isolated rock plateau. Masada in Hebrew means "fortress" and is a massive mountain rising up from the plain of the desert. David and his men are about to be taken captive when suddenly, out of the blue, a messenger comes to Saul with news that the Philistines have invaded the land (vs. 27). Saul is so preoccupied fighting a battle God never told him to fight that he's not doing the job he's supposed to do.

This news couldn't have come at a worse time for King Saul. Just a little bit more time and surely David would be in his grasp. Still, this news couldn't be ignored. Being who he was, one is made to wonder why Saul was even bothered by what the Philistines were doing. After all, he didn't care enough to rescue Keilah. This time, however, the situation is different for the invaders have come deeper into Israelite territory. The situation is so critical that he has to stop chasing David and go off in pursuit of the Philistines (vs. 28). It is interesting to note how God used His enemies, the Philistines, to save David. He is the Good Shepherd and He always watches over His sheep. David wrote in Ps. 23:4, "Yea, though I walk through the valley of the shadow of death, I will fear no evil; For You are with me." David was almost taken out by Saul's army but God intervened. They then called that place "The Rock of Escape" (vs. 28). Today, Jesus is your Rock of Escape. "Then David went up from there and dwelt in the strongholds at En Gedi" (vs. 29).

In the barren territory surrounding the Dead Sea there is a canyon that runs westward called En Gedi. It's about two hundred yards from the Dead Sea and its fresh water springs and waterfalls produce fragrant orchards and spicy gardens. It's a tropical paradise in the middle of the desert. It's a place of refreshing where one can find cool water on a hot day. There are only two places on the western shore where fresh water runs into the Dead Sea and En Gedi is one of them. At En Gedi the large mountains rise straight up from the shore and their steep, limestone cliffs are filled with honeycomb shaped caverns and caves. It was in twelve of these caves that the Dead Sea scrolls were found between 1946 and 1956. The name "En Gedi" means 'spring of the goats' because of all the wild goats that roam through the limestone caves in that area. There was plenty of water and wildlife at En Gedi making it a natural hideout for outlaws and inside the caves you could see anyone coming for miles around. Instead of reigning royally from a throne room in Jerusalem, David instead finds himself in one of the many caves at En Gedi.

David has found himself in a season of life where he didn't expect to be. Perhaps he thought he'd be on a smooth path to the throne but that is not how life is. On the way to the fulfillment of your destiny will be adversity, pitfalls, and dark cave experiences. What do you do when the path you're on takes you in a direction you didn't think it would go? What do you do when you're traveling north and life suddenly turns south? David is anointed to be king and he's destined to sit on the throne but here he is hiding with his men in the back of a cave. He's not living the life of the hero he is, but rather the life of an outlaw. He may have wondered how in the world he got to this place. Nothing makes sense anymore. God's ultimate plan for your life is love, joy, and peace, but why are so many tears shed along the way? Why can't life be easy? Why can't the pain just go away? Did David miss the mark somewhere or did he take a wrong turn in life? Or, perhaps, is he right where God wants him to be at this precise moment in his life?

The answer to all these questions is that it's in the dark caves of life where transformation takes place. It's where you develop the character it takes to reign on the throne and to fulfill your destiny. It's in the caves of life where you become the person God predestined you to become. It's where God prepares you for what He has prepared for you. There is a work in this life that God wants you to do. Eph. 2:19 (NIV) says, "For we are God's handiwork, created in Christ Jesus to do good works, which God prepared in advance for us to do." David was surrounded by his enemies and hunted down by those who hated him. He was betrayed by the very people he had saved and delivered. In spite of all that, David chose to trust in God's justice, in His timing, in His mercy, and in His divine protection. It is while David is in the back end of one of these caves that he'll be given an opportunity to take matters into his own hands. He'll be given a chance to take a shortcut to the throne, but deep in his heart he knows there are no shortcuts to character. Helen Keller once said, "There are no shortcuts to any place worth going."

In the wilderness, Satan gave Jesus an opportunity to take a shortcut to the throne. He showed Jesus all the kingdoms of the world and said, "All these things I will give You if You will fall down and worship me" (Matt. 4:9). Jesus didn't do it because He knew that reaching the throne of the universe would come by way of the cross. He knew that the Father had a plan and a time for Him to take the throne, the same plan He also had for David. A major detour has taken place in David's life until one day good fortune seems to be on his side. Or is it? When Saul was finished with the Philistine invasion he was told that David was at En Gedi. He then took three thousand warriors who were the best of the best "and went to seek David and his men on the Rocks of the Wild Goats" (1 Sam. 24:2). In his search for David, Saul came to a sheepfold by the road, a cave large enough to shelter a flock of sheep. A sheepfold was a large enclosure with a wall of shrubbery and thorn bushes around it to protect the sheep from wild animals and thieves. At a sheepfold there was only one entrance.

Of all the caves at En Gedi, Saul ends up at the one cave where David and his men were hiding. This was no coincidence but arranged by God to test David, to train him, and to display the godly heart inside of him. God is working in the lives of both David and Saul and great lessons will be learned in this cave. Saul is looking for David to kill him when all of a sudden nature calls and he has to relieve himself. He goes into the cave "to attend to his needs" (vs. 3) and soon finds himself in an undignified posture. It's dark in this cave and Saul is in a very vulnerable place. He went into this cave alone and he has no soldiers by his side to protect him. Unknown to him, David and his men are in the back recesses of this cave watching everything that is happening. This gives David a golden opportunity to get revenge on King Saul and become the king he is anointed to be. David's men tell him this opportunity is from the Lord and he should take advantage of it. Eye for an eye, tooth for a tooth. In their eyes, good fortune is smiling at them and they shouldn't let this opportunity pass.

David's men think today is the day everything changes. Today they will be free from persecution, suffering, and living life as a fugitive. They tell David that God is giving him the opportunity to take a shortcut to the throne (vs. 4). The problem is God did not say that. Revenge is forbidden in the Bible (Rom. 12:17-21) and even Jesus said in Matt. 5:44, "Pray for those who spitefully use you and persecute you." Yes, human nature is not inclined to do this but this is what makes Christianity different from all other religions in the world. It takes a changed heart and a renewed mind to pray for and genuinely love those who wish you harm. It can sometimes be confusing to distinguish between your own desires and the will of God, especially when you're in difficult times. Desires and circumstances are not good guides to determine which direction your life should take. You need to use the Word of God and the Holy Spirit to interpret your circumstances and to rule your passions. For sure, the worse thing David can do this day is take matters into his own hand.

How do you respond when you're mistreated? If you respond the right way, you will grow deep in God and the activity of the Holy Spirit will be released in your life. If you respond wrongly, a residue of bitterness will grow inside of you without you even knowing it. Having a godly love for others is the highest command there is. It looks good on paper and sounds good when your pastor preaches about it. But what about that mean neighbor who lives next to you? Or that coworker who gossips about you behind your back and spreads false rumors about you? It's easy to hear about loving these people but it's much more difficult to put it into practice. It's more fun to get revenge on the person who did you wrong. The problem with revenge is that it poisons the soul and lowers you to the level of the person who hurt you. Someone once said, "I love mankind, it's people I can't stand." It's easy to love humanity but what about your enemies? What is David going to do? With him are six hundred men who are tired of running, men who desperately want David to put an end to their plight by taking the life of King Saul.

With knife in hand, David quietly makes his way up to the front of the cave. What is going to determine the action he will take, his conscience or the voice of reason? Pontius Pilate didn't want to have Jesus killed for He had done nothing wrong. Still, the people cried out "Crucify Him! Crucify Him!" and Pilate eventually gave in to their demands. The voices of the people prevailed even though Pilate new what he was doing is wrong. The point is, don't give in to peer pressure. Don't do something wrong just because others want you to. When a person receives a promise from God, they must always let Him fulfill it His way. Don't take what God wants to give. The person who can wait on God is a person of power. This is why you need to be like Jesus who didn't take Satan's offer to win back the world at the expense of disobedience (Luke 4:5-8). Rom. 12:21 says, "Don't be overcome by evil, but overcome evil with good." What does David do? "And David arose and secretly cut off a corner of Saul's robe. Now it happened afterward that David's heart troubled him because he had cut Saul's robe" (vs. 4,5).

The conscience of David is tender. He is overcome with guilt and shame for cutting off a corner of Saul's robe. He is living in the fear of the Lord to the point that every little detail of integrity matters to him. Saul's robe was a symbol of his position as king. Cutting this robe showed a lack of respect and it made Saul look bad. David was wrong and he knew it. He makes his way back to his men and in whispered tones repents in front of them. "So David restrained his servants with these words, and did not allow them to rise against Saul" (vs. 7). David knew Saul was an evil man but that doesn't change the fact that he was anointed to be king. If a person in authority hasn't earned your respect as a person, respect them anyway because of the position they hold. Wives, respect your husband even if he's not the man you thought he would be. Children, respect your parents even if you have friends whose parents treat them better than yours do you. Give respect to government leaders, your boss at work, and your teachers at school. They've all earned your respect because of the position they hold.

Saul finished his business and left the cave with David following close behind. David could have remained in the cave but he didn't do that. He went out and surrendered himself to Saul to show him that he meant no harm. He showed great submission to Saul by bowing down before him and calling him "my lord the king!" (vs. 8). This made him vulnerable to Saul but David trusted that God would protect him and fulfill the promise. He shows Saul the corner of the robe that was cut away giving proof that he had the opportunity to kill him but didn't take it (vs. 11). Saul must have been reminded of when he grabbed Samuel's robe and tore off a piece of it. Samuel said to him, "The Lord has torn the kingdom of Israel from you today, and has given it to a neighbor of yours, who is better than you." As Saul looks at the corner of his robe in David's hand, he surely was reminded of what Samuel said to him. God's message was coming through loud and clear. David said, "Perhaps the Lord will kill you for what you are trying to do to me, but I will never harm you" (vs. 12 NIV).

Saul gets all choked up as he "lifted up his voice and wept" (vs. 16). He acknowledges that David is a righteous man and said in vs. 20, "And now I know indeed that you shall surely be king, and that the kingdom of Israel shall be established in your hand." Saul then asked for the same pledge Jonathan asked for, that David would show mercy to his descendants. "So David swore to Saul. And Saul went home, but David and his men went up to the stronghold" (vs. 22). Why didn't David go home also? Because he knew what the heart of Saul was like. Behind Saul was a trail of blood a mile long and David knew he couldn't be trusted. Forgiving someone doesn't mean you have to trust them or let them back into your life. You don't have to open yourself up to the same abuse you previously suffered. Be wise knowing it takes people a long time to change their behavior. If someone has hurt you repeatedly, forgive them but be careful not to run back to the same situation you were once in. David did not see this change in Saul's life so he went back to the stronghold.

-17-

"THE WAY OF ESCAPE"

Samuel was God's most influential man at this particular time in history. He was the last of the judges and was Israel's prophet and priest. He also served in the role of pastor to David. He had been David's counselor and was the one person to whom David could go in times of need and desperation. There was a time when Samuel was the only man holding Saul in check for he was the only person bold enough to stand up against him. Samuel had tremendous power in the land as he served as the mouthpiece of God. Suddenly, from out of nowhere, this great man of God who served the Lord from his youngest days, dies (1 Sam. 25:1). In recent times the people of Israel didn't appreciate him because they thought he was too old (1 Sam. 8:5) but now they honor him at his death. The whole nation gathered together and lamented for him. They then buried him at his home in Ramah. Samuel would later be listed in God's "Hall of Fame" of faith in Heb. 11:32. Scripture doesn't say that Saul or David attended his funeral. It does say that David arose and went to the Wilderness of Paran (vs. 1).

The wilderness of Paran stretched from Sinai to the border of Palistine in the southern territories of Judea. Hagar and Ishmael came to this region after leaving Abraham and Sarah (Gen. 21:21). It is also one of the places where the Israelites spent part of their forty years wandering after the exodus from Egypt. There is little or no soil formation in Paran because of the lack of rain and the ground is covered with much stones and gravel. The Bible doesn't say how long David stayed in this barren desert but eventually he and his men traveled north to the greener pastures of the wilderness of Judah. There were lush meadows there to which herdsmen brought their livestock during the grazing season. Wild animals and thieves were also in the area and protection was needed at all times. Those who provided this protection were given food and provisions for the service they rendered. Because David and his men were fugitives, they could not stay in one place long enough to plant and raise crops. Instead, they would provide the protection needed by these herdsmen and their flocks.

"Now there was a man in Maon whose business was in Carmel, and the man was very rich. He had three thousand sheep and a thousand goats. And he was shearing his sheep in Carmel" (1 Sam. 25:2). Carmel was a town on the edge of the hill country of Judah and was just up the road from Maon. The word "Carmel" means 'the vineyards of God' and was a lavish place to grow things like grapes. When Moses sent twelve spies into the Promised Land they brought back huge clusters of grapes from this area to show the people how prosperous the land was. Back then, wealth was measured by how much livestock you had which means this man was very rich for those days. This man was shearing his sheep and this was a cause of celebration. It was a time to work but it was also a time to eat, drink, and be merry. There was singing and dancing and the giving of gifts. It was a time of feasting with enough food to share with everybody. It was also the time when gifts of appreciation were given to those who helped protect the sheep and the shepherds watching over them.

1 Sam. 25:3 says, "The name of the man was Nabal, and the name of his wife Abigail. And she was a woman of good understanding and beautiful appearance; but the man was harsh and evil in his doings. And he was of the house of Caleb." Here's an evil man with money married to a beautiful woman with brains. All marriages are supposed to be made in heaven but so is thunder and lightning. In Biblical times,

women had little or no choice in who they married. Most marriages were arranged by the parents of the bride and groom, oftentimes when they're still children. Nabal was a rich man but wealth, power, and social position does not guarantee a happy marriage, especially with an evil man like he was. Nabal was a stubborn man, arrogant and evil in all his ways. He was a harsh man who was dishonest and deceptive. He was foul-mouthed, selfish, and greedy. He was also a drunkard and very, very rich. His name literally means "fool" which refers to somebody who is not morally sound. It was a name he lived up to.

In ancient times, a person's name was often connected to their character. Nabal was indeed a fool and Ps. 14:1 says, "The fool has said in his heart, 'There is no God.' They are corrupt, they have done abominable works, there is none who does good." The Message Bible says, "Their words are poison gas, fouling the air; they poison rivers and skies; thistles are their cash crop." The Hebrew word for "rich" means 'fail; heavy.' A fool with great wealth is capable of doing harsh and evil things. This was Nabal, a moral fool who over and over again didn't do what was right. He was unapproachable, unteachable, and hard-hearted. No one could talk or reason with this man and he was very foolish just like his name indicated. Abigail, on the other hand, was the direct opposite of her husband. She was a woman of good understanding and beautiful appearance. The only other women in the Bible who were given this Hebrew description of how they looked was Rachel (Gen. 29:17) and Esther (Esther 2:7).

Abigail, whose name means "praise of the father," personifies what strong character looks like. Notice that her wisdom and character are listed before her beauty. Always be more concerned with how you look on the inside than you do on the outside. Prov. 31:30 says, "Charm is deceitful and beauty is vain, but a woman who fears the Lord, she shall be praised." God cares more about your character than he does about how you look and the things you accomplish on the outside. There is a problem if you do many great and mighty things when your heart is not right with the Lord. As the story of Abigail unfolds it will be seen that, more times than not, character is revealed when things in life don't go the way you'd like. She is married to a foolish man, a man who is hostile, antagonistic, and very confrontational. This is the original beauty and the beast. Abigail is stuck in a dead-end marriage but still she stays loyal to her husband. Her life demonstrates what is pleasing to God in any person who claims to be a believer. Through her, a woman with a bright light of character, David will receive a taste of redemption.

David and his men were in the wilderness hiding from Saul when they encountered the shepherds of Nabal. They could have eaten these sheep then and there but they didn't. David was a godly man and it wasn't his nature to do such a thing. As time would soon tell, that nature would drastically change. Instead of eating the sheep, David and his men chose instead to protect these shepherds from thieves who would come in to steal the sheep and from all the wild animals that prowled in the area. It's shearing time and typically the owner of the sheep would have a big feast giving those invited wool and food. They would also compensate those who protected the sheep throughout the year. David heard that Nabal was shearing his sheep (vs. 4) and he knew it was time for he and his men to receive what was coming to them. Expecting a lot of food, David sent ten young men to Nabal and told them to "greet him in my name" (vs. 5). These men would be speaking on David's behalf and they were told to say to him who lives in prosperity, "Peace be to you, peace to your house, and peace to all that you have!" (vs. 6).

David sent messengers with a greeting full of warmth and kindness. Shalom! Shalom! Shalom! The threefold blessing of peace was wishing upon Nabal completeness and wholeness with nothing broken and nothing missing in every area of his life. This was a great and gracious blessing from David to Nabal and his household. He then gives Nabal an itemized list of services rendered, "Your shepherds were with us, and we did not hurt them, nor was there anything missing from them all the while they were in Carmel. Ask your young men, and they will tell you" (vs. 7,8). David and his men could have taken anything they wanted by force but they didn't. For this reason they ask Nabal to feed them willingly without thoughts of fear or intimidation. "Therefore let my young men find favor in your eyes, for we have come on a feast day. Please give whatever comes to your hand to your servants and to your son David" (vs. 8). David left the selection and size of the gift up to Nabal. It was a freewill offering so there was no threat or pressure of any kind. David made it as easy as possible for Nabal to give.

The truth be told, Nabal should have given food to David without him asking for it. He owed it to them for the work they had done. Notice also how David calls himself Nabal's son and his men Nabal's servants. He's being as friendly as possible. There is no extortion here and no threats are made. Without David's protection, Nabal would have lost men and livestock to thieves and raiding parties. David was providing a valuable service for Nabal and he simply comes to claim a share of the profits that are rightfully his and to celebrate with the others on this joyous occasion. David did not demand a specific amount from Nabal nor did he set a price for his services. He left that up to Nabal's generosity. The ten young men made this request on David's behalf and then waited for Nabal's reply. How shocked they must have been when Nabal responded, "Who is David, and who is the son of Jesse? There are many servants nowadays who break away each one from his master" (vs. 10). Nabal knew who David was. How else did he know that David was the son of Jesse? He's being very sarcastic.

Instead of responding graciously, Nabal the fool in essence asked, "Who does David think he is to come and ask provision from me?" One is reminded of what Pharaoh said to Moses in Ex. 5:2, "Who is the Lord, that I should obey His voice to let Israel go? I do not know the Lord, nor will I let Israel go." He then spitefully accuses David of being a rebellious servant who ran away from his master. To say this is very degrading, especially to the future king of Israel. Nabal then asks, "Shall I then take my bread and my water and my meat that I have killed for my shearers, and give it to men when I do not know where they are from?" (vs. 11). Nabal has a bad case of "Me, myself, and I." One can almost hear what Satan said in Is. 14:13,14, "I will ascend into heaven, I will exact my throne above the stars of God; I will also sit on the mount of the congregation on the farthest sides of the north; I will ascend above the heights of the clouds, I will be like the Most High." Like the devil, Nabal is a self-centered beast.

Benjamin Franklin once said, "He that falls in love with himself will have no rivals." People who are self-centered don't have a lot of friends because they're too focused on themselves. Nabal is an unapproachable egomaniac and he shouldn't have responded the way he did. David and his men had protected the sheep of Nabal and in return they received back harsh and evil mockery. They are insulted and smeared for a work well done. David's service has gone unrecognized and his motives and character has been slandered. The ten young men are very insulted by what was said but they don't try to reason with the man. Instead, they turned on their heels and went back to camp to tell David everything Nabal had said (vs. 12). The look on their faces was one of indignation and outrage. They weren't happy, but for sure they were hungry. Upon hearing the news David goes ballistic. He overreacts and in a deep rage says, "Every man gird on his sword" (vs. 13). David also girded on his sword and along with four hundred men he headed for the house of Nabal while two hundred men stayed with the supplies.

The Golden Rule of life is, "Do unto others as you would have others do unto you" (Matt. 7:12). Most people think this is a great rule until they're mistreated by others. They then ignore the Golden Rule and make one up of their own, a rule that says, "Do unto others as they have done unto you." They reason in their minds that this is the just and right thing to do. They even take this a step further. If they're not able to mistreat the person who did them wrong, they'll go off and mistreat someone else, someone who has nothing to do with the situation at hand. When this happens, the rule becomes, "Do unto others as someone else has done unto you." The problem with revenge and getting even with people who did you wrong is that it puts you on the same level they are. At the moment, David doesn't care about any of that. He is very angry and vows to wipe the name of Nabal and all his male servants off the face of the earth. David was no wimp. He was a warrior, a giant killer, and he wasn't going to take this fool-hearted response from an empty-headed, loud-mouthed rancher.

James 1:19,20 says, "Therefore, my beloved brethren, let every man be swift to hear, slow to speak, slow to wrath; for the wrath of man does not produce the righteousness of God." This is the first time in scripture that David ever lost his temper. He is very angry and he is out of control. He is about to commit mass murder; the same thing Saul did to the city of Nob. Prov. 29:11(NIV) says, "Fools give full vent to their rage, but the wise bring calm in the end." It's amazing what people will do when their anger is out of control. Because of uncontrolled rage, David is about to kill many innocent people. He's not showing Nabal the same longsuffering he showed to Saul who is the king. It seems to have been harder to do this with Nabal who is perceived to be equal to or lower than David. People usually treat superiors in a better way than those who are beneath them in one way or another. David had shown restraint with Saul but here he is about to do a deplorable act. He's set on revenge and his anger is about to turn him into a cold-blooded killer.

Matt. 26:14 says, "Watch and pray, lest you enter into temptation. The spirit is willing, but the flesh is weak." It doesn't take long for a person to ruin their life. One moment of uncontrolled anger can cause you to do something you'll regret for the rest of your life. Road rage has sent many people to prison for a long, long time. David just had a great victory in the cave at En Gedi but here he is consumed by fleshly feelings of rage and retribution. He didn't pray about it and he didn't hesitate to consider if what he's doing is right or wrong. He acted instinctively without conscious thought of what he was doing. Bringing four hundred men with him is overkill, it's like using a tank to kill a little bug. He was patient with Saul but has no tolerance with Nabal. Yesterday's victories don't carry you through today's testings. This is why Jesus said to pray, "Give us this day our daily bread" (Matt. 6:11). Daily battles require a daily filling of the Holy Spirit. God delivered David from Saul many times. Now He's about to deliver David from himself. Enter Abigail.

Nabal's servants heard what was said to these ten young men and they knew David wouldn't take this insult lying down. One of these servants go to Abigail and tell her how Nabal spoke to David's men with arrogant and scornful language. This servant tells how David's men were good to them, how they protected the shepherds and their sheep, and how not a single animal went missing while under their care. "They were a wall to us both by night and day, all the time we were with them keeping the sheep" (vs. 16). What this servant was saying is that Nabal wouldn't have had all this wealth had David not kept his sheep from being stolen or killed. The problem is Nabal didn't appreciate this blessing that was bestowed upon him. This servant knows Abigail is a woman of good understanding and he pleads with her to do something. "Now therefore, know and consider what you will do, for harm is determined against our master and against all his household. For he is such a scoundrel that one cannot speak to him" (vs. 17).

The word "scoundrel" means that Nabal was a worthless man, a man who was violent, harsh, and beastly. He is a man who can't be reasoned with, he can't be corrected, and he'll never apologize for anything. The Hebrew language calls him a "son of Belial," a description of a person characterized by worthlessness and corruption. The word "Belial" means 'without yoke' and a "son of Belial" would be someone who is lawless and rebellious. In 2 Cor. 6:15 the word "Belial" is used as a name for Satan but there is no indication in scripture that Belial is the proper name of a specific demon. Abigail heard what was happening and immediately takes action. She knows time is of the essence for she senses the roar of the hoofs beating a path directly to the front door of her home. Sometimes there is no time to think things through, to take a few days to meditate on the situation at hand. There are times when action must be taken right away. This is why you need godly character so you'll make the right decisions when these incidents occur. Abigail has such character and she went into action immediately.

Abigail was a woman stuck in an unhappy marriage and she could have done nothing and let her husband be killed. She has a chance to be vindicated and set free from the emotional prison she finds herself in. But she doesn't do that. Instead, she shows character and quickly gathers enough food to feed a small army. She's in panic mode as she takes upon herself the responsibility of protecting her household. She has all this food put on several donkeys and she sends her servants ahead of her with a promise that she will soon follow. It's not unusual in the Bible to send servants bearing gifts before one's arrival. Jacob sent gifts ahead before meeting Esau (Gen. 32) and the Queen of Sheba did the same thing before meeting Solomon (1 Kings 10). Prov. 18:16 says, "A man's gift makes room for him, and brings him before great men." Abigail is hoping all this food will cause David's wrath to subside before she gets there. This is a life and death situation and she wisely chose not to tell her husband. He was the one who just insulted the man who would one day be king. He doesn't realize that his household is doomed, that judgment is on its way.

Abigail gets on a donkey and sets off to meet David and four hundred hungry and angry men. David is still very angry and he vows that on this day heads are going to roll. "May God do so, and more also, to the enemies of David, if I leave one male of all who belong to him by morning light" (vs. 22). This shows how full of rage David is. This is a very serious sin he is about to commit. He's riding headlong into a situation that could affect him and his reign as king for the rest of his life. He is racing to slaughter fellow Jews because he was insulted by a fool. Thankfully, God sends to David a way to get out of the trap he's about to fall into. He sends Abigail. 1 Cor. 10:13 says, "God is faithful, who will not allow you to be tempted beyond what you are able, but with the temptation will also make the way of escape, that you may be able to bear it." The Message Bible says, "God will never let you down; He'll never let you be pushed past your limit; He'll always be there to help you come through it." There's a way out for every temptation you'll ever face. That is good news, especially for David.

David is on the warpath as these two caravans approach each other. One is a caravan of retaliation, the other a caravan of reconciliation. Suddenly, David and his men are confronted by an unarmed woman and several donkeys loaded down with food. "Now when Abigail saw David, she hastened to dismount from the donkey, fell on her face before David, and bowed down to the ground" (vs. 23). What a picture of reverence and humility this is. She didn't act like she was better than David like the rich and beautiful often do. No, she came to David as his humble servant. She's about to call David "my lord" thirteen times and herself "your maidservant" six times. Surely this made a startling impression on David. Here she is confronting an army of angry men all by herself. Indeed, she is an inspiring woman, a person of deep character. Immediately she takes the blame for her husband's actions. "On me, my lord, on me let this iniquity be" (vs. 24). She then asks for permission to speak and begins to speak words of wisdom to David and all his men. Here is David's way of escape.

Abigail quickly asks David to disregard the actions of her scoundrel husband. "For as his name is, so is he: Nabal is his name, and folly is with him" (vs. 25). She's saying that her husband is so worthless that he's not worth sinning over. He's not worth the time it would take to kill him. What Nabal did was wrong and what David is about to do is also wrong. She's saying that two wrongs don't make a right. Abigail is a smart woman as she then says, "Since the Lord has held you back from coming to bloodshed and from avenging yourself with your own hand" (vs. 26). David never said he wasn't going through with his plans. She's speaking to him as if he has already made a determination in his heart to change course. To say this is masterful. She then offers all this food to his men as she tries to correct a wrong that has taken place. She asks for forgiveness in a straightforward manner and then speaks of David's character in high terms. She gives recognition that David is to be king and she praises his future role as God's leader over Israel.

Abigail wisely reminds David of God's promises for his life. "For the Lord will certainly make for my lord an enduring house, because my lord fights the battles of the Lord, and evil is not found in you throughout your days" (vs. 28). She has him look beyond the circumstances at hand to the bigger promise of God. She's asking him not to do something he'll later regret. She asks him to let the Lord settle this matter instead of taking vengeance upon those who are innocent. "David, you are like a bundle that the Lord holds closely and securely to Himself. Your enemies are like rocks in a sling that the Lord will hurl away" (vs. 29). In her wisdom, Abigail turns David's attention from Nabal back onto the Lord. He is clearly in the wrong and God is using Abigail to be the way of escape from what he is about to do. God is using her to steer David back onto the right path. She didn't do this by tearing him down for how wrong he was. No, she emphasized the glorious calling on his life and the integrity he walked in. She gets him to consider if what he planned to do was consistent with that destiny and his integrity.

Abigail has become a brilliant light between two very angry men. Her intervention shows that you can't be an innocent bystander during the horrible disasters in other people's lives. You can't just stand there and do nothing. Roll up your sleeves and do something! Get involved! Share some wisdom, offer a helping hand, put your faith to work on someone else's behalf. Take a risk believing God will watch over you and give you the protection you need. Abigail's final words to David are found in 1 Sam. 25:31 (NLT), "Don't let this be a blemish on your record. Then your conscience won't have to bear the staggering burden of needless bloodshed and vengeance. And when the Lord has done these great things for you, please remember me, your servant!" Remember Abigail? How could he ever forget her? She had just said to him, "Think twice before you act. Don't do something you'll later regret. Always consider what the consequences will be for regret is one of the worst punishments there is. Don't do something that is beneath you. You're a bigger man than that."

Thankfully, David saw the light. He dodged a bullet here and he knows it. He knows he could have wrecked his entire future with this one rash act provoked by a fool. David acknowledges that Abigail is sent by God (vs. 32). He is amazed, delighted, and relieved all at the same time. He receives the food she brought him and says, "Go up in peace to your house. See, I have heeded your voice and respected your person" (vs. 35). Thank God for Abigail. David listened to her in his state of emotional turmoil and unrest, in his anger and resentfulness. He heeded the words of this saintly woman and pulled back from paying evil for evil. Abigail goes home and finds her husband drunk so she waits until the next morning to tell him what happened. When she does, he suddenly gets paralyzed by a stroke and dies ten days later (vs. 38). David hears about this, rejoices, and then takes Abigail to be his wife. David isn't finished though. Vs. 43,44 says, "David also took Ahinoam of Jezreel, and so both of them were his wives. But Saul had given Michal his daughter, David's wife, to Palti, the son of Laish, who was from Gallim."

The Shepherd King

-18-

"LAND OF THE ENEMY"

If not dealt with, old enemies have a way of coming back. David did nothing wrong and still Saul wants to kill him. He just won't let it go as he refuses to submit to the will of God. Saul was a man who sucked the life out of everything he was around. He drifted from one bad emotion to another and became a dark stain on the nation he ruled over. He continues to brood and dwell on David's popularity and how much the people love him. He appeared to have repented at En Gedi with a repentance that was sincere and emotional. Real repentance, however, doesn't linger or dwell on those things that can pull you down, things that can cause you to once again commit the same sin you repented of. In his evil mind, David must die and whoever finds him will be richly rewarded by the king. As fate would have it, the Ziphites came to Saul for the second time and told him that David is hiding in the hill of Hachilah (1 Sam. 26:1), the same place he was hiding in 1 Sam. 23:19. This hill was northwest of Carmel in the southern part of the desert, in the sun-drenched region between Ziph and En Gedi.

Upon hearing this news, Saul treacherously renews his pursuit of David. His cruelty knows no bounds. He's a beast of a man and there is no anchor of morality in his life. He gathers three thousand of his best warriors and heads out to seek for David in the wilderness of Ziph (vs. 2). As all this is happening, God continues to work on the heart of David, especially after what he almost did to Nabal and his household. David is still in training to be king and the strong heart of revenge must be purged out of him. Sometimes it takes a King Saul in your life to bring about godly change so that you might be purified, that the rough edges in your life might be knocked off, that you'll be transformed more and more into the image of Christ, that you'll be more patient and loving and kind and forgiving and tender-hearted. God works in your life through the people who cross your path. It may be your spouse with whom you have nothing in common or your boss at work who makes your life miserable. Believe it or not, God uses these people to mold and shape you into the person He wants you to be.

Saul was a weak man and knew what he was doing was wrong. He knew he was indulging in sin but he wouldn't stop himself thinking he can get away with it. He and his chosen men reach the hill of Hachilah and immediately set up camp. They are weary from the journey and rest and sleep are needed. Unknown to them, spies sent by David are watching their every move. They return to David and tell him what they've seen. David then rises up and goes to the camp where he sees everybody sleeping. No one is concerned about a big battle as they expect no resistance from David and his band of misfits. "Now Saul lay within the camp, with the people encamped all around him" (vs. 5). David is brave and very bold. He says he wants to go to Saul in the camp. At En Gedi he was hiding from Saul but here he actively seeks him out. This time he wants a confrontation with the king. He's going on what appears to be a suicide mission and he asks who wants to go with him. His nephew Abishai, the eldest son of his sister Zeruiah, steps forward and says, "I will go down with you" (vs. 6).

David couldn't have found a better warrior to go with him. Abishai was a fierce soldier, a combatant with an impulsive, bloodthirsty spirit. He was fearless in battle and bold as a lion. As the entire army sleeps, the two of them silently make their way to the center of the camp where they find Saul also asleep with his spear stuck in the ground by his head (vs. 7).

Once again Saul is in a vulnerable position. Just like at En Gedi, David is told by Abishai that this is no accident. Surely God is once again giving David an opportunity to take righteous vengeance upon Saul. Abishai makes it easier on David as he offers to kill Saul himself. That way David could say he never raised his hand against the king. Poetic justice would be served by killing Saul with the same spear he hurled at David multiple tomes in an attempt to kill him. David has a second chance to take matters into his own hand but he doesn't do it. Perhaps the sound words of Abigail are still ringing in his ears. He says to Abishai, "Do not destroy him; for who can stretch out his hand against the Lord's anointed, and be guiltless?" (vs. 9).

David again calls Saul "the Lord's anointed" even though he's disobedient and very wicked. Be very careful not to talk negatively about those who are called by God to do His work on the earth. In Acts 23:1-5 Paul was struck on the mouth and reprimanded for unknowingly reviling the high priest. David then assures Abishai that God will take care of Saul. "As the Lord lives, the Lord will strike him, or his day shall come to die, or he shall go out to battle and perish" (vs. 10). God forbid if David were to kill Saul himself. David tells Abishai to take the spear and jug of water that is by Saul's head, the two things he depends on most. Abishai is disgruntled with David and doesn't do what he is asked to do. David then takes the spear and water himself. All this is taking place in the midst of three thousand snoring soldiers. They weren't heard because "a deep sleep from the Lord had fallen on them" (vs. 12). This is the same Hebrew word that tells of God causing a deep sleep to fall upon Adam when He took one of his ribs and formed Eve (Gen. 2:21). God was protecting David all along.

The hill of Hachilah has deep valleys on its north and south borders. David and Abishai cross over one of these valleys "and stood on the top of a hill afar off, a great distance being between them" (vs. 13). David calls out loudly and reprimands Abner, the commander of the army, for not properly guarding Saul. The king could have been killed had David chosen to do so. Saul was a moral degenerate but still David knew it wasn't his place to seek personal vengeance against him. David's voice echoes off the hillside and down into the camp as he tells Abner he cares more for Saul then he does. "Are you not a man? And who is like you in Israel? Why then have you not guarded your lord the king? For one of the people came in to destroy your lord the king. This thing you have done is not good. As the Lord lives, you are worthy to die, because you have not guarded your master, the Lord's anointed. And now see where the king's spear is and the jug of water that was by his head" (vs. 15,16). All this commotion suddenly rouses Saul from his sleep.

Saul wakes up and right away recognizes the voice of David. He asks, "Is that your voice, my son David?" David answers, "It is my voice, my lord, O king" (vs. 17). David speaks with genuine humility as he asks Saul to think clearly about what he's doing. "Why does my lord thus pursue his servant? For what have I done, or what evil is in my hand?' (vs. 18). He makes it easier for Saul to repent. He says, "If the Lord has stirred you up against me, let Him accept an offering" (vs. 19). Saul is now able to admit he was wrong without admitting his plot originated with himself. David continues, "But if it be the children of men, may they be cursed before the Lord." David shares from his heart his own struggles, the pain he feels for not being able to go to the house of God and to live his life as God intended. David asks a request from deep inside his heart, "Now therefore, do not let my blood fall to the earth before the face of the Lord. For the king of Israel has come out to seek a flea, as when one hunts a partridge in the mountains" (vs. 20).

Saul immediately apologizes to David. He says, "I have sinned. Return, my son David. For I will harm you no more, because my life was precious in your eyes this day. Indeed I have played the fool and erred exceedingly" (vs. 21). This is the autobiography of Saul, spoken by the king himself. The Message Bible says, "And I've acted the fool - a moral dunce, a real clown." Saul repents but it's not from the heart. He says the right words but he's not overcome with emotion like he was at En Gedi. This time the feelings are not there as he bitterly realizes that David once again got the better of him. There is a difference between worldly sorrow and a heart that is truly repentant. Just because somebody acts sorrowful doesn't mean true repentance has taken place. People cry because they've been caught but tears are not proof that genuine sorrow has come. Godly sorrow always brings repentance that leads to salvation. 2 Cor. 7:10 (NLT) says, "For the kind of sorrow God wants us to experience leads us away from sin and results in salvation. There's no regret for that kind of sorrow."

There needs to be more preaching about repentance in the world today because you can't go to heaven without it. The Greek word "metanoia" means 'a change of mind, a change of heart, a change of your way of life.' Godly sorrow, true genuine repentance, is only real when it brings about change in your life. Emotional grief without godly conviction does not produce lasting change. Judas Iscariot wept bitterly for having betrayed Jesus and then went and hung himself. Peter, on the other hand, wept because he denied Jesus three times but he came back and served the Lord for the rest of his life. That was true repentance. Jesus said in Matt. 5:3,4, "Blessed are the poor in spirit, for theirs is the kingdom of heaven. Blessed are those who mourn, for they shall be comforted." He did not say, "Blessed are those who moan and shed many tears." Saul cried out, "I'm a fool!" What could have been in Saul's life never came to pass. He could have been a great king but it didn't happen. One day soon his potential will be buried with him. Saul is a prime example of a wasted life.

What happens next goes beyond the realm of human logic and spiritual comprehension. David has been having one highly charged emotional moment after another. He spared the life of Saul at En Gedi, he almost killed Nabal and his household, and he just spared Saul's life once again. In his life there is crisis after crisis after crisis. He then wakes up one morning weary and depressed. He asks himself, "When is this all going to end?" Every day he's running from Saul and he's weary from hiding in caves and being betrayed. On top of all that, he's also responsible for feeding six hundred man and their families. He's being stretched to the breaking point for his difficulties have wearied him to the point of hopelessness. He's tired, disgusted, and fatigued and this causes him to not think right. He feels on the inside that he can't take the pressure anymore. It's emotional overload. He snapped at the insult of Nabal and he's about to snap again. David is downcast and in low spirits from a loss of hope and courage. Nothing that happens next reveals that he is a man of God, a man after God's own heart.

It's a fact of life, men and women of God can get weary and depressed and fall into the pit of compromise. While in this condition it is not uncommon for smart people to make foolish decisions. David is having feelings of defeat, discouragement, and depression. He feels like God has forsaken him. He wrote in Ps. 13:1, "How long, O Lord? Will you forget me forever? How long will You hide Your face from me?" Again, he writes in Ps. 22:1, "My God, my God, why have you forsaken me? Why are You so far from helping me, and from the words of my groaning?" While in this condition, David makes a grave mistake. He makes the foolish decision to give up on God's plan for his life and sets off to live life on his terms. He is disillusioned and this bad decision will bring with it some serious and terrible consequences in his life. Instead of staying close to God, he walks away to a life of carnality and compromise. He'll become a doubter, a butcher, a liar, and a traitor. When you walk away from God, He appears smaller in your eyes while your enemies become bigger and bigger.

"And David said in his heart..." (1 Sam. 27:1). Be careful for what you say in your heart has the power to shape your thinking, your actions, and your destiny. Your thoughts carry tremendous power that brings forth good or evil, blessing or cursing. Prov. 23:7 says, "For as he thinks in his heart, so is he." Saying the wrong thing, especially in an emotionally charged crisis, will put you on a very slippery slope that can lead to a nightmare of the worst kind. David is about to say to himself something that is totally opposite of everything he knows about God. He's about to wipe away everything God has ever said or done in his life. David said in his heart, "Now I shall perish someday by the hand of Saul. There is nothing better for me than that I should speedily escape to the land of the Philistines; and Saul will despair of me, to seek me anymore in any part of Israel. So I shall escape out of his hand." This seems out of place for David to say this. Where was the David who boldly declared his trust in God against all his enemies (1 Sam. 17:45-47)?

David is now convinced that he'll die at the hand of Saul so he tells himself to leave and go live among the idol worshiping Philistines. At this moment in time it is David who is in despair, not Saul. Has he forgotten the many times God has delivered him from the deadly grasp of King Saul? How many prophecies and anointings and miracles has he had that revealed he was going to be the next king of Israel? He doesn't realize that when you're battling weariness and discouragement, this is the wrong time to make long-term decisions concerning your life. You need a clear mind and an open heart in order to hear from God and make wise decisions concerning the situation at hand. David didn't pray about this but believed in his heart that Saul was going to kill him. He reasons there is only one place he can go to where

Saul won't come after him and that was to the land of the enemy. The children of Israel had been miraculously delivered from slavery in Egypt but during a time of weariness and misery they said, "We should choose a leader and go back to Egypt" (Num. 14:4).

Always be afraid of being afraid. Charles Spurgeon said, "He who does not comfortably trust God will soon seek after comfort somewhere else." In his weariness, David is saying, "I give up. The stress of trusting God is too much. I must find protection somewhere else." This is total humanistic thinking. He's thinking horizontal and not vertical. He thinks God's way is not working so he decides to cross over to the side of the enemy. His despair was a more powerful enemy than Saul ever was. He doesn't pray about this for his faith in God has vanished. He is drowning himself in negative, faithless thinking, in his personal vision of the situation he is in. David's sin of unbelief turns into the logic of compromise. He's giving up the daily fight of faith and going back to the ways of the world, a world that is dark and sinful and contrary to the ways of God. He's tired of fighting. He's weary and depressed. Every day it's one crisis after another. He's overwhelmed and he's giving up the fight. Instead of looking to God, he looks to himself.

"Then David arose and went over with the six hundred men who were with him to Achish the son of Maoch, king of Gath" (vs. 2). David fled to Gath once before and ended up acting like a madman. Gath was the hometown of Goliath and there were still giants living in the city. Many of these giants were born through incestuous inbreeding in hopes of creating an entire army of giants. Not only do David and his men go to Gath but their families go with them. There are between two and three thousand people who follow David into the land of the enemy. Leaders come under stricter judgment from God because when they fall, they take others with them. David's compromise brought his men and their families down with him. On this day he became his own worst enemy. The buildup of anxiety caused negative counsel to come to his mind. He allowed wrong thinking to breed and be nurtured in his thinking to the point that in despair he decides to join forces with the enemy. He hopelessly expects the worse, that he'll die at the hand of Saul, and acts accordingly. He goes and lives with the pagans.

"And it was told Saul that David had fled to Gath; so he sought him no more" (vs. 4). Surprisingly, David's plan worked. The only thing worse than taking matters into your own hands and fighting your own battles is to be successful at it. David did the wrong thing but still he got the results he wanted. Sometimes you'll have success in the short term but ultimately the carnal responses to life will catch up to you and you'll be worse off than you were before. You can't follow animalistic instincts and be successful for very long. Sooner or later you'll fall into the pit of compromise, a pit of your own making, and everything pertaining to your life will crash and burn. What's more, you'll refuse to believe this disaster was of your own doing. You'll blame God, you'll blame other people, you'll blame everybody but yourself. You'll be self-deceived and nothing good happens when you are. You become blinded to the long-term consequences of bad decisions. David slipped into the flow of carnal living, the flow that leads deeper and deeper into sin. He is now on the path that leads to death and destruction.

Achish recognizes there is hostility between David and Saul. This means they both have the same enemy. He reasons that having David on his side will give him the extra leverage he needs with his own battle against Saul. David goes to the king and asks for a city in the country for him and his men to dwell in. He asks, "For why should your servant dwell in the royal city with you?" (vs. 5). It is an abomination, an atrocity of the worst kind, that David would call himself the servant of God's enemy. Beware for it's in the pit of compromise where you become the servant of the enemy, a servant of the devil himself. "So Achish gave him Ziklag that day" (Vs. 6). Ziklag did not belong to the Philistines. It was a city given to Judah by Joshua when the children of Israel took over the Promised Land. Judah never drove the enemy out of this city and it was later given to the tribe of Simeon. They also didn't destroy the inhabitants who lived there. The Philistines later came in and captured the city. It belonged to God's people but it was now controlled by the enemy.

The word "Ziklag" means 'winding.' This is a proper name for this city because at this time in David's life he is on a winding road. David and his men live here for sixteen months, all the while compromising with the enemy. For sixteen months David is taken out of the ministry. For sixteen months not a single psalm is written by the psalmist of Israel. They were now in a fortified city and would no longer have to find refuge in the wilderness. They still have to eat so David and his men go on a bloody rampage throughout the land killing those tribes that were the enemies of Israel (vs. 8). These people were Canaanites who should have been driven out of the land by Joshua and the children of Israel when they entered the Promised Land but they weren't. Although he's going against the ancient enemies of Israel, David is fighting for profit instead of for the honor of God. "Whenever David attacked the land, he left neither man nor woman alive, but took away the sheep, the oxen, the donkeys, the camels, and the apparel, and returned and came to Achish" (vs. 9).

This is not a pretty picture. David massacred men, women, and children, many of whom are innocent, in order to get their food and clothing. Yes, he was taking out the enemies of Israel but he did this to cover up his life of compromise. He returns to Achish with all this livestock and apparel and is asked, "Where have you made a raid today?" (vs. 10). David lies to the king and tells Achish he was fighting against Israel when in fact he was really fighting against the enemies of

Israel. He lied not because he was ashamed for what he did but because he wants to gain favor with the king. He wants to give the impression that he has attacked his own people and was forever loyal to the Philistine people. The devilish motive for what David did is revealed in vs. 11 (MSG), "He never left a single person alive lest one show up in Gath and report what David had really been doing. This is the way David operated all the time he lived in Philistine country." These people didn't have to die but David killed them all so that his lie to Achish would not be exposed.

In the back of his mind, Achish must have been thinking, "I've got him now!" If you remain in sin, if you stay in the pit of compromise, the devil will say the same thing about you. Achish believed the lie David told him and said, "He has made his people Israel utterly abhor him; therefore he will be my servant forever" (vs. 12). The Message Bible says, "He's made himself so repugnant to his people that he'll be in my camp forever." Achish believed that David had burned all his bridges with the people of God. David was now trapped in a dark web and Achish was the spider. 1 Sam. 28:1 says, "Now it happened in those days that the Philistines gathered their armies together for war, to fight with Israel." Why would the Philistines attack Israel at this time? Because they believe the strongest fighting force in Israel is now on their side. They believe the battle with Israel will now turn in their favor. Achish looks at David and says, "You assuredly know that you will go out with me to battle, you and your men." David is now forced to live out the lie he told to Achish.

Achish wants David to fight against his own people. He's going to be the next king of Israel and here he is standing shoulder to shoulder with the Philistines. He's pretending to be friends with the enemy while he's serving God. How many people keep secret their Christianity while they associate with the sinners of the world? You know you're a Christian but nobody else knows it because of your silence. You're living in the land of the enemy but inside you're a secret Christian. It has been said that Christianity will destroy your secret or your secret will destroy your Christianity. Ps. 107:2 says, "Let the redeemed of the Lord say so, whom He has redeemed from the hand of the enemy." The Message Bible says, "All of you set free by God, tell the world!" David appears to be completely surrendered to the ungodly Achish. He answers him in a round about way, "Surely you know what your servant can do" (vs. 2). Was that a yes or a no? David has come to a very low place even though he didn't say he would fight against Israel. Achish answers back, "Therefore I make you one of my chief guardians forever."

The Philistine army is now stronger than ever while Saul's army is weak and distracted because of all the time it spent looking for David. The people of Israel are now vulnerable so the Philistines gather their forces together to launch an apocalyptic war against Israel. This is the final showdown. The Philistines are encamped against Israel at Shunew and their army is bigger than anything Saul could ever imagine. Shunew is way up north just south of the Sea of Galilee and is the city where Elisha would later raise a godly woman's son from the dead (2 Kings 4). Up until this point the Philistines were down south but now, they've penetrated into the northern region of Israel. They've become a formidable foe, dividing the land in half. "When Saul saw the army of the Philistines, he was afraid, and his heart trembled greatly" (vs. 5). Saul's courage is completely gone. If you fear God, you won't fear anything else. If you don't fear God, you'll fear everything. "And when Saul inquired of the Lord, the Lord did not answer him, either by dreams or by Urim or by the prophets" (Vs. 6). Now what is he going to do?

-19-

"BACK FROM THE DEAD"

The Philistines mean business. They've become a formidable foe and are determined to make the land of Israel their own. Saul had fought the Philistines before but this time it's different. The fact that they had penetrated so far north is an indication of their dominance over Saul's kingdom. "When Saul saw the army of the Philistines, he was afraid, and his heart trembled greatly" (1 Sam. 28:5). Because of his sinful disobedience, the world is crashing in around him. He feels like his back is against the wall and there is no way out. He feels in his heart that this is the end of his reign as king. Samuel is dead and he killed all the priests of God at Nob. There is a spiritual vacuum in the land and now Saul doesn't have a faithful man to inquire of the Lord for him anymore. To make matters worse, he had heard that David had gone over to the other side and would now be fighting for the Philistines. His popularity has greatly declined and many of his soldiers defected and are now fighting with David.

Never has Saul felt so helpless. He is greatly afraid and doesn't know what to do. In desperation he cries out to the Lord for help. "And when Saul inquired of the Lord, the Lord did not answer him, either by dreams or by Urim, or by the prophets" (vs. 6). To his horror, Saul now realizes that the doors of heavenly communication have been closed and locked. There is nothing more devastating than the silence of God. It is a terrible thing to need God's help and to be cut off from Him. Is. 59:2 says, "But your iniquities have separated you from your God; And your sins have hidden His face from you, so that He will not hear." Saul's life of sin has finally caught up to him. He receives no answer from God because he refused to obey Him in the past. If you want guidance from God, you must do what He previously told you to do. In spite of his circumstances, Saul is not calling out to God because he was sorry for his life of sin. No, he selfishly wants God to get him out of trouble again.

It is important to know that the prayer for deliverance from sin must always precede the prayer for deliverance from your enemies. It is foolishness to seek God's help when you willingly and habitually live a life of sin. Ps. 66:18 says, "If I regard iniquity in my heart, the Lord will not hear." Saul is very desperate so he said to his servants, "Find me a woman who is a medium, that I may go to her and inquire of her" (vs. 7). Desperate people do desperate things. Saul is saying, "Find me a witch. She can help me!" He specifically asked for a woman because it is a fact that women are more drawn to the occult than men are. Paul said in 1 Tim. 2:14 that "Adam was not deceived, but the woman being deceived, fell into transgression." The Hebrew word for "medium" is "owb" and means 'to mumble; to speak with a strange, hollow sound.' A "medium" claims that a dead person would speak through them for they were a channel between the living and the dead.

Saul knew what he was doing is wrong. In Deut 18:11,12 God condemns "one who conjures spells, or a medium, or a spiritist, or one who calls up the dead. For all who do these things are an abomination to the Lord." When Samuel died Saul "put the mediums and the spiritists out of the land" (1 Sam. 28:3) even though Lev. 20:27 says these people were to be executed by stoning. Saul knew it was not right to "seek the dead on behalf of the living" (Is. 8:19) but he tells his servants to find him a medium anyway. He had removed witchcraft from the land but he didn't remove witchcraft from his heart. His servants say to him, "In fact, there is a woman who is a medium at En Dor" (vs. 7). En Dor was eight miles from where Saul was at. It was located four miles northeast of Shumen and was thus dangerously close to where the Philistines were encamped. "So Saul disguised himself and put on other clothes, and he went, and two men with him; and they came to the woman by night" (vs. 8).

Saul disguised himself but God sees everything. As Saul goes to the medium he brings upon himself a curse. God said in Lev. 20:6, "And the person who turns after mediums and familiar spirits, to prostitute himself with them, I will set My face against that person and cut him off from his people." Mediums claim they can bring people back from the dead and going to one reveals the depths of Saul's fall from grace. It has affected his mind and he's not thinking clearly. He has rejected the truth and is now opening himself up to the evil practices of a medium. Saul is in the wrong and he knows it. In the darkness of the night he arrives at En Dor and says to the medium, "Please conduct a séance for me, and bring up for me the one I shall name to you" (vs. 8). The woman is hesitant to return to her occultic practices as she reminds her visitors that Saul has "cut off the mediums and the spiritists from the land. Why then do you lay a snare for my life, to cause me to die?" (vs. 9).

Saul answers the suspicions of the medium and swore to her saying, "As the Lord lives, no punishment shall come upon you for this thing" (vs. 10). This is the last time Saul uses the name of the Lord and he uses it to swear to a medium that she will not be punished. Satisfied, the woman asks, "Whom shall I bring up for you?" Saul said, "Bring up Samuel for me" (vs. 11). He wants this witch to bring Samuel back from the dead. In the midst of his sin and demonic influence, Saul seems to have forgotten that Samuel was his biggest adversary. Considering all the times Samuel rebuked him, you would think that Samuel would be the last person Saul would want to see. To the medium's surprise, Samuel appears. "When the woman saw Samuel, she cried out with a loud voice" (vs. 12). Why was the woman shocked? Because most of her dealings with the spirit realm were tricks to fool those who came to her. She was a fraud and here she got more than she bargained for.

The Hebrew word for "cried out" means 'to scream.' She did not cause this appearance to happen and she is completely surprised to have a real encounter with the spirit realm. If this had been one of her tricks she wouldn't have been alarmed as she was. There are those who would say this was not the real Samuel but rather a demon impersonating the prophet of God. No where in scripture does it say a demonic spirit can impersonate a human being. The Bible says this was Samuel and that settles it. This is not the only biblical account of someone being visited by a person who was deceased. Matt. 17:3 says that Moses and Elijah spoke with Jesus on the Mount of Transfiguration. What is happening here at En Dor is real and was something allowed by God for His divine purposes. This passage of scripture does not give any reason to believe it was anyone other than the real Samuel. Fearing for her life, the woman turns to Saul and says, "Why have you deceived me? For you are Saul!" (vs. 12).

Saul said to the woman, "Do not be afraid. What did you see?" The medium answered, "I saw a spirit ascending out of the earth" (vs. 13). The Message Bible says, "I see a spirit ascending from the underground." The word "spirit" is the Hebrew word "elohim" meaning 'gods.' She saw something not of this world. She calls Samuel an elohim because in ancient times the dead could be referred to as gods because they lived in the realm beyond what was normal. Where did Samuel come from? He was in the heart of the earth in a place called "Abraham's bosom" (Luke 16:22) waiting for Jesus to die for his sins and then come and take him and all the other Old Testament saints to heaven. Both the medium and Saul physically saw Samuel standing there in front of them. This was not a hallucination or some make believe crystal ball experience. Saul then stooped with his face to the ground and bowed down. Coming from a better place, Samuel reprimands Saul and asks him, "Why have you disturbed me by bringing me up?" (vs. 15).

Samuel was called back from the dead but would rather be back where he came from. Who wouldn't? You need to live every day with an understanding of the world beyond, of the reality of eternity. Saul answers, "I am deeply distressed; for the Philistines make war against me, and God has departed from me and does not answer me anymore, neither by prophets nor by dreams. Therefore I have called you, that you may reveal to me what I should do?" (vs. 15). A logical question is then asked by Samuel, "Why then do you ask me seeing that the Lord has departed from you and has become your enemy?" (vs. 16). Is there anything more worse in life than having God as your enemy? If the Lord wouldn't tell Saul what he wanted, he didn't have any reason to believe that Samuel would. Samuel does confirm what God has already said to Saul previously. The kingdom has been torn out of his hand and given to David. The message to Saul is disturbingly consistent, no matter how God chooses to bring the message.

Samuel reminds Saul how he didn't obey God fifteen years earlier when he was told to attack Amalek and destroy all that they had (1 Sam. 15). His disobedience that day is the reason for the predicament he's in today. Perhaps Saul thought God had forgotten what happened and changed His mind. He didn't. Samuel then tells Saul what his fate will be. "Moreover the Lord will also deliver Israel with you into the hand of the Philistines. And tomorrow you and your sons will be with me. The Lord will also deliver the army of Israel into the hand of the Philistines" (vs. 19). When judgment feel upon Saul, it would include the people around him. His sons, including Jonathan, and all of Israel would suffer also.

Samuel never told Saul what to do because it was too late to do anything. God's judgment was already in motion. For Saul, time has run out. Never assume you'll have as much time as you want to repent. Surely, time is of the essence. If your heart convicts you to repent, do it now because you may not be here tomorrow.

When Samuel said "tomorrow you and your sons will be with me," he was saying they were going to die. Being with Samuel does not mean that Saul eventually went to heaven. Jesus said in Luke 16:19-31 that the blessed dead and the cursed dead are in the same general area. The Old Testament saints were in the place of comfort known as "Abraham's bosom" whereas the cursed dead were in a place of torment separated by a great gulf from the saints of God. Saul would be in the same general area as Samuel, in the heart of the earth, but not in the same specific place. Saul now knows that the Lord is his adversary. He disobeyed God and his fate has been sealed. Judgment is coming and his life is going to end. Knowing this is more that Saul can bear. "Then immediately Saul fell full length on the ground, and was dreadfully afraid because of the words of Samuel. And there was no strength in him, for he had eaten no food all day or all night" (vs. 20). The medium comforts Saul and offers him some food to eat. He refused and said, "I will not eat" (vs. 23).

It is a sad day when a witch comforts the king of Israel. The truth is, they were two of the same kind of people. Both lived in rebellion to God and each was under His divine judgment. The woman said to Saul, "I did what you said, now you do what I say. Eat something." Saul's servants likewise encouraged him to eat. He heeded their voice, arose from the ground, and sat on a bed. As Saul mourned, the woman made haste to kill a fatted calf and to bake unleavened bread. She made a meal for her uninvited guests, brought it before Saul and his servants, and they ate. This was like the last meal a man on death row eats before his execution. "Then they rose and went away that night" (vs. 25). Saul leaves this strange encounter resigned to his own fate. On the day when Saul was anointed to be king, the dawn of a new day was breaking forth (1 Sam. 9:26). Saul's reign began in the bright light of a new, promising day. Here he is seen going off at night under the cover of darkness revealing that a good start in life doesn't guarantee a good finish.

As Saul returns home in shame and defeat, the Philistines make their move by gathering together all their armies at Apheh. They are deep in Israelite territory and they're ready to deliver a death blow to Saul and his kingdom. Unfortunately, David and his men are with them. In the midst of great discouragement, David chose to fight alongside the Philistines against God's people. He is in a very compromising position as he finds himself in a place he never thought he would be. He is standing shoulder to shoulder with the enemies of God getting ready to attack the children of God, the same people he'll one day be king over. Jesus said in Matt. 6:24, "No one can serve two masters; for either he will hate the one and love the other, or else he will be loyal to the one and despise the other." He is saying that you can't be on both sides at the same time. This is why one of the first rules of warfare is to know who your enemy is. The Message Bible says, "Adoration of one feeds contempt for the other."

2 Cor. 6:14 says, "Do not be unequally yoked together with unbelievers. For what fellowship has righteousness with lawlessness?" It is a tragedy when you can't tell the difference between a child of God and a child of the devil, when there's no difference in the things they say and the things they do. They've compromised their beliefs, they've lowered their standards of living. Like David, they're dwelling in the land of the enemy and are now living a life of carnal hypocrisy. The Message Bible says, "Don't become partners

with those who reject God. How can you make a partnership out of right and wrong? That's not partnership; that's war. Is light best friends with dark? Does Christ go strolling with the devil? Do trust and mistrust hold hands?" Don't allow yourself to get too comfortable hanging around the wrong crowd. 2 Cor. 6:17 says, "Come out from among them and be separate, says the Lord." Don't link up with those who will pollute you (MSG).

Before the commencement of the battle, the prince rulers of the Philistines wanted to first review the troops. They watched with satisfaction as hundreds and then thousands of soldiers passed in front of them. Their delight was suddenly turned to alarm and dismay as they saw David and his men bringing up the rear with Achish the king of Gath. Immediately they asked, "What are these Hebrews doing here?" (1 Sam. 29:3). These leaders could see what David was blinded to. He shouldn't be here! David is not thinking right and he doesn't see as clearly as the enemy. He had started to think and act like a Philistine and had gotten deeper and deeper into compromise. Don't associate with ungodly people when you're in a backslidden condition. If you do, something on the inside of you will say, "You don't belong here! You should be with God's people." The rulers knew David shouldn't be among their ranks even if he couldn't. Achish steps in and defends David in the face of opposition from these rulers.

Achish said to the princes of the Philistines, "Is this not David, who has been with me these days, or these years?" (vs. 3). He knew who David was. He was a Hebrew, one of God's chosen people. Achish continues, "And to this day I have found no fault in him since he defected to me." David has identified himself so much with the ungodly that Achish believes David is surely on his side. The Message Bible says, "He's been with me a long time. I've found nothing to be suspicious of, nothing to complain about, from the day he defected from Saul until now." These words should have grieved David. They should have been a wake-up call to him, words that would bring him back to his senses. They didn't grieve David but they certainly grieved the Philistine leaders. They reject David and are angry with Achish for bringing him to the battle. They fear that in battle David will turn back into a godly man. They don't trust he'll stay on their side once the battle begins.

The Philistine officers said, "Send this man back to where he came from. Let him stick to his normal duties. He's not going into battle with us. He'll switch sides in the middle of the fight! What better chance to get back in favor with his master than by stabbing us in the back!" (vs. 4 MSG). David wants to fight but the Philistine rulers won't let him. Is this the intervention of God? Is this God's way of stopping David from doing something so evil and foolish that His plans for David's life will come to naught? These rulers don't trust David, nor should they. They're afraid that in the midst of the battle he'll attack them from the rear while Saul attacks them from the front. They ask Achish, "Is this not David, of whom they sang to one another in dances: 'Saul has slain his thousands, and David his ten thousands'?" (vs. 5). It's been more than ten years since this song was first sung and the enemy remembers it well. The song of David's victory over the Philistines in times past has come back to haunt him again.

Achish now tells David that he and his men must return home to Ziklag, a three-day journey from where they are now at. But first, he tells David that he is a good man in his sight. "Surely, as the Lord lives, you have been upright, and your going out and your coming in with me in the army is good in my sight" (vs. 6). In his mind, David is probably wondering why Saul never spoke to him like that. If he did, all these years of running and hiding in caves could have been avoided. If Saul would have embraced him like Achish did, David would now be fighting by the side of Saul instead of fighting against him. The Philistines would then have something to fear. It is interesting to note that Achish said "as the Lord lives." These words are unexpected in a Philistine oath because they don't believe in the same God that David believes in. Achish continues, "For to this day I have not found evil in you since the day of your coming to me. Nevertheless, the lords do not favor you."

David is being rejected by the ungodly Philistines and he doesn't like it. Achish then tells him to go home. "Therefore return now, and go in peace, that you may not displease the lords of the Philistines" (vs. 7). The truth is, David has no home. He is a man without a country. He ran away from the land of Israel and now the Philistine leaders won't accept him. He's trying to live in both worlds and you can't do that. Light and darkness don't mix. The problem with David is he has too much of the world in him to be at peace with God, and too much of the Lord in him to be at peace in the world. This is why Gal. 5:9 says, "A little leaven leavens the whole lump." In Jewish tradition, leaven was always symbolic of evil influence. Paul is saying that a little bit of sin and corruption will eventually destroy a person's life. David then appeals to Achish, "But what have I done?" (vs. 8). David used to be a mighty warrior for God but here he seems genuinely disappointed that he will not be able to fight with the Philistines against Israel.

David continues his plea to Achish, "And to this day what have you found in your servant as long as I have been with you, that I may not go and fight against the enemies of my lord the king?" David used to strike fear into the hearts of these people and now he's concerned about displeasing the lords of the Philistines. He is arguing to be allowed to fight the people of God! How low can he get? He even goes so far as to call Achish "my lord the king," the same words he reverently used to call King Saul. Achish answers David, "I know that you are as good in my sight as an angel of God; nevertheless the princes of the Philistines have said, 'He shall not go up with us to the battle.' Now therefore, rise early in the morning with your master's servants who have come up with you. And as soon as you are up early in the morning and have light, depart" (vs. 9,10). When the sun rises the next day, David sets off toward Ziklag while the Philistines prepare to fight Israel. What's it going to take for David to see the error of his ways? He's about to find out.

The Shepherd King

-20-

"THE VALLEY OF DESPAIR"

David has resigned himself to the fact that he won't be fighting with the Philistines. With the thoughts of battle fleeting from his mind, David and his men begin the long seventy-five-mile journey from Apheh to their home town of Ziklag. After three days of riding they are tired, hungry, and ready for all the comforts of home. The closer they get to Ziklag, the happier they become. They're about to receive a warm welcome from their wives and children and surely a nice hot meal will soon follow. Suddenly, their bright thoughts turn as dark as the night. From a distance they see black smoke rising into the air and immediately they knew something was wrong. What they didn't know is that while they were gone their city was left unguarded and the Amalekites took advantage of this. These were the people God told Saul to wipe out completely but he didn't do it. There is always a price to pay when you compromise with God. These savages attacked the city, burned it to the ground, and took captive all who were there.

"So David and his men came to the city, and there it was, burned with fire; and their wives, their sons, and their daughters had been taken captive" (1 Sam. 30:3). In front of these weary warriors is a pile of burned rubble with no sign of their families anywhere. David knows he is responsible for this and he's probably asking himself, "What have I done?" His two wives were taken captive along with all the others and he is greatly distressed and about as low as any man can be. He's like the prodigal son who found himself at the end of his rope sitting in a pigpen. All is lost. What is he going to do? "Then David and the people who were with him lifted up their voices and wept until they had no more power to weep" (vs. 4). The Message Bible says, "David and his men burst out in loud wails - wept and wept until they were exhausted with weeping." These are tears of great anguish, regret, and brokenness. Everything they've been fighting for is now gone.

Shock! Anger! Rage! These men are in the valley of despair. They've lost everything. Their families are gone, they're financially wiped out, nothing is left. They don't know if their loved ones have been killed or sold into slavery. Their grief turns to violent rage. They want someone to blame for this tragedy and soon all their eyes are pointed at David. "Then David was greatly distressed, for the people spoke of stoning him, because the soul of all the people was grieved, every man for his sons and daughters" (vs. 6). These men are very bitter over the loss of their families. They had followed David and remained by his side through thick and thin, through victory and compromise, and now they want to kill him. David is at the lowest point in his life. He realizes you can't disobey God and be immune from the effects of it. He's a man without a country. He has alienated himself from the people of Israel, the lords of the Philistines want nothing to do with him, his wives have been taken captive, and now his own men want to kill him.

David's cup has run dry. He's lost everything that has any meaning to him and now his life is on the line, held in the hands of six hundred grieving men. Its true, choices bring consequences. Sin and stubborn rebellion often bring brokenness into your life. When that happens, one of two things can occur. You can get bitter or you can get better. You can be humbled or get even more blind to the ways of God. Brokenness can bend you or break you. It can restore you back to God or make you even more resentful. For David, Ziklag was a place of compromise and disobedience, the place of do-it-yourself Christianity. It was at Ziklag where David hit rock bottom. He wrote in Ps. 18:4,5, "The pangs of death encompassed me, and the floods of ungodliness made me afraid. The sorrows of Sheol surrounded me; The snare of death confronted me." The Message Bible says, "The hangman's noose was tight at my throat; devil waters rushed over me. Hell's ropes cinched me tight; death traps barred every exit."

The scars of brokenness can last a long time but it's the consequences of one's fallen behavior that God uses to wake you up to the reality of His unending grace. It's where He takes a lemon and makes lemonade out of it. He loves you too much to allow you to continue living in sin and foolishness. It's His deep love for you that makes Him rebuke your sinful behavior along with divine discipline, followed by the correction you need to get back on the right path. There will be nothing to dread if you place your brokenness in the hands of the living God. He is a loving God and it is He who brings total and complete restoration to your life. Out of brokenness will come joy unspeakable and life forevermore. Shattered dreams can be reassembled and brought back to life more abundantly. The love of God is constant and unchanging. He'll take your mess and turn it into a message that will help prevent others from falling into the same pit of compromise you fell into. Thankfully, His love is not dependent on your failure or success. He loves you because that is who He is.

When you're at the bottom of the pit and all hope seems lost, never think it's too late for God to help you. David was out of God's will but he was never out of God's love and protection. He was in the burnt down city of Ziklag but he was never out of the sight of God. Know with certainty that God's eyes are always upon you and His hands are stretched in your direction. He said in Heb. 13:5, "I will never leave you nor forsake you." Bring your brokenness to God and watch what

He'll do in your life. It is in brokenness where God graciously begins His work of restoration. He used the natural consequences of David's sin to get his attention. It was here in the valley of despair when David turned back to God. His men wanted to kill him "but David strengthened himself in the Lord his God" (1 Sam. 30:6). It's because of this deep, distressing pain that David is now in that drives him to cry out to God in prayer. Because of his brokenness, David is ready to be filled with the strength of God.

You can reach a point in your life where there is no strength to be had except the strength that comes from God. Eph. 6:10 (CEV) says, "Let the mighty strength of the Lord make you strong." Standing here weeping in the charred ruins of Ziklag is the ultimate wake up call for David. It's the turning point in his life as he releases the anguish of his heart to his Lord and Master. Not once in the past sixteen months has he interacted with the Lord. It was because of the painful consequences of his compromise that brought David to the point of being made right with God. He's a hurting man but he knew where to go in his weakness. He is now ready for the strength of the living God to be made real in his life. God is his only strength and he knows it. Ps. 121:1,2 (GNT) says, "I look to the mountains; where will my help come from? My help will come from the Lord, who made heaven and earth." It's the strength of God that will give him the determination to take back what the enemy has stolen.

David is encouraged as he begins to worship God for who He is. Once again he meditates on the things God has already told him, the fact that he would one day be king of Israel. He went back to the firm foundation that God had built into his life. Don't wait until the storm is raging to build this foundation. The foundation for strengthening yourself in the Lord must be built before the valley of despair engulfs you and sweeps you away. Learn to pray and worship God and meditate on the Word before the trial comes. Build those walls of protection beforehand so you'll have the foundation in place on which you will stand. Do what David did. Rely on the eternal God and take courage. David now realizes that if he had not been rejected by the Philistine leaders it would have been weeks or months before he returned home. Who knows what would have happened to their loved ones if that had been the case? The truth is, God was working in his life and he didn't even know it.

Only when David hit rock bottom did he turn to the Lord. Many people never go to God unless a tragedy happens in their life. Thankfully, He's always there with opened arms. David's attitude of doing things his own way is finally broken. His consequences crushed his self-will. It broke him where he stood. He went from a terrible compromise to brokenness and crying out to God. Being at the end of yourself is the starting point where God can strengthen you and use you for His glory. From this point forward things will happen in rapid succession that will lead David straight to the throne. David is strengthened in the Lord and it's now time to take action. He is standing in the midst of a self-ruined life, in the rubble of a city that's been burned down. He stops in the midst of these smoking ruins and inquires of the Lord (vs. 8). This is the mark of true repentance. David has finally been brought to the end of himself as he now seeks the will of God, something he should have done in the first place. Indeed, man's extremity is God's opportunity.

David told Abiathar the priest to bring the ephod to him where he asked the Lord if he should pursue the troop of soldiers and overtake them. It would be a natural thing to pursue the enemy and rescue their loved ones but David would not go without God's approval and direction. David wouldn't have done this a few days earlier. He is a warrior and when a soldier is attacked, he attacks back. Today is different. He is a broken man and desperately needs God's help. The moment he is broken is the moment God steps in and gives him the answer he's looking for. God now brings revival to the life of David. British evangelist Alan Redpath once said, "Revival is getting God's vision and God's passion for God's action." Revival is all about God. David understands that and it leads him to God's will and purpose. He's broken and annihilated and is right where God wants him. God then answers David and says, "Pursue, for you shall surely overtake them and without fail recover all" (vs. 8).

God would not answer the inquiry of Saul but here He tells David what to do along with a promise that all would go well. David's spirit is lifted high and he immediately goes back to living in the confidence of the Lord instead of the compromise of the flesh. Vs. 9 says, "So David went..." David did what God told him to do. Obedience to God is often that simple. People should never call Jesus their Lord unless they're willing to do what He tells them to do. After having just traveled seventy-five miles, David and his men now travel an additional sixty miles to the Brook Besor. David's band of misfits are once again standing by his side when not long before they wanted to kill him. They saw he had faith in God and this is what compelled them to follow him on this mission to rescue their loved ones. There wasn't an army in the world who could stop them now. When they reached the Brook Besor a third of his men were too exhausted to continue so David allowed them to stay behind with the supplies (vs. 10).

David's army has just gotten smaller but he had God on his side and that is all that mattered. Gideon's army was reduced to three hundred men because God didn't want his soldiers to claim the glory of their victory for themselves (Judges 7). As they traveled, they unexpectedly came across a helpless Egyptian alone in a field. They were on a mission of much greater importance but still they stopped to render aid to this man. He was near death for he had not eaten any bread or drank any water for three days and nights. His strength returned after being given food and water, after which David asked him, "To whom do you belong, and where are you from?" (vs. 13). The young man said he was a servant of an Amalekite and was left behind when he fell sick. Not realizing who he was talking to, he then proceeds to say that he helped with the burning of Ziklag. He was fortunate that he wasn't killed then and there. David knew it was no coincidence that they found this man sitting in the middle of nowhere. The Lord is about to give him the direction he needs.

David asks him, "Can you take me down to this troop?" (vs. 15). The Egyptian agrees to take David to the Amalekites in exchange for his life. They soon come upon the enemy camp and "there they were, spread out over all the land, eating and drinking and dancing, because of all the great spoil which they had taken from the land of the Philistines and from the land of Judah" (vs. 16). The last thing these people expected was to be attacked for they reasoned all the Philistine and Israelite armies were in the far north preparing to fight each other. David and his men got some rest and attacked at first light. The Amalekites were still hung over from the feast the previous night and were least able to defend themselves. "And David attacked them from twilight until the evening of the next day. Not a man of them escaped, except for four hundred young men who rode on camels and fled. So David recovered all that the Amalekites had carried away, and David rescued his two wives" (vs. 17,18). God's promise proved true. Everything He said would happen, did happen.

The Lord fulfilled His promise for not one person was harmed or killed. David also received a great spoil from this battle that went beyond what had been taken from Ziklag. He also took that which the Amalekites had taken from the other cities. Charles Spurgeon said, "Now, in the great battle of

Christ on our behalf, He has not only given us back what we lost, but He has given us what Adam in his perfection never had." Everything was going fine until they get back to the two hundred men at the Brook Besor. It was there that David decided to divide the spoil equally among those who fought with him and those who stayed behind. The "wicked and worthless men" (vs. 22) who went with David did not agree with this. These "mean-spirited men" (MSG) said they could have their families back but none of the spoil. David is about to teach them about the grace of God. He openly declares that the supply lines are just as important as the soldiers who go to battle and both should be rewarded equally.

In Matt. 20:1-16 Jesus told the parable of the laborers. Some went to work for the master early in the morning, some at noon, some an hour before quitting time. At the end of the day everybody received the same amount of pay. The ones who started early in the morning complained and said, "That's not fair. We should have gotten more." Grace is not about fairness. If it were, nobody would receive anything "for all have sinned and fall short of the glory of God" (Rom. 3:23). In God's kingdom, not all people are called to do the same thing. Not everybody is called to be a pastor or a missionary. Not everybody is called to go out to the front lines of battle. Some are called to stay with the supplies. In other words, some are called to vacuum the floor and clean the toilets. When you support those who do battle on the front lines, you'll share the same rewards they receive. Jesus said in Matt. 10:41 (BSB), "Whoever receives a prophet because he is a prophet will receive a prophet's reward, and whoever receives a righteous man because he is a righteous man will receive a righteous mans reward."

Many people serve the Lord behind the scenes and are often out of the public eye. God rewards the hidden servant as much as He does the ones who stand behind a pulpit. David's men said they fought for the spoil and it was theirs.

David looked at the same spoil and said, "Look at what the Lord has given us" (vs. 23). The principle of rewarding those who stayed behind with the supplies was so important that it was declared to be a statute and an ordinance for Israel to this day (vs. 25). Charles Spurgeon said, "You that have a great heart for holiness, but feel beaten back in your struggles, the Lord shall give you His love, His grace, His favor, as surely as He gives it to those who can do great things in His name." David became rich and he sent part of the spoil to his fellow countrymen. He knew his time with the Philistines had strained his relationship with God's people. He must now do whatever it takes to make things right again. Over thirteen cities were blessed by David's generosity. He is now back serving the Lord like he did in times past.

As all this is happening, Saul is in his own valley of despair. The Philistines are deep in Israelite territory and Saul is not ready for battle. He is greatly afraid as he remembers the words of Samuel who told him this would be the day he and three of his sons would die. The enemy is attacking Saul at the Valley of Jezreel, the very place where the Battle of Armageddon will be fought. The men of Israel are greatly outnumbered so they begin to retreat up the slopes of Mount Gilboa. An uphill retreat is very difficult. It's slow and grinding work and their backs are fully exposed to the weapons of the enemy. The massive number of Philistines are relentlessly pressing upon them. Blood is everywhere and dead bodies cover the ground as far as the eye can see. Many have been slashed with swords and others have been pierced with arrows. Screams of terror are heard as Saul's soldiers cry out in pain and agony. The Philistines step over thousands of mutilated bodies as they spot Saul and make their advances toward him.

"Then the Philistines followed hard after Saul and his sons. And the Philistines killed Jonathan, Abinadab, and

Malchishua, Saul's sons" (1 Sam. 31:2). It is a tragedy that Jonathan had to die in the same battle where judgment came upon his father. He was a brave soldier, a man worthy of honor and respect. He died fighting for his God, his country, and his father the king. Saul watched three of his sons die at his feet. Samuel's prophecy is coming true, death after agonizing death. He is all alone with only his armorbearer by his side. The archers are closing in and one by one they pull back their bows and let the arrows fly. "Now the battle became intense against Saul; and the archers hit him, and he was severely wounded by the archers" (vs. 3). He knew he would die from his wounds and that it would be a long and painful death. He also knew how brutal and vicious the Philistines were. When they captured Samson, they gouged out his eyes and mocked him openly. Surely Saul didn't want this to happen to him.

Saul said to his armorbearer, "Draw your sword, and thrust me through with it, lest these uncircumcised men come and thrust me through and abuse me" (vs. 4). The Message Bible says, "Draw your sword and put me out of my misery, lest these pagan pigs come and make a game out of killing me." As Saul is dying, he offers up no prayer of repentance. He was told the previous day that he would die yet he does nothing to prepare his soul to meet God in any way. His heart had become so hardened to sin that he didn't want to repent. Instead, he's more interested in his appearance. He doesn't want to be embarrassed. He doesn't want the enemy to make sport of his body, to gloat over him and parade his body around. Even as he is dying, he is more concerned about his reputation than he is with his character and his relationship with God. He asks his armorbearer, "How do I look? Is my tie on straight? Is my hair combed just right? Do I look good? Great. Now kill me." The armorbearer wouldn't do it so he took a sword and fell on it (vs. 4).

Once again, Saul did things his own way. He committed the abominable act of suicide because he thought it was the best way to serve his ego. British evangelist G. Campbell Morgan said, "Suicide is always the ultimate action of cowardice. In the case of Saul, and in many similar cases, it is perfectly natural; but let it never be glorified as heroic. It is the last resort of the man who dare not stand up to life." Few people have had the potential and the promise Saul had. He was a handsome man, well-liked by the people, and the Spirit of God was upon him. He had everything going for him yet time and time again he disobeyed God and tried to do things his way. He was a man who played the fool and erred exceedingly. He neglected the friendship of Samuel and David, along with Jonathan his son. He often disobeyed God and made religious excuses for doing so. He allowed jealousy and hatred to master and enslave his soul. His last days were filled with fear, terror, and regret. His life personifies the tragedy of a wasted life.

"And when his armorbearer saw that Saul was dead, he also fell on his sword, and died with him" (vs. 5). With Saul now dead, panic spread across the nation. So devastating was this defeat that even those on the other side of the Jordan fled in terror. Mark 14:27 says if you strike the shepherd, the sheep will be scattered. The Philistines crossed over the river and dwelt in those cities, thus cutting Israel in half. The land that rightfully belonged to God's people is now occupied by the enemy. What's more, because of their victory over Israel, the Philistines now believe their god is stronger than their God, the God of Israel. Saul's tragic death gave the Philistines an opportunity to disgrace the name of the Lord. "So it came to pass the next day, when the Philistines came to strip the slain, that they found Saul and his three sons fallen on Mount Gilboa. And they cut off his head and stripped off his armor, and sent word throughout the land of the Philistines, to proclaim it in the temple of their idols and among the people" (vs. 8,9).

The Philistines did not need Saul alive to mock him. Part of the spoils of war was to strip those who were killed of their clothes, weapons, and money. They cut off Saul's head, perhaps in retaliation for Goliath, and put his armor on display in the temple of the fertility goddess Ashtaroth. They then nailed the body of Saul and the bodies of his three sons to the wall of Beth Shan, a wall that sat high on a hill for all to see. It was here that the Philistines hung the headless body of Saul in total humiliation, openly seen by all to mock and ridicule. The very thing Saul didn't want to happen came to pass anyway. In a time of disgrace and loss, God still has valiant men to do His work. The men of Jabesh Gilead heard what happened so they took down the bodies of Saul and his sons from their place of humiliation and gave them a proper burial. They then fasted seven days. It is interesting to note that Saul's first battle as king was to save the men of Jabesh Gilead (1 Sam. 11). His body was burned and buried at the same place his ministry began. Where he started was where he finished.

-21-

"THE MIGHTY HAVE FALLEN"

The death of Saul brought about the end of a tragic life. His reign as king began in humbleness but ended with a bitter heart toward God and man. When he died, he left behind a fractured country with broken ideals. The Philistines are occupying not only the southern area of Israel but they've now infiltrated to the north. They've even won control over Galilee because of their victory over Saul on Mount Gilboa. David knew the Philistines were going to battle against Israel. He knew because he wanted to fight alongside them but was not allowed to do so. Instead, he had to go fight the Amalekites who had burned down his city and taken captive the loved ones of he and his men. As this battle was going on he had no knowledge of what was happening in the war between the Philistines and Israel. Surely, he must have pondered the outcome of that battle. After attending to the business at hand, David and his men, along with their loved ones, return to Ziklag perhaps with thoughts of rebuilding their burned down city.

David is still living among the Philistines but he is now a changed man after he was compelled to strengthen himself in the Lord. Three days later an unexpected quest comes to their camp. He is out of breath and his clothes are torn and there is dust on his head. David knew this was bad news because the messenger had the traditional expressions of one mourning for the dead. In his hands are two strange objects, a crown and a bracelet. "So it was, when he came to David, that he fell to the ground and prostrated himself" (2 Sam. 1:2). David wants to know where the man came from and is told he had just escaped from the camp of Israel. This sparks the interest of David and he says to the man, "How did the matter go? Please tell me" (vs. 4). The messenger answers him, "The people have fled from the battle, many of the people are fallen and dead, and Saul and Jonathan his son are dead also." This news pierced the heart of David. Oh, how he loved Jonathan. He was his best friend, his covenant brother. He even loved and gave great respect to King Saul.

David asks, "How do you know that Saul and Jonathan his son are dead?" (vs. 5). The young man answers, "As I happened by chance to be on Mount Gilboa, there was Saul leaning on his spear; and indeed the chariots and horsemen followed hard after him." Something is wrong here. You don't "by chance" stumble upon a battle scene halfway up a mountain. The Bible says Saul fell on a sword, not a spear. It would be hard to fall on a spear with a long handle. This man probably wasn't even at the battle. What he tells David next is a complete fabrication. He says he found Saul wounded and is asked by the king to kill him. "So I stood over him and killed him, because I was sure that he could not live after he had fallen. And I took the crown that was on his head and the bracelet that was on his arm, and have brought them here to my lord" (vs. 10). This messenger is probably smiling as he says this. He assumes David will be delighted to hear that his enemy is dead. David can now place the crown on his own head and wear it himself, along with the king's bracelet on his arm.

This man is clearly lying to the future king of Israel. 1 Sam. 31:4,5 says Saul committed suicide and that his armorbearer saw that he was dead. This messenger is lying for he hopes to receive a financial reward from David for killing his enemy King Saul. There would be no reward or recognition if Saul was already dead when he found him. Besides, Saul's armorbearer was still alive and surely he wouldn't let this man finish him off. It was only after he knew Saul was dead that he fell on his own sword and died. What actually happened is that this man was the first person to come upon Saul's body. The Philistines didn't come back to take Saul's body until the next day. It was during this time that the messenger found Saul's body and took his crown and bracelet. He then brought them to David in hopes of getting recognition and some kind of reward. He thought David would be happy to hear of Saul's death. He was wrong, dead wrong. "Then David took hold of his own clothes and tore them, and so did all the men who were with him" (vs. 11).

This is a picture of David's greatness. He is in deep anguish and grief as he mourns for the man who hunted him down and tried to kill him several times. Bitterness will poison your soul and this is why David always looked at Saul through the lens of his calling. He was the anointed servant of the Lord, the top leader of the nation. David is weeping because the king of Israel is now dead. One is reminded of when Jesus stood over the city that would in a few days kill Him. He wept and cried aloud saying, "O Jerusalem, Jerusalem, the one who kills the prophets and stones those who are sent to her! How often I wanted to gather your children together, as a hen gathers her chickens under her wings, but you were not willing!" (Matt. 23:37). Jesus lamented as David does here for Saul. How do you respond to a fallen adversary, when those who despise you have a setback in their lives? Prov. 24:17,18 says, "Do not rejoice when your enemy falls, and do not let your heart be glad when he stumbles; Lest the Lord see it, and it displeases Him, and He turns away His wrath from him."

Never seek the downfall of any person for it will not go well for you if you do. Prov. 17:5 says, "He who is glad at calamity will not go unpunished." The Message Bible says, "Gloating over misfortune is a punishable crime." David's response to the death of Saul can be used as a way to measure the degree of bitterness that you might have in your soul toward somebody who is troubling you. Instead of rejoicing if and when they stumble, view that person the way God sees them. See what God sees and feel how God feels. 2 Cor. 5:16 says, "Therefore, from now on, we regard no one according to the flesh." The NLT says, "So we have stopped evaluating others from a human point of view." You can't determine who a person is based on their natural abilities or actions. You view them according to how God views them. It will help if you'll remember that God loves those who have fallen the same way He loves you. He said in Ezek. 33:11, "I have no pleasure in the death of the wicked, but that the wicked turn from his way and live. Turn, turn from your evil ways!"

Saul had stolen the best years of David's life yet David cried and agonized over the death of Saul, and his men did also. They had their own reasons to hate Saul but they followed their leader and wept with him. The throne of Israel is now vacant but David expressed little thought in himself being made king. Instead he mourned for Saul, for Jonathan, and for all the people of Israel who had fallen by the sword. Later that evening he asked the messenger who came to him with this bad news, "Where are you from?" This young man probably thinks David is going to reward him as he answers, "I am the son of an alien, an Amalekite" (vs. 13). This is the worst thing the man could have said. The Amalekites were a terrorist organization and David doesn't like them. These were the people who burned down their city and took captive their wives and children. Sadness turns to anger as David asks, "How was it you were not afraid to put forth your hand to destroy the Lord's anointed?" (vs. 14). It was God's job to end the reign of Saul. Woe to the person who puts forth his hand to destroy a God-appointed leader.

Saul was God's representative and David is saying to the young man he should have known better than to touch the king of Israel. David gives the command to have the messenger executed as he says to him these final words, "Your blood is on your own head, for your own mouth has testified against you, saying, 'I have killed the Lord's anointed'" (vs. 16). This man died for something he didn't even do. He thought it would be to his advantage to lie to David and make himself look good. He thought wrong. This lie got him killed. Prov. 6:2 says, "You are snared by the words of your mouth." It is never to your advantage to lie. Ananias and Sapphira lied to Peter and both fell over dead immediately (Acts 5:1-11). Prov. 6:16-19 lists "a lying tongue" and "a false witness who speaks lies" as two of the seven abominations to the Lord. Over and over again the Bible tells stories of how lying leads to misery, loss, and judgment. Be a person of character and always tell the truth. Ps. 120:2 says, "Deliver my soul, O Lord, from lying lips and from a deceitful tongue."

2 Sam. 1:17 says, "Then David lamented with this lamentation over Saul and over Jonathan his son." David's sorrow is sincere so he writes a song to express how deep his anguish is (vs. 17-22). This song is called "The Song of the Bow," a fitting title because the bow and arrow are symbols of warfare and is a reminder of the wounds one can receive in battle. In this song David praises Jonathan as you would expect him to. Surprisingly, he also praises Saul, the man who hunted him down and tried to kill him for many, many years. Vs. 18 says this song is also found in the Book of Jasher. Also known as the "Book of the Upright One," this book is a collection of ancient Hebrew songs and poems praising the heroes of Israel and their exploits in battle. The Book of Jasher is also mentioned in Josh. 10:13 when the Lord stopped the sun in the middle of the day during the battle of Beth Horon. David wants this song to be taught to the people of Judah (vs. 18). God can use sorrow as a means of teaching valuable lessons to people. Wisdom can be gained from the weeping people do.

David begins his song in vs. 19, "The beauty of Israel is slain on your high places! How the mighty have fallen!" He calls Saul and Jonathan "the beauty of Israel." David had great love for the king of Israel and he saw beauty in Saul. 1 Cor. 13:5 says love "thinks no evil" and 1 Peter 4:8 says, "And above all things have fervent love for one another, for 'love will cover a multitude of sins.'" Through all the years of being hunted by Saul and hiding in caves, David always kept his heart free from bitterness toward this man. He wanted no rejoicing over the death of Saul but rather mourning and weeping. Saul was promoted to the "high places" and he didn't handle it well. The enemy attacks those in high places and this caused Saul to suffer a tragic end to his life. The tragedy that took place in Israel is very great. Not only did ordinary soldiers fall, the mighty fell also. Three times David says, "How the mighty have fallen!" (vs. 19,25,27). Saul fell on Mount Gilboa but the truth is he fell long before this fateful day. He fell the day he hardened his heart against God and His faithful servants Samuel and David.

David wants this song of lamentation to be censored. He doesn't want the death of Saul to become an occasion for the enemies of God to rejoice. Vs. 20 (MSG) says, "Don't announce it in the city of Gath, don't post the news in the streets of Ashkelon. Don't give those coarse Philistine girls one more excuse for a drunken party!" These were the two main cities of the Philistines and David doesn't want these people to brag and gloat over what happened. Some people can't keep quiet when bad things happen, either to themselves or others. Don't wear all your problems on your sleeve for all the world to see. Don't give the ungodly in the world cause to dishonor God and His people. Saul had hunted David like an animal but in this song, David doesn't say one bad word about him. It's as if the memory of what Saul tried to do to him has been erased from his mind. Love keeps no records of wrong done to it (1 Cor. 13:5) and this is what forgiveness is all about. Refusing to keep a record of wrongs done to you is a clear expression of God's love working in your life.

David then curses the mountain Saul died on. Vs. 21 (MSG) says, "No more dew or rain for you, hills of Gilboa, and not a drop from springs and wells, for there the warrior's shields were dragged through the mud, Saul's shield left there to rot." Saul did not come back from the battle. Those who did return would clean their dirty and bloody shields with oil to make them shine again. As David continues his song of lamentation, he focuses on three of Saul's admirable traits. He first praises Saul's courage in battle. "From the blood of the slain, from the fat of the mighty, the bow of Jonathan did not turn back, and the sword of Saul did not return empty" (vs. 22). Saul did some great things early in his reign as king and David focused on this as he gives honor to the king. He wouldn't assassinate Saul with his sword, and now he won't assassinate him with his words. In the eyes of David, Saul and Jonathan were great warriors who fought side by side to the very end. They lived their lives together and they died together. David said, "They were swifter than eagles, they were stronger than lions" (vs. 23).

After telling of Saul's courage and his close relationship with his son Jonathan, David now tells how Saul caused prosperity to come to the nation. "O daughter of Israel, weep over Saul, who clothed you in scarlet, with luxury; Who put ornaments of gold on your apparel" (vs. 24). David is bragging on Saul. Nowhere in this eulogy does David mention Saul's faults and the things that brought his life to a disgraceful end. He's not denying the evil Saul did, he just wants no part in tarnishing his memory. Just like you can always find something negative to say about somebody, so can you find something good to say. Eph. 4:29 (NLT) says, "Don't use foul or abusive language. Let everything you say be good and helpful, so that your words will be an encouragement to those who hear them." The Message Bible says, "Watch the way you talk. Let nothing foul or dirty come out of your mouth. Say only what helps, each word a gift." Watch what you say about people no matter how good or bad they are. Say things that will build them up and not tear them down. Be known as a person who always encourages people.

David next turns his thoughts and words toward Jonathan, one of the greatest men in the Old Testament. "How the mighty have fallen in the midst of the battle! Jonathan was slain in your high places" (vs. 25). Out of all the relationships David had in his life, Jonathan was his greatest friend. He was a person David could always depend on. They sacrificed for one another and were free to express their deepest emotions with each other. "I am distressed for you, my brother Jonathan; You have been very pleasant to me; Your love to me was wonderful, surpassing the love of women" (vs. 26). The Message Bible says, "I'm crushed by your death. Your friendship was a miracle-wonder, love far exceeding anything I've known or ever hope to know." The death of Jonathan was a great tragedy. David talks about his pleasant personality, how he was honest, true, and faithful. His love for David was a superior love. He was David's best friend and they were two men of a kindred spirit. David ends his song by saying, "How the mighty have fallen, and the weapons of war perished!" (vs. 27).

Now that Saul is dead, David's rise to the throne should have gone smoothly because everybody knows he's been anointed to be king. Unfortunately, that didn't happen. Just because you live for God doesn't mean you won't have trials and hardship in your life. You're going against the grain of the rest of the world and your journey upstream will be a rough one filled with many unpleasant experiences. Remember, you're a soldier in the army of the Lord and going to battle is what a soldier does. Nobody knows this better than David. He knows he'll one day be king but he's not going to force his way onto the throne of Israel. Instead, he seeks the will of God. This is the key to success in any person's life. No longer is David making his own plans for he now wants to be in the middle of God's plan. He is still in Ziklag, in the territory of the Philistines. He now wonders if it's time to return to his homeland. He asks the Lord, "Shall I go up to any of the cities of Judah?" (2 Sam. 2:1). The Lord answers and tells him to go up to the city of Hebron.

David didn't leave Ziklag until the Lord told him to. There is value in waiting on the Lord for divine direction. Don't allow the pressures of life to cause you to make decisions in haste without seeking God's will in the matter. David knew the promise for him to be king would soon be fulfilled. Still, he didn't want to seize the throne on his own efforts but chose instead to let God bring it to pass on His terms. He doesn't do anything without inquiring of the Lord first. Jesus said in John 5:30, "I do not seek My own will but the will of the Father who sent Me." It is to the glory of God that He was faithful to answer David even after his time of spiritual decline. God tells David to go to Hebron where he'll be among his own people. "And David brought up the men who were with him, every man with his household. So they dwelt in the cities of Hebron" (vs. 3). Hebron is twenty miles south of Jerusalem in the Judean hills and in Joshua 20 is listed as one of the six cities of refuge. If you accidentally killed somebody you could flee to a city of refuge and get a fair trial. By divine law, nobody could kill you there.

The name "Hebron" comes from the Hebrew word for "friend" referring to Abraham who was called the friend of God (James 2:23). Hebron was one of the first places Abraham resided after his arrival in Canaan. Sarah later died in Hebron so Abraham bought from Ephron the Hittite the field and cave of Machpelah to serve as a family tomb. This cave is known as the Tomb of the Patriarchs (Gen. 23) and is the traditional burial place of Abraham and Sarah, Isaac and Rebecca, and Jacob and Leah. "Then the men of Judah came, and there they anointed David king over the house of Judah" (2 Sam. 2:4). This is the second time David is anointed. Everybody needs a fresh, ongoing experience with the Holy Spirit. The first anointing with Samuel was a private event but this is a public anointing. These elders wanted David to be king because he was from their tribe, the tribe of Judah. Notice also that David did not seize the throne, the elders approached him. Always seek to advance God's kingdom but leave the promotion of yourself in His capable hands.

David is not yet king over the whole nation of Israel but he is the anointed king over one of the twelve tribes, the tribe of Judah. In Deut. 17:14-20, God gave His qualifications for the man who would be Israel's king. First and foremost, he must be chosen by the Lord (vs. 15) and he must be chosen from among his own brethren. He must not multiply horses for himself for he was not to rely on military strength but on the Lord (vs. 16). He must not have multiple wives (vs. 17), a qualification David did not meet because he's already been married three times. Before his story is finished, David will have close to twenty wives. God also said that the king must not greatly multiply silver and gold for himself (vs. 17) for the love of money is a root of all kinds of evil (1 Tim. 6:10). He is to read the Law, study the Law, know the Law, lead by the Law (vs. 18,19). Like David, he should be a man after God's own heart. Finally, his heart is not to be lifted above his brethren (vs. 20) for pride goes before destruction, and a haughty spirit before a fall (Prov. 16:18).

David is now king over the southern region of Israel and the first thing the elders tell him is that the men of Jabesh Gilead were the ones who buried Saul. Why would the elders tell him this? These men were from the northern territory and were very loyal to Saul. How will they respond to David being made king of Judah? David sent messengers to them saying, "You are blessed of the Lord, for you have shown this kindness to your lord, to Saul, and have buried him. And now may the Lord show kindness and truth to you. I also will repay you this kindness, because you have done this thing. Now therefore, let your hands be strengthened, and be valiant; for your master Saul is dead, and also the house of Judah has anointed me king over them" (vs. 5-7). David blesses these men with a covenant love and he tells them to be strong. These men were loyal to Saul and David now wants them to be loyal to him. Surely, he will need brave and valiant men in his kingdom, especially after what happens next.

Even though Saul is now dead, he still has many loyal followers, chief among them is Abner the son of Ner. Abner was Saul's cousin (1 Sam. 14:50) and the commander of Saul's army for many years. This is the man David called out for not protecting Saul when David had the opportunity to kill him. Abner said since Saul is dead, Saul's remaining son Ishbosheth should be king. There is no previous mention of Ishbosheth among the sons of Saul so it's possible he was an illegitimate son or the son of a concubine. He's not a warrior like his three brothers who died with their father on Mount Gilboa. He's a softy, a palace boy, a puppet on a string. Abner takes the forty-year-old Ishbosheth and makes him king over the remaining eleven tribes of Israel (vs. 9). Ishbosheth was not the Lord's anointed like Saul was but Abner makes him king anyway so he could be the real power behind the throne. There is a conflict here because God said David would be the next king. The country of Israel is now divided. The north is following Ishbosheth and the south is following David.

David did nothing to stop Ishbosheth from being made king over the northern tribes. He chose to leave everything in God's hands just like he did concerning the removal of Saul.

He doesn't realize it yet, but it's going to be seven and a half years before he becomes king over all of Israel. Even so, he would not force his reign on anyone but, unfortunately, Abner did not feel the same way. He had aspirations of his own and, like Saul before him, he took matters into his own hands. 2 Sam. 2:12 says he gathered the remains of Saul's army and "went out" to Gibeon which is about seven miles northwest of Jerusalem. This was not a casual going out but an aggressive posture of attack. They went out armed for battle to fight the tribe of Judah. Joab, David's nephew and chief military commander, took his troops and met Abner at the pool of Gibeon, a thirty-foot-wide circular shaft cut into bedrock that was over eighty feet deep. Abner and Joab were both mean, tough military men who were devoted to the cause which they fought for. You wouldn't want to cross paths with either one of them.

Abner sat on one side of the pool and Joab sat on the other side, both daring the other to make the first move. The tension was growing by the second when Abner suggests a duel between twelve of his men and twelve of Joab's men. In the Valley of Elah, Goliath also proposed a duel. He told the army of Israel to choose a man to fight him and the winner would determine the outcome of the battle. Joab thought this was a good idea so they chose twelve of the best warriors from each side and let them fight. "And each one grasped his opponent by the head and thrust his sword in his opponent's side; so they fell down together" (vs. 16). This duel turned into a bloodbath as these warriors butchered each other and all died at the same time. So bloody was this fiasco that they named the place where they fought the Field of Sharp Swords. A fierce battle followed this duel where David's men fought Abner and his men. This was the start of a civil war among God's people that would last many years. This happened at a time when there should have been victory and peace.

-22-

"TIME OF CIVIL WAR"

As twenty-four soldiers lay dead at the pool of Gibeon, killed by the hand of their fellow brethren, the armies of Joab and Abner begin to battle one another. This turns into a bloody civil war, Jews fighting Jews. As the bodies begin to fall, Abner quickly realizes that Joab's men were more skilled in the art of warfare than his own. "So there was a very fierce battle that day, and Abner and the men of Israel were beaten before the servants of David" (2 Samuel 2:17). Scripture goes on to say that David lost twenty men in this battle while Abner lost three hundred and sixty men (vs. 30,31). Abner is being defeated so he and his men turn and retreat from the battle. Joab and his men, along with his two brothers Abishai and Asahel, give chase. Asahel was a fast runner, "as fleet of foot as a wild gazelle" (vs. 18), and he outruns his fellow soldiers as he closes in on Abner. The first century historian Josephus wrote that Asahel, whose name means "made by God," was so fast he could outrun a horse. "So Asahel pursued Abner, and in going he did not turn to the right hand or to the left from following Abner" (vs. 19).

Abner and his men are in full retreat when he turns around and sees a lone figure quickly closing in on him. He thinks he recognizes who it is so he asks, "Are you Asahel?" The man answers, "I am" (vs. 20). Abner pleads with Asahel to turn away because he doesn't want to kill him. Abner is a great fighter and Asahel is a young man with little experience in the art of warfare. Besides that, they're supposed to be on the same side. Abner tells him to kill somebody else and not him for there will be trouble if he tries. "But Asahel would not turn aside from following him" (vs. 21). Young men full of zeal sometimes do stupid things. Abner and Joab know each other and Abner doesn't want to kill his younger brother. He pleads with Asahel a second time to turn away. "However, he refused to turn aside. Therefore Abner struck him in the stomach with the blunt end of the spear, so that the spear came out of his back; and he fell down there and died on the spot. So it was that as many came to the place where Asahel fell down and died, stood still" (vs. 23).

Abner killed Asahel in self-defense. It was the only thing he could do. If he did nothing, he would be the one laying on the ground dead. Justified or not, this act of war will create bad blood between two sides of God's people. It causes a civil war, a war of revenge, to take place in the house of Israel. Joab and his brother Abishai keep chasing Abner. Remember, Abshai was the man who volunteered to sneak into Saul's camp at night with David. Both of these men were fierce, scoundrel-like warriors. The day was drawing to a close when they came to a hill with Abner and his men standing on top of it. A good strategy of warfare is to be on higher ground than your enemy. Abner calls out to Joab asking for the battle to end. He asks, "Are we going to keep killing each other till doomsday? Don't you know that nothing but bitterness will come from this? How long before you call off your men from chasing their brother?" (vs. 26 MSG). It never ends well when there is division among God's people. There will be spiritual separation, hurt, and loss of testimony.

Joab stopped and considered what Abner was saying. Thinking his troops could use the rest, he agrees to the cease-fire but not before saying, "As God lives, if you hadn't spoken up, we'd have kept up the chase until morning!" (vs. 27 MSG). So Joab blew a trumpet made out of ram's horn and all the army of Judah stood still and ceased in their pursuit of Abner and his men. Joab stopped fighting but in his heart he knew that Abner killed his younger brother. He would not forget this and thoughts of revenge filled his mind. He knew that he would forever be looking for the opportunity to kill this man. The fighting stopped, at least for now, and Abner and his soldiers returned to Mahanaim while Joab went to Bethlehem and buried Asahel in his father's tomb. Joab and his men then traveled all night and came to Hebron at daybreak. He was home but he knew the battle was far from over. 2 Sam. 3:1 says, "Now there was a long war between the house of Saul and the house of David. But David grew stronger and stronger, and the house of Saul grew weaker and weaker."

As David's kingdom grew stronger and stronger, his personal family grew bigger and bigger. When he came to Hebron he had two wives, not including Michal, and now he has four more. He would later marry Bathsheba and many other women, this on top of all the concubines he had. A man in those times would show his magnificence by having many wives. It's one way that a king expressed his power and status. Solomon had three hundred wives and seven hundred concubines. It has always been God's will for one man to be married to one wife (Gen. 2:24; Matt. 19:4-6). David went against God's command that Israel's king should not have multiple wives (Deut. 17:17) and he later reaped the penalty for disobeying this command. This was not a good situation for David and it did not produce good fruit. While in Hebron each of David's six wives bore him a son (vs. 2-5). Three of these sons would later become a living nightmare for David. His was a household out of order. Disorder always creates chaos that harms people. In like manner, tornadoes and hurricanes happen when the weather gets out of order.

When there is order, there is peace and harmony. When there is disorder, when you don't apply the order of God's Word to your life, there is chaos and danger. David was a great man of God and he would set the standard by which all the other kings of Israel would be measured. He was a godly man but his fleshly passions often got the best of him and he didn't always make the right decisions. This is why Prov. 4:23 (NLT) says, "Guard your heart above all else, for it determines the course of your life." David will become a good king but he was a poor husband and father and this caused him to have a very dysfunctional family. His son Amnon would later rape his half-sister and get murdered by his half-brother. Absalom led a civil war against his father David and tried to kill him. Adonijah tried to seize the throne from David and his successor. He then tried to take one of David's concubines and was executed for his arrogance. All this happened because David spent no time with his children as they were growing up. He didn't discipline his children and he failed to show them love. The result of such negligence is always chaos.

Chaos was also brewing in the northern kingdom. "Now it was so, while there was war between the house of Saul and the house of David, that Abner was strengthening his hold on the house of Saul" (2 Sam. 3:6). Ishbosheth, the weak-willed son of Saul, is the king of the eleven northern tribes but Abner is the real power behind the throne. He didn't have this power while Saul was alive but with Ishbosheth as king he is now getting stronger and stronger. It was at this time that Ishbosheth accuses Abner of having relations with one of his dead father's concubines (vs. 7). Not only was this a sin of sexual immorality, it was also a crime of high treason. Taking the king's concubine is seen as a gesture of claiming authority over the kingdom for yourself. Ishbosheth is accusing Abner of being a traitor. It is not told if this actually happened but the accusation is made anyway. Naturally, Abner becomes very angry. He asks Ishbosheth, "Am I a dog's head that belongs to David? A traitor? A worthless contemptible dog? Is this the thanks I get for sticking by the house of your father, Saul, and all his family and friends?"

Suddenly, in mid-stream, Abner switches sides. He is so mad that he tells Ishbosheth he will now support David and help him fulfill what God has promised. This is pride talking. Abner is saying, "I made you king, now I'll make David king. I can do whatever I want." No, Abner is not in control, God is. It is He "who works all things according to the counsel of His will" (Eph. 1:11). Yes, one day David will be king over all of Israel and God doesn't need Abner's help to make this happen. For sure, He is the sovereign ruler over all things. Abner knows that God promised the kingdom to David but still he continued on in disobedience until now. Why didn't he obey God from the very beginning when Saul died? A lot of lives could have been spared had he done so. Why do people do wrong when they know they shouldn't do it? Abner's reason is that he craved the power he had with Ishbosheth as king. He did not know what God would later say in Jer. 9:23, "Let not the mighty man glory in his might." He knows David is getting stronger so he reasons to himself, "If you can't beat them, join them."

All over Israel it is a time of civil war. It is a time of division, conflict, death, sorrow, and defeat. The entire nation is in turmoil and this is mankind at its worse. There are weaknesses, anger, sin, pride, and vengeance in the hearts of all the people in this divided nation. Jer. 17:9 (NLT) says, "The human heart is the most deceitful of all things, and desperately wicked. Who really knows how bad it is?" Abner is switching sides but still he has dreams of power and glory. Surely he'll want to be a military commander in David's army. The problem with that is David already has a commander. His name is Joab, the brother of the man Abner had slain with the blunt end of the spear. With Ishbosheth quaking in fear, Abner sends messengers to David saying, "Whose is the land? Make your covenant with me, and indeed my hand shall be with you to bring all Israel to you" (vs. 2). Abner is ready to transfer the eleven tribes over to the authority of David who needs to realize he doesn't need Abner's help to be made king. Even so, David agrees to make a covenant with Abner but first he wants one thing in return.

David said, "Good, I will make a covenant with you. But one thing I require of you: you shall not see my face unless you first bring Michal, Saul's daughter, when you come to see my face" (vs. 13). David received Michal in marriage for killing Goliath but Saul took her away to spite him. She's now married to a second husband but David wants her back anyway. She was his first wife and had the right to be his wife above all the others. In truth, does David need another wife? He's got his hands full with the six wives he already has. Perhaps he wants to see if Abner was sincere in his willingness to help him. Maybe he wants to see if Abner has the power to get Michal for him. Either way, David sent messengers to Ishbosheth telling him to give him Michal. Being a puppet on a string that he was, Ishbosheth did what David asked not realizing that he's helping Abner join forces with David. Michal's husband followed behind them weeping and Abner, strong and powerful as he was, tells him to turn around and go home and he returned (vs. 16). If he stayed and argued with Abner, he surely would have lost his life.

Abner keeps his end of the deal as he rallies support for David among the other tribes. He tells the elders to make David their king for he couldn't reign over them until they submitted to him freely. He said, "In time past you were seeking for David to be king over you. Now then, do it! For the Lord has spoken of David, saying, 'By the hand of My servant David, I will save My people Israel from the hand of the Philistines and the hand of all their enemies'" (vs. 17,18). Once again Abner shows that he knew what the will of the Lord was. The prophecies about David were widely known but not widely obeyed. It was this lack of obedience that plunged the nation into a bloody civil war. Abner then goes and speaks personally to the people of Benjamin. This was the tribe Saul was from and they might be harder to win over than the other tribes. After gaining their support, Abner goes to Hebron where David makes a feast for him and the twenty men who came with him. Abner now considers himself a friend of David. Surely he'll now be made David's right hand man, the second-in-command over all of Israel.

Abner leaves to make preparations to ensure the kingdom goes to David and he is sent away in peace. It was not very long before this that Abner was an adversary of David, the man who led an army against him. Something does not seem right about his motive and intentions for wanting David to be made king over all of Israel. Still, he leaves to gather all Israel together so that David can reign over them. It was at this moment when Joab comes back from a raid with much spoil and he finds out that Abner had spoken to David. He becomes very angry because this was the man who killed his brother. He goes straight to David and says to him, "What have you done? What do you think you're doing? This guy is an enemy!" He tells David that Abner's only motive for coming to see him was "to know your going out and your coming in, and to know all that you are doing" (vs. 25). He accuses Abner of being a spy working on behalf of Ishbosheth in order to deceive David. Joab also thinks to himself, "This guy is trying to take my place." Overcome with a spirit of vengeance and pride, Joab decides to take matters into his own hands.

Unknown to David, Joab sends messengers to Abner and tells him to return to Hebron. He must have been told David wants to see him for this is the only reason he'd come back. Joab feels justified in what he is about to do. When vengeance consumes a person's heart, all sound reasoning flees and is not considered. Only one thing is on his mind and he will not be deterred from what he plans to do. "Now when Abner had returned to Hebron, Joab took him aside in the gate to speak with him privately, and there stabbed him in the stomach, so that he died for the blood of Asahel his brother" (vs. 27). Joab took Abner outside the gate of Hebron because this was a city of refuge and it was against the law to kill anybody inside the city limits. Joab knew Abner killed his brother in self-defense, in an act of war, but he murdered him anyway. Joab's thirst for revenge did not justify what he did. Charles Spurgeon once said, "We may even deceive ourselves into the belief that we are honoring our Lord and Master when we are, all the while, bringing disgrace upon His name."

David had no part in this gruesome act and when he found out about it he pronounced a severe curse on Joab and his family. "Before God I and my kingdom are totally innocent of this murder of Abner son of Ner. Joab and his entire family will always be under the curse of this bloodguilt. May they forever be victims of crippling diseases, violence, and famine" (vs. 28,29 MSG). The NLT says, "May the family of Joab be cursed in every generation with a man who has open sores or leprosy or who walks on crutches or dies by the sword or begs for food!" David doesn't want anybody to think he's responsible for Abner's murder. By cursing Joab, he's saying what he did was wrong and he doesn't want to be connected to this diabolical act. David cursed Joab but he took no action to punish him for what he did. Perhaps he didn't want to lose Joab as commander of his troops. He was not a nice man but you wanted him on your side in time of war. What he did do is demand that Joab and all the people with him openly mourn the death of Abner (vs. 31).

"So they buried Abner in Hebron; and the king lifted up his voice and wept at the grave of Abner, and all the people wept" (vs. 32). David leads the mourning for Abner because he does not want his kingdom established by violence. He believes that vengeance belongs to the Lord and he then sings a lamenting song for Abner, another song for the dead. "Should Abner die as a fool dies? Your hands were not bound nor your feet put into fetters; As a man falls before wicked men, so you fell" (vs. 33,34). What a song to sing at a warrior's funeral. Should Abner die as a fool? He was a fool. Like Saul before him, Abner only lived to serve his own interests and he died "like a nameless bum" (MSG). After this song the people wept over Abner all over again. David is too sad to eat and the people now know he had no part in the death of Abner. If David had not acted properly this day, the people surely would have rebelled thus creating another civil war that never would have ended. David then calls Abner a great man when in truth he was a power-seeking scoundrel, a man of pride.

Then David said to his servants, "Do you not know that a prince and a great man has fallen this day in Israel?" He commends Abner the same way he did Saul. No matter how bad these men were, David always found something good to say about them. The words that come out of your mouth need to build up and not tear down. You can always find something good to say about people. Ignore the bad and focus on the good. David continues, "And I am weak today, though anointed king; and these men, the sons of Zeruiah, are too harsh for me. The Lord shall repay the evildoer according to his wickedness" (vs. 39). Vengeance belongs to the Lord (Rom. 12:19) so always let God deal with evil in His own way. Justice will get done for what a man sows, he will reap (Gal. 6:7). Many years later, when David was about to die, he tells his son Solomon to have Joab killed for his past betrayals and the blood he was guilty of shedding. Solomon then ordered his death and Joab died at the hands of a man named Benaiah (1 Kings 2:29-34). Eventually justice gets served.

As life goes on, you can have the assurance that God is always at work behind the scenes so that ultimately His will gets done on the earth. All rebellion against God's will must in the end submit and give way to the glory of God. Ps. 76:10 says, "Surely the wrath of man shall praise You."

Man's wicked fury and hostility will give occasion for great deeds to be done on behalf of the will of God. When all is said and done, circumstances will show that the enemy was able to bring nothing to pass for God will bridle their rage so that they will not accomplish their evil purpose. For the moment, Ishbosheth is still king of the eleven northern tribes and when he "heard that Abner had died in Hebron, he lost heart, and all Israel was troubled" (2 Sam. 4:1). Ishbosheth doesn't know what to do now that Abner is dead. He was the king but Abner was the leader, the force behind the throne. Ishbosheth was a weak man because he trusted in a man more than in the living God. He knows his day as king is about over and those under his rule know it also.

Ishbosheth had an army under him but he had no loyalty among his troops. Their loyalty was to Abner and now that he is dead the weakness of Ishbosheth is fully exposed. His soldiers want no part in serving a king who was as weak as a rabbit. Two brothers, Bacnah and Rechab, were captains in the northern army but they were not of the Jewish bloodline. Their forefather Beeroth was a Canaanite who lived in the Promised Land when Joshua and the children of Israel entered in (Josh. 18:25). He lived in the land that was given to the tribe of Benjamin and began to live and dwell among the Jewish people there. "Then the sons of Rimmon the Beerothite, Rechab and Baanah, set out and came at about the heat of the day to the house of Ishbosheth, who was lying on his bed at noon. And they came there, all the way into the house, as though to get wheat, and they stabbed him in the stomach. Then Rechab and Baanah his brother escaped. For when they came into the house, he was lying on his bed in his bedroom; then they struck him and killed him, beheaded him and took his head, and were all night escaping through the plain" (vs. 5-7).

Baanah and Rechab kill Ishbosheth as he was taking his midday rest and they cut off his head. English Bible commentator John Trapp said in the seventeenth century, "To sleep at noon, and without a guard, speaketh him both sluggish and secure. He died therefore in his sloth, who had lived slothfully all his days." These two brothers know David is getting stronger and stronger. They want to get on his good side so they bring the head of King Ishbosheth to him as proof that they killed him. Ishbosheth was not a good leader but he was not a bad man. He just happened to be Saul's son and got caught up in the evil scheme of Abner's choosing. This good man was killed by these two evil brothers who said to David in Hebron, "Here is the head of Ishbosheth, the son of Saul your enemy, who sought your life; and the Lord has avenged my lord the king this day of Saul and his descendants" (vs. 8). They said, "We are God's servants, defeating your enemies as instruments of God." They were proclaiming they had God's approval for what they did, as if they acted on direct orders from Him.

Throughout history, many evil things have been done in the name of God, things He had nothing to do with. This is one of those times. Baanah and Rechab tell David that through their actions God has given him vengeance on Saul his enemy. These two men underestimated David's loyalty to God and to the house of Saul. He never thought of Saul as his enemy and he even made a pledge to honor and preserve his family and descendants. It did not sit well with David as he looked at the severed head of Ishbosheth in the hands of these two men. In no way would David accept their evil deed even though it seemed to be for a good purpose. G. Campbell Morgan said, "While it is true that God overrules all the doings of men, and compels them ultimately to serve His high purposes, it is equally true that no servant of His can ever consent to do evil that good may come. It's an arresting truth that our Lord, in the days of His earthly life, would not accept the testimony of demons." These wicked men just killed a good man for the purpose of personal gain. They can't get away with this

Baanah and Rechab were not soldiers fighting for David, they were murderers who deserve to die. David tells them what he did to the Amalekite who said he killed Saul. He then says, "How much more, when wicked men have killed a righteous person in his own house on his bed? Therefore, shall I not now require his blood at your hand and remove you from the earth?" (vs. 11). David swiftly makes an example of these men for he wants to keep his conscience void of offense toward God and man. "So David commanded his young men, and they executed them, cut off their hands and feet, and hanged them by the pool in Hebron. But they took the head of Ishbosheth and buried it in the tomb of Abner in Hebron" (vs. 12). These men used their hands and feet to shed innocent blood so David cut them off. Prov. 6:17,18 says God hates "hands that shed innocent blood, a heart that devises wicked plans, feet that are swift in running to evil." It is God's will that you live righteously in this fallen world. He wants you to "provide people with a glimpse of good living and of the living God" (Phil. 2:15 MSG).

-23-

"CITY ON A HILL"

It is a time of great transition in Israel. Saul and Jonathan are dead and so is Abner and Ishbosheth. David is ruling in Hebron over the tribe of Judah while the northern kingdom has collapsed. Their leaders have been killed and there is disarray, chaos, and division in the government. For five and a half years the eleven northern tribes have been without a king. Then one day "all the tribes of Israel came to David in Hebron" (2 Sam. 5:1). These were the same people who stood beside Saul as he chased David and tried to kill him. They've been resisting him for many, many years but now they come to him because there is nobody else to turn to. Surely they should have come to David outright and not when their other choices crumbled and fell. 1 Chron. 12:23-40 says 339,600 people came to David at this time. The elders of these people knew in times past that the incoming king would purge and execute all those who resisted him along with their loved ones. They brought such a vast number of people with them thinking David couldn't kill them all.

As a way of greeting, the elders say to David, "Indeed we are your bone and your flesh" (vs. 1). This is why civil war is so bad. They were brothers who all came from father Abraham. They were God's people fighting one another making this one of the darkest periods in Israel's history. Instead of unity, there was civil war. It is the cunning plan of the devil to get believers to fight and argue among themselves. If there is division in the church, the people won't have the wherewithal to fight the real enemy who is

Satan himself. A great multitude of people stood before David but still he had the upper hand because God was on his side. How will he respond to what they're about to say to him? The greatest indicator of one's personal maturity is how well you handle authority, power, and influence. How do you act and respond if you're the most powerful person in the room, when all the eyes of those around you are focused on you and you alone? There is nothing more disturbing than when a person of power uses their authority for their own benefit to the neglect of the people they're responsible for.

David had always been destined to be great. Eight hundred years earlier Jacob, just prior to his death, spoke a prophetic blessing over his son Judah. He said in Gen. 49:8, "Judah, you are he whom your brothers shall praise; Your hand shall be on the neck of your enemies; Your father's children shall bow down before you." Vs. 9 (MSG) says, "You're a lion's cub, Judah, home fresh from the kill, my son. Look at him, crouched like a lion, king of beasts; who dares mess with him?" David is from the tribe of Judah and standing before these elders he is bold and has great confidence in God. He listens as the elders continue to speak, "Also, in time past, when Saul was king over us, you were the one who led Israel out and brought them in; and the Lord said to you, 'You shall shepherd My people Israel, and be ruler over Israel'" (vs. 2). The elders openly acknowledge the hand of God upon David's life. They knew David was supposed to be king so why did they follow Ishbosheth? Why didn't they make David king when Saul died? Defeated, they now want to unite under David's authority.

David was once a shepherd boy watching over his father's flocks in Bethlehem. Now he's going to shepherd the people of Israel. He's going to love them and nurture them. He's going to watch over them and protect them from the lions and bears and giants of life. He is also going to rule over them. The best rulers are always shepherds, those who have a loving heart, one who rules by serving and serves by ruling. This is David, the shepherd king of Israel. Saul was a ruler but he was not a shepherd. On the other hand, some people may be good caregivers but not show much leadership skills. In government you need both, skillful leadership as well as skillful caring for the people. These elders recognize David has both these qualities and they know he can unify the nation and heal the wounds between the north and the south. There comes a time when the Lord causes the value of your past work for Him to come to light and be seen by others, especially God's people. This will happen when you realize that everything that happens must be in accordance to God's will and His timing.

"So all the elders of Israel came to the king at Hebron, and King David made a covenant with them at Hebron before the Lord" (vs. 3). At this moment, David shows his true greatness. He applies everything he's learned in the wilderness. He shows extraordinary maturity that he gained all those years running and hiding from King Saul. What did he do? He made a covenant with these people before the Lord. He made promises to them, something he didn't have to do. He didn't allow bitterness to consume him. James 2:13 says, "Mercy triumphs over judgment." On this day, David was wise as a serpent and gentle as a dove. He was the king even without the crown. His word is law and on this day he is the most powerful person in the nation. He's facing a group of elders who did not support him when he was on the run from Saul. He could have had every one of them put to death and nobody would have blinked an eye. Instead of doing that, he made a covenant with them, an oath that was both sacred and serious. Why?

At this time there is no king over the northern tribes. David could have forced these people to submit to him and make him king but he didn't do that. He instead waited for God to make it happen. In Hebron, the elders of Judah came to him

(2 Sam. 2:4) and here the elders of the remaining tribes also come to him. This is important. David never demanded his position of authority over these people. He wasn't being passive about it, he just chose to let God make it happen. Now, on this day, it was all coming together so David made a covenant with these people "before the Lord." David recognized that he would be a king under the authority of God. In his wisdom, David saw the big picture of God's ultimate plan. His graciousness was rooted in his revelation of God's heart toward him and this is what would cause the nation to prosper. He submitted himself to God's law which meant that as a leader he was submitting himself to the people over which he would rule. Even though he was a king, he knew that God was the true King of Israel.

David learned that leadership is a stewardship. When you're the most powerful person in the room, you use your power for the benefit of the other people in the room. Jesus washed the feet of the disciples and told you to do likewise. If you're a person of authority, look for some feet to wash. If you're a Christian, if Jesus is Lord of your life, this is what is required of you. Imagine what the world would be like if everybody lived this way. David stood by these people in spite of their failures just like God stood by him in his failures. He was generous to those who opposed him. Twice he spared the life of Saul when he had the chance to kill him. He now makes a covenant with the northern tribes because he wants everybody to be equally yoked in the vision God mandated to him. The word "division" means 'two visions' and David insisted they all follow the same vision. Amos 3:3 asks, "Can two walk together, unless they are agreed?" This covenant increased their loyalty to him and impacted the way they would serve with him.

"So they anointed David king over Israel" (vs. 3). This is the third time David is anointed and 1 Chron. 12:39,40 describes the joyfulness of the occasion, "And they were there with

David three days, eating and drinking, for their brethren had prepared for them. Moreover those who were near to them, from as far away as Issachar and Zebulun and Naphtali, were bringing food on donkeys and camels, on mules and oxen - provisions of flour and cakes of figs and cakes of raisins, wine and oil and oxen and sheep abundantly, for there was joy in Israel." This was one big celebration of extravagant proportions. On this day the people were saying to David, "It's your time now!" David had held on to his calling with faith and patience and now his dream was fulfilled. Like David, you need to see yourself as a leader. The call to leadership is found in all ages, in all seasons of life, and all spheres of influence. You can be a leader in life even if you're not the boss of the company you work for. Anybody can be a leader, from teenagers to those nearly a hundred years old.

You can rejoice knowing that God's call on your life supersedes whatever limitations you may have. It eclipses all of your inadequacies. It's bigger than all your past failures and mistakes, it's stronger than all your shortcomings. Leadership is not confined to your age or your job status, or if you're married or single. Leadership is meant to be used by God in every sphere of life. David will soon set out to change the atmosphere of the nation. He wants to bring revival to the land, an awakening to the goodness of God. He wants to change the culture of the land for under Saul the nation was spiritually dead. The people weren't worshiping God and they weren't reading the scriptures. Likewise, it is your time to take authority of the atmosphere God has placed you in and shift it back to Him. 2 Sam. 5:4,5 says David was thirty years old when he became king over Judah. He reigned in Hebron seven and a half years and after that all of Israel for thirty-three years for a total of forty years. Saul before him also reigned forty years as did Solomon after him. The first three kings of Israel each reigned forty years.

The Shepherd King

David is now king over all of Israel and his first recorded act was that he captured Jerusalem and made it the capital city of Israel. This was one of David's greatest accomplishments because of the eternal significance involved. Jerusalem was close to the border between the north and the south. It was and always will be the most important city in all the world. It used to be called "Salem" meaning "peace" but was later named "Jerusalem" which means "Jehovah's Peace." It's the place where God told Abraham to offer his son Isaac to Him as a burnt offering. It's the city where Jesus died on the cross, the place where Jesus will set up His throne at His second coming. David loves Jerusalem as does the Lord. Ps. 87:2 (NLT) says, "He loves the city of Jerusalem more than any other city in Israel." Jerusalem sits on a hill and there are valleys all around it. It was hard to conquer Jerusalem because you had to charge up a hill to do so. You'd be an open target for the archers who fired their arrows from the walls around the city. There is no safe way to attack a city on a hill.

Ps. 125:2 says, "As the mountains surround Jerusalem, so the Lord surrounds His people from this time forth and forever." These mountains were a great fortification from attack. Walls could be built on the slopes that surrounded the city and this would stop an invasion from the enemy. It was also strategic to move to Jerusalem because of the water source. Not a lot of rain fell but there was an underwater spring called the Gilion Spring. Coming out of the ground was cool, fresh water and this is what made human settlement in Jerusalem possible. This spring was not only used for drinking water but also for the irrigation of gardens and the adjacent Kidion Valley that provided food for the people who lived there. Jerusalem is built on two hills, Mount Moriah and Mount Zion, and the water supply for the city was in the valley between these two hills. The people built a tunnel through the rocks, later to be known as

"Hezekiah's Tunnel." This tunnel led to the Gilion Spring and this is where the people got their water. As David moves to take command of this city, a critical, eternal event is taking place.

In the Old testament, God always wanted a place where His glorious presence could dwell. Deut. 12:5 says, "But you shall seek the place where the Lord your God chooses, out of all the tribes, to put His name for His habitation; and there you shall go." God would later say in 2 Chron. 6:6, "But I have chosen Jerusalem, that My name may be there; and I have chosen David to be over My people Israel." The children of Israel had been in the land of Canaan for almost five hundred years but still Jerusalem was not under their authority. The city was controlled by the idol-worshiping Jebusites. They live in a fortified city and they think David is no threat to them. They mock him saying, "You shall not come in here; but the blind and the lame will repel you" (2 Sam. 5:6). The Jebusites who lived there thought their city was so invincible that even the blind and the lame could keep David and his men out. They had convinced themselves that David couldn't break through the walls surrounding the city. What they didn't realize is that the water shaft leading down to the spring was the one weak link in the city.

David realizes that people on the outside can get into the city by climbing up this fifty to a hundred foot long water shaft. He then puts forth a challenge to his men, saying, "Whoever climbs up by way of the water shaft and defeats the Jebusites shall be chief and captain over my army" (vs. 8). 1 Chron. 11:6 says David's nephew Joab, the man who killed Abner, accepts this challenge. He and his men climb up this narrow, wet, slimy shaft and captured the city. They persisted through difficult circumstances to defeat an overconfident enemy. Territory that should have been controlled by Israel long ago is now conquered. Jerusalem is now David's capital city. "So David dwelt in the stronghold and called it the City of David" (vs. 9). Forty times in the Old Testament, Jerusalem is referred to as the City of David. No other city in the Bible is called by that name until Luke 2:4 where Bethlehem is called by the same name. Luke reminds his readers that David didn't come from a place of great power but from a little town known as least of all the cities of Judah (Matt. 2:6).

"So David went on and became great, and the Lord God of hosts was with him" (vs. 10). David knew greatness but by no means was he an overnight success. Samuel anointed him when he was a teenager and he spent approximately fifteen years in preparation for the throne. It is a fact that there is a price to pay for greatness. Often those who become great in God's kingdom will experience much pain and difficulty in the training camp of spiritual development. David was God's representative on the earth and he came to the place of greatness because God was with him. He was a man after God's own heart and he knew the kingdom belonged to Him. Yes, he made many mistakes, several really, but down in his heart was the continual desire to abide in the presence of God. He had a relational intimacy with God that opened his heart to all that God had planned for his life. Many times he got off course. He stumbled, he fell, but God was always there to pick him up. Eventually he always found himself back on the path God wanted him to be on.

David is now precisely where God wants him to be. He's in the city of God, the stronghold of Zion (vs. 7). Ps. 87:1-3 says, "His foundation is in the holy mountains. The Lord loves the gates of Zion more than all the dwellings of Jacob. Glorious things are spoken of you, O city of God!" The Message Bible says, "He founded Zion on the Holy Mountain - and oh, how God loves His home! Loves it far better than all the homes of Jacob put together! God's hometown - oh!

Everyone there is talking about you!" God continues to bless David. "Then Hiram king of Tyre sent messengers to David, and cedar trees, and carpenters and masons. And they built David a house" (vs. 11). This shows David's influence and importance. A neighboring king north of Israel honors him with the finest craftsmen and wood to build him a palace. This royal palace was built on Mount Zion on the southeast side of the city on a plot of ground eleven acres big. It overlooked the city and David could see the city spread out before him. This palace on Mount Zion became the seat of power in David's kingdom.

"So David knew that the Lord had established him as king over Israel, and that He had exalted his kingdom for His people Israel's sake" (vs. 12). It was not for David's sake that he became king, it was for the sake of the people of Israel. At first, David was anointed to bring pleasure to God who said to Samuel in 1 Sam. 16:1, "For I have provided Myself a king among his sons." Here, in vs. 12, David is anointed to benefit the people. God is going to use him as a channel to bless His people. David also knows that it was God who made him king. John the Baptist once said, "A man can receive nothing unless it has been given to him from heaven" (John 3:27). If heaven gives something to you, the devil can't take it away. David then, however, took something heaven did not give him. Vs. 13 says, "And David took more concubines and wives from Jerusalem." He had many sons with these women, among them Nathan and Solomon (vs. 14). Through Nathan came Mary, the mother of Jesus, and through Solomon came Joseph, the husband of Mary. Jesus was related to David through both his mother and His adoptive earthly father.

Once again, David disobeyed the command given in Deut. 17:17, "Neither shall he multiply wives for himself, lest his heart turn away." Some people might see having this many wives and children as a blessing in disguise. It's not. Far from it. Most of the trouble David would later experience came from his relationships with women and from his children. Never let your guard down during good times. It is a fact of life that future troubles often come from what is sown in times of great prosperity and success. If you're not careful, what you do in good times can bring about your downfall in latter times. David's troubles from within his family would come later but his success now will bring new challenges from the outside. Unknown to him, the Philistines are mad. They thought David was on their side and here he is king over all of Israel. The Philistines had settled in the south, defeated Saul in the north, and now they're ready to battle David. When David was king over Judah, he never attacked the Philistines and they never attacked him. David is now king over all of Israel and they want to take him out before he gets deeply rooted in his kingship.

David was one of the greatest warriors to ever walk the planet. A great call was placed on his life when Samuel poured the anointing oil on his head when he was still a young lad. From that day forward, he went out to defend the honor of his God. Throughout his ministry, the storms of life raged against him but he was able to stand strong in the heat of battle because he knew the Lord was always with him. "Now when the Philistines heard that they had anointed David king over Israel, all the Philistines went up to search for David" (vs. 17). The Philistines arrived and spread out across the Valley of Rephaim which was one mile southwest of Jerusalem. They reason it's only a matter of time before David wipes them out so they're here to kill him before that can happen. As they mobilize their troops for battle, David goes to God in prayer. He inquired of the Lord, "Shall I go up against the Philistines? Will You deliver them into my hand?" (vs. 19). God honored David's dependence on Him and gave him the promise of victory. He said, "Go up, for I will doubtless deliver the Philistines into your hand" (vs. 19).

Full of confidence, David goes out and defeats the Philistines with an overwhelming force, like a breakthrough of water. He said in vs. 20 (NLT), "The Lord did it! He burst through my enemies like a raging flood!" David called the name of that place Baal Perazim which means "Master of Breakthroughs." In David's eyes, God would always be the Lord of the Breakthrough. This is why he could write in Ps. 23:4,5, "Yes, though I walk through the valley of the shadow of death, I will fear no evil; For You are with me; Your rod and Your staff, they comfort me. You prepare a table before me in the presence of my enemies; You anoint my head with oil; My cup runs over." David was a man after God's own heart and this was his greatest strength. He wrote in Ps. 34:4, "I sought the Lord, and He heard me, and delivered me from all my fears." In vs. 8 he wrote, "Oh, taste and see that the Lord is good; Blessed is the man who trusts in Him." It is no surprise that the Philistines brought their idols to the battle, thinking they would help them defeat the Israelites. They left the idols there and David and his men burned them (1 Chron. 14:12).

If getting defeated by David wasn't enough, the Philistines decide they want to fight him a second time. After recovering from their wounds, they once again return to the same Valley of Rephaim. Knowing what brought him success the first time, David again inquires of the Lord, asking what he should do. God always gives guidance and supernatural direction but so often in life His help is not asked for. Due to a lack of faith, people don't seek God's help because they don't believe He'll give it to them. British theologian Adam Clark said this happens "because they are under a refined spirit of atheism, and have no spiritual intercourse with their Maker." David always had fellowship with the Lord, excluding the sixteen months he spent with the Philistines, and sure enough, God once again gives him the answer he's looking for. This time, however, God gave him a different strategy. Even against the same enemy, not every battle is the same.

Instead of attacking the enemy head on, the Lord said to "circle around behind them, and come upon them in front of the mulberry trees" (vs. 23).

"So it shall be, when you hear the sound of marching in the tops of the mulberry trees, then you shall advance quickly. For then the Lord will go out before you to strike the camp of the Philistines" (vs. 24). At this battle, David waited for the Lord to strike the enemy's camp first before he made his move. Ancient rabbis believed it was the celestial footsteps of angels walking along the top of the mulberry trees that made the sound David needed to hear. This was the sign for David and his men to rise up and fight. At the signal that God was at work, David rushed forward and won a great victory. "And David did so, as the Lord commanded him; and he drove back the Philistines from Geba as far as Gezer" (vs. 25). Here is the key to success. Do what the Lord tells you to do! Trust Him, obey Him, and He will give you the victory. This is what will cause Jesus to say to you one day, "Well done, good and faithful servant; you have been faithful over a few things, I will make you ruler over many things. Enter into the joy of your lord" (Matt. 25:23).

-24-

"WITH ALL HIS MIGHT"

David is now king over the entire nation of Israel. Saul is dead, the civil war is over, and now he tries to unite the nation through the worship of God. Worship is all about putting God first. Jesus said in Matt. 4:4, "You shall worship the Lord your God, and Him only you shall serve." Worship is to glorify and exalt God, to show your loyalty to Him and your admiration for Him. It reminds you that He is bigger and more powerful than anything and everything in your life, whether good or bad. Worship will change your life and the way you look at the world. You'll be so overwhelmed by how good God has been to you that it will affect the way you treat people and how you do business. It will motivate you to live your life for the glory of God. Rom. 12:1 (NLT) says, "And so, dear brothers and sisters, I plead with you to give your bodies to God because of all He had has done for you. Let them be a living and holy sacrifice - the kind He will find acceptable. This is truly the way to worship Him." David knew that for the people to be unified, the God of heaven must be glorified.

God meant everything to David. Ps. 42:1,2 says, "As the deer pants for the water brooks, so pants my soul for You, O God. My soul thirsts for God, for the living God." David's main desire in life was to worship God which is how one expresses the worth God has in their life. He wants Jerusalem to be known as the City of God, the center of worship and the religious capital of the nation. During the reign of Saul, the people of Israel lost their reverence, respect, and fear of God. David wants to change all that so he decides to bring the Ark of the Covenant to Jerusalem.

The ark, which means "box" or "chest," was a wooden box covered with gold and on its golden lid was the mercy seat where the presence of God would be manifested. When God told Moses to build the ark, He was saying, "I want to be in your midst." Not once did Saul make an attempt to bring the ark to his capital city because he did not have a heart for God. He was a man of the flesh and he wanted to be the center of attention, not God. He had no desire to have a place where all the people could gather together and worship God.

God gave the Ark of the Covenant to Israel as a symbol of His presence. It was a thing of beauty, blessing, and security. It gave you a sense of belonging as you were able to identify with the great God of the universe. Israel, unfortunately, has not possessed the ark for over seventy years. It was last seen in the house of Abinadab in 1 Sam. 7:1,2 where it has been for the past twenty years. His house was less than ten miles from Jerusalem and David decides to go there and get it. He considered it a high priority to bring the ark out of obscurity and back into prominence. By bringing the ark to Jerusalem, this city on a hill will become the home of God on the earth. It will be the spiritual center of the entire planet for the ark was the literal place where God manifested His glory. For the occasion an elaborate celebration was planned. "Again David gathered all the choice men of Israel, thirty thousand" (2 Sam. 6:1). There were musicians there, as well as singers and dancers. The Ark of the Covenant was coming to Jerusalem and all the people were going to shout and sing and dance joyfully.

Music is important to worship for it draws your emotions out of you. If your love for God is true and sincere, you won't be able to keep it bottled up inside of you. Cymbals and tambourines and other instruments will be played loudly for this is going to be a glorious celebration, a time of happiness and good cheer. Bringing the ark to Jerusalem is a huge, significant moment for the people of Israel. This is a national gathering for a glorious event. David and all the people are excited because the manifested glory of God is coming to the city. When they got to Abinadab's house they loaded the ark onto a new cart and headed for Jerusalem (vs. 3). Two of Abinadab's sons who had lived with the ark all this time went with them. Ahio drove the ox cart and Uzzah walked beside it. "Then David and all the house of Israel played music before the Lord on all kinds of instruments made of fir wood, on harps, on stringed instruments, on tambourines, on sistrums, and on cymbals" (vs. 5). Little did they know that God was about to rain on their parade.

The exact requirements regarding the ark were given to Moses on Mount Sinai in Ex. 25:10-22. When Moses went up there, the very first instructions God gave him was regarding the Ark of the Covenant. That alone shows the significance of the ark when it came to worshiping God. He told Moses how to build it and how to carry it. With God, detail is important and this is why He gave very clear and strict instructions on how to handle the ark. It was to be covered when moving so no one would look at it, touch it, or defile it. God said the ark was to be carried with poles on the shoulders of four Levites from the family of Koath, two in front and two in back. On the four bottom corners of the ark were four gold rings put there to accommodate the poles. No where in these detailed instructions did God say anything about a cart. The Philistines transported the ark on a cart in 1 Sam. 6:10,11 and got away with it because they were Philistines. God expects more from His people. He wants His people to follow Him and not the example of the world. The world says put the ark on a cart, God said to carry it on poles.

The presence of God was on its way to Jerusalem and a great celebration is taking place. In heaven, music is continually playing around the throne of God. What's happening here is worship on earth as it is in heaven. Loud, jubilant music is being played. Singing and dancing is taking place all around. On the surface, things appear to be going wonderful just like David hoped it would. They were all very sincere but they were sincerely wrong. God is a holy God and you must respect Him, His word, His will, and His ways. In other words, you must always do things on His terms. Thirty thousand people were singing and shouting and dancing but because of the sin of ignorance it was all done in vain. Suddenly, at the threshing floor of Nachon, the oxen that were pulling the cart stumbled. Instinctively, Uzzah reached out to steady the ark and touched it. "Then the anger of the Lord was aroused against Uzzah, and God struck him there for his error; and he died there by the ark of God" (vs. 7). The Message Bible says, "God blazed in anger against Uzzah and struck him hard because he had profaned the Chest."

Does God ever get angry? You better believe it. There are people who assume that since God is a God of love, He never gets angry. They probably never read Is. 30:27 (NLT), "Look! The Lord is coming from far away, burning with anger, surrounded by thick smoke; His lips are full of fury, and His tongue is like a devouring fire." Willful and habitual sin provokes God to a righteous anger which is justified when His holiness is disrespected and when there is a violation of His character. He is forever righteous, just, and holy and none of these attributes can be compromised. You can't play games with sin and expect to survive the experience. This is why Heb. 10:31 says, "It is a terrible thing to fall into the hands of the living God." Aaron's sons Abihu and Nadab were destroyed by fire when they offered a profane sacrifice in the tabernacle, a sign of their disregard for the holiness of God and the need to honor Him in reverence and holy fear. Jesus got angry with the religious teachers and leaders of that day for using religion for their own gain and keeping the people in bondage.

Ps.7:11 says, "God is a just God, and God is angry with the wicked every day." The Message Bible says, "God in solemn honor does things right, but His nerves are sandpapered raw." This goes along with Rom. 1:18 (NLT), "But God shows His anger from heaven against all sinful, wicked people who suppress the truth by their wickedness." You don't think God gets angry? Deut. 4:24 says, "For the Lord your God is a consuming fire, a jealous God." God's holiness is the reason for Him being a fire that utterly consumes and destroys, a fire that burns up anything unholy. The good news is you don't have to fear this consuming fire of God's wrath if you are born again and covered by the purifying blood of Christ. The grace of God is a wonderful message but you still can't play games with sin. Gal. 6:7 says, "Do not be deceived, God is not mocked; for whatever a man sows, that he will also reap." Vs. 8 (NLT) says, "those who live only to satisfy their own sinful nature will harvest decay and death from that sinful nature. But those who live to please the Spirit will harvest everlasting life from the Spirit."

Too many people have a faulty concept of who God is. He is a good God but, more than that, He is a holy God. The four living creatures in front of the throne in heaven do not rest from saying night and day, "Holy, holy, holy, Lord God Almighty, Who was and is and is to come!" (Rev. 4:8). On the surface, what happened to Uzzah seems like an exceeding, severe penalty for a well-meaning yet unlawful act. God knew Uzzah meant well but He couldn't overlook His disobedience. The nation under David was being established at this time and God couldn't let the people think they could sin and get away with it. God is using this disaster to bring David and the people to a better and deeper understanding of who He really is. He is laying a foundation of holiness and not foolishness. By touching the ark, something God said not to do, Uzzah was showing a lack of respect for the majesty of God as symbolized by the ark.

Matthew Henry wrote in his commentary, "Let none think the worse of the gospel for the judgments on those that reject it, but consider the blessings it brings to all those who receive it."

The presence of God can be awesome, or it can be awful. The problem this day is that the people wanted the presence of God without the holiness of God. Uzzah and all the people there with him were unaware of their own sinfulness. God's message throughout the entire Bible is the seriousness of sin. People don't understand this message because they don't want to understand it. It's a crucial message but people are offended by it. They hate it and are insulted when they're told they're doing something wrong. This doesn't change the fact that sin is serious because it separates you from God. Many people are in denial over this and falsely believe the grace of God gives them permission to do whatever they please. They minimize how serious the problem of sin is. They make light of their wrong doing by saying, "It's not that big a deal." It was a big deal to Uzzah. He had an insensitivity to the sacredness of the ark not realizing that even the Levitical priests were forbidden to touch it. Num. 4:15 clearly states, "But they shall not touch the holy thing, lest they die." Uzzah touched the ark and died for doing so.

It's true, Uzzah meant well and he was trying to do an honorable thing. Unfortunately, he made a hasty decision to disregard God's command and did what seemed right to him. He thinks the ark will be defiled if it falls and touches the ground but not if it touches him. He wrongly assumed the ground was dirty and unclean but he is not. German theologian Otto von Gerlach said in the nineteenth century, "Uzzah was a type of all who, with good intentions, humanly speaking, yet with unsanctified minds, interfere in the affairs of the kingdom of God, from the notion that they are in danger, and with the hope of saving them." The Bible says God struck him "for his error." The ark had been in Uzzah's house for twenty years and it became a common thing to him. He had seen the ark for so long that he no longer saw it for what it was, the place where God would meet and have fellowship with the people and make atonement for their sins. So often familiarity breeds contempt and God saw presumption and irreverence in Uzzah's heart. In other words, the ark had become just a box to him.

As Uzzah lay dead on the ground, all the singing and dancing and playing of instruments stopped. There was dead silence all around. "And David became angry because of the Lord's outbreak against Uzzah" (vs. 8). David reacts with anger and fear. He's confused. He doesn't understand how God could do such a thing. Uzzah was doing something honorable and here God strikes him down dead. In David's eyes, the punishment didn't fit the crime. Uzzah meant well. Didn't God see his heart? Yes, Uzzah was sincere but he was sincerely wrong. God's law is law and Uzzah's motive did not give him the right to do what God said not to do. If you disobey God, there will be consequences. Rom. 6:23 says, "For the wages of sin is death." David must have thought the end justifies the means. No, it doesn't. Consider the story of Abraham and Sarah. God promised them a son but when he wasn't born in their timing they devised a plan of their own. Abraham had a relation with Sarah's handmaid Hagar and nine months later Ishmael was born. They had good intentions but went about it the wrong way.

David is mad at God and goes three months without having fellowship with Him. That's three months without being blessed by God. Because of what happened to Uzzah, David felt he couldn't do what God wanted him to do. David was initially mad at God but eventually he became mad at himself for one day he would know he hadn't followed the instructions of God. He allowed his anger and fear to motivate him to seek more insight into the heart of God. He asked, "How can the ark of the Lord come to me?" (vs. 9).

Until his question was answered, vs. 10 says, "So David would not move the ark of the Lord with him into the City of David; but David took it aside into the house of Odeb-Edom the Gittite." Obed-Edom was a Levite of the family of Koath (1 Chron. 26:4). This was the family within the tribe of Levi that God commanded to transport and take care of the ark. "The ark of the Lord remained in the house of Obed-Edom the Gittite three months. And the Lord blessed Obed-Edom and all his household." Blessings always follow when God is obeyed and His holiness is respected.

It had always been God's intentions for the ark to be a blessing to the nation and not a curse. All He asked from the people was holy fear and reverence and a willingness to obey Him at all times. To obey God properly you must pay attention to the details. If God put them there, pay attention to them. Good intentions are not enough if you ignore the details. During those three months David read the scriptures where it was told how the ark was to be carried. He didn't stay angry but went and learned how to do it right the second time. He gathered the heads of the Levites together and said to them, "For because you did not do it right the first time, the Lord our God broke out against us, because we did not consult Him about the proper order" (1 Chron. 15:13). David heard that the house of Obed-Edom was blessed and he decides to get the ark to Jerusalem as quickly as possible. This time, however, he was going to do it the right way. "And the children of the Levites bore the ark of God on their shoulders, by its poles, as Moses had commanded according to the word of the Lord" (1 Chron. 15:15).

David had realigned his heart with the heart of God. He recognized what he did was wrong and corrected it. This is what you do when you're a person after God's own heart. "So David went and brought up the ark of God from the house of Obed-Edom to the City of David with gladness. And so it was, when those bearing the ark of the Lord had gone six paces, that he sacrificed oxen and fatted sheep" (2 Sam. 6:12,13). No sacrifices were made when they wrongfully transported the ark the first time. David now knows it's only by sacrifice that you come into the presence of God. He knew that something had to die in order for him to really live. On this day David got a glimpse of what God was going to do with the death, burial, and resurrection of the Lord Jesus Christ (Rom. 5:1,2). He also learned the meaning of Prov. 3:11,12, "My son, do not despise the chastening of the Lord, nor detest His correction; For whom the Lord loves He corrects, just as a father the son in whom he delights." The Message Bible says, "It's the child He loves that God corrects; a father's delight is behind all this."

One thing was certain, this celebration would be more elaborate and excessive than the first one. On this joyous occasion David would hold nothing back. "Then David danced before the Lord with all his might; and David was wearing a linen ephod. So David and all the house of Israel brought up the ark of the Lord with shouting and with the sound of the trumpet" (2 Sam. 6:14,15). The Message Bible says David "danced with great abandon before God." This shows the genuine emotional link he had with God as he twirled around and whirled about. He didn't sit on the throne and watch this celebration unfold before him. No, he got involved and led the procession. The first time David looked like a king with his crown and royal robe. This time he dressed like all the other priests. He set aside his royal garments and dressed like everyone else. He's dancing and spinning around before the Lord, having a good time. To this day, Israel still talks about this glorious event and its significance. David did the right thing, the right way, and God is happy.

Many biblical scholars believe Psalm 68 was written at this time. Vs. 3 says, "But let the righteous be glad; Let them rejoice before God; Yes, let them rejoice exceedingly." The

Message Bible says, "When the righteous see God in action, they'll laugh, they'll sing, they'll laugh and sing for joy." This is what David is doing now. He's received grace and he's responding to the goodness of God. He's the lead worshiper for he's been chosen by God to do so. David loves God and doesn't care what anybody else thinks about it. Vs. 4 (MSG) says, "Sing hymns to God; all heaven, sing out; clear the way for the coming of Cloud-Rider. Enjoy God, cheer when you see Him!" Joy is one of the first evidences of a person who has given their life to Christ. There's an overwhelming excitement that can't be contained. When Philip went and preached in Samaria, the people listened and they believed. Acts 8:8 says, "And there was great joy in that city." Salvation always leaves its mark. There is nothing more fun than loving God and worshiping Him with all your heart, mind, soul, and strength.

Worship is supposed to be fun. Ps. 118:24 says, "This is the day which the Lord has made; We will rejoice and be glad in it." Worship is responding to God and all He has done as you sing and dance and shout for joy. Some people may look down on dancing as a form of worship but it is definitely biblical. Ps. 149:3 says, Let them praise His name with the dance; Let them sing praises to Him with the timbrel and harp." Ps. 30:11 says, "You have turned for me my mourning into dancing" and Ps. 150:4 urges you to "Praise Him with the timbrel and dance." In Matt. 11:17 Jesus describes dancing as a symbol of joy that accompanies music. As long as the dance is worshipful, God-focused, and praiseworthy, it can have a proper place in worship. 1 Cor. 10:31 says, "Do all to the glory of God." Dancing is used as an act of worship in scripture and can be used in church services today as long as the focus is on worshiping God rather than drawing attention to one self. Dancing in the context of worship is not self-expression and anything that distracts from a focus on Christ should be left out. This is why 1 Cor. 14:40 says, "Let all things be done decently and in order."

A person with a sincere heart to praise God won't seek attention from the crowd nor will they demand to be allowed to dance in front of the church. They'll be just as happy to dance in a back corner of the room as on the front stage. If a person desires attention for their dancing, then they have ceased to praise God and are seeking praise for themselves. Dancing is a mode of expression that can be used for good or for evil (Ex. 15:20; 32:19). This is why each congregation bears the responsibility to structure its worship service in a way that honors God and encourages those within their group. If you want to dance in a church service, speak to the pastor about it first. Heb. 13:17 says Christians are expected to be in submission to their leaders. The Message Bible says they "work under the strict supervision of God." The pastor and elders of the church should pray about this and be confident in the direction the Holy Spirit gives them. The introduction of the dance as part of the worship service should be done purposely as a result of the thoughtful and prayerful decision on part of the leadership.

2 Sam. 6:16 says, "And as the ark of the Lord came into the City of David, Michal, Saul's daughter, looked through a window and saw King David leaping and twirling before The Lord; and she despised him in her heart." Most wives would thank God for giving them what they prayed for, a husband that loves and worships God. Not Michal for she is a very bitter woman. Her father is dead, her brothers are dead, and she's been pulled away from the husband she was living with. She looks out her window and views what David is doing in a bad light. She didn't appreciate David's exuberant form of worship. She felt it wasn't dignified for the king of Israel to take off his royal robe and express his emotions before God. David knew, however, that the true and appropriate response to God's presence is always worship. Indeed, David was a man who made God his top priority. To him, God was number one. He sought first the kingdom of

God and all His righteousness (Matt. 6:33) and Michal doesn't like it. Charles Spurgeon said, "From the window of their superiority they look down upon us."

The ark was placed in the midst of the tabernacle and set in the most holy place. "Then David offered burnt offerings and peace offerings before the Lord." (vs. 17). The burnt offerings spoke of consecration and the peace offerings spoke of fellowship. Afterward, David blessed all the people in the name of the Lord with food for a thanksgiving banquet. What a great king he was. David then returns home to bring a blessing to his household and he is hit with the wrecking ball of sarcasm, an icy blast of criticism from Michal that catches him completely off guard. She mocks him saying, "How glorious was the king of Israel today, uncovering himself today in the eyes of the maids of his servants, as one of the base fellows shamelessly uncovers himself!" (vs. 20). Her complaint was that David wasn't wearing royal attire. He wore no crown or royal robe. Her father Saul was a man of pride who liked to make an outward showing of his position as king. He was into pomp and circumstance, David wasn't. He was a man of the people and he dressed down like one of them.

Michal is venting her feelings toward David face-to-face. She's saying to him, "How dare you do what you did! No king has ever done this before." Michal stands as a sad example of the person who is too proud to worship God, a person who will not humble themselves before the King of kings and Lord of lords. She doesn't realize that worship is an expression of what's in your heart. It's a way of showing what God means to you, a way of showing your hunger for Him and your gratitude for all He's done. David doesn't care what Michal thinks, he only cares what God thinks. He then rebukes Michal and puts her in her place. He said in vs. 21,22 (MSG), "In God's presence I'll dance all I want! He chose me over your father and the rest of our family and made me prince over God's people, over Israel. Oh yes, I'll dance to God's glory - more recklessly even than this." Vs. 23 then says, "Therefore Michal the daughter of Saul had no children to the day of her death." This is the formal end of their relationship showing there is always barrenness in the life and ministry of the overly critical.

The Shepherd King

-25-

"THANKS BUT NO THANKS"

Bringing the Ark of the Covenant into Jerusalem was one of the most epic events in all of human history. David established that day a new worship order on the earth, worship like it is in heaven. Nothing like this had ever been seen in Israel or anywhere else on the earth. God alone is worthy to be praised and David wants Him to receive the worship due His name. He wrote in Ps. 29:1,2, "Give unto the Lord, O you mighty ones, give unto the Lord glory and strength. Give unto the Lord the glory due to His name; Worship the Lord in the beauty of holiness." The Message Bible says, "Stand at attention! Dress your best to honor Him!" True worship involves at least three important elements. It requires sincere reverence, giving to the Lord the honor and respect He rightfully deserves. It also includes public expression. This was prevalent in the Old Testament because sacrifices were to be made openly in front of others. Worship also includes the joyful service Christians render to their Lord and Savior. The concept of worship embraces an entire life of devotion and obedience to God.

When the children of Israel were wandering in the wilderness for forty years, God instructed them to build a tabernacle (Ex. 26), a tent made out of animal skins. Called the tabernacle of Moses, this was mainly a place for animal sacrifices and offerings. At no time did God reveal to these people how they were to worship Him. Their hearts were not right for they continually murmured and complained about the conditions they were forced to live in. In order to worship God, your heart must be pure and your spirit needs to be continually sensitive to the things of God. You can't have a hardened heart like the children of Israel and still worship God. David, however, was different. God revealed to him the power of worship because he was a man after His own heart. Yes, Moses knew God face-to-face and Abraham was called the friend of God. Still, God waited until the time of David to reveal the power of worship because it was through his bloodline that the Messiah would come to the earth, born in the little village of Bethlehem.

David will forever be known for his extravagant commitment to worship God. By reading the many psalms he wrote, you can see the spirit in which he loved and worshiped his Lord. The ark was put in a tent that David had built in Jerusalem and this is called the tabernacle of David. After burnt and peace offerings were made unto God, David appointed a group of Levites to minister continually around the Ark of the Covenant, to record what was said there, to thank and to praise the Lord God of Israel (1 Chron. 16:4). Many of the psalms were recorded by a scribe as David sang songs in the presence of God at the tabernacle. He also appointed singers and musicians to sing continually around the ark. There were four thousand musicians on his staff for he wanted a lavish, spiritual symphony that would worship God day and night. He wants all of Israel to be filled with the glory of God. A new worship order was established as thousands of the most skilled and highly gifted singers and musicians were mobilized in one place for the purpose of praising God.

Everything that is happening here is an expression of the passion in David's heart. He wrote in 1 Chron. 16:23-25, "Sing to the Lord, all the earth; Proclaim the good news of His salvation from day to day. Declare His glory among the nations, His wonders among all peoples. For the Lord is great and greatly to be praised." So special is this that God said in the last days He would raise up the tabernacle of David which had fallen down (Amos 9:11). David had conquered Jerusalem and now the Ark of the Covenant is the center of attention in all the city. He understood the significance of this city and its need to worship the God of the universe. So convinced is he of this need that in Ps. 132:1-5 he made a vow that changed history. The psalmist writes, "Lord, remember David and all his afflictions; How he swore to the Lord, and vowed to the Mighty God of Jacob: 'Surely I will not go into the chamber of my house, or go up to the comfort of my bed; I will not give sleep to my eyes or slumber to my eyelids, until I find a place for the Lord, a dwelling place for the Mighty God of Jacob.'"

Most times scripture tells people to remember God but here the psalmist is telling God to remember David. He knows that God was moved by David's dedication and the way he lived his life before Him. He wants God to remember all of David's afflictions that were related to his obedience, the reproach he bore for the decisions he made. David wrote in Ps. 69:7-9, "Because for Your sake I have borne reproach; Shame has covered my face. I have become a stranger to my brothers, and an alien to my mother's children; Because zeal for Your house has eaten me up, and the reproaches of those who reproach You have fallen on me." David has so much zeal for God that he is going to make an all out effort to find a dwelling place for the glory of God. He is referring to a temple in Jerusalem with the ark in the middle of it. It will be a place where the manifested glory of God would dwell, a place of miracles and signs and wonders, a place where the fullness of God's purpose is released, a place where God's will is done to the fullness of what He ordained.

David was a mighty warrior and will be a successful king. However, the top priority of his heart was that he wanted to be a worshiper of God. He wrote in Ps. 70:4, "Let all those who seek You rejoice and be glad in You; And let those who love Your salvation say continually, 'Let God be magnified!'" It is the desire of his heart to establish a dwelling place where the glory of God would be manifested on the earth.

Ps. 132:7-9 says, "Let us go into His tabernacle; Let us worship at His footstool. Arise, O Lord, to Your resting place, You and the ark of Your strength. Let Your priests be clothed with righteousness, and let Your saints shout for joy." In vs. 5 he calls this a dwelling place and here in vs.8 it's called a resting place. God said in Gen. 6:3, "My Spirit shall not strive with man forever." God rests when people are in agreement with Him, when they don't resist Him or His will for their lives. They don't contend with Him but are forever pressing into the things of God. Their whole desire is for revival, an awakening that breaks forth on the earth. These are the people who seek the fame of His name.

The psalmist said David wanted a dwelling place for the Mighty God of Jacob. It was Jacob who dreamed of a ladder that reached into heaven. Gen. 28:12 says, "Then he dreamed, and behold, a ladder was set up on the earth, and its top reached to heaven; and there the angels of God were ascending and descending on it." He later said in vs. 17, "How awesome is this place! This is none other than the house of God, and this is the gate of heaven!" David wanted a place where the God of the open heaven would be manifested, where the grace of God would be readily available. This won't be a casual undertaking but he'll go at it with all his strength, with all his heart and soul. He has no other vision in his life than to see God glorified and His people blessed fully and completely. Is. 62:6,7 (MSG) says, "I've posted watchmen on your walls, Jerusalem. Day and night they keep at it, praying, calling out, reminding God to remember. They are to give Him no peace until He does what He said, until He makes Jerusalem famous as the City of Praise."

At this time, all is well in the life of David. There is nothing missing, nothing broken. There are no wars to fight because "the Lord had given him rest from all his enemies all around" (2 Sam. 7:1). David is at rest but there is no diminishing of his spiritual pursuits. He refuses to be content where he is now at for he doesn't want to sit around and do nothing. He refuses to draw back and live a life of ease and comfort. No, he wants to go to the next level with God, to press in to whatever it is God would have him do. He wants a greater measure of what God set before him. He never got to the place where past victories were enough to satisfy him. He wants to do more and more for the kingdom of God. He wants to advance the kingdom all the days of his life for there is no retirement for the servant of God. Surely there is more he can do for his Lord and Master. Having nothing serious to deal with, David one day is having fellowship with Nathan the prophet. He looks at his beautiful palace and then begins to think about the Ark of the Covenant sitting in a tent. David thinks to himself, "This is not right."

David is living in an expensive, beautiful palace built from the best cedar trees in the land while the ark is in a tent. David is troubled that he lives in a nicer home than the ark. He says to Nathan, "See now, I dwell in a house of cedar, but the ark of God dwells inside tent curtains" (vs. 2). More than four hundred years prior to this conversation, God told Moses to build a tent of meeting, also known as the tabernacle, according to a specific pattern (Ex. 25:8,9). He never asked for a permanent building to replace the tent. Back then, a tent was necessary because the people were constantly moving. Now that Israel is secure and the tabernacle is in Jerusalem, David reasons that it would be more appropriate to build a temple to replace the tabernacle. He wants God to have a house much more grand than the one he is living in. He is so filled with gratitude and concern for God's glory that he is inwardly driven to do something special for God. This seems like a good and reasonable thing to do so Nathan tells him, "Go, do all that is in your heart, for the Lord is with you" (vs. 3).

Throughout the history of Israel, God had always raised up prophets to serve as His voice to the people. He never intended for the kings and other civil leaders to have absolute and unquestioned authority. They were required by God to listen to His voice through the Word and the voice of His prophets. Samuel was God's voice through whom He spoke to Saul and Nathan served as the prophet to King David. He listens to David as he expresses his desire for God to have the best that man can offer. Surely, the church buildings where people go to worship God should be the most beautiful and best kept buildings in the community. David tells Nathan he wants to build a house for God and the prophet answers him, "David, that's great! Do it!" The problem here is that he spoke to David before he spoke to God. Not once did he say, "Thus says the Lord..." Be careful when you counsel people with good ideas. Encourage them but also tell them to pray about it and see if this is what God wants. Later that night, God tells Nathan to go back and tell David his heavenly building permit is denied.

Nathan is a great prophet of God who was used mightily by God at different times. This day, however, he didn't seek counsel from God concerning David's desire. His response was presumptuous. He answered according to human judgment and common sense. G. Campbell Morgan wrote, "It is of the utmost importance that we should ever test our desires, even the highest and holiest of them, by His will. Work, excellent in itself, should never be undertaken, save at the express command of God. The passing of time will always vindicate the wisdom of Divine will." Nathan was wrong to say what he did to David and God is about to tell him so. That night the word of the Lord came to Nathan telling him to ask David the question, "Are you the one to build Me a house?" (vs. 5 NIV). God must have been pleased with the desire of David's heart. People everywhere should be asking the question, "What can I do for God?" It would be a better world if everybody had the heart and attitude of David. Most people do nothing for God and, if they do, they do as little as they can hoping God may still be pleased.

God never commanded anybody to build Him a permanent dwelling place. He reminds Nathan that He moved about in a tent and tabernacle when He brought the children of Israel out of Egypt (vs. 6). Never once did He command anyone to build Him a house of cedar (vs. 7) but here David wants to go the extra mile, to do more than what is asked or required of him. It was a good idea but it was not a God idea. Solomon would later ask, "But who is able to build Him a temple, since heaven and the heaven of heavens cannot contain Him?" (2 Chron. 2:6). Yes, His presence was manifested on top of the Ark of the Covenant but He didn't live there. The entire universe cannot contain God, much less some temple of church building. These buildings are built as a token for the people, to remind them of God rather than God actually living in them. God identifies with people, not buildings. When Jesus came to the earth, John 1:14 says, "And the Word became flesh and dwelt among us." This verse literally says Jesus "tabernacled among us." He pitched His tent of flesh among the people and was able to identify with them and they with Him.

God then tells Nathan to remind David of all the things He has already done for him. 2 Sam. 7:8,9 says, "I took you from the sheepfold, from following the sheep, to be ruler over My people, over Israel. And I have been with you wherever you have gone, and have cut off all your enemies from before you, and have made you a great name, like the name of the great men who are on the earth." David lived three thousand years ago and people today still know his name. Next to Jesus, he is the most written about man in all the Bible. David knows God has been good to him and this is the reason why he wants to build God a temple to dwell in. David has a good heart and he did well for wanting to do this. God said to him in 2 Chron. 6:8, "Whereas it was in your heart to build a temple for My name, you did well in that it was in your heart. Nevertheless you shall not build the house, but your son who will come forth from your own loins, he shall build the temple for My name." God is saying to David, "Forget the house. Forget the temple. Instead, listen to My plans for you."

God promises two things to David. He says in 2 Sam. 7:10, "Moreover I will appoint a place for My people Israel, and will plant them, that they may dwell in a place of their own and move no ore; nor shall the sons of wickedness oppress them anymore." God promises to establish a permanent, secure Israel under the reign of David. He had the heart of a shepherd, he was the shepherd king, and God knew he was concerned for the welfare of the people. This was a great promise for the nation of Israel. The second promise, however, goes beyond the borders of Israel for it will have eternal significance. Vs. 11 says, "Also the Lord tells you that He will make you a house." God is not referring to a physical house because David already has one. He is telling David that He will establish through him a royal dynasty that will last forever. It will be an everlasting throne and kingdom, an enduring legacy for David long after his death. God was saying, "Thanks, but no thanks. Let Me build you a house instead." David's house would last longer and be more glorious than the temple he wanted to build.

David wants to build God a house but here God says He will build David a house, a kingdom that is never going to end. Why did God say no to David's offer? Because David was a man of war and God wanted a man of peace to build His temple. He said to David in 1 Chron. 22:8-10, "You have shed much blood and have made great wars; you shall not build a house for My name, because you have shed much blood on the earth in My sight. Behold, a son shall be born to you, who shall be a man of rest; and I will give him rest from all his enemies all around. His name shall be Solomon, for I will give peace and quietness to Israel in his days. He shall build a house for My name, and he shall be My son and I will be his Father; and I will establish the throne of his kingdom over Israel forever." God promises a hereditary monarchy for the house of David. The family of Saul became extinct but the family of David remained till the birth of Christ and beyond. The Messiah will come through the bloodline of David and through Him the entire world will be blessed.

God promises David a son whose name will be Solomon. He will have a special relationship with God and he will be the one who builds God's temple in Jerusalem (vs. 12,13). If he sins, God will not reject him. Instead, He will chasten him and purge his iniquity (vs. 14). Mercy will follow Solomon all the days of his life and his throne will be established forever (vs. 13,15). God then makes a promise to David that is one of the greatest promises in all the Bible. He said in vs. 16, "And your house and your kingdom shall be established forever before you. Your throne shall be established forever." This promise is why 2 Sam. 7 is one of the most important chapters in the entire Bible. God makes a covenant with David, called the Davidic covenant, that contains promises referred to throughout all of scripture. In Is. 9:6,7 the prediction of the coming Messiah is given and it's a promise referring to 2 Sam. 7. The New Testament begins (Matt. 1:1) and ends (Rev. 22:16) with a reference to 2 Sam. 7. In these verses, Jesus is introduced as the offspring of David, showing that He is the fulfillment of the promise God made to David.

The purpose of all of God's covenants with man is that He wants to do good things to those who follow Him in the obedience of faith. You can have the confident assurance that God is a loving God who is working everything together for your good, that His grace will have a positive affect in every area of your life. God's job description includes the responsibility to withhold no good thing from those who walk uprightly, to work everything out for your eternal benefit. Three times the word "forever" appears in this promise (vs. 13,16). With this promise, all of eternity is being shaped. Beyond any shadow of doubt, the promise to David that his descendant would rule forever is fulfilled in Jesus Christ. The angel Gabriel said to Mary in Luke 1:32,33, "He will be great, and will be called the Son of the Highest; and the Lord God will give Him the throne of His father David. And He will reign over the house of Jacob forever, and of His kingdom there will be no end." As the Son of David (Rom. 1:3) and the Lord of David (Matt. 22:45), Jesus now reigns as king in heaven (1 Cor. 15:25) over the house of David.

How did David respond to all this? He is overwhelmed, speechless. 2 Sam. 7:18 says he went in and sat before the Lord and acknowledged what God told Nathan to tell him. He said, "Who am I, O Lord God? And what is my house, that You have brought me this far?" He is saying God is great and he is not. Ten times in this prayer David will refer to himself as "Your servant" revealing his humble reception of the covenant God made with him. Charles Spurgeon said, "There are some professors who would do a great thing if they might, but if they are not permitted to act a shining part they are in the sulks and angry with their God. David when his proposal was set aside found it in his heart not to murmur, but to pray." David continues, "Now what more can David say to you? For You, Lord God, know Your servant" (vs. 20). In other words, "Who am I to question God?" He's not rationalizing his desire and he's not trying to change God's mind. He doesn't have a critical spirit as he says, "What more can Your servant say? You are God and I am not."

"For Your word's sake, and according to Your own heart, You have done all these great things, to make Your servant know them" (vs. 21). David acknowledges the great work

God has already done, and the great work He is about to do. He now realizes that what he wanted to do for God is not as great as what God wants to do for him. David then magnifies the greatness of God. "Therefore You are great, O Lord God. For there is none like You, nor is there any God besides You, according to all that we have heard with our ears" (vs. 22). When David heard his kingdom would be established forever, he didn't think it made him any greater. On the contrary, in David's eyes it made God greater. Giving always reflects the greatness of the giver, not the receiver. David changes his focus for a moment and acknowledges that there is no nation on earth like Israel. "For You have made Your people Israel Your very own people forever; and You, Lord, have become their God" (vs. 24). Jesus was a Jewish man and this is why there is no nation like Israel and never will be.

David then boldly asks that the promise be fulfilled as spoken. "And now, O Lord God, the word which You have spoken concerning Your servant and concerning his house, establish it forever and do as You have said" (vs. 25). Nothing pleases God more than to hear His children say, "Lord, do as You have said." David is asking God to fulfill His promise. He wants God's will to be done on earth as it is in heaven. He now knows God has a better plan so he says, "Do as You have said and I'll stay out of the way." David is most sincere for he is praying from his heart (vs. 27). Some people say prayers written in a book while others pray from off the top of their head. No, when you pray you must do so from your heart. David ends his prayer by saying, "And now, O Lord God, You are God, and Your words are true, and You have promised this goodness to Your servant. Now therefore, let it please You to bless the house of Your servant, that it may continue forever before You; for You, O Lord God, have spoken it, and with Your blessing let the house of Your servant be blessed forever" (vs. 28,29).

David's desire to build a house for the Lord is noble, but God had other plans. David's reaction to God is a model for all to follow. When God closes the door on your plans and desires, don't expect or demand an explanation. There is always a reason why God says "no" but He doesn't always tell you what that reason is. God said "no" to David without any explanation at this time. He just said "no." He would later give David the reason why but scripture doesn't say when this happened. He also may give you a reason but it may come later. Sometimes you'll have to wait until you get to heaven to find the reason for God's denial. Of course, by then it won't matter. Sometimes God says, "Just trust Me." In David's closing remarks, he asks God three times to bless his house. God said "no" but David was still blessed. When you accept the fact that God has a better plan, you also will be blessed. Thank Him for having a better plan than you. Praise Him and then move on in a new direction of His choosing. Rather than complaining about what you can't do, do what God says you can do, giving all the glory to Him.

-26-

"AT THE KING'S TABLE"

God told David he couldn't build Him a temple in Jerusalem because he was a man of war and his hands were stained with blood. This decision did not take away David's desire to be involved in the advancement of God's righteous rule on the earth. The Lord had given him many breakthroughs in his life and, the greater the victory, the greater his determination and zeal to serve in the kingdom of God. Paul had this same tenacity. He was "bound in the spirit" (Acts 20:22) and never looked back. He wrote in Phil. 3:13,14, "One thing I do, forgetting those things which are behind and reaching forward to those things which are ahead. I press toward the goal for the prize of the upward call of God in Christ Jesus." There comes a day and an hour when the servants of God determine they're not going to count their lives dear to themselves, that they're not going to coast through life and do nothing for God. Paul said, "But none of these things move me; nor do I count my life dear to myself, so that I may finish my race with joy, and the ministry which I received from the Lord Jesus, to testify to the gospel of the grace of God" (Acts 20:24).

God's decision did not mean He didn't have a job for David to do. When God takes something away, He multiplies something back in return. He does exceedingly, abundantly over what you can ask or think if you're in a position to receive it. David was the ruler over an entire nation and God made him a warrior for a reason. He didn't want David to build Him a temple but He did want him to increase Israel's territory. God promised Abraham in Gen. 15:18 that Israel's borders would expand from the Nile River in Egypt all the way north to the Euphrates River which passes through

The Shepherd King

Syria and Iraq. Saul never conquered this territory and this promise to Abraham is now going to be fulfilled by David and his mighty men. In the days that follow, David is going to conquer more land than any other king in Israel. He'll increase Israel's territory ten times over. Nobody in all of scripture used his resources for the advancement of the kingdom more than David. Instead of defending Israel when attacked by the enemy, David now becomes the aggressor seeking a greater breakthrough of God's purpose in his life.

"After this it came to pass that David attacked the Philistines and subdued them. And David took Metheg Ammah from the hand of the Philistines" (2 Sam. 8:1). When David became king, the Philistines were taking territory from God's people. Now, under the leadership of David, this territory is taken back. Metheg Ammah means "the bridle of the Mother City" and refers to the city of Gath, the hometown of Goliath. This was the key city of the Philistines and they tried to control and bridle the people of Israel. David then goes east of the Jordan River where he defeated Moab (vs. 2). These were the people who in Num. 22-24 tried to get a prophet named Balaam to place a curse on the people of God. When the prophet opened his mouth to curse them, blessings came out instead. David had trusted the king of Moab to care for his parents in 1 Sam. 22:3,4. Jewish tradition says this king went back on his vow to David and killed his entire family except for his brother Elihu (1 Chron. 27:18). This is likely true because David would not attack Moab if his parents were still there.

God made David great. He is a conquering ruler and the borders of Israel are expanding. David didn't just take new territory, he recovered old ground that had been lost to the enemy. Syria was a great heathen nation to the north, divided into two groups with capitals in Zebah and Damascus. They united together for protection but found themselves helpless against the might of David for "the Lord preserved David wherever he went" (vs. 6). David honored God as he conquered the enemy in every direction. The Philistines were in the west, Moab was in the east, Syria was in the north, and Edom was in the south. Neighboring nations saw the hand of God on David and brought him honor and gifts (vs. 9,10). When David received this acclaim and wealth from the nations, he dedicated it all to the Lord (vs. 11). He knew the praise and glory belonged to God, not himself. David's victories are now complete. Israel now possessed more of the land promised to Abraham than at any other time. David then selected gifted men and made them leaders of various departments in the government (vs. 16-18).

David had just been to war with at least eight nations and he won great victories over all of them. At this time in his life he is wealthy and very powerful. There is joy and peace, his cup is running over. He is at rest once again and, as he meditates on God, he decides he wants to do something good in the name of his God. He asked in 2 Sam. 7, "What can I do for God?" as he expressed his desire to build a temple for God to dwell in. Here he asks another question, "What can I do for others?" David is at the pinnacle of his career and he wants to show grace to someone. Grace is a one-sided event. It's when a blessing is given to a person who does not deserve it. This blessing can't be earned and can't be repaid. It's unmerited, undeserved favor. David wants to show someone else the same kindness God showed to him. He is a man after God's own heart and he's about to give you a window into the heart of God. Sad to say, what happens next is the last good deed David does before his life begins to crumble. 2 Sam. 9:1 says, "Now David said, 'Is there still anyone who is left of the house of Saul, that I may show him kindness for Jonathan's sake?'"

No other king would have asked this question. They would have looked for people from the previous king's house to kill, not show kindness to. Not David for he was a man of great passion. Yes, he was a fierce warrior but he had a tender heart, a heart of feeling and emotion. He goes against the common principles of self-preservation and revenge as he seeks a way to bless the family of his former enemy, King Saul. He remembered his relationship with Jonathan and the covenant they made with one another not long after he killed Goliath (1 Sam. 20:14,15). David and Jonathan were more than best friends. They were soul mates and had a kindred spirit with one another. More than that, they both loved God with all their hearts. Even though Jonathan was next in line to be king, he knew David was God's choice and he backed him up all the way. He only asked one thing of David, to show kindness to his family when he came to the throne. Three times David made a covenant promise to do so, twice to Jonathan and once to Saul (1 Sam. 24:21,22). What happens next is David at his best for this is his finest hour.

David knew that when you make a promise, you keep the promise. He wrote in Ps. 15:4 (MSG), "Keep your word even when it costs you." Serving David was a man from the house of Saul named Ziba. David asked him, "Is there not still someone of the house of Saul, to whom I may show the kindness of God?" (vs. 3). David doesn't want to just show kindness, he wants to be a living demonstration of the love and kindness of God. The Hebrew word for "kindness" is "chesed" and is often translated as 'loving kindness; loyal love.' It is used throughout the Old Testament and is equivalent to the New Testament Greek word for love, "agape." This Hebrew word refers to God's unconditional, steadfast, loyal, and unfailing love for His people, a love that cannot be earned, is not deserved, can never be repaid. It's the unmerited love, mercy, and favor of God toward the undeserving. This love is shown in His unfailing grace that is poured out on those who belong to Him, on those who will receive it. This is the love David wants to show to any member of Saul's family. Nobody is excluded.

Ziba answers David, "There is still a son of Jonathan who is lame in his feet" (vs. 3). David could have had Ziba killed for withholding this information from him. It was customary to kill the heirs from the previous kingdom so why did Ziba wait until now to tell David an heir of Saul was still alive? You can almost hear the sarcasm in Ziba's voice. It's as if he's saying, "There is one guy but he's not very kingly. He's crippled, he's broken, he's lame. You don't want him here." Jonathan's son is named Mephibosheth and his name means "to be ashamed." 2 Sam. 4:4 tells how the five-year-old Mephibosheth was in the care of a nurse while his father was fighting alongside King Saul on Mount Gilboa. When the nurse heard that Saul and Jonathan had died in battle, she rightly feared that the leader of the new dynasty would execute every potential heir of the previous dynasty. The nurse grabbed the child in her arms and ran in panic. As the nurse was running, the boy fell to the ground and broke both his ankles. There were no doctors to reset the bones properly and they healed deformed, causing him to be a cripple for life.

Mephibosheth was a member of a disgraced family. He is the last living relative from the house of Saul, a man God rejected. Being lame hindered the way he lived. His strength, his self-worth, and the joy of life was taken away from him at an early age. He is in his mid-twenties now and has the right to be king according to the custom of the land. He is the son of the first-born son of Saul, and the other potential heirs are dead. It is not hard to understand why Ziba may have thought there was no place in the royal court for this crippled man. David, on the other hand, didn't care about any of that and he didn't ask Ziba what condition Mephibosheth was in. All he asked was, "Where is he?" to which Ziba replied, "Indeed, he is in the house of Machin the son of Ammiel, in Lo Debar" (vs. 4). Mephibosheth is married, has a son (vs. 12), and he doesn't even have his own house to live in.

Instead, he lives in the house of a man named Machin. Later, when one of David's sons led a rebellion against him, Machin supported and helped David at great danger to himself (2 Sam. 17:27).

Lo Debar is about seventy miles northeast of Jerusalem in the foothills on the west side of the Jordan River. It's as far from Jerusalem as you can go and still be in Israel. Even the name of this city sounds depressing. Lo Debar. In Hebrew the name means "no pasture; no life." It is a land of desolation, a dark and barren place where there is no pasture to feed the animals. Mephibosheth has found a place that resembles the condition his life is in. He's hiding there because any heir of Saul would be anticipating judgment from David the new king. He's afraid that David will find him and kill him. When Adam and Eve sinned in the Garden of Eden, they hid from God and didn't go to Him seeking forgiveness. God came looking for them, they were not looking for God (Rom. 3:11). In like manner, David sent messengers to Lo Debar looking for the living son of Jonathan. Mephibosheth must have been terrified when these messengers knocked on his door and demanded that he come with them to see the king. He thinks he's been hiding long enough and now he's about to die.

Fear covered the face of Mephibosheth as he is brought before the king. Immediately "he fell on his face and prostrated himself" (vs. 6). This is a sign of submission as he shows David great respect and reverence. The Message Bible says, "He bowed deeply, abasing himself, honoring David." Mephibosheth is on his face expecting the punishment he's been hiding from in that dark, desolate place. Fearing the worst, he hears David call his name, "Mephibosheth." For the Hebrews, a person's name was associated with the person and his presence. To call on someone's name was to seek his presence. Take comfort knowing that God is pursuing you and your presence. He said in Is. 43:1, "Fear not, for I have redeemed you; I have called you by your name; You are Mine." God is calling you to the honor of enjoying His presence while He enjoys being in yours. He said in Rev. 3:20, "Behold, I stand at the door and knock. If anyone hears My voice and opens the door, I will come in to him and dine with him, and he with Me."

Mephibosheth responds to David calling his name by saying, "Here is your servant!" (vs. 6). What he hears next is the last thing he expected to hear. David said to him, "Do not fear, for I will surely show you kindness for Jonathan your father's sake, and will restore to you all the land of Saul your grandfather; and you shall eat at my table continually" (vs. 7). Mephibosheth is on his face expecting judgment but he receives grace instead. David is saying, "I'm not going to give you what you deserve, I'm going to give you what you don't deserve. I'm going to give you mercy and grace. I'm going to show you the unfailing love and kindness of God. This is the reason I brought you here, just as you are. Yes, you're a wreck but you're also the son of my best friend and I'm going to bless you abundantly." People say God helps those who help themselves. That is found nowhere in the Bible. The truth is, God helps those who can't help themselves. Rom. 5:6 (NLT) says, "When we were utterly helpless, Christ came at just the right time and died for us sinners."

Mephibosheth feared death but David promised him a life full of peace and abundance. He promised to show him the kindness of God. God's kindness is so great that He spared not His own Son to save all humanity (Rom. 8:32). When Jesus walked the earth, He showed kindness to a leper, a woman caught in adultery, a hated tax collector, and a thief dying on a cross. He showed kindness to people who didn't deserve His kindness. This is what grace is all about. Rom. 8:15 (MSG) says, "This resurrection life you received from God is not a timid, grave-tending life. It's adventurously expectant, greeting God with a childlike 'What's next, Papa?'" What's next for Mephibosheth? First, he's going to get all the land that belonged to his grandfather Saul. As Saul's heir, this land rightfully belonged to him. David, however, goes beyond giving Mephibosheth what was rightfully his. He also gave him the honor of eating at the king's table continually, to have a close relationship with the king of the nation. He is now part of the king's family. On this day, Mephibosheth becomes royalty.

Eating at the king's table is one of the greatest blessings in all the Bible. A similar promise is given to those who give their life to Jesus. He said in Luke 22:30 that the disciples would eat and drink at His table in heaven. Paul later wrote in Eph. 2:6 (NLT), "For He raised us from the dead along with Christ and seated us with Him in the heavenly realms because we are united with Christ Jesus." The Message Bible says, "Then He picked us up and set us down in highest heaven in company with Jesus, our Messiah." Mephibosheth was broken and lame and this made him a perfect candidate to sit at the king's table. Jesus said in Luke 14:12-14, "When you give a dinner or a supper, do not ask your friends, your brothers, your relatives, nor your rich neighbors, lest they also invite you back, and you be repaid. But when you give a feast, invite the poor, the maimed, the lame, the blind. And you will be blessed, because they cannot repay you; for you shall be repaid at the resurrection of the just." When it comes to God's grace, all you can do is accept the invitation to sit with Him at His table.

Mephibosheth didn't feel worthy of such generosity for he considered himself a worthless and insignificant person. He bowed before David and asked, "What is your servant, that you should look upon such a dead dog as I?" (vs. 8). David asked a similar question in Ps. 8:4, "What is man that You are mindful of him, and the son of man that You visit him?" The Message Bible says, "Why do You bother with us? Why take a second look our way?" Mephibosheth was asking, "Who am I to deserve this grace, wretched man that I am?" Mephibosheth may have considered himself as worthless as a dead dog but he was still a living, breathing soul. Eccl. 9:4 says, "But for him who is joined to all the living there is hope, for a living dog is better than a dead lion." Mephibosheth is facedown in the dirt. He's lame and undeserving of all this kindness. Little does he know that David isn't finished. In fact, he's just getting started. As he looks upon the son of his best friend, he's probably thinking to himself, "Mephibosheth, you haven't seen anything yet."

David does not respond to Mephibosheth's low opinion of himself. Instead, he turns to Ziba and commands him, his sons, and his servants to work the land he had given to Mephibosheth so that he may have food to eat (vs. 10). Ziba responds, "According to all that my lord the king has commanded his servant, so will your servant do" (vs. 11). This was a good thing to say. He probably would have been killed had he said differently. Mephibosheth has so much grace poured out on him that he now has thirty-six servants at his disposal. David still has one more blessing to give him. "As for Mephibosheth, he shall eat at my table like one of the king's sons (Vs. 11). David was adopting Mephibosheth as one of his own sons just like Christ adopts you to become one of the children of God (Rom. 8:15). Mephibosheth is lame but he's eating like royalty at the king's table. When he sits down, the table covers his feet. Nobody can tell what's wrong with him. He looks like the other people at the table. Yes, he's lame but people see him as the son of the king.

Right about now David is feeling like he's on top of the world. That's one of the benefits of being a blessing to someone else, to work on behalf of the weak and not exploit them. Paul wrote in Acts 20:35 (NLT), "And I have been a constant example of how you can help those in need by working hard. You should remember the words of the Lord Jesus: 'It is more blessed to give than to receive.'" God is a loving and generous God and you are made in His image. As a child of God, you are called to imitate Him. Eph. 5:1 (MSG) says, "Watch what God does, and then you do it, like children who learn proper behavior from their parents." Giving to others is a demonstration of God's character and a response to what He has done for you. Ps. 116:12 says, "What shall I render to the Lord for all His benefits toward me?" The Message Bible says, "What can I give back to God for the blessings He's poured out on me?" God loves a cheerful giver (2 Cor. 2:7) because giving is rooted in His character. It's a reflection of who He is and He takes delight when His children gladly open their hands and hearts to others.

Jesus said in Matt. 5:14, "You are the light of the world." This happens when you become more loving, more gracious, and more giving. Because God is generous, you also are called to be generous. You reaching out to others can change homes, relationships, entire countries, and the eternal destiny of many souls. David is a generous giver and his kindness to Mephibosheth doesn't end his passion to do good works for other people. He now wants to take God's kindness beyond the borders of his own kingdom. 2 Sam. 10:1,2 says, "And it happened after this that the king of the people of Ammon died, and Hanun his son reigned in his place. Then David said, 'I will show kindness to Hanun the son of Nahash, as his father showed kindness to me.'" Ammon is a pagan city east of the Jordan River. The Ammonites were one of the two tribes that were born as a result of Lot's drunken incestuous relationship with his two daughters, the other tribe being the Moabites. The Ammonites were not good people for they worshiped a false god named Moloch and offered their children up to him.

David wants to show kindness to Hanun because his father showed kindness to him. Perhaps Nahash protected David when he was hiding from King Saul. It is recorded that David did flee to the other side of the Jordan River when he was running from Saul. Hanun is a pagan king but David wants to show him kindness anyway. Rom. 12:18 says, "If it is possible, as much as depends on you, live peaceably with all men." David sends messengers to comfort the new king of Ammon whose father just passed away. Unfortunately, his good intentions are grossly misunderstood. The princes of the people questioned David's motives as they say to Hanun their lord, "Do you think that David really honors your father because he has sent comforters to you? Has David not rather sent his servants to you to search the city, to spy it out, to overthrow it?" (vs. 3). The people don't want David's kindness. Instead, they believe he wants to spy on them and do them harm. They couldn't picture themselves showing kindness to others, so they couldn't imagine anybody showing kindness to them.

Hanun, unfortunately, listens to these men and their wrong assessment of what David's motives are. This shows you must always be careful who you listen to. Instead of receiving David's generous offer, Hanun treats David's men shamefully and makes a public spectacle of them. "Therefore Hanun took David's servants, shaved off half their beards, cut off their garments in the middle, at their buttocks, and sent them away" (vs. 4). In that culture, a man would rather die than have his beard shaved off. To the Hebrews, the value of one's beard was great for it was considered to be man's greatest ornament. It was a sign of their manhood. To be clean shaven was the mark of a slave, to cut of half their beards was to show that each one of them were half a man. Doing this was one of the greatest insults they could have done to these men who came in peace. They also had their garments cut off so their back sides were showing. They're standing there embarrassed, humiliated, and greatly ashamed. In this condition they are sent back to King David.

2 Sam. 10:5 says, "When they told David, he sent to meet them, because the men were greatly ashamed. And the king said, 'Wait at Jericho until your beards have grown, and then return.'" David isn't going to take this sitting down. Sometimes you have to take a stand for what you believe in. Sometimes you have to be firm and harsh as you draw a line in the sand and say, "No more!" Don't worry what the world thinks about your stand. After all, they only think you're nice if you agree with them. To insult the ambassadors of the king is as if they had done this to David himself. Jesus said in John 15:18, "If the world hates you, you know that it hated Me before it hated you." Before going into battle, David takes care of his own men first. Sometimes you have to take one step back before you take two steps forward. He tells his men to stay in Jericho until their beards grow back, until their manhood returns. The shame of these men were seen by all and David cares for their dignity and honor. This is why he allowed them to wait for their beards to grow back before they returned to Jerusalem.

The Ammonites heard "they had made themselves repulsive to David" (vs. 6) so they hired the Syrians to fight for them. David heard about this so he sent Joab and his mighty men to go fight them. As they approached the enemy they found themselves surrounded. In front of them were the Ammonites in battle array at the entrance to the gate of the city, behind them were the Syrians in a field. This was a battle bigger than themselves and these warriors had to remember that the outcome was ultimately in God's hands (vs. 12). In faith Joab and his men pressed on. The Syrians turned out to be very weak and fled when they saw Joab coming. When the Ammonites saw this they also fled back to their own city. The Syrians would later regroup and lose forty thousand men in a battle against David (vs. 18). After this defeat the Syrians no longer helped the people of Ammon. They made peace with Israel and served them (vs. 19). The Ammonites are still in their city and David decides to wait until spring to send Joab to deal with them. He'll stay home for this battle, a mistake he'll regret for the rest of his life.

-27-

"THE ABYSS OF SIN"

At this time in David's life, he is an extremely blessed man. It's a time of great prosperity and Israel is the strongest nation in the known world. David is a mighty and powerful king, a great warrior, and the sweet psalmist of Israel. He is a man after God's own heart, a man who loved and served God with all his heart and soul. The Lord was his shepherd and he knew the supernatural power of being in the presence of God. He's seen more in his life than a hundred men combined. Things are so good for David that he made the unfortunate mistake of letting his guard down. He relaxes his grip on what's right and what's wrong. Worse than that, he doesn't maintain his walk with God. No longer does he fellowship with Him on a daily basis. He's become like the church of Laodicea described in Rev. 3:17 (NLT), "You say, 'I am rich. I have everything I want. I don't need a thing!' And you don't realize that you are wretched and miserable and poor and blind and naked." Little does David realize he's about to enter the darkest hour of his life.

When you get comfortable and satisfied there is a danger that you'll forget about God. A warning is given in Deut. 6:11,12, "When you have eaten and are full, then beware, lest you forget the Lord who brought you out of the land of Egypt, from the house of bondage." The devil will get you when you're down but he'll also get you when you're up. More people are destroyed with prosperity than they are with poverty. As David was enjoying the rewards of victory and success, his soul was rotting away on the inside of him. Why is that? Because you can't ignore spiritual growth on the inside just because you're healthy, wealthy, and wise on the outside. You can never be stagnant in your walk with the Lord. If you're not growing and going forward, you'll backslide and go backward. The deceiving thing about backsliding is you don't have to do anything for it to happen. Doing nothing causes you to backslide and fall from grace. It's while David is doing nothing that he plays with the fire of temptation and gets badly burned and scarred.

David is about fifty years old at this time. Middle age can be a dangerous time for men. If they haven't reached their life's goals yet, if they haven't fulfilled their destiny, they run the risk of getting bored with life. This, in turn, causes them to seek new thrills elsewhere. On the other hand if, like David, they have reached their goals, they may get disappointed because they don't have the sense of fulfillment they hoped they would have. To the downfall of many, this leaves a void in their life, a barren emptiness that needs to be filled. They long to be young again and free so they act like it. They have what is called a mid-life crisis and go looking for excitement wherever they can find it. It's at this time in David's life that he falls into the abyss of sin. He falls and he falls hard, farther than anybody has ever fallen. For a few minutes of pleasure David, a man after God's own heart, will lose everything he's worked for all his life. His name will be stained and blemished, men will lose their lives, those he trusted most will betray him, and his marriages will be destroyed.

G. Campbell Morgan said, "In the whole of the Old Testament literature there is no chapter more tragic or full of solemn warning than this." This season in David's life will cause you to realize just how powerful, deceitful, and devastating the consequences of sin really is. David is about to find out that sometimes the enemy will attack you when things are going well with you, when you're over-confident, when you think the enemy can't touch you, when you're head and shoulders above the circumstances of life. It's times like this that 1 Cor. 10:12 warns, "Let him who stands take heed lest he fall." The Message Bible says, "Don't be so naive and self-confident. You're not exempt. You could fall flat on your face as easily as anyone else." Paul is saying to always be on guard, to take heed, pay attention, be aware, open your eyes, seek to understand. 1 Peter 5:8 says, "Be sober, be vigilant; because your adversary the devil walks about like a roaring lion, seeking whom he may devour." The Message Bible says, "Keep a cool head. Stay alert." Never let your guard down when it comes to the devil.

David is blessed but he's also disengaged. 2 Sam. 11:1 says, "Now it came to pass in the spring of the year, at the time when kings go out to battle, that David sent Joab and his servants with him, and all Israel; and they destroyed the people of Ammon and besieged Rabbah, But David remained at Jerusalem." Instead of attacking, David is home relaxing. He should have been with his men, leading them to victory. After all, it was the perfect time to go to war. In that part of the world, there were seasons of the early rain and the latter rain. The early rain took place in the winter months and the latter rain ended around April of the beginning of May. After the latter rain the ground dries up and this prevents the chariots from getting stuck in the mud. The latter rain also brought about an abundant harvest of all the crops that were planted. Good weather and plenty of food made spring the best time to go to war and expand your borders. David knew this but he stayed home anyway. He's about to learn the hard way that idleness is the devil's playground.

David is older now and he's been fighting since he was a teenager. He decides to stay home from this battle and let the younger men do the fighting, to let others do what he's supposed to do. Rest is good but realize that the devil never goes on vacation. You can get in trouble if you're not actively involved with the things of God, if you don't do what you've been called and anointed to do. It's when you're disengaged that you're the most vulnerable to the wicked schemes of the enemy. The best way to resist temptation is to be busy with a higher purpose. You have got to be caught up in something bigger and greater than your own life. There is a call on your life, a mission from God, that you can't turn away from. Every day you need to be continually engaged with the fulfillment of your destiny. So many people live pointless lives of quiet desperation. Their lives are shallow for they have no vision beyond themselves. They become bored with life and turn to sin hoping it will fill the void in their soul. They falsely believe sensual pleasures will give them the fulfillment they need.

David lived for the purpose of giving glory to God until one day he got bored with life. He wasn't doing anything purposeful because he stayed home from the battle. Perhaps he got tired of fighting because he'd been doing it all his life. He reasoned that now would be a good time to relax and take it easy. Contrary to what your flesh will tell you, the safest place for any Christian to be is on the frontlines of battle. The enemy hasn't stepped away from the battle and neither should you. If you remove yourself from life's battles, you'll be an open target for the devil and all his evil cohorts. Like Saul before him, David has taken his eyes off God and began to focus his attention completely on himself. He laid aside his higher purpose and this is about to get him in deep trouble. Be aware that boredom is one of the first signs that trouble is lurking at your door step. Doing nothing always gives the devil the upper hand. Like a well-trained sniper, he'll wait to make his move and at the most opportune moment he'll pick you apart piece by agonizing piece.

Life is tough and you can't put your weapons down. You must stay in the battle for it's the only safe place you'll ever be. Not going to war is going to get David in serious trouble. The spears and arrows that he would have faced on the battlefield pale in comparison to what is about to happen to him. Like Adam and Eve, David is about to learn it doesn't take long to ruin a person's life. How do you destroy your life? One step at a time. On this quiet spring night, David is about to take the first step. "Then it happened one evening that David arose from his bed and walked on the roof of the king's house. And from the roof he saw a woman bathing, and the woman was very beautiful to behold" (vs. 2). David is bored so he decides to take a late afternoon nap. He's restless and he can't sleep because he wasn't where God wanted him to be. Perhaps he's lonely. Ps. 102:7 says, "I lie awake, and am like a sparrow alone on the housetop." He decides to get out of bed and go for a walk on the roof. The Hebrew word for "walked" suggests David paced back and forth on the roof.

David is restless and he's bored. Idleness has consumed his life and temptation is lurking around the corner. God does not use people who are lazy and idle to do His work but the devil certainly does. He knows where there is room for idleness, there is room for sin. Ezek. 16:49 says one of the many sins of Sodom and Gomorrah was an "abundance of idleness." Eccl. 4:5 (MSG) says, "The fool sits back and takes it easy. His sloth is slow suicide." The NLT says, "Fools fold their idle hands, leading them to ruin." Many people in today's world are being idle and doing nothing with their lives. They would rather play video games and sleep than be productive. Paul told the church in 1 Thess. 5:14 to "encourage the stragglers" (MSG), "warn those who are lazy" (NLT), "admonish the idle" (ESV). With nothing better to do than pace back and forth on the roof of his house, David takes a moment to look over the vastness of the city spread out before him. He notices movement on another rooftop nearby and sees it is a beautiful woman taking a bath.

Bathing on a rooftop was not unusual for that culture for water was stored on the roof to be warmed by the midday sun. Still, she was an incredibly attractive woman and surely more discretion could have been used. 1 Tim. 2:9 says, "The woman should adorn themselves in modest apparel, with propriety and moderation." Such was not the case here. David glanced down and saw what this woman was doing. In truth, he couldn't help what he saw. He went up on the roof and there she was. He quickly noticed that "the woman was very beautiful to behold." He saw and then he beheld. Things are quickly going from bad to worse. The word "behold" does not suggest an innocent glance but a deliberate gaze. The first look was not a sin, the second one was. He could have turned away and went back into his house but he didn't do that. He looked and then he looked again. That gaze, that second lingering forbidden look, inflamed him with lust and a sexual longing that would have to be satisfied at any cost. Unfortunately, that's what happened.

Men, be careful what you look at. Jesus said in Matt. 5:28, "But I say to you that whoever looks at a woman to lust for her has already committed adultery with her in his heart." If you don't take charge of your flesh, your flesh will take charge of you. James 1:14,15 (NLT) says, "Temptation comes from our own desires, which entice us and drag us away. These desires give birth to sinful actions. And when sin is allowed to grow, it gives birth to death." To continue to look lustfully at a woman puts you on the path that leads to the abyss of sin. This is why Job 31:1 says, "I have made a covenant with my eyes; Why then should I look upon a young woman?" The word "look" means 'to look intently; to gaze; to look lustfully.' The Message Bible says, "I made a solemn pact with myself never to undress a girl with my eyes." What you allow yourself to look at for a long time will eventually control your life. Remember, temptation reveals the heart and mind of the one being tempted. Joseph ran away from his temptation, David did not.

Because of the way God wired men, when he looks at a beautiful woman all sorts of chemical and electrical reactions takes place. A man is visually stimulated because God made him that way. God's first command to Adam and Eve was to be fruitful and multiply. For this to happen, God gave man sensual desires when he looked upon his wife and this is what brings them together to have children. God also gave man control over those impulses. They're to be for his wife and her only. Yes, these same cravings will come when you look at a woman not your wife but you can and must control them. You can't stop a bird from flying over your head but you can prevent it from building a nest in your hair. At the same time, women can help by modestly dressing in such a way as to not encourage those chemical reactions. Don't add fuel to the fire. English Bible teacher Arthur Pink said in the early twentieth century, "If lustful looking is so grievous as sin, then those who dress and expose themselves with the desire to be looked at and lusted after are not less, but perhaps more guilty."

The more David looked at this beautiful woman, the more sinful his thoughts became. He had many wives but even that didn't satisfy his sexual cravings. If one woman wasn't enough, neither will several women be enough. That's the danger of being controlled by fleshly appetites. It always wants more and more. At this moment David has lost all sense of right and wrong. All he's thinking about is himself. The absence of moral restraint cause him to pursue this temptation even further. "So David sent and inquired about the woman" (vs. 3). There is always a progression to sin. It begins with a thought before it becomes an action. One thing leads to another. Notice the downward steps David takes from fantasy to reality. He saw, he beheld, he sent, he inquired. The wheels are turning and they're headed straight to the abyss of sin. David could have just walked away but he instead put himself into a more tempting situation. He's got to have her so he asks who she is. Someone said to him, "Is this not Bathsheba, the daughter of Eliam, the wife of Uriah the Hittite?" (vs. 3).

God is warning David here. This woman is somebody's daughter, somebody's wife. David learns that she came from a notable family. Her father Eliam was one of David's mighty men (2 Sam. 23:34). His father was Ahithophel who was one of David's chief counselors, a man greatly renowned for his deep insight and wisdom (2 Sam. 15:12). She was also the wife of Uriah the Hittite, another of David's mighty men (2 Sam. 23;39) whose name means "fire of Jehovah." Each of these men were very loyal to David and continually put their lives on the line for him. Learning this did not stop David from embracing this temptation. He doesn't care if she's married or not. At this point, God is totally absent from his thoughts. All that's real to him is that image of Bathsheba on the rooftop. When sin takes over, all thoughts of God are pushed away. The devil doesn't try to get you to hate God, he tries to get you to forget Him. David did not heed the warning of God as sexual desire takes control of his flesh. The flame is kindled and a raging fire consumes him. Adam ate the forbidden fruit and David is about to do the same thing.

The problem with David is he wasn't busy fighting the Lord's battles. Neither was he fighting the temptations of his flesh. In the past, David tried to satisfy his fleshly desires with a harem of women. He showed no regard for God's plan for marriage when he married several women instead of just one. This showed a lack of restraint on his part and a willingness to indulge in his passions at all costs. This is about to catch up to him in a tragic way. You can't sow wild oats at night and pray for crop failure in the morning. David doesn't realize it yet but the hammer of destruction is about to smash his life into pieces. He's about to learn the hard way that it's much easier to avoid temptation than it is to resist it. It's easier to squash an acorn than it is to bring down a giant oak tree. God told Cain in Gen. 4:7, "If you do well, will you not be accepted? And if you do not do well, sin lies at the door. And its desire is for you, but you should rule over it." God is saying you must master your temptations. You must kill sin or sin will kill you. David didn't do this. The same man who conquered a giant is about to be conquered by the beauty of a woman.

David knew Joab and all his mighty men were away fighting the Ammonites and this made the situation all the more tempting. "Then David sent messengers, and took her; and she came to him, and he lay with her, for she was cleansed from her impurity; and she returned to her house" (vs. 11). David ignored every warning and the way of escape God had given him. Instead, he took Bathsheba and plunged into the abyss of sin. There is no evidence that she was taken by force and nothing is said about her being reluctant to come to David. Perhaps she was lonely because of all the time her husband was away fighting the enemy. She came without any hesitation proving she was a willing participant. She wasn't like Abigail who years before told David he was too godly a man to kill her husband. Bathsheba could have refused his advances and screamed but scripture says she did neither of these. It does say she laid with David because she was cleansed from her impurity. This confirms that she just went through her monthly menstrual cycle proving she wasn't already pregnant when she laid down with him.

That night, for a brief moment of time, David enjoyed the temporary, fleeting pleasures of sin (Heb. 11:25). That's the lure of sin. For a moment it's fun and exciting. What is so deceptive about sin is that it promises so much but delivers so little. You give in to temptation and quickly realize it doesn't give you the satisfaction you thought it would. The more you do as you please, the less you are pleased with what you do. Sin looks good on the surface but underneath is a world of hurt. You can sin and pay the price for what you did for years to come. Sin is expensive and its dividends have destroyed many lives. It has the potential to take from you everything you've got. David lost his integrity as a leader, his fidelity as a husband, his standing as a father. He ruined everything, but boy, was it fun. But only for a moment. His entire life will be scarred by this one momentary, passing pleasure of sin. "And the woman conceived; so she sent and told David, and said, 'I am with child'" (vs. 5). She is pleading with David to do something because the law of Moses required both the adulterer and adulteress be put to death (Lev. 20:10).

In rapid succession, things for David begin to spiral out of control. He can't let it be known what he had done so a plan to cover up his sin begins to unfold in his mind. With self-preservation foremost in his thoughts, David reasons there is no better way to hide his evil deed than to have Bathsheba's husband sleep with her. This way, all the people will think the child is his and not David's. It is very deceptive to try to hide your sin for God sees and knows everything (Prov. 15:3). With futile effort people may try to hide their sin from their conscience and memory but rarely, if ever, are they successful. Charles Spurgeon said, "As soon as ever we are conscious of sin, the right thing is not to begin to reason with the sin, or to wait until we have brought ourselves into a proper state of heart about it, but to go at once and confess the transgression unto the Lord, there and then." What's especially sad here is that David shows no remorse for what he did. There is no inner struggle or deep-rooted conviction to plague his soul. Instead of repenting, David tries to hide his sin and cover up the cruel and wicked thing he had done.

David sets his plan in motion by sending word to Joab to have Uriah sent back home to see him (vs. 6). First century historian said Uriah was Joab's armorbearer, a man who did what he was commanded to do. "When Uriah had come to him, David asked how Joab was doing, and how the people were doing, and how the war prospered" (vs. 7). This was David's attempt to pretend nothing happened and all was normal. He then told Uriah, "Go down to your house and wash your feet" (vs. 8). People washed their feet just before they went to bed. David is telling him to go home, clean up, and go to bed with your wife. He even sends a gift of food to follow him home. Unexpectedly, things didn't go as planned. To the chagrin of David, Uriah didn't go home but instead slept at the door of the king's house with all the other servants of David. The next day David asked him why he didn't go home. Uriah said the ark was in a tent and his fellow troops were in the open fields. "Shall I then go to my house to eat and drink, and to be with my wife? As you live, and as your soul lives, I will do no such thing" (vs. 11).

Ironically, David was ready to throw away his honor and integrity in order to lay with Bathsheba but Uriah was not. David had been feeding his flesh for twenty years but Uriah was a one-wife man who had a passion for the glory of God even though he was a Hittite and not a native Jew. Uriah is the hero of this story. His principle concern is the ark of God and his fellow soldiers. You don't sleep with your wife when your comrades in arms are fighting in the field. His first loyalty was to the king's interests and not his own pleasure. David is listening to a better man than he is. Through the words of Uriah, God is piercing David in the heart because of what he had done. Uriah had a right to have Bathsheba but didn't take it. David had no right but took her anyway. Apparently, the words of Uriah didn't sting enough to cause David to cease from his cover-up and his downward fall into the abyss of sin. He tells Uriah he can return to the battle the next day and then decides to get his drunk. Surely in a state of drunkenness Uriah will spend his last evening before returning to battle with his wife.

David was drunk with lust when he slept with Bathsheba. He hopes making Uriah drunk with wine will bring the same result. When drunk, your guard is definitely down but Uriah held on to his integrity anyway. "And at evening he went out to lie on his bed with the servants of his lord, but he did not go down to his house" (vs. 13). Once again David's plan was brought to naught by the integrity and loyalty of Uriah. Having failed to cover his sin, David now wants Uriah dead. If Bathsheba was to have a child, Uriah wouldn't be around to claim the child wasn't his. David writes a death warrant for Uriah and has him deliver it to Joab himself. He wrote in the letter, "Set Uriah in the forefront of the hottest battle, and retreat from him, that he may be struck down and die" (vs. 15). David trusted the integrity of Uriah so much that he made him the carrier of his own death sentence. That's about as despicable as you can be. British theologian Adam Clarke wrote, "This was the sum of treachery and villainy. He made the most noble man the carrier of letters which prescribed the mode in which he was to be murdered."

As a servant to Saul, David feared killing the king because he was God's anointed. But as a king himself, he didn't hesitate to kill one of his most faithful warriors. David goes from lust to adultery to deception to murder. There's no end to his evil deeds. He saw, he beheld, he sent, he inquired, he took. One sin led to another and still he thinks he can get away with what he did. He needs to reconsider those thoughts because Job 34:21,22 says, "For His eyes are on the ways of man, and He sees all his steps. There is no darkness nor shadow of death where the workers of iniquity may hide themselves." David tells Joab to send Uriah on a suicide mission so he'll die. This is an act of betrayal because no good military commander would ever deliberately kill a good soldier. Joab, however, had killed Abner so he also had blood on his hands. He's used to doing treacherous things so he obeys David's command. Uriah charges the walls of the city, Joab's men pull back, the archers hit Uriah and he dies. Not only Uriah but other men die also, men who didn't need to die were it not for David's despicable plan to cover his sin.

Joab sends word of Uriah's death back to David. He quickly defends himself because rushing the walls of an enemy city was a bad strategy of military warfare. Joab didn't want David to remind him that in Judges 9:50-57 Abimelech was killed by getting too close to the walls of a city under siege (vs. 21). Many men were murdered under Joab's command and David's wrath might rise when he found out about it. Joab tells his messengers if David questions his strategy to tell him that Uriah also died in the battle. The messengers did this and David tells them to tell Joab, "Do not let this thing displease you, for the sword devours one as well as another." (vs. 25). This was a proverb regarding the misfortunes of war. It's one way of saying, "These things happen." When Bathsheba heard her husband was dead, she mourned for him" (vs. 26). There is no reason to believe she knew that David had arranged the death of her husband. When her mourning was over, David married her and she bore him a son. Vs. 27 (CEV) then mentions God for the first time in this chapter, "The Lord was angry because of what David had done."

Randall J. Brewer

-28-

"YOU ARE THE MAN"

One year has passed since David cheapened the marriage covenant by committing adultery with Bathsheba. He didn't casually fall into sin, he stepped into it consciously and deliberately. He knowingly and willingly sinned again and again and again. Sin promises you warmth and satisfaction but it leaves you cold and empty and barren. David now finds himself a prisoner of his own lust. He has no peace, he writes no psalms, he sings no songs. No longer does he dance before the Lord with all his might. He's like salt that lost its flavor because of the poisonous contamination of sin. Jesus said in Matt. 5:13 (MSG), "You're here to be salt-seasoning that brings out the God-flavors of this earth. If you lose your saltiness, how will people taste godliness? You've lost your usefulness and will end up in the garbage." David married Bathsheba and they now have a young son they both love dearly. David is acting like nothing bad happened, as if he has gotten away with murder, literally. He's living a lie, a double-life. He's living in a reality of his own choosing as he refuses to deal with the horrible things he has done.

Only a few people know what happened. David and Bathsheba know and Joab knows to a certain extent. David thinks his sins were done in secret. He thought they were covered up, that nobody knew the dastardly things he had done. He thought wrong for God sees and knows everything. Prov. 5:21 (NLT) says, "For the Lord sees clearly what a man does, examining every path he takes." Vs. 22 (MSG) says, "The shadow of your sin will overtake you; you'll find yourself stumbling all over yourself in the dark." The Lord had seen everything David did and He is greatly displeased by it. In a moment of passion, David committed the most unspeakable atrocity. He did things he never imagined he would ever do. His life is stained with sin and he falsely believes he has gotten away with what he did. David is in a place of extreme denial as he refuses to acknowledge he has fallen into the abyss of death and destruction. Sin always takes you deeper than you want to go. David has shunned brutal honesty and the confession of his sin. Instead, he chose to live a life of denial and act like all is well.

The truth is, everybody sins. "For all have sinned and fall short of the glory of God" (Rom. 3:23). The question is, what do you do when you do sin? Will you humble yourself and admit you did wrong or, in pride and rebellion, will you deny the fact that you sinned? Denial is when you don't want to deal with reality. It's a defense mechanism which people use when faced with facts too uncomfortable to accept. They reject reality when it's too painful to do so in spite of overwhelming evidence. It's pretending all is well in life when it really isn't. Denial is leaving that bill you received in the mail unopened on the desk because you know you don't have the money to pay it. Alcoholics deny they have a drinking problem even after they've lost their job and as their health and marriage is crumbling. Their life is a wreck but they won't admit it. They say, "Everything is fine. I've got this under control." They don't want to face reality. They run from the humiliation and embarrassment of admitting they have a problem. Prov. 28:13 says, "He who covers his sin will not prosper. But whoever confesses and forsakes them will have mercy."

Mark Twain once said, "It's easier to deceive a person than it is to convince a person they're already deceived." There are people who live in denial so long they can't see they're deceived. They openly disagree with the facts even when the truth is staring them in the face. They're not interested in hearing the truth that will help them with the reality of their situation. People who can't handle the truth have settled on a course of their own choosing regardless of what the facts tell them. They defend themselves believing they've made the right decisions, refusing to admit they're denying that which is really true. They then go off and keep busy doing other things so they'll be distracted from dealing with the issue at hand. They become workaholics because they don't want to slow down and deal with the realities of life. David is in denial and in his heart he is miserable. In graphic detail he later wrote in Ps. 32:3 (NLT), "When I refused to confess my sin, my body wasted away, and I groaned all day long." He is feeling the pain of denial, the consequences of carrying the guilt and stress of what he had done nearly a year ago.

David is living a life separated from God. Is. 59:2,3 says, "But your iniquities have separated you from your God; And your sins have hidden His face from you, so that He will not hear. For your hands are defiled with blood, and your fingers with iniquity; Your lips have spoken lies, your tongue has muttered perversity." Sin separates you from God and this is called death. Adam was told if he ate of the tree of the knowledge of good and evil that he would die (Gen. 2:17). Adam ate of the tree and immediately his soul was separated from God. He died spiritually and began to die physically. The proof that all people sin is found in the fact that all people die. Where there is sin, there is death. The only way to escape the death penalty of sin is to confess it and forsake it. This David has not done. He didn't listen to the conviction of his own heart and has shown no outward appearance of sorrow and remorse. God has been patient for a year as He gave David a chance to repent and make things right. When he didn't repent God said, "Enough is enough" and He sent Nathan to talk to him (2 Sam. 12:1).

Nathan is David's friend and God's faithful prophet and it is only by grace that God sent him to David. One can never presume that God will speak to an unrepentant sinner. He said in Gen. 6:3, "My Spirit shall not strive with man forever." When a person sins they must respond to the conviction of the Holy Spirit because it might not always be there. After a while, God will step back and wait for you to make the first move. James 4;7-10 says, "Therefore submit to God. Resist the devil and he will flee from you. Draw near to God and He will draw near to you. Cleanse your hands, you sinners; and purify your hearts, you double-minded. Lament and mourn and weep! Let your laughter be turned to mourning and your joy to gloom." Sin is nothing to laugh at. The Message Bible says, "Hit bottom, and cry your eyes out. The fun and games are over. Get serious, really serious. Get down on your knees before the Master; it's the only way you'll get on your feet." Surprisingly, God makes the first move here. He's seeking David the same way a good shepherd goes looking for a lost lamb.

Fellowship between God and man is what the Bible is all about. This is why Rom. 5:8 (NLT) says, "But God showed His great love for us by sending Christ to die for us while we were still sinners." A whole year has gone by and God wants to bring His wayward son home. He wants to restore fellowship with David, a man after His own heart. God didn't send Nathan to David right away. He waited a full year because He was preparing David through his inner turmoil for this upcoming confrontation. He knew that David would not have received what Nathan had to say if he was approached immediately after his sin. The grinding wheel of guilt and shame is what made David receptive to what God had to say to him through Nathan the prophet. Nathan was a close friend of David, probably his best friend. If you need to be confronted, pray that God will use a close friend to do it. Prov. 27:6 says, "Faithful are the wounds of a friend, but the kisses of an enemy are deceitful." It's hard to confront an enemy. They won't listen to you but a friend will. This is why God sent Nathan to David.

Nathan is about to do what Gal. 6:1 says you should do, "Brethren, if a man is overtaken in any trespass, you who are spiritual restore such a one in a spirit of gentleness, considering yourself lest you also be tempted." To confront a king about his sin takes courage, compassion, and wisdom. Nathan didn't come to David in anger and self-righteousness, he came in a spirit of love and with a broken heart. David considered Nathan a friend and this made him receptive to what he was about to say. In a cunning way, Nathan confronts David and begins to tell him a parable, a story David thinks is true. Why a parable? Because a parable will take David completely off guard so that he'll see the severity of his sin by seeing it on someone else. It's also common knowledge that people get defensive when confronted directly. Nathan begins by saying, "There were two men in one city, one rich and the other poor. The rich man had exceeding many flocks and herds. But the poor man had nothing, except one little ewe lamb which he had bought and nourished" (2 Sam. 12;1-3).

So far, so good. Surely David remembered his life as a shepherd boy in the fields of Bethlehem. Now that Nathan has David's attention, he continues by saying, "And it grew up together with him and with his children. It ate of his own food and drank from his own cup and lay in his bosom; and it was like a daughter to him" (vs. 3) Certainly there is a smile on David's face as he relates to what Nathan is saying. He also loved those lambs he watched over and more than once he laid down his life for them. Now comes the bad news, "And a traveler came to the rich man, who refused to take from his own flock and from his own herd to prepare one for the wayfaring man who had come to him; but he took the poor man's lamb and prepared it for the man who had come to him" (vs. 4). This rich man took the poor man's lamb, butchered it, and fed it to the traveler. He refused to take from his own, as did David who had a harem of women to choose from. He allowed his lust to run wild and took for himself the one ewe lamb, the only wife of Uriah the Hittite.

The message of this story is that David stole something precious and valuable from Uriah. Lev. 18 describes in great detail the sin of "uncovering the nakedness" of those other than your spouse. The nakedness of others doesn't belong to you and you're a thief if you take it. David's anger is greatly aroused for he doesn't yet see himself in this story. There is fire shooting out of his eyes and smoke coming out his ears. He was a shepherd at one time and he knows what it's like to have a little lamb to love and cherish. His blood boils over and in rage he says to Nathan, "As the Lord lives, the man who has done this shall surely die! And he shall restore fourfold for the lamb, because he did this thing and because he had no pity" (vs. 5.6). David is proving that people often try to rid themselves of a guilty conscience by passing judgment on someone else. They judge people for doing the same thing they've done. Jesus said in Matt. 7:3, "And why do you look at the speck in your brother's eye, but do not consider the plank in your own eye?"

David had the anxious desire to do the right thing. As king, he had the obligation to administer justice, to protect the innocent and condemn the guilty. Because his passions were aroused, David passes a death sentence on this rich man when stealing a lamb wasn't a capital crime. He also thought death wasn't enough punishment for this thief. Before being put to death he would have to restore fourfold what he took from the poor man. David knew that true repentance brings with it restitution. Without realizing it, David is signing his own death sentence. He is pronouncing judgment on himself because there was a death penalty for adultery. He is willing to level the highest possible judgment on a lamb thief but overlook his own far greater sin. David said, "The man shall die!" Nathan looks at him and says, "You are the man!" (vs. 7). Suddenly, this story broke through the wall of denial and penetrated into David's heart. All David can do is sit there and stare at Nathan as his terrible sin passes through his heart and soul.

What Nathan said to David are some of the most epic words in all the Bible. One is reminded of what Jesus said at the last supper, "Truly I tell you, one of you will betray Me" (Matt. 26:21). When Nathan said, "You are the man!" he wasn't seeking to crush or humiliate David. No, Nathan knew the heart of God and the richness of His grace and kindness. Rom. 2:4 says, "The goodness of God leads you to repentance." The Message Bible says, "In kindness He takes us firmly by the hand and leads us into a radical life-change." Nathan understood the best way to reach the heart of David was not to point a finger at him but to share a story he could relate to. If there is any hope that a person can be persuaded that they've done wrong, God will use conviction and conversion to turn them around, not condemnation. God never confronts a person to set them up for failure. He confronts sin to restore, not humiliate, to set free and not condemn. Rom. 5:20 says, "But where sin abounded, grace abounded much more." Through grace, conviction takes place, conversion happens, restoration comes.

God is in the restoration business. This is why He showers you with undeserved love and grace. He wants to bring you to a place where you can hear and receive the truth. John 3:17 says, "For God did not send His Son into the world to condemn the world, but that the world through Him might be saved." God knew David's heart and that he could be persuaded to come to a place of confession and repentance. This is why Nathan was sent to confront him. Personal salvation requires personal conviction of sin so Nathan had to shock David into seeing his sin for what it was. What Nathan said is totally unexpected and David is hit like a train in a dark tunnel. He didn't see it coming. Suddenly, David's eyes are opened to the seriousness and enormity of what he had done. The finger of God is pointed at him and his sin is now out in the open. For sure, secret sin on earth is an open scandal in heaven. All David can do now is sit still and listen to what else has to be said. Sad to say, David will pay a terrible price for what he has done for God's justice is just as real as His mercy.

Don't let yourself be fooled; sin always has consequences. Gal. 6:7,8 is a New Testament verse that says there will be, "Do not be deceived, God is not mocked; for whatever a man sows, that he will also reap. For he who sows to his flesh will of the flesh reap corruption." The NLT says, "Those who live only to satisfy their own sinful nature will harvest decay and death from that sinful nature." Mocking God is believing you can sin and get away with it. The Message Bible says, "No one makes a fool of God." Yes, the cleansing power of God's grace to forgive and restore can and will come on you like a flood. You can be cleansed on the inside, but on the outside there will be consequences that won't go away, situations that must be faced and dealt with. The choices you make always have consequences. It may take months or years for them to catch up to you but make no mistake about it, one way or another, your sin will find you out. What David did was evil in the eyes of the Lord and there will be consequences. In the moments that follow, David will learn how horrible those consequences will be.

God, in His exalted holiness, says to David, "I anointed you king over Israel, and I delivered you from the hand of Saul. I gave you your master's house and your master's wives into your keeping, and gave you the house of Israel and Judah. And if that had been too little, I also would have given you much more" (vs. 7,8). David had everything and still God was willing to give him much more, to give him exceedingly, abundantly above all he could ask or think (Eph. 3:20). God is saying here that David's sin was an expression of ingratitude. God had given him so much but instead of being thankful, he chose to sin instead. God asks him, "Why have you despised the commandment of the Lord, to do evil in His sight?" The Message Bible says, "So why have you treated the word of God with brazen contempt, doing this great evil?" David wrote in Ps. 19:8, "The statutes of the Lord are right, rejoicing the heart; The commandment of the Lord is pure, enlightening the eyes." David wrote this yet, by his sin, he showed that he hated and despised God's commands. This is true of anybody who deliberately sins against God.

Nathan said to David, "You are the man!" God now says the same thing, "You have killed Uriah the Hittite with the sword; you have taken his wife to be your wife, and have killed him with the sword of the people of Ammom" (vs. 9). God won't allow David to blame anyone else but himself. Who killed Uriah? "You did! You are the man!" The skeletons in David's closet are there for all to see. Nothing is hidden. What he did in secret is out in the open. Jesus said in Luke 12:2,3, "For there is nothing covered that will not be revealed, nor hidden that will not be known. Therefore, whatever you have spoken in the dark will be heard in the light, and what you have spoken in the ear in inner rooms will be proclaimed on the housetops." The Message Bible says, "You can't keep your true self hidden forever; before long you'll be exposed. You can't hide behind a religious mask forever; sooner or later the mask will slip and your true face will be known. You can't whisper one thing in private and preach the opposite in public; the day's coming when those whispers will be repeated all over town."

God now tells David the punishment he must bear for his sin. What he has sown, he must now reap. "Now therefore, the sword shall never depart from your house, because you have despised Me, and have taken the wife of Uriah the Hittite to be your wife" (vs. 10). God doesn't even use Bathsheba's own name. God wants David to see this woman as the wife of another man. David despised God when he chose to sin and for that there will be heavy consequences. To whom much is given, much is required (Luke 12:48). God promised from that day forward there will be violence and bloodshed among his own family members. David demanded a fourfold restitution from the rich man in Nathan's parable. In the days that follow a fourfold restitution for Uriah will be paid from four of David's sons. His baby son with Bathsheba, Ammon, Absalom, and Adonijah will each die and pay a heavy price for the sins of their father. "Behold, I will raise up adversity against you from your own house; and I will take your wives before your eyes and give them to your neighbor, and he shall lie with your wives in the sight of the sun" (vs. 11).

The Living Bible translates "adversity" as "rebellion." God told David that because he troubled another man's house, trouble and rebellion will come from his own house. Also, just as David violated another man's wife, so will his wives be violated for all to see. "For you did it secretly, but I will do this thing before all Israel, before the sun" (vs. 12). God had given much to David so he could further God's kingdom and proclaim His glory. This is what all people are created to do. For that to happen, Jesus said in Matt. 16:24 (NLT), "If any of you wants to be My follower, you must turn from your selfish ways, take up your cross, and follow Me." When it came to his sensual desires, David did not deny himself and turn from his selfish ways. Because he didn't do that, he must now bear the cross for what he had done. David says to Nathan what he should have said a year earlier, "I have sinned against the Lord" (vs. 13). Open rebuke brought open confession. David didn't minimize his sin as he placed the blame solely on himself. He acknowledged that by sinning against Uriah, he was in fact sinning against the Lord.

David speaks few words here and this is a sign of a spirit that is truly broken. He acknowledges his guilt with no denial of the truth. This is the lowest point in David's life as he hits rock bottom. He is broken and devastated as he dwells in the depths of despair. His life and the lives of his family will never be the same. When Nathan said, "You are the man," David's eyes were opened to the horrible reality of what he had done. The Holy Spirit brought deep conviction of sin to his soul. He now feels guilty for the sins he has committed. He is crushed and filled with remorse and sorrow. There is anguish in his soul as he takes full responsibility for his sin. He feels shame before a holy God. This is to David's credit for some people have no shame at all. Jer. 6:15 says, "Were they ashamed when they had committed abomination? No! They were not at all ashamed; Nor did they know how to blush. Therefore, they shall fall among those who fall; At the time I punish them, they shall be cut down." The Message Bible says, "There's no hope for them. They've hit bottom and there's no getting up."

Sad to say, David didn't wake up one day and realize all that he had done and decided to ask God to forgive him. No, God initiated the process of repentance by sending Nathan to expose David's sin and to open his eyes to the travesty of justice he has committed. Through denial, the eyes of the sinner can be closed to the reality of their actions but God has a way of opening those eyes. Many times this will happen through the wounds of a faithful friend or the words of a loving spouse, people who will share the truth with you in love. It's when you see what you have done that opens you up to the power of repentance that brings with it healing and restoration. True repentance brings about a change of course, a change of action, a change of heart and soul, a change of lifestyle. Too many people want to be forgiven without changing the sinful way they are living. They want to be free from guilt yet have the freedom to keep doing what they felt guilty of in the first place. Repentance replaces a self-centered life with a life that is submitted to the will of God in everything you say and do.

The most miserable people in the world today are not unbelievers living in their sin. In fact, many sinners appear to be quite happy. They ask, "Why give my heart to Jesus if I can be happy doing anything I want to do?" These people are deceived for there is a judgment day coming. Sooner or later, what you sow is what you'll reap. No, the most miserable people in the world are believers who have lost their fellowship with God. Unlike sinners who enjoy their sin, God makes it impossible for one of His children to sin and enjoy it. Slowly but surely David was dying on the inside and he was most sincere when he confessed that he had sinned against the Lord. Sincere repentance is not regret or remorse. Saul cried with remorse when confronted by Samuel but his heart never did submit to God. Real repentance is about transformation, a radical change of mind that leads to a transformation of life. God didn't send Nathan to humiliate or destroy David but to bring him to the place of repentance. A drastic and immediate change had to take place because a tumor of sin had taken root in David's heart.

-29-

"DO NOT BE DECEIVED"

Without repentance there is no hope for the willful sinner. David knows this as he sits down and writes Psalm 51. As the words flow out of him, his mind is being engaged, his will is being acted upon, and his heart is involved. "Have mercy upon me, O God, according to Your lovingkindness; According to the multitude of Your tender mercies, blot out my transgressions" (vs. 1). The word "transgressions" is plural and means 'willful rebellion; to revolt; to break away from authority.' Yes, sin is sin but there is a huge difference between slipping and falling into sin unintentionally and sins done deliberately. David didn't stumble into sin, he knew exactly what he was doing. "Wash me thoroughly from my iniquity, and cleanse me from my sin" (vs. 2). The word "iniquity" means 'moral crookedness.' Sin is always devious and every unsaved heart is crooked in some way. For sure, a sinful heart is complicated and never simple. Jer. 17:9 (MSG) says, "The heart is hopelessly dark and deceitful, a puzzle that no one can figure out."

David feels dirty on the inside as he pours his heart out to God. He's asking Him to beat every last bit of dirt out of his life. The Message Bible says, "Scrub away my guilt, soak out my sins in Your laundry." It's like taking dirty clothes to the river and beating them with a stick until they are thoroughly clean and fresh again. David admits his sin and asks God to deal with it. The word "sin" means 'to fall short of the mark.' God has given all people one life to live. Everybody has one arrow to shoot, one chance to hit the target of godly fulfillment. The problem in the world today is what was once considered repulsive a few years ago is now accepted as normal behavior. The concept of what's right and wrong is constantly changing in today's society. People no longer let their conscience be their guide. They don't feel guilty for the wrongs they do and this stops them from seeking forgiveness from God. How do you determine what's right and wrong and if you should feel guilty or not? The bottom line is if God says something is wrong, then it's wrong.

Because David has been confronted, he now knows there is only one true standard that matters, one point of view that all others are judged by. He says in vs. 3,4, "For I acknowledge my transgressions, and my sin is ever before me. Against You, You only, have I sinned, and done this evil in Your sight." Charles Spurgeon wrote, "The virus of sin lies in its opposition to God. To injure our fellow men is sin, mainly because in so doing we violate the law of God. Where there is grace in the soul it reflects a fearful guilt upon every evil act, when we remember that the God whom we offend was present when the trespass was committed." David makes no excuses for what he did wrong nor does he try to justify his actions. A plea for mercy is a confession of guilt. Some people, when confronted with reality, try to come up with some form of excuse or justification for why they did what they did. When they lose their temper and break something, they blame the type of home they were raised in. They blame everybody but themselves.

Repentance is taking full responsibility for what you've done wrong. David does this and in his heart an emptiness and spiritual void consume him. How can he recover from all this? Will he ever have credibility among those under his rule? Will his confidence ever return? With a sorrowful heart that is truly repentant, David cries out, "Create in me a clean heart, O God, and renew a steadfast spirit within me" (vs. 10). He is asking God to give him a fresh start. "Do not cast me away from Your presence, and do not take Your Holy

Spirit from me" (vs. 11). David doesn't want to be exiled from God's face and favor like Cain was. Neither does he want the Spirit to depart from him like he did with Saul. He is saying, "God, don't throw me away as being worthless. Don't leave me to my folly, don't desert me to my own weakness. You are my only hope of salvation." He pleads, "Restore to me the joy of Your salvation" (vs. 12). The heart is the rudder of the soul and David is most sincere as he seeks for things to go back to the way they once were.

God is merciful and through repentance you can be put back on your feet no matter how far you have fallen. Precious in the eyes of God is a heart that mourns because of sin. A crushed heart that has been humbled is a fragrance of pure delight in the nostrils of God. Vs. 17 (MSG) says, "Heart-shattered lives ready for love don't for a moment escape God's notice." No matter how broken you are, repentance can put the pieces back together. Martin Luther once said, "The entire life of believers should be one of repentance." David is truly repentant and as soon as he confesses his sin, he is immediately forgiven. Nathan said to him, "The Lord also has put away your sin; you shall not die" (2 Sam. 12;13). God's forgiveness came in the blink of an eye and David is spared the death penalty for adultery commanded under the law of Moses. David was forgiven but he still had to face the consequences of his sin. Even if you confess your sins and get forgiven, this doesn't mean you'll live happily ever after. Sin has consequences as David is about to painfully find out.

Nathan then says to David, "However, because by this deed you have given great occasion to the enemies of the Lord to blaspheme, the child who is born to you shall surely die" (vs. 14). David's confession was sincere and it came from a broken heart. God forgave him but still there are consequences that won't go away. Jesus forgave the thief on the cross but he still died for the crimes he committed. It is foolish to think you can willfully sin and not face the consequences that surely will follow. David took someone's wife in secret, his own son will take his wife publicly. David defiled someone's daughter, one of his own sons will defile his daughter. David killed someone's son, one of David's sons will kill his brother, another son of David. Charles Spurgeon said, "Long before his sin with Bathsheba, there were various indications as to David's liability to temptation. That sin only threw out upon the surface the evil that was always within him; and now God, having him see that the deadly cancer is there, begins to use the knife to cut it out of him."

Nathan's job is finished so he departs and goes to his home. The truth is, he is lucky to be alive. Other kings, when confronted by a prophet, would have the prophet put in jail (1 Kings 22:27). They would point their finger at the man of God and say, "How dare you talk to me like that?" Other prophets were killed for standing up to the king. Nathan had confronted David and told him the sword would never depart from his house and that he would be shamed in public. He looked David in the eye and told him he had become a stumbling block for others. He had given the enemies of God the opportunity to scorn, blaspheme, and ridicule God and His people. For all that, a heavy price must be paid. He's about to learn that the terrible consequences of sin give a person a reason not to sin. "And the Lord struck the child that Uriah's wife bore to David, and it became very ill" (vs. 15). Bathsheba is now married to David but she is still referred to as Uriah's wife. This is because when the child was conceived Uriah was still alive and married to Bathsheba.

The law of Moses was given so that Israel could reflect God's character to the world. David's sin was observed by the nations and it resulted in them dishonoring God. Paul said in Rom. 2:23,24 (NLT), "You are so proud of knowing the law, but you dishonor God by breaking it. No wonder the Scriptures says, 'The Gentiles blaspheme the name of God because of you.'" Make no mistake about it, God is very concerned about His reputation. He couldn't look the other way when David sinned for his disobedience was a matter of public knowledge. For God to allow David's sin to have no consequences would enable the wicked to conclude that God does not really hate sin, nor does He do anything about it when people do sin. By taking the life of this child who was conceived in sin, God is making a statement to those looking on. If He does not deal with this sin, the people will mock Him with the confidence that they can get away with their sin. The death of this child will silence those who would use David's sin as an occasion to blaspheme the name of God.

Some people shun taking responsibility for their sin by saying, "David lived under the law, we're under grace." That's true but don't forget that Paul said, "Do not be deceived!" He wouldn't have said that if the possibility of being deceived wasn't there. He said those words to people who think they can sin without dealing with the consequences that are sure to follow. These people are deceived into thinking that the law of sowing and reaping (Gal. 6:7,8) doesn't apply to those under grace, to those whose sins have been forgiven. They're wrong, dead wrong. Just ask David. For the rest of his life David is going to reap what he has sown. His remaining days on earth will be filled with grief and misery, beginning with the death of an innocent child who was the evidence and monument of his guilt. Yes, God removes all sin but He doesn't remove the consequences of what you've done wrong. If He did, people would never learn the seriousness of sin and would continue to sin all the more.

English church leader Robert William Dale said in the nineteenth century, "It is partly because sin does not provoke our own wrath, that we do not believe that sin provokes the wrath of God." Many people don't learn the easy way by being forewarned in advance. Instead, they continue sinning and learn the hard way. Heb. 10:29 (MSG) says, "This is no light matter. God has warned us that He'll hold us to account and make us pay." Because David regarded the Lord with contempt, the son Bathsheba had conceived with him during one night of lustful pleasure would die. David's sin, like all sin, in never worth the price one has to pay. There are people who play with sin, thinking they can do what they want and that God is obligated to forgive them. Sure, they may suffer some consequences here in this life but their eternal future is secure no matter what they intentionally do. This is presumptuous sin, the most serious and dangerous kind there is. Heb. 10:31 (NLT) says, "It is a terrible thing to fall into the hands of the living God."

Robert Louis Stevenson, the noted Scottish novelist who wrote "Treasure Island," once wrote, "Everybody, sooner or later, sits down to a banquet of consequences." He was right, yet many don't believe that. They're disillusioned and shrug off serious sin thinking they're under grace. The fact remains, sin is never worth the price you have to pay, even for those whose sins are forgiven. If you've sinned in the past and you now want to make things right with God, confess your sin to Him (1 John 1:9) and be willing to submit to His discipline. If you'll do that, you can believe that, in time, God will bring beauty out of your ashes (Is. 61:3). Many psalms were written by David in his latter years as he once again drew close to God even as he experienced the discipline of reaping what he had sown. It's true, you can't undo your past but you can do something about the present and the future. Gal. 5:16 says, "Walk in the Spirit, and you shall not fulfill the lust of the flesh." If you sow to the Spirit by walking in the Spirit, you will eventually harvest a crop of the fruit of the Spirit (Gal. 5:22,23).

People need to wake up and realize that the negative consequences of sin far outweigh the momentary pleasures it often brings. The son David's sin produced is about to die and there is nothing he can do to change the inevitable although he'll desperately try. "David therefore pleaded with God for the child, and David fasted and went in and lay all night on the ground" (vs. 16). There are times in scripture when people earnestly sought the mercy of God causing Him to pull back from what He planned to do. He wanted to wipe out the stiff-necked children of Israel and Moses talked Him out of it. The people of Ninevah repented and God relented from His judgment on them. David is hoping God will do the same thing here so he pleads with Him mightily. Whatever David did, he did it with all his might (Eccl. 9:10). He fought Goliath when nobody else would. He sang louder and danced harder than anyone else. Here he repents with all his might, all his heart, all his soul. He is extremely brokenhearted as he lays on his face for seven long days.

"When David saw that his servants were whispering, David perceived that the child was dead. Therefore David said to his servants, 'Is the child dead?' And they said, 'He is dead'" (vs. 19). Sadly, there are times when the innocent suffer because of the sins of the guilty. David fasted and prayed and the child died anyway. You need to understand that fasting and prayer are not tools to get whatever you want from God, they're demonstrations of your surrender to His will. Even when sin is forgiven, a price must be paid. Although the child died and went to heaven, the chastisement was upon David and Bathsheba. If the child had lived, he would have been a living reminder of the terrible sin that brought about his birth. Not only did God want to forgive David of his sin, He also wanted to heal him of the presence of his sin. The baby was innocent and represents another innocent baby who came into the world and died so people could be forgiven of their sin. This baby was the son of David just like Jesus is called the Son of

David. They both died so forgiveness could come and the kingdom salvaged and restored.

Never again will David commit adultery because the consequences of doing so drove those desires out of him. The death of this child will be the first of a number of painful events David will experience as a result of his sin. A burden was lifted off of David when he heard the baby had died and a sense of peace came over him. "So David arose from the ground, washed and anointed himself, and changed his clothes; and he went into the house of the Lord and worshiped. Then he went to his own house; and when he requested, they set food before him, and he ate" (Vs. 20). David's servants questioned him for doing this and he said to them, "While the child was still alive, I fasted and wept, for I said, 'Who can tell whether the Lord will be gracious to me, that the child may live?' But now he is dead; why should I fast? Can I bring him back again? I shall go to him but he shall not return to me" (vs. 22,23). David was confident he would meet his son in heaven. Here is biblical proof that young babies go to heaven when they die.

"Then David comforted Bathsheba his wife, and went in to her and lay with her. So she bore a son, and he called his name Solomon. And the Lord loved him" (vs. 24). Before the child died, Bathsheba was called Uriah's wife. Now, after the chastisement for sin, she is recognized as the wife of David. Not one word is said to her in this narrative concerning her guilt in all of this but she was severely punished in the calamities that fell upon David, namely the death of her son. This child was the only connection she had with David and perhaps she thought she would be cast away the same way David no longer had any relation with Michal. Would she be left alone to bear the shame and punishment that had come upon her? No doubt she was very distressed on account of the sin she had committed, because of the wrath and displeasure of God, and especially because of the death of her child. Thankfully, God did not tell David to forsake her. God is saying to repent of whatever sin they committed and move on.

David patiently submitted to the will of God in the death of his child, and God made up for it with the birth of another. God loved this child and will make his name great. It will be this new son who will succeed David on the throne and build a house for the Name of God, a temple where His glory will be manifested. The name "Solomon" means 'God is peace' and his birth was a confirmation of the peace and reconciliation between God and his parents. There will be peace during Solomon's reign as king in which he'll be a type of Christ, the Prince of Peace. "And He sent word by the hand of Nathan the prophet; so he called his name Jedidiah, because of the Lord" (vs. 25). This new name means 'Beloved of the Lord.' The changing of the child's name revealed God's favor on his life, just like the names of Abraham, Sarah, and Jacob were also changed. It is interesting to note that David felt no animosity toward Nathan the prophet, the messenger of bad news. In fact, he and Bathsheba would later name a son after him (1 Chron. 3:5) and it is through this son that the Messiah would be born (Luke 3:31).

The past couple of years have been very traumatic for David. He cheated on his many wives and Prov. 11:29 says, "He who troubles his own house will inherit the wind." The Message Bible then says, "Common sense tells you it's a stupid way to live." Yes, David did many stupid things. He sowed the wind and he's about to reap the whirlwind (Hos. 8:7). Evil deeds done in the past have a way of coming back to haunt you. Foolish things willfully done will result in an intense storm of severe consequences. Along with the law of sowing and reaping comes the principle of multiplication. You always reap more than you sow. You sow the wind; you reap the destructive forces of the whirlwind. In other words, those who live in unrepentant sin can expect to suffer the consequences of their wrongdoing magnified many times over. Sin has the potential to bring forth an amplified series of calamities into your life that can sweep you away with stunning intensity into the pit of doom and gloom. Sin has no mercy and, if not dealt with and forsaken, will lead to a life of ruin and despair.

A whirlwind is a powerful and destructive force that brings with it unavoidable consequences over which you have no control. Concerning disobedience, God said in Lev. 26:14,16, "But if you do not obey Me, and do not observe all these commandments, I will even appoint terror over you, wasting disease and fever which shall consume the eyes and cause sorrow of heart. And you shall sow your seed in vain, for your enemies shall eat it." Do not be deceived! If you sow the wind, you will reap the whirlwind. A simple breeze of sin can turn into a mighty tempest of fury, a whirlwind of powerful destruction. Marriages disintegrate and careers get ruined because of the crushing annihilation that comes as a result of sin. God continues, "I will set My face against you, and you shall be defeated by your enemies. Those who hate you shall reign over you, and you shall flee when no one pursues you. And after all this, if you do not obey Me, then I will punish you seven times more for your sins. I will break the pride of your power" (vs. 17-19).

There is something terribly wrong in the world today. Gone are the grandmothers and great-grandmothers who taught their children to do the right thing and not sin. The humble and moral generation of yesterday where people knew right from wrong has been replaced by an atheistic generation of people who say it's acceptable to sin. A culture of permissiveness runs rampant in today's world where people say, "If it feels good, do it." They say sex outside of marriage is okay and it's not that big a deal to cheat on an exam at school. They even say it's barbaric to discipline your children. Good is bad and bad is good. They ignore the biblical fact that the wages of sin is death. Like a train out of control, sin always brings with it death and destruction, a whirlwind of social trauma and heartache. Devastating consequences are being experienced by those who willfully and habitually sin. Even so, people still will not admit they're wrong as they continue to fight for the right to do what is evil in the eyes of God.

The state of the world today is the result of over sixty years of social madness. People reject the values and moral standards of their ancestors who clung to a way of life many fought and died for. They now make their own rules that are twisted with devilish intent. They legalize drugs, prostitution, and same-sex marriages. They fight to protect seals in the Arctic but demand the right to abort their babies whenever they want to. These people are described in 2 Tim. 3:2-5, "For men will be lovers of themselves, lovers of money, boasters, proud, blasphemers, disobedient to parents, unthankful, unholy, unloving, unforgiving, slanderers, without self-control, brutal, despisers of good, traitors, headstrong, haughty, lovers of pleasure rather than lovers of God, having a form of godliness but denying its power." People get this way because liberals in the media, schools, and even in some churches have taught a new morality contrary to the will of God. They tell people they can live any way they want to with no penalty or consequence for wrong behavior.

Abraham Lincoln said in 1863, "We have been the recipients of the choicest bounties of heaven. We have been preserved these many years in peace and prosperity. We have grown in numbers, wealth, and power as no other nation has ever grown. But we have forgotten God." It is foolish to think you can sin and get away with it. Look around you. You don't have to look far to see the result of all the evil compromise and greed that is in the world. Everywhere you look there are wars and rumors of wars. Earthquakes happen almost weekly. Famines and pestilence are everywhere and wildfires consume the land. Teenage suicides are at an all-time high and over fifty percent of marriages end in divorce. Sexually transmitted diseases is running rampant and children don't even know who their real fathers are. Craving attention, people both young and old are covering themselves with tattoos and body piercings. They join cults that offer them free love and an acceptance they don't get at home. A cyclonic wind of destruction is ripping their lives to pieces.

Is. 33:14 (MSG) asks the question, "Who among us can survive this firestorm? Who of us can get out of this purge with our lives?" The answer is found in the next two verses, "Those who are honest and fair, who refuse to profit by fraud, who stay far away from bribes, who refuse to listen to those who plot murder, who shut their eyes to all enticement to do wrong. These are the ones who will dwell on high. The rocks of the mountains will be their fortress. Food will be supplied to them, and they will have water in abundance" (vs. 15,16 NLT). God wants you to prosper and be happy. He surely doesn't want you to die because of your sins. Humbly seek God and step away from worldly thinking. Set your hearts and minds on Him and walk in obedience at all times no matter what others around you choose to do. People who ignore the warnings of God do so at their own peril. He said in Jer. 18:11, "Return now every one from his evil way, and make your ways and your doings good." If you don't do this, if you sow the wind, be forewarned for you will reap the whirlwind.

-30-

"ALL IN THE FAMILY"

The storm in David's life has begun. God said it would when He had Nathan tell him, "The sword shall never depart from your house" (2 Sam. 12:10). An element of violence will always be there, tragic events that will rip his family apart. David no longer has anything good to look forward to. For the rest of his life, David will be on a journey of one heartache after another as he reaps the whirlwind of what he has sown. He will reap the harvest in the lives of his children as they pattern their lives after his weaknesses and failures, as they follow in their father's footsteps. It is a sad but true reality that, if not dealt with right away, children will have a tendency to follow in the weaknesses of their parents instead of their strengths. C. S. Lewis said, "Pain is God's megaphone to rouse a deaf world." He also said, "God whispers to us in our pleasure, but He shouts to us in our pain." God is about to do a lot of shouting because all in the family of David will be pain and nothing but pain from this day forward.

What is about to happen is one of the darkest and most tragic chapters in all the Bible. David is about to learn the hard way that the love of God is a double-edged sword. One edge is forgiveness and the other edge is the consequences of sin that are sure to follow. Both edges are the result of God's amazing grace toward those who belong to Him. David wrote about this grace in Ps. 103, "The Lord is merciful and gracious, slow to anger, and abounding in mercy" (vs. 8). "For as the heavens are high above the earth, so great is His mercy toward those who fear Him; As far as the east is from the west, so far has He removed our transgressions from us" (vs. 11,12). When you go to God in confession and repentance, by His grace you'll be forgiven. This same grace will carry you through the consequences that come to teach people the horrors of sin. God is first and foremost a holy and just God. He forgives people of their sin but He also allows them to reap pain and sorrow so they won't go back and sin again.

Heb. 12:5,6 says, "My son, do not despise the chastening of the Lord, nor be discouraged when you are rebuked by Him; For whom the Lord loves He chastens, and scourges every son whom He receives." There is a massive difference between judgment and chastisement. Judgment is what you receive as a result of sin that has never been confessed and forgiven. Chastisement is a refining process that comes from the loving hand of God and His grace toward you. Called the "refiner's fire," chastisement burns away the impurities in your life that ruin your value as a child of God. God's refining fire are the consequences of the sin you willfully choose to do. Rom. 8:28 says God is at work in all things for your good. You need to realize that these consequences are for your good, for your refinement. "Now no chastening seems to be joyful for the present, but grievous; nevertheless, afterward it yields the peaceable fruit of righteousness to those who have been trained by it" (Heb. 12:11).

In the days ahead, history will repeat itself as a reenactment of David's sin with Bathsheba and Uriah is about to be played out in the lives of some of his children, as well as a replay of his confrontation with Nathan. But first, there is unfinished business to be taken care of. Joab, David's military commander, is about to complete the defeat of the Ammonites, the war that was taking place while David was gazing at Bathsheba from the rooftop of his palace. The people of Ammon are ready to surrender and Joab provoked David into returning to battle by saying, "I'll take all the credit myself if you don't come and finish the war" (2 Sam. 12:28). David went back to doing what he should have done all along. He captured the city, took the spoil, and set the people to forced labor (vs. 31). The crown of Ammon's king was placed on the head of David, a crown worth over a million dollars in today's currency. David and all the people then returned to Jerusalem where a whirlwind was waiting there to confront him.

"Now after this it was so that Absalom the son of David had a lovely sister, whose name was Tamar; and Amnon the son of David loved her" (2 Sam. 13:1). Amnon was David's eldest son making him the crown prince, the next in line to be king. Absalom was the third son of David whose mother was Maacah, the daughter of the king of Geshur. In biblical times, kings would marry the daughters of other kings to form alliances with them. Maacah was the daughter of a foreigner and was not of the covenant people of Israel. Tamar was the full sister of Absalom for they both had the same mother. David's second son was Chilead whose mother was Abigail. He must have died at an early age because no record of his life is found anywhere in scripture. The name "Amnon" means 'faithful, stable.' The name "Absalom" means 'his father's peace' and "Tamar" means 'palm tree' signifying fruitfulness. Because their father David is reaping the whirlwind, none of these three children of his will live up to the meaning of their names.

"Amnon was so distressed over his sister Tamar that he became sick; for she was a virgin. And it was improper for Amnon to do anything to her" (vs. 2). Amnon became infatuated with his half-sister. Tamar was about sixteen or seventeen years old and was very beautiful. All of David's sons and daughters were handsome and beautiful because he selfishly only married the best looking women. Being a virgin meant Tamar was available for marriage but not to Amnon because marriage between half-brother and half-sister was forbidden by Mosaic law. Yes, Abraham married his half-sister Sarah (Gen. 20:12) but that was before the Mosaic law was given. Lev. 18 mentions three sins that are described as abominable sins, sins that are very serious in the eyes of God. Those sins are incest (vs. 6,9), homosexuality (vs. 22), and bestiality (vs. 23). Adultery is a perversion but sex with a family member is a perversion of a perversion. Amnon was a very wicked and immoral man. He was so tormented by his lustful craving for Tamar that he became sick.

Like his father, Amnon had a weakness in his flesh, an unholy passion for women. Being the king's son, he surely could have his pick of eligible women. Instead, he wanted a woman the Mosaic law said he could not have (Lev. 18:18). The Bible says Amnon loved Tamar. The Hebrew word for "love" in this verse means 'an attraction; a carnal desire; a sexual craving.' What is often called love is not love at all. Underneath the outward show of passion is hate and disregard. Lustful men who say to a woman "I love you" are really in love with themselves. They use women for the satisfaction of their sensual desires and the gratification of their uncontrolled lusts. Lust is powerful and seductive. It's selfish and opposed to real love. The more selfishly a man feeds his lusts, the more isolated, lonely, insecure, and empty he will be. These feelings will cause the man to hate the woman he just had sex with. Lust and hatred are kindred spirits. This is why you often read about men who rape women and then murder them afterward.

A woman will use sex to get love while a man will use love to get sex. Because a woman wants the security of unconditional love, she'll compromise in the area of sex so the man will love her. A man, on the other hand, will use love to get his lust satisfied. He'll tell a woman everything she wants to hear. "I love you and will always be there for you. We're one and nothing can separate us." And then, after he gets what he wants, he no longer wants to be with her. He leaves to go find another woman to seduce with his deceitful, charming ways. Lust can satisfy but only for a moment. The excitement soon goes away because lust can never satisfy beyond the physical. Sex before marriage undermines a stable relationship. It erodes the godly foundation on which marriage is to be built on. It lessens the effectiveness, power, and ability to stay committed to one another. It makes the relationship unstable and this is why those who have sex before marriage are more likely to get a divorce than those who wait until they are married.

Amnon lusted after Tamar and called it love. Thoughts of his half-sister are consuming him night and day. Tamar this, Tamar that. He is bothered by all this so much that he became sick. The word "sick" means 'tied up.' His stomach is in knots over the way he feels. He's not eating, he's not sleeping. He's burning with lust just like his father once did with Bathsheba. Like father, like son. Biblically and morally, Amnon is not supposed to have anything sexual to do with Tamar. Lev. 18:11 (MSG) says, "Don't have sex with the daughter of your father's wife born to your father. She is your sister." Just like Adam and Eve in the Garden of Eden, it is the sinful nature of man to desire and crave what is forbidden. The more forbidden something is, the more your flesh wants to have it. Amnon was used to getting whatever he wanted and nothing would stop him from getting that which was forbidden. So much does he want Tamar that he becomes depressed. He looks worn out and haggard, becoming thinner and thinner by the day.

Amnon's condition catches the attention of a friend of his who happens to be his cousin. Jonadab was a sly, crafty man and he asked Amnon why he was feeling so down and depressed. Amnon answered him and said, "I love Tamar, my brother Absalom's sister" (vs. 4). The world today says love is a feeling, an emotion that comes in and overtakes you. You can see a stranger across the room and if they have a favorable outward appearance you can feel like you're suddenly in love with that person. You feel like you have no control over love. It comes and it goes. One moment you're in love, the next moment you're not. Surely, this is not the love of God. 1 Cor. 13:4 says love is patient. Lust can't wait, it demands immediate gratification. Love is gentle and kind, lust is abusive verbally and physically. Love does not insist on its own way, lust is selfish and demanding. Love does not think evil or rejoice over iniquity, lust wants to dwell on and fulfill evil, immoral thoughts. Love desires what's best for the other person, lust desires what's best for you.

Amnon called Tamar "my brother's sister." If Absalom was his brother, then clearly Tamar was his sister. Why didn't he call her that? Because sin has the power to twist the way you see reality. It will cause you to redefine the situation you're in. The world today takes the stigma out of wrong doing. Songs are sung that say, "It can't be wrong when it feels so right." Jonadab should have told Amnon what he was thinking is wrong. He was a shrewd man who was very clever, sharp, and highly intelligent. But was he a true friend? No real friend will help you get involved with sin. Instead of directing the gullible Amnon onto the right path, he cunningly gives him a plan to fulfill his lust. He advised Amnon to deceitfully arrange a private meeting with Tamar. Be careful who you make friends with because the last thing you need is a friend who helps you satisfy the lusts of the flesh. Jonadab was a crafty man and his wicked, twisted advice to Amnon begins a disastrous chain of events that will lead to rape and murder.

Back then, the virgin daughters of a king were kept from men, including relatives, for their own safety. The sons of the king had their own house while the daughters lived in the palace until the time they got married. To get Tamar out from under her father's care, Jonadab told Amnon to pretend he was sick and then ask David to have Tamar come to his house and cook some food for him to eat. Amnon took Jonadab's advice and, with much moaning and groaning, pretended to be sick. Amnon's behavior is clearly childish, and he's next in line to be king. Not long after this, David comes to check up on his son. Amnon continues to act like a baby and David stood by and permitted this to happen. He wasn't a good father and was often indulgent and complacent with his children. Amnon asks his father, "Please let Tamar my sister come and make a couple of cakes for me in my sight, that I may eat from her hand" (vs. 6). She is now his sister, not his brother Absalom's sister. Surely David should have comprehended that something was not right here.

"And David sent home to Tamar, saying, 'Now go to your brother Amnon's house, and prepare food for him'" (vs. 7). David, what are you thinking? Can't you discern something isn't right here? Amnon, this spoiled brat of a prince, won't eat anything unless his sister feeds it to him? David is the king, the ruler of the people. He's supposed to be able to discern right from wrong. He should have seen what was coming next. Tamar did as she was told and not long after she is kneading flour and baking cakes at the house of her brother Amnon. She took the food she had prepared and placed it before her brother. To her surprise, he refused to eat it but instead told the servants to leave the house. They obeyed him because he was the king's son but didn't they suspect that something was wrong? He then said to Tamar, "Bring the food into the bedroom, that I may eat from your hand" (vs. 10). Why on earth would he want to eat in the bedroom and why does he want her to feed him? Can't he feed himself? What is going on in the twisted mind of Amnon?

This unusual request by her brother should have told Tamar that something was amiss. Bring the food into the bedroom? Be alone with a man of the opposite sex? It is so important that you think before you act. If you sense inside that something isn't right, don't do it. Going into the bedroom alone with Amnon was not a wise thing to do but Tamar did it anyway. "Now when she had brought them to him to eat, he took hold of her and said to her, 'Come, lie with me, my sister'" (vs. 11). The Hebrew language says he powerfully grabbed her and wouldn't let go. Like a dog in heat, Amnon is acting on those feelings that won't go away. The world today encourages people to put action to their sensual impulses. They don't look at you as a person who can resist temptation. This is why condoms are being handed out at schools, something that was unheard of a few short years ago. They treat teenagers as people who can't help themselves, people who are overcome with a physical urge that is beyond their ability to resist. How foolish is that?

Tamar answered him, "No, my brother, do not force me, for no such thing should be done in Israel. Do not do this disgraceful thing!" (vs. 12). This should have been Jonadab's advice. Tamar saw how terrible and evil this was so she desperately tries to reason with him. The problem is, you can't reason with lust because it blinds your eyes to what's right and what's wrong. Amnon wants his desires fulfilled with no regard for the will of God or the welfare of his sister. People say, "Let's make love" when all they want to do is satisfy a biological impulse and have sex. Yes, this impulse is God-given but it must also be God-controlled. This lustful impulse is not the same as love. Any animal can mate but it takes a deep commitment to love. Like his father before him, Amnon doesn't see the consequences that will come as a result of his sin. Heb. 13:4 says, "Marriage is honorable among all, and the bed undefiled; but fornicators and adulterers God will judge." The Message Bible says, "God draws a firm line against casual and illicit sex."

Tamar continues her plea, "And I, where could I take my shame? And as for you, you would be like one of the fools in Israel" (vs. 13). She pleads with Amnon to consider the result of what he wants to do. She appeals to him on the basis of her own honor. It would shame her because she is supposed to be a virgin when she gets married. This action would also destroy his reputation because what he wants to do would reveal him as a fool. Blinded by lust, he could not see that he also will one day reap the whirlwind. Like father, like son. Grasping at straws, Tamar is trying to stop the inevitable. In desperation, she tries one more tactic. She says to him, "Now therefore, please speak to the king; for he will not withhold me from you" (vs. 13). The law of Moses forbade this type of marriage and she said this hoping she'd stop him from what he is about to do. She's doing everything she can to stop this gross sin from happening. "However, he would not heed her voice; and being stronger than she, he forced her and lay with her" (vs. 14).

David defiled someone's daughter and now his daughter is defiled. To make matters worse, his own son did it. Indeed, lust is powerful. It clouds your thinking and causes you to do things you wouldn't normally do. Your flesh powerfully pulls you to do what is contrary to the will of God. It pulls on you until you give in to it and do the wrong thing. Amnon raped his sister because he couldn't control his lust just like his father couldn't. Ex. 20:5 says "the iniquity of the fathers" is carried on by "the children to the third and fourth generation." A child will often model a parent's sinful behavior, getting worse and more worse with each passing generation. Amnon got what he wanted and his lust now turns to extreme hatred. "Then Amnon hated her exceedingly, so that the hatred with which he hated her was greater than the love with which he had loved her. And Amnon said to her, 'Arise, be gone!'" (vs. 15). Amnon used his sister to satisfy his sensual desires. He got what he wanted. He pressed in, he conquered, and now he's off for new conquests.

Amnon had said earlier, "I love Tamar. I can't live without her." As soon as the sexual act was committed, he said, "I hate you. Get out of my sight. I never want to see you again." He retreats into his own world as Tamar is left isolated as the stigma of being a rape victim is placed upon her. Her life is damaged and destroyed. Her future has been shattered into many broken pieces for no man will want to marry now since she is no longer a virgin. According to Mosaic law, Amnon could either marry Tamar or pay her bride-price according to Ex. 22;16,17 and Deut. 22:28,29. This payment was meant to compensate for the fact that Tamar was less likely to get married and this money would go for her future financial support. Her only hope of being married is if Amnon marries her so she pleads with him in vs. 16, "No, indeed! This evil of sending me away is worse than the other that you did to me." Amnon would not listen to her desperate plea and he said to his servants, "Here! Put this woman out, away from me, and bolt the door behind her" (vs. 17).

Tamar made an emotional and earnest appeal to her brother. She said to Amnon, "Please, don't send me away. Let's go through with this relationship." The Mosaic law says a man who rapes a woman is supposed to marry her but Amnon throws her out like she's a tramp. He doesn't call her "sister" or "Tamar" but instead he calls her "this woman." In Hebrew he was saying, "Get this thing out of here." Tamar deserved to be treated with honor and respect because she was an Israelite and the daughter of the king. She was a princess but Amnon spitefully calls her a very degrading name. "Now she had on a royal robe of many colors, for the king's virgin daughters wore such apparel. And his servant put her out and bolted the door behind her" (vs. 19). This was a robe extending all the way down to the wrists and ankles. It was a garment of privilege and status, a royal robe. "Then Tamar put ashes on her head, and tore her robe of many colors that was on her, and laid her hand on her head and went away and wept bitterly" (vs.19).

Tamar feels like dirt, like garbage. She wants people to know that a great wrong was done to her so she put ashes on her head and tore her robe. She feels completely broken, shattered, ruined, and crushed. She correctly treats this as an abominable calamity and does not hide the fact that a terrible atrocity was committed against her. It should come as no surprise that Tamar didn't go back home to the king's palace but instead stayed in the house of Absalom her brother. She knew her father tended to be indulgent with his sons and he excused all kinds of evil in them. Absalom knew something was wrong and immediately he suspects Amnon. He asks his sister, "Has Amnon your brother been with you? But now hold your peace, my sister. He is your brother; do not take this to heart" (vs. 20). He's telling her to not worry about it for he'll deal with it in his own way and in his own time. From that point on, Absalom plots revenge for what happened to his sister not realizing that vengeance belongs to the Lord. Amnon must die and that's all there is to it.

"So Tamar remained desolate in her brother Absalom's house" (vs. 20). The word "desolate" means 'a state of bleak and dismal emptiness; depressingly empty or bare.' This describes Tamar's life from this moment forward because Amnon stole her virginity from her. She disqualified herself from marriage because now she is a stained, defiled, tainted woman. No man will want her now. No longer will she wear the colors declaring her availability. Eventually her father heard what happened and vs. 21 says, "But when King David heard of all these things, he was very angry." David got very angry but he didn't confront or discipline Amnon in any way. Why not? Because not too long ago he did the very same thing. He took a woman who didn't belong to him and violated her sexually. Perhaps he was conscious of his own guilt and felt a lack of moral authority to discipline his own son. Bible commentator F. B. Meyer said, "Certainly a man never sees the worst of himself until it reappears in his child." If David won't do anything, for sure Absalom will.

The Shepherd King

-31-

"AN ACT OF VENGEANCE"

David's family is spiraling out of control and he's doing nothing about it. He refused to bring upon Amnon the rightful consequences for what he had done wrong. He didn't even rebuke his son who did this horrible thing. He was a passive, preoccupied father. He was angry, he got emotional, but he did nothing to his son over what happened. What good is David's anger if he doesn't bring justice to the situation? Is he feeling guilty because this came about as a result of his sin with Bathsheba? Guilt from your past can cause you to not discipline your children when they do the same thing you did. This is paralysis by guilt, a recipe for sin to continue from generation to generation. Doing nothing is one of the worst things a parent can do. You can't allow your past mistakes to prevent your children from experiencing the consequences of their sin. How else will they learn right from wrong? By doing nothing, David is setting his children, as well as the entire nation of Israel, up for destruction. He'll later regret this lack of action very deeply.

At one time or another, all parents have failed and done things they are now ashamed of. Even so, they can't let the devil tell them they have no right to correct and discipline their children. Do these parents want their children to go down the same wrong path they did? Parents must step forward and raise the standard of righteousness in the lives of their children even if they didn't follow the same standard in their younger years. It's not hypocritical to expect your children to live better lives than you did. That's called being a good parent. The truth is, children need to hear about the shame and heartache you went through as a result of your moral failure. Even though you don't have a perfect background, the lives of your children can prosper and succeed if you'll allow yourself to be an example to them of what happens when a person misses the mark and does something wrong. Both Absalom and Tamar are waiting to see what their father is going to do. Since David did nothing, Absalom decides to take matters into his own hands.

"And Absalom spoke to his brother Amnon neither good nor bad. For Absalom hated Amnon, because he had forced his sister Tamar" (2 Sam. 13:22). Absalom didn't say anything to Amnon who is thinking he got away with this evil deed, just like David thought he got away with his sin. The truth is, nobody gets away with anything that violates the Word of God. Absalom is being quiet as his devious heart is setting the stage for getting back at his older brother for what he did. How long can hatred and bitterness go on before something bad happens? If left unchecked, hatred can be like a volcano that can erupt at any moment and go great damage. There is nothing more dangerous than a smoldering anger that is waiting for its time to attack. The hate and anger in Absalom's heart is boiling over as he patiently waits for the opportunity to take vengeance on Amnon for violating his sister. "And it came to pass, after two full years, that Absalom had sheepshearers in Baal Hazor, which is near Ephraim; so Absalom invited all the king's sons" (vs. 23).

For two years, Absalom had a root of bitterness in his heart toward Amnon. Heb. 12:15 (NLT) says, "Look after each other so that none of you fails to receive the grace of God. Watch out that no poisonous root of bitterness grows up to trouble you, corrupting many." The Message Bible says, "Keep a sharp eye out for weeds of bitter discontent." This is a warning not to treat holiness lightly or to be presumptuous with the grace of God. Don't be fooled like those in Deut. 29:19 (ESV) who said, "I shall be safe, though I walk in stubbornness of my heart." The NIV says, "I will be safe, even though I persist in going my own way." In the Hebrew culture, any poisonous plant was considered a bitter plant. The Hebrew word translated "bitter poison" refers either to the unfaithful (Deut. 29:18) or to their judgment (Jer. 8:14). Peter rebuked Simon the Sorcerer saying, "I see that you are full of bitter jealousy and are held captive by sin" (Acts 8:23). God considers pulling up bitter roots essential to living a sin-free life.

Vengeance is on the mind of Absalom. He is bitter, angry, and full of hatred because his precious sister had been violated. It is human nature to want to get even with somebody who has done you or one of your loved ones wrong. Both the Hebrew and Greek words translated "vengeance" have as their root meaning the idea of punishment. The word means 'to vindicate, to reestablish the cause of justice.' Vengeance and justice go together and it all starts in the church. 1 Peter 4:17 says, "For the time has come for judgment to begin at the house of God; and if it begins with us first, what will be the end of those who do not obey the gospel of God?" The Message Bible says, "If good people barely make it, what's in store for the bad?" People often overlook the sin they do but God does not do this. He can't act like nothing is wrong. He'll be patient with you as He gives you time to repent and submit to His will. If sin continues, it may be long in coming but God's vengeance and justice will come on those who don't walk uprightly.

Heb. 12:29 says, "For our God is a consuming fire." Yes, God is a God of love and mercy but scripture clearly states that He is also a God of vengeance. Nahum 1:2 says, "God is jealous, and the Lord avenges; The Lord avenges and is furious. The Lord will take vengeance on His adversaries, and He reserves wrath for His enemies." The Message Bible says, "God is serious business. He won't be trifled with. He avenges His foes. He stands up to His enemies, fierce and raging." Vengeance is retribution against evildoers and without it there can be no justice in the world. If there is no vengeance, there is no hell. Jesus said to the Pharisees, "Serpents, brood of vipers! How can you escape the condemnation of hell?" (Matt. 23:33). Without vengeance, evildoers prosper at the expense of the innocent. The fact is, those who speak against vengeance deny justice and support evil. You can't set justice aside for the sake of love and compassion. Rom. 3:5,6 says, "Is God unjust who inflicts wrath? Certainly not! For then how will God judge the world?"

Unlawful acts require vengeance and it is very tempting to play God and seek to punish those who have hurt you. Personal vengeance and Christianity do not go together for it is impossible to take revenge with pure motives. The Mosaic law says, "You shall not take vengeance, nor bear any grudge against the children of your people, but you shall love your neighbor as yourself: I am the Lord" (Lev. 19:18). Leave vengeance in the hands of God for He promises to pay back the evildoer in His own way and in His own time. Deut. 32:35 says, "Vengeance is Mine, recompense; Their foot shall slip in due time; For the day of their calamity is at hand, and the things to come hasten upon them." The ministry of vengeance is not placed in the hands of individuals but in the hands of God and God alone. The Message Bible says, "I'm in charge of vengeance and payback, just waiting for them to slip up; And the day of their doom is just around the corner, sudden and swift and sure."

Rom. 12:17-19 (MSG) says, "Don't hit back; discover beauty in everyone. If you've got it in you, get along with everybody. Don't insist on getting even; that's not for you to do." There are only two times in the Bible when God gives men permission to avenge in His name. After the Midianites committed violent acts against the children of Israel, God commanded Moses to lead the people in a holy war against them. The Lord said in Num. 31:2, "Take vengeance for the children of Israel on the Midianites." Second, Christians are to be in submission to the civil rulers God has set over them because they are His instruments for vengeance on evildoers (1 Peter 2:13,14). God gave the right of vengeance only to the civil government. They alone have the right to take life. Rom. 13:4 (NLT) says, "The authorities are God's servants, sent for your good. But if you are doing wrong, of course you should be afraid, for they have the power to punish you. They are God's servants, sent for the very purpose of punishing those who do what is wrong."

There are many reasons why the world today is falling apart. First, righteous judgment is delayed. Eccl. 8:11 says, "Because the sentence against an evil work is not executed speedily, therefore the heart of the sons of men is fully set in them to do evil." The Message Bible says, "Because the sentence against evil deeds is so long in coming, people in general think they can get by with murder." Is this what Amnon was thinking, that he had gotten away with raping his sister? After all, nobody had said or done anything to him for two years. He needs to think again because without biblical vengeance against the evildoer, anarchy will reign. Another reason for the calamity in the world is found in Rom. 3:18, "There is no fear of God before their eyes." Where there is no fear of God, there is no fear of vengeance. Ps. 36:1,2 (MSG) says, "The God-rebel tunes in to sedition - all ears, eager to sin. He has no regard for God, he stands insolent before Him. He has smooth-talked himself into believing that his evil will never be noticed."

The problem today is that society doesn't want godly vengeance and justice. They pass laws that give them the right to do things that are an abomination to God. They defy the holiness of God and this brings about the spiritual decline in the world and in many churches. There are spiritual leaders who think it's better to go along with the world than stand against the sin they are doing. They say,

"Hate the sin but love the sinner." That's true but that doesn't mean you let sin continue. You love the sinner, you get him saved, and then you work with him to help him stop sinning. Jesus talked about this in Matt. 18:15-17. He said if the brother refuses to turn from his sin after much effort has been extended to help him do so, then "let him be to you like a heathen and a tax collector." You don't embrace the person who continues to willfully sin, you cast him out of your fellowship and have nothing more to do with him. Light and darkness don't mix. 1 Cor. 15:33 says, "Evil company corrupts good habits." One bad apple can indeed spoil the whole bushel.

Heb. 10:26 (NLT) says, "Dear friends, if we deliberately continue sinning after we have received knowledge of the truth, there is no longer any sacrifice that will cover their sin." If God's people don't take a stand against sin, how can they expect the civil government to do it? The breakdown of lawful vengeance and justice works to benefit the ungodly sinners in the world. As the king, it was David who should have taken vengeance out on Amnon but he didn't do it. Because he did nothing, Absalom held on to those feelings of hatred and bitterness until an opportue time for an act of vengeance came his way. That time has now arrived. Shearing sheep was a festive time, a yearly event where people came together to work, to party, to celebrate. It was expected that Absalom would have a great feast at this time of year, and it was only natural that he would invite the king along with all his sons and servants. To Absalom's surprise, David refused his offer saying, "No, my son, let us not all go now, lest we be a burden to you" (vs. 25).

Absalom, sensing his chance for revenge is slipping away, persisted but still David refused to go. After being blessed by his father, Absalom makes one final request, "If not, please let my brother Amnon go with us" (vs. 26). Something doesn't seem right so David asks, "Why should he go with you?" Does David suspect ulterior motives behind Absalom's strange request? Why just Amnon and not the other brothers? Absalom urged him all the more until David gives in. Thinking there is safety in numbers, David allowed all his sons to go to the party. To Absalom's delight, his evil plans for vengeance are coming to fruition right before his very eyes. He commands his servants, "Watch now, when Amnon's heart is merry with wine, and when I say to you, 'Strike Amnon!' then kill him. Do not be afraid. Have I not commanded you? Be courageous and valiant" (vs. 28). What a thing to say to people who are about to commit murder. Secretly killing a drunk man takes no courage. It's a cowardly act to kill a man who can't defend himself.

Absalom was cunning as he waited until Amnon was relaxed and vulnerable. At just the right moment he gave the command for his rapist brother to be killed. "So the servants of Absalom did to Amnon as Absalom had commanded. Then all the king's sons arose, and each one got on his mule and fled" (vs. 29). This was a partial fulfillment of God's promise to David that the sword shall never depart from his house. He doesn't realize it but more bloodshed will come. There are many similarities in the way David killed Uriah and the way Absalom killed Amnon. In each case, the murder was a means to an end. David wanted Bathsheba and Absalom wanted revenge. Also, both Uriah and Amnon died at the hands of other people. David didn't commit murder directly nor did Absalom. They both put a contract out on their lives and used other people to achieve their goals. Interestingly, there was the use of alcohol in both of these murders. Uriah was made drunk and so was Amnon. Like father, like son.

David's other sons fled the scene wondering if Absalom is going to kill them too. "And it came to pass, while they were on the way, that news came to David, saying, 'Absalom has killed all the king's sons, and not one of them is left!'" (vs.

30). This is not true for only Amnon is dead. Whenever a tragedy occurs, news that filters back isn't always accurate. Be careful what you listen to. Prov. 18:13 says, "He who answers a matter before he hears it, it is folly and shame to him." The Message Bible says, "Answering before listening is both stupid and rude." In other words, don't act without investigating the matter fully. Listen to both sides before action is taken. Sad to say, it is human nature to listen to something and believe the very worst. "So the king arose and tore his garments and lay on the ground, and all his servants stood by with their clothes torn" (vs. 31), David hears this bad news, believes it, and mourns. He didn't respond with disbelief because he sensed that Absalom was capable of such evil. This is why he reacted with mourning instead of disbelief.

Finally, David is told the truth about what happened. Jonadab, the man who set these events in motion with his wicked advice to Amnon, tells David that only his oldest son is dead. He then said, "For by the command of Absalom this has been determined from the day that he forced his sister Tamar" (vs. 32). David is grieved at learning Amnon is dead yet his lack of correction against him contributed to his murder. If David had done something, Absalom wouldn't feel the need to administer his own brutal form of justice. Absalom then fled and went to Geshur where he stayed with his grandfather the king. He's going to a non-believing city for refuge and protection just like David did when he went to Gath when he fled from Saul. Like father, like son. After three years, David longed to be reconciled to Absalom with no intention of correcting him for the evil he had done. David's indulgence toward Amnon is repeated toward Absalom who, like his father and brother, will one day reap the whirlwind and meet a similar end.

According to the Mosaic law, David should have had Absalom put to death for killing Amnon just like he should have put Amnon to death for raping his sister. Both times David did nothing. In time, he will face even more painful consequences for his failure to follow God's law in regards to both his evil sons. He wasn't showing compassion to them, he was showing compromise. The consequences he'll soon face for this will be almost more than he can bear. "So Joab the son of Zeruiah perceived that the king's heart was concerned about Absalom" (2 Sam. 14:1). David was obviously troubled by his estranged relationship with Absalom. Joab saw that he was emotionally distraught and it was affecting his leadership ability. Slowly but surely the people were losing their confidence in David to be their king. Neither David or Absalom wanted to make the first move toward reconciliation so Joab decides to so something to bring them back together. He decides to appeal to David by bringing before him a widow with a story similar to his own.

Joab knows David has a soft spot in his heart for Absalom. He also knows David does not respond well to direct confrontation so he devises a plan to reconcile father and son. He sends for a wise woman from the city of Tekoa, a village in the hill country of Judea about ten miles south of Jerusalem. History records that the tomb of Amos the prophet is in Tekoa. Joab wants this woman to act out a parable, much like the story Nathan told David about the poor man and his beloved ewe lamb. He said to her, "Please pretend to be a mourner, and put on mourning apparel" (vs. 2). Joab sent this woman to David and told her what to say. Nathan used a story to get David to do something right. This wise woman, however, is going to use a tale to get David to do something wrong, to receive a son back without repentance. She goes to David acting the role of a widowed mother who is grieving because one of her sons has killed the other. Her family wants to execute the murdering son but the woman wants mercy granted to him.

The Mosaic law demands that this son be killed, but the woman wants to preserve her dead husband's name and her sole means of survival. She is pleading with David for she understands that "with patience a ruler may be persuaded, and a soft tongue can break bones" (Prov. 25:15). Her whole family wants her to deliver her son so that he may be executed (vs. 7). In the Bible, an avenger of blood is a person legally responsible for carrying out vengeance when a family member has been unlawfully killed (Num. 35:19). The avenger of blood is usually the nearest male relative of the person who was murdered. This woman is asking David to pardon her killer son with no consequences for his actions. She wants David to set aside the law and let her son live so he can take care of her since she is a widow. Not only that, if this son is put to death then the family name would be extinguished forever. David then said to her, "Go to your house, and I will give orders concerning you" (vs. 8). In other words, "Don't call me, I'll call you."

The woman is relentless. She knows what she's asking David to do is wrong so she says to him, "My lord, O king, let the iniquity be on me and on my father's house, and the king and his throne be guiltless" (vs. 9). She's telling David that she is willing to take the blunt of the punishment for letting her son off the hook with no consequences for his actions. The woman pleads with him, "Please let the king remember the Lord your God, and do not permit the avenger of blood to destroy anymore, lest they destroy my son" (vs. 11). Being a widow was an invitation for symphony from David. He makes his decision and says to her, "As the Lord lives, not one hair of your son shall fall to the ground" (vs. 11). David ignores the cause of justice for the sake of family sympathy and loyalty. He is forsaking his responsibility as king and chief judge of Israel. British evangelist Alan Redpath said, "He guaranteed safety at the expense of justice, and immediately the farsighted woman captured him in her trap."

As Joab had hoped and planned, this actress from Tekoa now has David where she wants him. He's painted himself into a corner and the woman asks permission to say one more thing. David said, "Say on" (vs. 12). The woman then applies her story to David and Absalom. She speaks boldly to David as she confronts him for not initiating reconciliation with Absalom. In so many words she says to him, "You're a hypocrite! You don't practice what you preach. You've extended mercy to my imaginary son but you have not extended mercy to your own son. He's banished and you won't bring him back." She appeals to him according to the nature of God saying, "Even God will devise a means to bring the banished ones back" (vs. 14). This is true, God has devised a way for estranged men and women to be brought back to Him. It's by being born again by the saving grace of Jesus Christ. However, this is not automatic. Forgiveness is never granted without repentance, without change, without a desire to leave the old sinful life behind.

David's eyes are now opened and he sees through the whole charade. He asks the woman, "Is the hand of Joab with you in all this?" (vs. 19). He knew a plan this subtle had to come from the hand of Joab. The woman confessed that yes, it was Joab who put the words in her mouth. David gives in and tells Joab to bring Absalom back home. Joab got what he wanted so he fell to the ground before David and said, "Today your servant knows that I have found favor in your sight, my lord, O king, in that the king has fulfilled the request of his servant" (vs. 22). Why is Joab so interested in Absalom coming back? Is it because he knows David is hurting for his son and longs to see him? Maybe, but Joab is not that kind-hearted. He's a little more treacherous than that. More than likely, he remembered the curse David put on him for killing Abner (2 Sam. 3:29). This is probably his attempt to make a favorable impression on Absalom who he thinks will be the future king, thus preserving his own position of authority in the kingdom that is to come.

David had one condition regarding the return of Absalom. He said, "Let him return to his own house, but do not let him see my face" (vs. 24). There should have been remorse and repentance on Absalom's part so a real reconciliation could take place but that didn't happen. At the same time, David should have initiated a true reconciliation with Absalom. He should have gone to him right away and said he loved him and was ready to forgive. He needed to encourage Absalom to repent and change what was in his heart. David didn't do that but instead shut him out of his life. David was being a stern king instead of a loving, caring, forgiving father. This irritated and frustrated Absalom immensely and resentment began to boil over on the inside of him. Seeds of indignation started to grow as bitterness and hatred for his father began to simmer. Absalom then began a deliberate campaign to win the hearts of the people. He would use his good looks and charm to turn the hearts of the people away from his father to himself.

-32-

"REBEL IN THE HOUSE"

David was tricked by the wise woman from Tekoa into bringing Absalom back to Jerusalem. Absalom did come back but David doesn't want to see him because he doesn't want to deal with Absalom's sin. Out of sight, out of mind. David did nothing to Amnon for raping Tamar but is very harsh with Absalom, refusing to see him after he had been exiled in Geshur for three years. David is avoiding the issue at hand, the issue of there always being consequences for sin. He's avoiding conflict at all costs because he doesn't want to deal with it. When parents don't discipline their children right away, they tend to be more rough later on when they do correct them. This often provokes the children to wrath (Eph. 6:4) and puts a heavy strain on their relationship making it worse than it was before. David is turning his back on Absalom's sin, acting like it never happened. This is wrong and will eventually bring great heartache to David's life. With God, no sins are ever swept under the rug. He deals with each and every one of them.

"Now in all Israel there was no one who was praised as much as Absalom for his good looks. From the sole of his foot to the crown of his head there was no blemish in him" (2 Sam. 14:25). This explains his growing popularity in all of Israel. The people were attracted to King Saul because he was a very good-looking man (1 Sam. 9:2). Absalom also had long, flowing hair which he cut once a year. Five pounds were taken off because it was heavy on his head. He had three sons and a beautiful daughter whom he named Tamar in honor of his sister who had been wronged. "And Absalom dwelt two full years in Jerusalem, but did not see the king's face" (vs. 28). It's been five years since the murder of

Amnon but still David did nothing about it. Absalom is a spoiled brat and during this time he's growing more and more bitter toward David. He felt more than justified in killing Amnon who raped his sister and this made his bitterness toward David more intense. Deep inside of him was a volcano waiting to erupt.

"Therefore Absalom sent for Joab, to send him to the king, but he would not come to him. And when he sent again the second time, he would not come" (vs. 29). Absalom is mad because he's not getting what he wants. Frustrated that he can't see his father, he tells his servants to burn Joab's fields of barley in order to get his attention. In the Lord's parable, the prodigal son came back home humble and repentant, Absalom came back bitter and angry, burning Joab's fields. This shows how brutal of a man he was. David created this monster because he didn't deal with his sin. He created a whirlwind that is going to blow his life apart even more than it's already been. Absalom's plan worked. He got Joab's attention and told him to say to the king on his behalf, "Why have I come from Geshur? It would be better for me to be there still" (vs. 32). Absalom looked Joab in the eye and demanded, "Now therefore, let me see the king's face; but if there is any iniquity in me, let him execute me" (vs. 32).

This is not repentance. There is no confession of sin here. There is no broken spirit inside of him. This is pride and contempt for he believes he was fully justified in what he did. The problem when sin is ignored is it plants the seed for further rebellion. "So Joab went to the king and told him. And when he had called for Absalom, he came to the king and bowed himself on his face to the ground before the king. Then the king kissed Absalom" (vs. 33). Absalom outwardly submits to David but being ignored all these years made him a very bitter man. David offered him forgiveness without any repentance for the wrong he had done. Alan Redpath said, "If the pardon you want is that God should wink at your sin,

He will not do it." To think this is what God does is blasphemy. You're mocking God if you think He gives you a clean slate so you can sin all over again at will. What David did was wrong and this will lead to further outbreak of sin. Things will soon turn out badly for David, Absalom, and all Israel.

There's a rebel in the house of David and his name is Absalom. Eph. 6:4 tells fathers to not live in such a way that their children will grow up resenting them. David was a harsh father and for many years he turned his back on Absalom. The differences between them were irreconcilable and Absalom came to resent his father with great bitterness. The problem with bitterness is that it almost always leads to rebellion. God told David that He would raise up adversity from his own house (2 Sam. 12:11) and this will happen in the form of Absalom. He pretends all is well between him and his father but deep in his heart is discontentment and division as he sets out to overthrow his father from the throne. Absalom, whose name means "father of peace," is in reality a two-faced tyrant of a man who became intoxicated with vengeance and power. He's not honest, he's not real, and he definitely can't be trusted. Unfortunately, because David was not a good father, he is partially responsible for Absalom becoming the person he now is.

In order for Absalom's plan to work, he must first steal the hearts of the people away from his father David. He's going to elevate himself and look good before the people while he becomes critical of David, thus making the king look bad. It is the scheme of the enemy to sow division in the house of God from the inside out. Many innocent believers get hurt because of the spirit of division as good spiritual leaders fall by the wayside. Absalom is a bitter, horrid, unsightly man and he camouflaged a bad heart with good looks. He was a very handsome man on the outside but diabolically ugly and deceitful on the inside. The first thing Absalom does is he makes himself look important. "After this it happened that Absalom provided himself with chariots and horses and fifty men to run before him" (2 Sam. 15:1). Whenever Absalom went before the people these runners would go before him and shout, "Make way for Absalom!" He would be riding tall in his chariot and the people would think, "Wow, this guy must be important."

Absalom is carefully cultivating an exciting and enticing image of himself. Not only is he a very handsome man, something he knows will work in his favor, he must also appear to be sensitive and caring, to be concerned deeply for the people and the problems they have. "Now Absalom would rise early and stand beside the way to the gate. So it was, whenever anyone who had a lawsuit came to the king for a decision, that Absalom would call to him and say, 'What city are you from?'" (vs. 2). The gate was where all legal transactions were settled and it was here that Absalom called out to the people and got personal with them. He's acting very concerned as he talks to the people about what's troubling them. The truth is, the king was the supreme court justice of the land, but here Absalom is putting himself in a position of perceived power. He's sitting there in all his splendor and glory, acting so concerned for all the people. He's coming across as a perfect politician, stealing your heart with a willingness to stab you in the back.

Absalom would say to the man who had a lawsuit to be settled, "Look, your case is good and right; but there is no deputy of the king to hear you" (vs. 3). He is sympathizing with the people as he stirs up dissatisfaction with David's government. He's saying, "No one in the king's court will listen to you, but I will." Absalom knows that he is going to undermine his father's authority by acting like he really cares about the people. He's making David look bad, acting like he doesn't care about their troubles. He would say, "You're right! It's a shame the king won't hear your case. I care but

David doesn't care. If I were king, I'd take care of all your problems" (vs. 4). Politicians always say that in an effort to get the people's vote. The truth is that it would be physically impossible for any one person to hear and fix every complaint and every problem in the land. It can't be done but it sure sounds good. By saying this, Absalom is planting seeds of division among the same people who once swore their allegiance to David.

"And so it was, whenever anyone came near him to bow down to him, that he would put out his hand and take him and kiss him" (vs. 5). He is flattering the people for this is how a king would treat a royal visitor. Absalom is acting like he's king and he's treating people like they're royalty. Encouragement is when you build somebody up for their benefit, flattery is when you build somebody up for your benefit. You tell people what they want to hear so they'll do what you want them to do. In Hebrew, the word "flatter" means 'smooth.' You flatter people with smooth talk so they'll do whatever you ask. Prov. 29:5 says, "A man who flatters his neighbor spreads a net for his feet." The Message Bible says, "A flattering neighbor is up to no good; he's probably planning to take advantage of you." Absalom was projecting himself to be a man of the people. This was an illusion for he regularly acted as if he was better than everyone else. He was better looking, the son of the king, and he had gotten away with murder.

"In this manner Absalom acted toward all Israel who came to the king for judgment" (vs. 6). This wasn't real. He's acting, he's deceiving the people. It's true, most people are more impressed with image than they are with reality. To them, image is everything. David is getting old and Absalom represents the dawning of a new day. David is the hero of the people but Absalom is the new celebrity in town. He's handsome, exciting, skilled, and very cunning. "So Absalom stole the hearts of the men of Israel" (vs. 6). His sly, manipulative plan worked. Absalom became more popular and more trusted than David and the people are thinking he should be king. How did this deceitful plan come to pass? Absalom knew that people will always follow the person who promises them the most. People are self-centered by nature and Absalom used this to his advantage. Promise to give the people what they want and they'll follow you anywhere. David served the people while Absalom used the people in his quest to overthrow his father from the throne.

Absalom next gets religious, thinking a showing of spirituality will work in his favor. He makes a request of his father saying, "Please, let me go to Hebron and pay the vow which I made to the Lord. For your servant vowed a vow while I dwelt at Geshur in Syria, saying, 'If the Lord indeed brings me back to Jerusalem, then I will serve the Lord'" (vs. 7,8). What a deceiving hypocrite Absalom is. He's using serving the Lord and paying a vow as a means to fulfill his evil plan. He doesn't want to worship God, he wants to go to Hebron to claim he's the new king. He's already stolen the hearts of the people in Jerusalem. He now starts his military coup in the same place where David first became king, in a town just a few miles from Jerusalem. Ironically, David says to him, "Go in peace" (vs. 9). Instead of saying that, he should have asked, "Why did it take you so long to fulfill this vow?" Also, "Why go to Hebron since the ark and tabernacle are here in Jerusalem?" David should have known something was not right about Absalom's request.

David doesn't get it. He loves Absalom and his eyes are blinded to what's going on. He tells his son, "Go ahead and go to Hebron. Do whatever you want to do. Have a good time. Live long and prosper." Telling Absalom to go in peace are the last words David will say to him. With his father's blessing, Absalom went to Hebron and right away he sent spies throughout all the tribes of Israel saying, "As soon as you hear the sound of the trumpet, then you shall say,

'Absalom reigns in Hebron!'" (vs. 10). Why would Absalom do this? Because people believe what they hear themselves say. If they say that Absalom reigns in Hebron, then Absalom must be reigning in Hebron. Their words turned the situation into a reality and this is what Absalom wanted to happen. He also brought two hundred men with him from Jerusalem who didn't know that a rebellion against David is about to take place. They were invited to Hebron because Absalom wants a crowd around him when he announces to the people that he's the new king.

Next, Absalom sent for Ahithophel the counselor of David, one of the wisest men in the land. Why would Ahithophel leave David and go to be with Absalom? Because he was the grandfather of Bathsheba and he knows what David did to her and Uriah her husband. He's got an axe to grind with David and no longer has any loyalty toward him whatsoever. If he can get back at David by joining forces with Absalom, then so be it. Absalom recruited Ahithophel "while he offered sacrifices" to the Lord (vs. 12). He's still acting spiritual and he's doing this for the sake of his image. He wants the people to think he's somebody he's not. He's pretending to worship God when John 4:24 says you are to worship Him in spirit and truth. Worship is responding to God, it's showing "worth" to who He is. Absalom is not being truthful in his worship yet his evil plan is working anyway. "And the conspiracy grew strong, for the people with Absalom continually increased in number" (vs. 12). The revolt is coming for more people are with Absalom than are with David.

A messenger came to David saying, "The hearts of the men of Israel are with Absalom" (vs. 13). What started out as a trickle of support turned into a raging flood as more and more people started coming over to Absalom's side. David knew that Absalom was a ruthless man who valued power over principle. He didn't want the city of Jerusalem to become a battleground where innocent lives would be lost so he said to his servants who were with him, "Arise, and let us flee; or else we shall not escape from Absalom" (vs. 14). David was a mighty warrior and along with his mighty men he could have stayed and fought against Absalom. He didn't do that because he never forced his leadership on anybody. He served the Lord before he became king and he's not going to fight to lead the people of God now. It's God he serves, not them. Israel's greatest king steps aside without a fight because he will not strive for control over God's people. As always, he trusts God to protect him no matter what Absalom does.

Thankfully, David still has many followers who will stay by his side no matter what. His servants say to him, "We are your servants, ready to do whatever my lord the king commands" (vs. 15). Their lives may be in danger but they will stay with David anyway. David and his followers flee Jerusalem but he left ten of his concubines behind to take care of the house, In his heart he believed he'd be coming back some day. At the outskirts of the city he stops and looks back as all those with him pass by. This shows David who's on his side and who isn't. He's finding out who his real friends are. Sad to say, there are very few Israelites among them. Men from foreign lands rally around David when his own countrymen are nowhere to be found. As expected, his mighty men stay by his side. They'd been with David in the wilderness and were in the trenches of battle with him. They knew him like nobody else and what type of man he was deep inside his heart. They were sticking by his side through thick and thin with a willingness to do anything for him.

As David watches this procession leave Jerusalem his heart is in great turmoil. He wrote in Ps. 55:4,5, "My heart is severely pained within me, and the terrors of death have fallen upon me. Fearfulness and trembling have come upon me, and horror has overwhelmed me." His own country has rejected him but by his side are friends who will carry him through the valley of rejection and despair, through conspiracy and rebellion. One of these men was named Ittai the Gittite, a man who had only joined David's troop the day before. A Gittite is somebody who used to live in Gath, the hometown of Goliath. A Gittite is a Philistine warrior which means this guy was once David's enemy. David can't understand why this newly arrived foreigner would risk such loyalty to him. He tells Ittai, "Go, be blessed. Return to the new king, have a nice life, and take your brethren with you." David, what are you saying? Wake up! Don't call Absalom the king. You're the king! How surprised was David when he heard Ittai's response?

Ittai answered David and said to him, "As the Lord lives, and as my lord the king lives, surely in whatever place my lord the king shall be, whether in death or life, even there your servant will be" (vs. 21). David called Absalom the king but here Ittai calls David the king. He vows his loyalty to the real king of Israel even when it appeared that it would cost him everything, maybe even his life. The man isn't even Jewish but he believes in the God of Israel. He's saying the fate of David will become his fate. If David dies then Ittai will die with him. True loyalty isn't proven until it costs you something to be loyal. On this day Ittai became a great friend to David. Intimate friends are your shelter in a time of crisis. They're the ones you call in the middle of the night because you know they'll be there. David said to him, "Go, and cross over" (vs. 22). To leave Jerusalem you had to cross over the Brook Kidron. David is saying to him, "Come with us." Ittai and all those with him crossed over, friends to the end (vs. 22).

"And all the country wept with a loud voice, and all the people crossed over. The king himself also crossed over the Brook Kidron, and all the people crossed over toward the way of the wilderness" (vs. 23). The masses were swayed by

Absalom but the chosen few stayed with David. They left Jerusalem through the eastern gate, walked down Mount Moriah, crossed over the Brook Kidron toward the way of the wilderness, and now they're going up the Mount of Olives. Surely David remembered how many years ago he left the safety of Saul's palace to live life as a fugitive in the wilderness. What goes around, comes around. One thing all the people knew about David is that wherever he went, he wanted the presence of the Lord to be with him. Knowing this, Zadok and all the Levite priests came to David and they brought the ark with them. These priests were spiritually sensitive to the evil of Absalom and the good of David. They knew who was right and who was wrong. If David and his people are leaving Jerusalem, they want God to go with them.

Like David's mighty men, these priests were loyal to David even though they might be killed if Absalom succeeds in his quest to become king. Everybody needs friends who are close to the Lord, friends who serve Him and know the Word of God. To their surprise, David tells them to bring the ark back into the city (vs. 25). Why would he do that? The ark was the sign of assured victory. It manifested the presence of God and contained the power needed to defeat any enemy. David knew Jerusalem was the center of spiritual worship and the ark belonged there. It doesn't belong on some battlefield. He told the priests, "If I find favor in the eyes of the Lord, He will bring me back and show me both it and His habitation" (vs. 25). David trusted in God, not the ark of the covenant. He was willing to let the ark go back to Jerusalem and put his fate in God's hands. He's saying whatever God wants will come to pass. He then said, "But if He says thus: 'I have no delight in you,' here I am, let Him do to me as seems good to Him" (vs. 26).

David wrote in Ps. 62:5,6, "My soul, wait silently for God alone, for my expectation is from Him. He only is my rock and my salvation; He is my defense; I shall not be moved." David's humble and chastened spirit proves he knew God dealt with him righteously. He doesn't know what's going to happen but he trusts God anyway. He knows God is the God of love, grace, and mercy. He's saying, "God is in control whether He lets me come back or not." Since Zadok was a priest and a prophet, David realizes that a man of insight that is supernatural might be a valuable source of information for him. He says to him, "See, I will wait in the plains of the wilderness until word comes from you to inform me" (vs. 28). He's saying, "Go back, see what's happening, and then send word and tell me what I should do." Zadok went back to Jerusalem with the ark and did what David told him to do. "So David went up by the ascent of the Mount of Olives, and wept as he went up; and he had his head covered and went barefoot" (vs. 30).

David is weeping on the Mount of Olives. He is overcome by the greatness of the whirlwind that brought tragedy to the nation, his family, and himself. He is crushed knowing his punishment is deserved. His sin was ever before him and because of the horror of what is now happening he never did it again. It was at this time that David hears of Ahithophel's defection to Absalom so he prayed, "O Lord, I pray, turn the counsel of Ahithophel into foolishness!'" (vs. 31). Prayers are powerful. The Queen of Scotland once said she feared the prayers of John Knox more than an army of fighting men. "Now it happened when David had come to the top of the mountain, where he worshiped God, that there was Hushai the Archite, coming to meet him with his robe torn and dust on his head" (vs, 32). David's life was in danger and he's running for his life. Still, he took time to stop at the top of the Mount of Olives, turned around and looked upon the city of Jerusalem, and worshiped God. He worshiped God in a crisis, which is what you should do.

Next to David as he worshiped was another friend of his, an older man named Hushai the Archite. His robe was torn and dust was on his head, symbolizing his sharing in the suffering of David. It is a time of shame and sadness with mush weeping. Hushai is there to give David his support. David says to him, "If you go with me, then you will become a burden to me" (vs. 33). Because of his age, Hushai wouldn't be able to travel as fast as the others and David didn't want him to slow them down. However, David does have a plan for his faithful friend. He tells him to go to Absalom and offer to be his servant. Hushai was a wise man and David sent him back for the purpose of defeating the counsel of Ahithophel (vs. 34). "So Hushai, David's friend, went into the city. And Absalom came into Jerusalem" (vs. 37). It is interesting to note that Absalom came into Jerusalem as a cunning, wicked rebel. On the other hand, David came into Jerusalem as a brave, noble conqueror (2 Sam. 5:6,7) and Jesus came into the city as a servant-king (Matt. 21:4-10).

-33-

"THE BATTLE FOR TRUTH"

David is in flight. He is running away from Absalom and what could turn into a bloody battle where many innocent lives would be lost. This concerns him more than anything Absalom could possibly do so he flees Jerusalem with no hesitation. As he and those with him cross over the top of the Mount of Olives, they are met by Ziba, the servant of Mephibosheth, with provisions of food that were essential for their journey. On the surface, Ziba appears to be doing a good thing but underneath he is a snake in disguise who will do anything to gain the favor of the king. David asks him where Mephibosheth is at and Ziba replies, "Indeed, he is staying in Jerusalem, for he said, 'Today the house of Israel will restore the kingdom of my father to me'" (2 Sam. 16:3). Ziba is lying as he tells David that Mephibosheth is in Jerusalem waiting to be made king. Saul is dead and his father Jonathan is dead. This means he is next in line to be king. Ziba was a self-seeking heathen who shamelessly lied and slandered the good name of Mephibosheth.

What Ziba said doesn't sound like Mephibosheth at all. Once again, David should have suspected that something was wrong. Ziba is trying to use David's dilemma to his advantage. He lies to make himself look good while making Mephibosheth look bad. G. Campbell Morgan said, "Ziba was utterly despicable, and the more so because at the moment the sorrow he brought to the heart of David was his feeling that his kindness toward Mephibosheth was ill requited." Some people take opportunities when other people are in trouble to advance themselves. This is precisely what Ziba is doing. He knows David is too preoccupied fleeing from Absalom to investigate and see if he is telling the truth or not. All people, believers especially, have a need for discernment, something David did not have on this day. He believes Ziba and says to him, "Here, all that belongs to Mephibosheth is yours" (vs. 4). This is the response Ziba craved. He says to David, "I humbly bow before you, that I may find favor in your sight, my lord, O king!"

Ziba wickedly used a crisis for his own benefit. He lied to David and belittled the name of Mephibosheth. Worse than Ziba's trickery was how gullible David was on this day. Prov. 14:15 (NIV) says, "The simple believe anything, but the prudent give thought to their steps." The Message Bible says, "The gullible believe anything they're told; the prudent sift and weigh every word." The word "gullible" refers to someone who is easily deceived or cheated, easily taken in or tricked. The root word for "gullible" means 'to swallow.' The person who is gullible will swallow anything that's said to them. Those who are gullible aren't necessarily bad people but the Bible calls them the simple ones. Proverbs says there are fools who are consumed with stupidity and wickedness. On the other hand, there are those who are wise and faithfully follow God each and every day. The simple ones are those who can go either way. They don't have the experience or the knowledge to make wise decisions so they become gullible and believe whatever is told them.

Christians today live in a world that is filled with deception and non-truths. There are too many shades of gray where people don't have a clear understanding of what's right and what's wrong. What was considered horribly evil in generations past is sadly considered acceptable today. The world says it's okay for couples to live together before marriage, and to marry a person of the same gender is an acceptable thing to do. God is taken out of schools and universities and students are taught that man evolved from monkeys and a big bang created the planet on which they live. Is. 8:20 says, "If they do not speak according to this word, it is because there is no light in them." The world today is being overwhelmed with information but not all of it is the truth. One news channel says one thing while another says something completely different. Without godly discernment people don't know what to believe anymore. 1 Cor. 3:19 says, "The wisdom of this world is foolishness with God." The Message Bible says, "What the world calls smart, God calls stupid."

Be careful what you hear and what you believe. People swear to "tell the truth, the whole truth, and nothing but the truth" but do they really? The time is drawing near where people in court will no longer have to swear on the Bible that the truth is being told. Never in the history of the world have people been more religious while being so non-Christian. The New Testament continually warns the church to be aware of false teachers and false prophets. 1 John 4:1 says, "Beloved, do not believe every spirit, but test the spirits, whether they are of God; because many false prophets have gone out into the world." The truth be told, the most gullible people in the world are Christians because they strive to expect the best in people. Because they want to love and trust their fellow man, believers sometimes become vulnerable to the deceptive motives of others. People need to be more discerning than they are. The devil is a liar and he transforms himself into an angel of light. This is why you must investigate everything that's being said to you.

Many believers today are like pilots who fly with no windows or equipment that lets them know where they are going and what to believe. They blindly go through life not able to tell right from wrong, truth from error, good from bad. This is why 1 Thess. 5:21,22 says, "Test all things; hold fast what is good. Abstain from every form of evil." The Message Bible says, "Don't be gullible. Check out everything, and keep only what's good. Throw out anything tainted with evil." The world today will tell you that anything goes, that everything is acceptable whether it is right or wrong. This way of thinking has slowly crept into the church because many spiritual leaders lack righteous discernment, a spiritual quality that should characterize Christianity. They don't want to rock the boat so they go along with the flow of the world instead of swimming upstream against it. Fear prevents them from standing up and publicly condemning the gross evil that the world accepts as normal behavior. They reason if you can't beat them, join them.

The devil knows better than to oppose God directly. What he does do is sneak into the church where he tries to deceive the children of God from the inside out. His servants become ordained ministers who dress nicely and are eloquent in speech. They preach ear-tingling messages with words that are soothing to those listening. They use smooth words and flattering speech to deceive the hearts of the simple (Rom. 16:18). It's true, deception comes in a very convincing fashion. It wears the garment of authenticity and is supported by church credentials. Satan takes a grain of truth and mixes it with a truckload of falsehood. He then serves it to the body of Christ on a silver platter. Those who are non-discerning will go home saying, "Didn't Pastor Fungus preach a good sermon today?" Jesus warned the church in Matt. 7:15 saying, "Beware of false prophets who come to you in sheep's clothing, but inwardly they are ravenous wolves." Paul said, "Savage wolves will come in among you, not sparing the flock" (Acts 20:29).

Those who call themselves a believer don't like to admit this but there is a world of chaos and confusion in the church today. Why? Because Christians are so gullible. They think if something is spoken from the pulpit then it must be true. They overlook 1 Tim. 4:1 which says, "Now the Spirit expressly says that in latter times some will depart from the faith, giving heed to deceiving spirits and doctrines of demons." The Message Bible says some will "chase after demonic illusions put forth by professional liars." The lack of discernment has left more scars on the church than those heroic martyrs who were beaten and suffered at the whipping post. These brave saints suffered outwardly but not knowing right from wrong will cause you to suffer a much greater fate than those who were tortured for their faith. This is why you must examine everything you hear very carefully. Test everything to see if it is genuine or not, to see what is true and what is false. Judge and evaluate everything so you can hold fast to that which is good and acceptable to God.

The battle for truth is continually being fought in the church today. German scholar Richard Lenski wrote, "The worst form of wickedness consist of perversion of the truth. Spiritual lies are looked upon with indifference and are regarded as being harmless. Moral perversions work to destroy the spiritual life and appear in many forms." It is the will of God that all believers have a discerning spirit, the ability to look beneath the surface of what's being presented so you'll be able to tell what's true and what's not. Ps. 119:66 (CSB) says, "Teach me good judgment and discernment, for I rely on Your commands." The Message Bible says, "Train me in good common sense; I'm thoroughly committed to living Your way." Information that is not true can be very destructive. Without discernment bad decisions will be made based on faulty reasoning and superficial understanding. Yes, widespread ignorance can be very costly. Decisions made because of doctrinal confusion and biblical infidelity can and will affect you for the rest of your life.

In 1 Kings 3:5 God appeared to Solomon in a dream and said to him, "Ask! What shall I give you?" God was willing to give Solomon anything he asked for. Instead of requesting fortune and fame, Solomon asked in vs. 9, "Therefore give to

Your servant an understanding heart to judge Your people, that I may discern good and evil." The word "discern" in Greek means 'to distinguish; to search out by diligent search; to examine.' Discernment gives wisdom and insight that goes beyond what is seen or heard. It helps you make wise decisions and sound moral judgments. Guided by the Holy Spirit, discernment takes the time to think things through so that good and wise decisions can be made. Paul wrote in Phil.1:9-11, "And this I pray, that your love may abound still more and more in knowledge and all discernment, that you may approve the things that are excellent, that you may be sincere and without offence till the day of Christ, being filled with the fruits of righteousness, which are by Jesus Christ, to the glory and praise of God."

A lack of discernment has led to more anguish in the church than all the persecution that has come against those who believe. For the sake of spiritual survival, you will need discernment in your life. Sound, biblical doctrine must be the foundation that sets the standard for what you believe. Rom. 12:9 says to "hate what is evil, cling to what is good." It's discernment that helps you tell the difference. Discernment is supernatural wisdom that comes from God and it must be exercised diligently, At the same time it must also be exercised forcefully. You must be able to quickly distinguish between truth and error, even if the error is dressed up nicely to look like truth. Discernment separates the wheat from the chaff and unmasks Satan for who he is, the master of trickery and deception. Discernment allows you to see the world through God's eyes. Those with discernment can spot a false teacher a mile away. They don't operate on the basis of emotion or sentimentality but solely on the Word of God and the leading of the Holy Spirit.

It's discernment that protects you from being swayed by false doctrine. Facing life without discernment is like going to battle without any weapons. Some people believe anything and everything and the lack of discernment causes many believers to commit spiritual suicide. It's what leads to mental chaos which in turn leads to spiritual chaos. The weakening of doctrinal clarity and conviction is one reason there is such a terrible lack of discernment in the church today. At one time Christians were told to search the scriptures thoroughly, to speak biblically, and to test everything they see and hear. They were told to take a stand when the truth was revealed and be immovable. In today's world, those who stand up for biblical doctrine are frequently criticized for being unloving and not accepting people for the way they are. They're told to stop being so narrow-minded and be more open to the ways of the world. God's Word will never pass away but sadly it has been bypassed to the point where doctrine and conviction is scorned.

The Word of God is the foundation and basis for wise discernment. Paul told Timothy, "Hold on to the pattern of wholesome teaching you learned from me - a pattern shaped by the faith and love that you have in Christ Jesus. Through the power of the Holy Spirit who lives within us, carefully guard the precious truth that has been entrusted to you" (2 Tim. 1:13,14 NLT). He then said in 2 Tim. 2:15, "Be diligent to present yourself approved to God, a worker who does not need to be ashamed, rightly dividing the word of truth." If you don't have discernment, if you don't rightly divide the word of truth, then you should be ashamed. Stop being preoccupied with the way the world looks at you. You're not here to make the world comfortable, you're here to proclaim and defend what is right and to condemn and shun what is wrong. You're not attacking people when you speak the truth in love, you're preserving the Word of God as you discern what it says and interpret its accuracy.

The truth be told, the place where discernment is needed most is within the four walls of the local church. There are many preachers today who are popular with the people even though God disapproves of the message they are giving. Paul said in Acts 20:29-31, "For I know this, that after my departure savage wolves will come in among you, not sparing the flock. Also from among yourselves men will rise up, speaking perverse things, to draw away the disciples after themselves. Therefore watch, and remember that for three years I did not cease to warn everyone night and day with tears." Paul knew that in the church there would be wolves in sheep's clothing, and you must know this also. Because of this, there is a call for discernment in the church today. Too many people go to church for the sake of being entertained. They embrace pleasure and warm fuzzy feelings as they ignore that which brings conviction to their soul. It's discernment that has the ability to set people free, to help you overcome in times of spiritual warfare.

The church must hold up a higher standard of living than the rest of the sinful world. It is of the greatest importance that those who believe be called back to a life of holiness. A line has to be drawn in the sand. This means that sin must be confronted and dealt with for the absence of church discipline will render discernment useless. Rich believers are not confronted out of fear they'll no longer give their money to the church. In cases like this, sin is allowed to run rampant for the sake of financial gain. 1 Peter 4:17 says, "The time has come for judgment to begin at the house of God." A wall must be put up that separates the church from the rest of the world. This is why Ananias and Sapphira were judged and died in front of the whole church. Too many people want the blessings of being a Christian but not the discipline that goes with it. Those who are not discerning are "children, tossed to and fro and carried about with every wind of doctrine, by the trickery of men, in the cunning craftiness by which they lie in wait to deceive" (Eph. 4:14).

Job was a man of discernment because he "was blameless and upright, and one who feared God and shunned evil" (Job

1:1). This shows that discernment and maturity go hand-in-hand. Prov. 16:21 (NIV) says "The wise in heart are called discerning, and gracious words promote instruction." Discernment can perceive what is birthed through human desire or thought. It knows right from wrong. Prov. 14:33 (NET) says, "Wisdom rests in the mind of the discerning." Make discerning what God is doing your main point of focus. Seek Him out for His redemptive plan and what He would have you say and do. You must desire to do the right thing, the right way, so that God will be pleased with what you're doing. Discernment is needed before you get in trouble, not after. It adds the power of God's Spirit to natural knowledge and wisdom in order to make good decisions. Prov. 14:6 (NIV) says, "The mocker seeks wisdom and finds none, but knowledge comes easily to the discerning."

David was a man after God's own heart but on this day, he lacked discernment as he believed the lie Ziba told him. He was told Mephibosheth was in Jerusalem waiting to be made king. Scripture later reveals that clearly this wasn't true. Surely David should have known better. He gives to Ziba what rightfully belongs to Mephibosheth and goes on his way. Not long after this, rocks began raining down on his head. Literally. When David came to Bahurim, a distant relative of King Saul named Shimei came out, cursing continually as he came. "And he threw stones at David and at all the servants of King David" (2 Sam. 16:6). Shimei is an angry man and he resented David for replacing Saul as king. Once David became king all preferential treatment given to Shimei disappeared. Because of this, he carried some deep-rooted bitterness toward David. He's as offensive as a person can be and he's using David's misfortune to get back at him. He wants to do to David harm because he wrongly believes David did Saul wrong.

Shimei continues to curse David saying, "Come out! Come out! You bloodthirsty man, you rouge!" (vs. 7). He is accusing David of taking the throne by force, using bloodshed to become king. He thinks God is now judging him for doing so. It helps his anger to believe he was an instrument to carry out God's judgment in this matter. Shimei thinks his behavior is justified but he is totally wrong. None of this came upon David because of what he did to Saul and his family. Bible commentator Matthew Henry said, "See how forward malicious men are to press God's judgments into the service of their own passion and revenge." Shimei next proclaims that the Lord delivered the kingdom into the hand of Absalom. He then said, "So now you are caught in your own evil, because you are a bloodthirsty man!" (vs. 8). Again Shimei says something that is not true. The Lord did not deliver the kingdom into the hands of Absalom. Still, these words stab David in the heart. He did do evil and he's experiencing the consequences for what he had done wrong.

David's mighty men are with him and they're more than ready to kill Shimei if David would only give the word. His nephew Abishai says to him, "Why should this dead dog curse my lord the king? Please, let me go over and take off his head!" (vs. 9). It was Abishai who sneaked into Saul's camp with David and wanted to pin Saul to the ground with his own spear. He was a very zealous man and David often had to reign him in so he wouldn't do something he'd later regret. David said, "No, vengeance belongs to the Lord. Let him curse." He wrongly thinks God told Shimei to curse him and was willing to hear what God might say to him through a cursing critic. Matthew Henry wrote, "As it was Shimei's sin, it was not from God but from the devil and his own wicked heart, nor did God excuse it much less justify it. However, as it was David's affliction it was from the Lord. David looked beyond the instrument of his trouble to the supreme director. There is nothing more proper to quiet a gracious soul under affliction than an eye to the hand of God in it."

David let Shimei speak because he saw the hand of God in every circumstance. He trusted God to work all things out for his good. He said, "It may be that the Lord will look on my affliction, and that the Lord will repay me with good for his cursing this day" (vs. 12). Like a person lifting weights, you only get stronger if somebody adds resistance to your life. You grow in strength through adversity, not comfort. No pain, no gain. Almost never do blessings add to your strength as a Christian. It's the resistance from the enemy that causes spiritual growth to take place. You can't be refined without going through the refiner's fire. The truth is, sometimes you just have to let people vent, to give you a piece of their mind, to get what's bothering them out of their system. Consider the source and let them do it. Smile at them if you can. Say you're sorry and offer to pray for them. Shimei continues to curse David and throw rocks at him (vs. 13). He believes David will not return to Jerusalem and regain his throne. Guess again.

Whenever you deal with people you need the heart of a child, the wit of an ambassador, and the hide of a rhinoceros. Be open, be loving, be willing to forgive. David knew his real problem was Absalom and not Shimei. He never lost his perspective. He knew if he did what was right now, God would take care of the future. "Now the king and all the people who were with him became weary; so they refreshed themselves there" (vs. 14). David was able to receive comfort because he was at peace knowing God was in control of Israel. It was at this time that he penned the words of Psalm 3. His life is in danger because Absalom seeks to kill him so he writes in vs. 1, "Lord, how they have increased who trouble me! Many are they who rise up against me." Suffering, difficulty, and hardship are universal experiences for all people. Everybody goes through hard times but how you respond to those trials is what determines victory of defeat. David never once blamed God for his hardship but goes to Him in awe and reverence.

David says in vs. 2, "Many are they who say of me, 'There is no help for him in God.'" Why would he say that? Because the people think what he's going through is some form of punishment from God. Charles Spurgeon said, "If all the trials which come from heaven, all the temptations which ascend from hell, and all the crosses which arise from the earth, could be mixed and pressed together, they would not make a trial so terrible as that which is contained in this verse. It is the most bitter of all afflictions to be led to fear that there is no help for us in God." David will not accept what the people say so he writes, "But You, O Lord, are a shield for me, my glory and the One who lifts up my head" (vs. 3). He knows it is God who honors and vindicates. It is He who will prevent David from walking in shame and defeat. God lifts the weights that hold you down and causes you to look to Him. Don't look down at your problems, look up to your vindicator. By looking up, God will stop your life from being consumed with difficulty and hardship.

"I cried to the Lord with my voice, and He heard me from His holy hill" (vs. 4). Don't worry and complain. Cry out to God! Draw near to Him and He will draw near to you. He'll meet you at the place of your greatest need. "I lay down and slept; I awoke, for the Lord sustained me" (vs. 5). David is full of confidence and peace. He is running for his life yet he's determined to not give in to the fear that is trying to grip his heart. "I will not be afraid of ten thousands of people who have set themselves against me all around" (vs. 6). Fear was just as big of an enemy as Absalom was. Confess out loud, "I will not give in to fear!" Walk in the confidence that God will keep you and sustain you. "Arise, O Lord; Save me, O my God! For you have struck all my enemies on the cheekbone; You have broken the teeth of the ungodly" (vs. 7). God is the God who delivers. Don't try to save yourself because you can't do it. "Salvation belongs to the Lord. Your blessing is upon Your people" (vs. 8) Victory comes when you know it is God who saves and delivers.

-34-

"THE HAND OF JUSTICE"

Absalom is standing tall and proud as he enters Jerusalem to begin his reign as the new king of Israel. Those who were once loyal to David are now giving their support and allegiance to him. Chief among these traitors is Ahithophel, the former counselor of David. As the grandfather of Bathsheba, he wanted nothing more to do with David. In his heart, Ahithophel vowed to do anything and everything to bring shame upon David and all he stood for. It wasn't long after this that Hushai, a friend of David's, came to Absalom vowing his support saying, "Long live the king! Long live the king!" (2 Sam. 16:16). Absalom doesn't realize it but Hushai came to him by design for the purpose of turning the counsel of Ahithophel to foolishness. David sent him to spy on Absalom and give him bad advice. Absalom is suspicious of Hushai so he asks him, "Is this your loyalty to your friend? Why did you not go with your friend?" (vs. 17). Hushai responds, "I want to be with the person God and all Israel has chosen. Him I will serve."

Absalom knows nothing about being a king so he says to Ahithophel, "Give counsel as to what we should do" (vs. 20). Now is Ahithophel's chance to get back at David in the worst possible way. He tells Absalom to do something so offensive and despicable that it would eliminate any possibility of reconciliation with David. "Go in to your father's concubines, whom he has left to keep the house; and all Israel will hear that you are abhorred by your father. Then the hands of all who are with you will be strong" (vs. 21). The Hebrew word for "abhorred" means 'to stink.' In the ancient world, taking the king's concubines was not only immoral but was considered an act of treason. Ahithophel wanted to see David's concubines violated the same way his granddaughter was violated. This shows the power of bitterness. Ahithophel was willing to see these women raped and abused for the purpose of satisfying his longing for revenge. Absalom thought he could establish his kingdom through immorality so he did what Ahithophel told him to do.

Having sex with David's concubines will show the people that Absalom is the new king. "So they pitched a tent for Absalom on the top of the house, and Absalom went in to his father's concubines in the sight of all Israel" (vs. 22). It should come as no surprise that this tent was set up at the same place where David saw Bathsheba bathing. Absalom violated these women in the sight of all Israel which was the fulfillment of the prophecy Nathan gave to David in 2 Sam. 12:11,12. God told David this was going to happen and it did. As wicked as Ahithophel was, he had one advantage over the people. Everybody believed that when he spoke it was as if God Himself was speaking (vs. 23). This is why everybody was ready to do whatever Ahithophel said needed to be done. This is the reason Absalom did not hesitate to take his father's concubines for himself. Ahithophel must have been well pleased that Absalom was so willing to do what he advised him to do. David is now disgraced but Ahithophel wants more than that. He wants David dead.

Ahithophel is a wicked man and is well pleased with the downfall of David. He can't wait to see him dead so he says to Absalom, "Now let me choose twelve thousand men, and I will arise and pursue David tonight" (2 Sam. 17:1). This is a peculiar request because Ahithophel is a counselor, not a warrior. What must Absalom be thinking? He thinks the world revolves around himself and here his chief counselor wants to be a leader. Something's not right here. Ahithophel continues, "I will come upon him while he is weary and weak, and make him afraid" (vs. 2). The word "afraid" means 'to tremble with fear.' He is suggesting a surprise attack while David was still west of the Jordan River. He advised urgency because surely David is bone tired from his flight out of Jerusalem. "And all the people who are with him will flee, and I will strike only the king" (vs. 2). Absalom is the new king but deep in his heart Ahithophel knew who the real king was. He also underestimated the loyalty of those with David for they would never flee his side in time of battle.

What Ahithophel said pleased Absalom and all the elders of Israel. In the natural this was a good plan. It was bold and the probability of success was very high. As Ahithophel was patting himself on the back, he was suddenly overcome with shock and dismay when Absalom said, "Now call Hushai the Archite also, and let us hear what he says too" (vs. 5). Ahithophel can't believe that Absalom would want a second opinion. What he doesn't realize is that God is at work here answering David's prayer that he requested in 2 Sam. 15:31. Why else would Absalom ask for another opinion after receiving such good advice from Ahithophel? Hushai is a friend of David's and he's working undercover as a spy for the purpose of turning the counsel of Ahithophel into foolishness. As Hushai is brought to stand before Absalom, the world of Ahithophel is about to fall apart. Absalom says to Hushai, "Ahithophel has spoken in this manner. Shall we do as he says? If not, speak up" (vs. 6). Hushai quickly has to come up with a counter plan.

Hushai said to Absalom, "The counsel that Ahithophel has given is not good at this time" (vs. 7). It is a good plan but Hushai tells Absalom it's not. He says this is not a good idea because David is a mighty warrior. He's brilliant and he's strong. "For all Israel knows that your father is a mighty man, and those who are with him are valiant men" (vs. 10). If Ahithophel's plan is followed, if they pursue David now, surely the battle will be lost. David and his men are dangerous and shouldn't be attacked too quickly. If they are, then without a doubt Absalom's army would be torn to pieces. People would then hear that Absalom was defeated and what would that do to his credibility? They wouldn't want to follow him anymore because nobody likes a loser. Hushai said, "Go after David but not now. Organize your army and train them. Then you go to battle in person" (vs. 11). In Ahithophel's plan he led the army into battle, in Hushai's plan Absalom leads the army. This fed the huge ego of Absalom and Hushai's advice was favored over the counsel of Ahithophel.

Absalom liked Hushai's advice because it appealed to his pride and vanity. His eyes were blinded to the fact that this plan bought David some time so he could get farther out into the wilderness where he would come up with a battle plan of his own. The greater reason the advice of Ahithophel was rejected was because God is in control. "For the Lord had purposed to defeat the good counsel of Ahithophel, to the intent that the Lord might bring disaster on Absalom" (vs. 14). Absalom had the smartest man in Israel on his side, David had the God of the universe on his. G. Campbell Morgan wrote, "This is one of the great principles of life which every page of the Bible emphasizes and illustrates. Men cannot escape God. They go their own way, but that way never sets them free from the authority and invincible power of God." It was David's prayer that moved the hand of God. He was a man after God's own heart and God did not forsake him during this time of chastening. He was not out to destroy David but rather to correct him.

As prearranged by David, Hushai goes to the priests Zadok and Abithar and tells them what Absalom plans to do. He says David should cross over the Jordan River as quickly as possible. This will give him time to regroup before Absalom's attack. The priests sent a maidservant to tell their sons what Hushai had said so they could go and give the information to

David. The two sons, Jonathan and Ahimaaz, were staying in En Rogel on the outskirts of Jerusalem hiding from Absalom. A young lad saw them there and reported their location to Absalom. The sons then fled to a man's house in Bahurim near the Mount of Olives and hid in a well on the man's property. The man's wife put a covering over the top of the well and spread grain over the top of it. When Absalom's guards came looking for the two men this woman sent them off in another direction. When the sons couldn't be found the guards returned to Jerusalem. The two men then came out of the well and went to David and told him what Hushai said he should do.

David wisely followed Hushai's advice and all during the night he and those with him crossed over the Jordan River. Back in Jerusalem, Ahithophel was beside himself. He knew that under Hushai's plan that Absalom would fail and all would be lost. He wasn't going to wait around and see that happen. "Now when Ahithophel saw that his counsel was not followed, he saddled his donkey, and arose and went home to his city. Then he put his household in order, and hanged himself, and died; and he was buried in his father's tomb" (vs. 23). Like Absalom, Ahithophel was also a man of pride. When Absalom did not take heed to his counsel, he went home and killed himself. Charles Spurgeon wrote, "To put his house in order showed that he was a prudent man; to hang himself proved he was a fool. Herein is a strange mixture of discretion and desperation, mind and madness. Shall a man have wisdom enough to arrange his worldly affairs with care, and yet shall he be so hapless as to take his own life afterwards?"

Absalom "crossed over the Jordan, he and all the men of Israel with him" (vs. 24). Pursuing David was good for his pride but bad for his success on the battlefield. G. Campbell Morgan said, "Absalom's vanity ensured his ruin." Absalom replaces Joab as commander of the army with Amasa, a nephew of David and a cousin of Joab. He and his followers encamped in Gilead while ten miles northwest of there, David is finding refuge in the city of Mahanaim. God supplies David and his men with food through the efforts of three obscure men sent to help David in a time of great need and to bring comfort in his time of affliction. One of these men was Machir from Lo Debar, the man who graciously allowed Mephibosheth to stay in his home in his lame condition. The other men were named Shobi and Barzillai. A war was about to take place and David needed his men to be strong and healthy so that victory would come their way. These three men were not widely known but their efforts this day would help change the course of history.

Absalom is coming so David prepares for battle. He is a seasoned warrior and he knows what to do in time of war. At this time, he and his men are in the wilderness north of Jericho in a fortified city. There he divides his army into three units as he faces the gut-wrenching possibility of fighting and perhaps killing his own son. Thousands of people have remained loyal to David and he sets battle-scarred commanders over them, men who know how to fight and how to win. The leaders of these three units are Joab, his brother Abishai, and the non-Jew Ittai the Gittite. David knows that Joab is a treacherous man and somewhat of a scoundrel. He also knows that if you're in a battle, you'd want Joab on your side. Absalom's soldiers, on the other hand, have little or no experience in war and are led by untrained leaders. David offers to lead the army into battle because he didn't want to repeat the same mistake of not going to war when he should have. The last time he stayed home he sinned with Bathsheba and this led to the predicament he's now in.

To David's surprise, the people say to him, "You shall not go out. For if we flee away, they will not care about us; nor if half of us die, they will care about us. But you are worth ten thousand of us now. For you are more help to us in the city" (2 Sam. 18:3). The people know how valuable David is and they don't want a wayward arrow to kill him. They also know how difficult it would be for him to have to fight against his own son. David responded by saying, "Whatever seems best to you I will do" (vs. 4). It must have been hard for David to say this. He wants to go to battle and make sure nothing happens to Absalom. At the same time, he knew how to submit to the good advice of others. He is still their leader as he stood by the gate of the city and watched the people pass by before him. He knew they were devoted to him and that each and every one of them were willing to risk their lives for his sake. He spoke these final words to the three army captains in front of all the others, "Deal gently for my sake with the young man Absalom" (vs. 5).

Even though Absalom wants to kill him, David still loves his son. He made it clearly known that he wanted Absalom captured alive and not mistreated in any way. These words revealed his heart as a father who was hoping to be reconciled with his wayward son. David gave this command in the presence of all the people so the captains would feel greater pressure to do what David said. "So the people went out into the field of battle against Israel. And the battle was in the woods of Ephraim" (vs. 6). An ancient Chinese book called "The Art Of War" says a key to success in any battle is to choose the terrain in which the fighting will take place. David's men chose the wooded area of Ephraim to wage a guerilla-type war against Absalom. This eliminated the advantage Absalom had with all his chariots and heavy equipment. They were totally unprepared for this type of war. Not only that, Absalom did not have his father's heart, his father's strategic mind, and his father's commitment to the Lord. What he wanted was to be king over his own life.

"The people of Israel were overthrown there before the servants of David, and a great slaughter of twenty thousand men took place there that day" (vs. 7). What a sad day this was. Thousands of people died in a civil war as those loyal to David fought against those who had been seduced by Absalom's charisma and power. "For the battle there was scattered over the face of the whole countryside, and the woods devoured more people that day than the sword devoured" (vs. 8). Those who fought for Absalom were swallowed up by the woods with its many cliffs and great caverns. They fell into pits and swamps and were attacked by wild animals. Charles Spurgeon said, "Perishing not only by sword, but among the thick oaks and tangled briers of the woods, which concealed fearful precipices and great caverns, into which the rebels plunged in their wild fright when the rout set in." Absalom is good at looking good but he is not a fighter. Unlike those navy captains who vow to go down with their ship, Absalom gets on a donkey and flees the battle scene.

"The mule went under the thick boughs of a great terebinth tree, and his head caught in the terebinth; so he was left hanging between heaven and earth. And the mule which was under him went on" (vs. 9). Absalom ran away from the battle and here he is with his head caught in an oak tree, swinging back and forth. Bible commentator John Trapp said, "So he hung between heaven and earth, as rejected by both." This is the same position of a carnal, lukewarm Christian. He has one foot in heaven and the other foot in the world. God said in Rev. 3:16, "So then, because you are lukewarm and neither cold nor hot, I will spew you out of My mouth." The Message Bible says, "You're stale. You're stagnant. You make Me want to vomit." A certain man saw what happened to Absalom and he went and reported it to Joab. Showing no regard for David's command to deal gently with Absalom, Joab said to the man, "Why didn't you kill him when you had the chance? I would have rewarded you handsomely and given you a promotion" (vs.11).

This man knows that Joab is the commander of the army unit he is in but he also knows that David is the king and outranks him. David said to deal gently with Absalom and the man replied that he did not kill him out of obedience and faithfulness to David. He said to Joab, "I don't care how much money you'll give me, I will not kill the king's son." He knows Joab very well as he next says, "Even if I did kill Absalom, you would set yourself against me for disobeying the command of the king" (vs. 13). Joab wasn't going to waste any more time talking to this man. He knew sparing Absalom would please David but would be harmful for Israel. "And he took three spears in his hand and thrust them through Absalom's heart, while he was still alive in the midst of the terebinth tree. And ten young men who bore Joab's armor surrounded Absalom, and struck and killed him" (vs. 14,15). Absalom defiled the ten concubines of David, there are ten commandments, and ten men killed him. For every commandment you break, there is always a corresponding judgment.

Joab was a ruthless man and he knowingly and deliberately disregarded the orders given to him by David. He didn't hesitate to strike Absalom even though David commanded him not to. He knew that as long as Absalom was alive, he'd always be a threat to David's throne. He also knew it was in the best interest of Israel to show Absalom justice, not mercy. In truth, Absalom got what he deserved. He was a murderer, a traitor, and a rapist. According to the Mosaic law, he should have died by the hand of justice long ago. Joab knew David would never punish Absalom so he did it himself. It is ironic that the rebel Absalom was killed by a rebellious act performed by Joab who disobeyed the command of the king. Joab was not right in disobeying David and would later be held accountable for what he did, both by God and eventually by David (1 Kings 2:5,6). With Absalom now dead there was no need for the battle to continue.

"Then Joab blew the trumpet, and the people returned from pursuing Israel. For Joab held back the people" (vs. 16).

Absalom's body was thrown into a large pit in the woods and was covered by a large heap of stones. Joab wanted to make sure his body was not memorialized as an inspiration to other followers or future rebels. "Then all Israel fled, everyone to his tent" (vs. 17). Joab doesn't hunt down and kill those who followed Absalom but lets them return home. Absalom is dead and the revolt has ended. The only thing left is to get the news to David. Ahimaaz, the son of Zadok the priest, said to Joab, "Let me run now and take the news to the king, how the Lord has avenged him of his enemies" (vs. 19). Right away Joab said, "No, you don't want to give the king bad news that his son is dead." He knows David has a history of not doing well with bad news. When he heard from a messenger that Saul had died in battle, he had the messenger killed. Joab was looking out for Ahimaaz for he wanted to spare him the burden of being the messenger of bad news. If a messenger brought good news, he might get a reward. If bad news, he might get killed.

Joab then turned to a Cushite and said, "Go, tell the king what you have seen" (vs. 21). The people of Cush came from the southern region of Egypt and the northern part of Ethiopia. This Cushite is a foreigner and Joab doesn't care if he gets killed or not. "So the Cushite bowed himself to Joab and ran." Ahimaaz watches the Cushite leave and this only increased his desire to be the one to go to David. He has no concern about what may happen to him as he pleads with Joab saying, "But whatever happens, let me run" (vs. 23). Joab gives in and says to him, "Run." Ahimaaz took off and along the way he outran the Cushite. The direct route to David went over many hills and valleys. It was a shorter route but much more difficult. This is the route the Cushite took. Ahimaaz, on the other hand, took the longer route by way of the plain which was not as rugged as the shorter route. This is how he was able to outrun the Cushite. Back at the city a watchman saw a man running alone and reports this to David.

David thinks good news is coming. He said, "If he is alone, there is news in his mouth" (vs. 25). Several runners would have indicated bad news. Just then the watchman sees another man running alone. David said, "He also brings news." The watchman identifies Ahimaaz as the runner in the lead and reports this to David who responds, "He is a good man, and comes with good news" (vs. 27). A good man will bring good news, or so it is assumed. Concerning David, there is both good news and bad news to tell. Ahimaaz chooses to tell the good news. He called out and said to the king, "All is well!" He bows down before David and continues, "Blessed be the Lord your God, who has delivered up the men who raised their hand against my lord the king!" (vs. 28). David has little or no interest in this news. Instead of rejoicing over this good news, he asks the question, "Is the young man Absalom safe?" Ahimaaz is not sure how to answer David's inquiry so he lies to him saying, "When Joab sent the king's servant and me your servant, I saw a great tumult, but I did not know what it was about" (vs. 29).

Absalom is dead but Ahimaaz doesn't want to be the one to give this bad news to David. He is told to stand aside until the other runner arrives. The Cushite soon stood before David and proclaimed he had good news to tell, "The Lord has avenged you this day of all those who rose against you" (vs. 31). That is indeed good news but there in only one concern on the mind of David. He asks about Absalom and the Cushite says to him, "May the enemies of my lord the king, and all who rise against you to do you harm, be as that young man is!" (vs. 32). Without saying it directly, the Cushite tells David that Absalom is dead. David is deeply moved and he went up to his chamber and wept. The words "deeply moved" implies a violent trembling of the body. David is so grieved that he shook all over. His moanings are echoing off the stone walls for all to hear. He knows it was his sin of adultery and murder that sowed the seeds of hate and rebellion in Absalom, that his son's death was the consequences he paid for his own sinful behavior.

David is completely undone over what happened. He can't control the tears that are gushing down his face. He is heartbroken, overcome with grief. Charles Spurgeon said, "Our children may plunge into the worst sins, but they are our children still. They may scoff at our God; they may tear our heart to pieces with their wickedness; we cannot take complacency in them, but at the same time we cannot unchild them, nor erase their image from our hearts." In his agony and sorrow David seems oblivious to the grief of others. Twenty thousand men lost their lives and their families are lamenting also. He cries out, "O my son Absalom - my son, my son Absalom - if only I had died in your place! O Absalom my son, my son!" (vs. 33). G. Campbell Morgan said, "This surely had a deeper note in it than that of the merely half-conscious repetition of words occasioned by personal grief. The father recognized how much he was responsible for the son. It is as though he had said, 'He is indeed my son, his weaknesses are my weaknesses, his passions are my passions, his sins are my sins.'"

-35-

"BRING BACK THE KING"

David is grieving excessively for his dead son as he continually cries out with a loud voice, "O my son Absalom! O Absalom, my son, my son!" (2 Sam. 19:4). He is no stranger to loss and death, yet on this day he is paralyzed by his feelings of pain and sorrow. He watched in horror as his own sins were acted out in his young son's life. He felt guilty for things left unsaid and undone, for the years he neglected Absalom and wanted nothing to do with him. His sense of loss is so overwhelming that he became self-absorbed to the point of ignoring his responsibilities to those still living. There is always an emotional response to death, but a superabundance of grief can lead to self-centeredness. David's grief blurred his vision to the point that he didn't know who his friends were or his enemies. He wasn't able to grasp the seriousness of the situation he and the nation were in. The kingdom was deeply divided and Jesus said in Matt. 12:25, "Every kingdom divided against itself is brought to desolation and every city or house divided against itself will not stand."

There can be excessive mourning that is rooted in unbelief and self-indulgence. Some people express sorrow during times of tragedy as if there is no hope in God (1 Thess. 4:13). This is why during times of trial you must continually resist the temptation to worship the problem. Loss is inevitable and endlessly focusing on it and refusing to get over it is a form of idolatry. There is a grief so disproportionate that it causes you to take your eyes off of God. This in turn makes your circumstances appear to be bigger than He is. Charles Spurgeon said, "A Christian is expected to be more self-possessed than those who have no God to fly to." Don't dwell on the problem but "give all your worries and cares to God, for He cares about you" (1 Peter 5:7 NLT). Pray about your situation believing that God can handle whatever you're going through. Keep His supernatural ability on the forefront of your mind. Focus on God and on who He is and what He's done for you in the past. Do that and He will return to you the joy and peace you so desperately need.

On this day David was held captive by his excessive mourning and his lack of perspective. He forgot that God was still in control. When someone is overcome with sorrow, the problem is not what they know but what they forget. What David is doing is not good for his mourning is getting completely out of hand. The victory over the rebellion is not celebrated for the people also mourned because David is excessively grieving for his son. David's loyal supporters just won a great victory but they return home as if they'd been defeated. 2 Sam. 19:3 (MSG) says, "The army straggled back to the city that day demoralized, dragging their tails." What David needs now more than anything is to be called back to reality. There are times when everybody needs to hear the truth no matter how painful the truth may be. He needs to be called back to the land of the living and the concerns of the nation. Surprisingly, the unlikely person God used to shock David back to reality is none other than the rude and arrogant Joab.

Joab was the commanding general of the armies of Israel and he had a mind of his own. He wasn't the type of person to season with salt the words that he spoke. Like it or not, he always said what was on his mind. He goes to David and says, "Today you have disgraced all your servants who today have saved your life, the lives of your sons and daughters, the lives of your wives and the lives of your

The Shepherd King

concubines, in that you love your enemies and hate your friends" (vs. 5,6). This was a stern rebuke that David needed to hear. Evangelical teacher Arthur Pink said, "Sometimes God uses a rough hand to awaken us from our lethargy." As David wallowed in sorrow, he lost sight of the need to put the concerns of the kingdom first. Yes, he lost a son but he's still the king of Israel. There are matters that need looking into, issues to be dealt with. This is a harsh wake-up call as David is told his excessive mourning is selfish. Joab continues, "I perceive that if Absalom had lived and all of us had died today, then it would have pleased you well" (vs. 6).

Joab is giving David no respect here. How you treat people is a reflection of who you are. If you are kind, you'll treat people with kindness. If you're rude, you'll be rude to other people. If you're disrespectful, you'll treat people in a disrespectful manner. This is a sharp rebuke delivered with precise and accurate words. David is being foolish in his excessive grief and it takes a man like Joab to show him how selfish he's being. He tells David, "Get hold of yourself; get out there and put some heart into your servants! I swear to God that if you don't go to them they'll desert; not a soldier will be left here by nightfall. And that will be the worst thing that has happened yet" (vs. 7 MSG). In other words, "Wake up! Snap out of it! You've got a country to lead! Get back to what God called you to do!" This is truly the best advice David could have received. Bible commentator Matthew Henry said, "A wise man will accept good advice no matter what the source; no matter how insensitive it may have been given."

David's grief doesn't go away but he receives Joab's rebuke. He let his understanding of what was right be bigger than what he felt. He acted on the advice Joab gave him and rose up and sat in the gate of the city. The people needed to see David sitting as king in the place of authority. This told them that he recognized all the sacrifices they made for him and the kingdom. He honors and respects all they've done and it was highly appreciated. "So all the people came before the king. For everyone had fled to his tent" (vs. 8). These are the same people who were loyal to Absalom. For them, it is a time of defeat and sorrow. They are filled with shame because they know it's God's will for David to be king and not Absalom. Both the loyal and disloyal are mingled together in front of David as he sits in the gate of the city. Before any sense of normalcy can take place, David knows he must initiate and maintain good communication with these people. He sits before them knowing that without good communication there are no good relationships.

The quality of any relationship is measured by how well the two parties communicate with one another. Indeed, good communication is the life flow of any relationship. It goes way beyond talking to one another for it is the art of listening, watching, and sharing. In other words, it is a matter of the heart. Jesus said in Luke 6:45, "For out of the abundance of the heart his mouth speaks." For good communication to happen, a transformation in your heart must first take place. If not, you'll put yourself and the other person on a collision course that will lead to hurt, anger, and unforgiveness. It will be like a head-on collision of two trains going at full power. Most Christians who are doing damage with their tongues are blind to the sinful condition of their heart. This makes them just like unbelievers. Don't be like the sinners of the world having your mind darkened and being far from God. Eph. 4:17,18 (NLT) says, "For they are hopelessly confused. Their minds are full of darkness; they wander far from the life God gives."

Your words reveal what's in your heart. If you're harboring poison and resentment in your heart, it will spill out and pollute and devastate what God made to be beautiful. A bitter heart brings forth bitter words while a loving heart brings forth loving words. The first step to godly communication is not to become a better talker, it's dealing with the sin in your heart. It's sin that causes the breakdown of good communication in any relationship. It's what causes you to spew forth toxic words toward the person you're talking to. If you don't repent of your sin and allow God to transform you, you'll never be able to communicate well with anybody. 1 Peter 3:10-12 (NLT) says, "If you want to enjoy life and see many happy days, keep your tongue from speaking evil and your lips from telling lies. Turn away from evil and do good. Search for peace, and work to maintain it. The eyes of the Lord watch over those who do right, and His eyes are open to their prayers. But the Lord turns His face against those who do evil."

Once the sin problem has been dealt with and transformation has taken place, James 1:19 gives you the key to success when communicating with other people. "Therefore, my beloved brethren, let every man be swift to hear, slow to speak, slow to wrath." That is the total opposite of what your flesh wants to do. Communication breaks down when you're slow to hear and swift to speak. The Message Bible says, "Lead with your ears, follow up with your tongue, and let anger straggle along in the rear." Controlling your tongue is a big deal. James said to be slow to speak. The word "slow" means 'inactive in mind.' You need to slow down for a moment, be inactive, and put all your effort and focus into receiving what the other person is saying. Be sensitive to their thoughts and feelings concerning that which they're sharing with you. Don't just listen, listen actively. Do your best to understand where they're coming from. Let them talk without interruption instead of pushing your own agenda onto them.

Being a good listener doesn't mean you never talk. It is not a conversation if only one person does all the talking. Just listen first without interrupting and, when you do talk, speak the truth in love (Eph. 4:15). If, by chance, you feel anger building up inside of you, stop talking and take a break. Walk away and then fall on your knees and pray. Once you get angry, all good communication ends and this will eventually lead to the end of all good relationships. Anger that boils over resulting in cruel words and actions gives the devil permission to wreak havoc in your life. It is vital that people communicate with one another. Just do it the right way. Slow down before you talk and then speak the truth in love. This does not mean you're to be blunt with cruel judgments and harsh criticism. You can't tell a person he's a fool even though he may very well be one. Eph. 4:29 (NLT) says, "Don't use foul or abusive language. Let everything you say be good and helpful, so that your words will be encouragement to those who hear them."

As important as good communication is, there was much arguing going on throughout all the tribes of Israel. The nation is divided and fractured. A civil war has taken place and twenty thousand people died in battle. There is inner turmoil as the people talked among themselves about what had transpired. They remembered what David did in the past saying, "The king rescued us from our enemies and saved us from the Philistines, but Absalom chased him out of the country. Now Absalom, whom we anointed to rule over us, is dead. Why not ask David to come back and be our king again?" (vs. 9,10 NLT). The Message Bible says, "So what are you waiting for? Why don't you bring the king back?" The only reason these people want to bring back the king is because Absalom is dead and his attempt to overthrow David failed. Clearly they were on the wrong side, for their allegiance to Absalom only brought misery and confusion. This is a sign something is not right for there will always be turmoil when God's will is not being done.

David is hearing what the people are saying and he wonders why the tribe of Judah isn't saying the same thing. Matthew Henry writes, "We do not always find the most kindness from those we have the most reason to expect it from." He sends the priests Zadok and Abithar to ask the elders of Judah, "Why are you the last ones to welcome back the king into his palace? For I have heard that all Israel is ready. You are my relatives, my own tribe, my own flesh and blood! So why are you the last ones to welcome back the king?" (vs. 11,12 NLT). David didn't assume the throne was his to once again take and he wasn't going to force his reign on anybody. He would only come back if the tribes who rejected him for Absalom agreed to bring him back. He's waiting for an invitation, for the relationship to be restored. Still, he's heard no word from the tribe of Judah. Arthur Pink said, "How often we find that those who are bound to us by the closest ties and upon whom we have the greatest claims, are the first to fail and the last to help us."

David is showing sound wisdom in getting Zadok and Abithar to help negotiate peace and to bring about a reconciliation between himself and the tribe of Judah. These were godly men who were trusted by David and respected by Judah and all of Israel. Everybody knew they would promote the will of God above the interests of any one individual or tribe. David and his army are marching back to Jerusalem to reorganize the government and bring peace back to the nation. He will soon begin negotiations to reunite the people, to seek unity and a sense of brotherhood among the people. He is still outside the city and he's not sure what the people of Judah are thinking. Did they take Absalom's side in the rebellion? Do they think David will take vengeance on them if and when he returns to the city? Some people have been so hurt by the past that they lose the will to expect a better future. If they lower their expectations, they reason they can deal better with what they think is the inevitable disappointment.

David has one more thing to say to the two priests. He commands them to tell Amasa, the son of his sister Abigail (1 Chron. 2:17), "Are you not my bone and my flesh? God do so to me, and more also, if you are not commander of the army before me continually in place of Joab" (vs. 13). This is a shocking move. Amasa took Absalom's side and was the commander of his army during the rebellion. It was he who led the army that fought against David. Why is David making him commander over his entire army? Is this a way to punish Joab for killing his son? Or is this his way of trying to reunite the nation that has been fractured and torn apart? Eph. 4:3 (MSG) says to be "alert at noticing differences and mending fences." The NLT says, "Make every effort to keep yourselves united in the Spirit, binding yourselves together with peace." Did David make this appointment for personal or political reasons? Perhaps it was a little of both. One thing is certain. Joab is a scoundrel and he won't respond well to being demoted by David.

For unity to take place, you must be willing to forgive those who have done you harm. Mark Twain said, "Forgiveness is the fragrance that the violet sheds on the heel that has crushed it." By promoting Amasa, David is showing the nation that he is willing to forgive his enemies, to pardon those who raised their hands against him in battle. Isn't this what Jesus does? He is willing to forgive sinners and allows them to enlist in the army of the Lord. Rom. 5:8 says, "But God demonstrates His own love toward us, in that while we were still sinners, Christ died for us." Never is a person more like God than when he loves and forgives. Prov. 19:11 says, "The discretion of a man makes him slow to anger, and it is to his glory to overlook a transgression." The pinnacle of being a human being is to forgive the same way God forgives you. Forgiveness is a marvelous, liberating, loving attitude and action. It is a healthy and wholesome thing to forgive. It frees you from tension and anxiety. It brings peace and solicits love.

In the world today, forgiveness is desperately needed like never before. The problem is that people are too self-centered. They're consumed by their selfish desires and this causes them to do harm to others who stand in their way of getting what they want. James 4:1,2 (NLT) says, "What is causing the quarrels and fights among you? Don't they come from the evil desires at war within you? You want what you don't have, so you scheme and kill to get it. You are jealous of what others have, but you can't get it, so you fight and wage war to take it from them." By nature, the hearts of most people are filled with hostilities, and this makes them prone to anger, bitterness, and resentment. Eccl. 7:9 says, "Anger rests in the bosom of fools." People today are angry about so many things. Their mother did this to them and their father did that. The children scream too loud and the wife wants to talk during the championship ballgame. Taxes are too high, their boss don't like them, and the driver in front of them is going too slow. On and on it goes.

Jer. 17:9 (MSG) says, "The heart is hopelessly dark and deceitful, a puzzle that no one can figure out." Sin has the power to bury the world in an avalanche of hate, vengeance, and violence. Anger is everywhere and for many people crime and violence has become a way of life. If not controlled, these vast flaws of demonic proportions will erupt and destroy the world as people know it today. What's missing in the lives of most people today is forgiveness. Mother Angelica said, "Our lack of forgiveness makes us hate, and our lack of compassion makes us hard-hearted. Pride in our hearts makes us resentful and keeps our memory in a constant whirlwind of passion and self-pity." Unforgiveness imprisons people and chains them to their past. It pours gasoline on the fire of what somebody did wrong to them. It produces a deep-seeded bitterness that causes anger to rage out of control. Thoughts of revenge consume their mind and every conversation becomes a channel through which they'll vent their rage and hostility.

Unforgiveness is a wall often built one brick of hurt at a time until eventually it turns into a massive crisis. It destroys all relationships but the good news is there is no offense that cannot be overcome by God's divine forgiveness. Eph. 4:31,32 (NLT) says, "Get rid of all bitterness, rage, anger, harsh words, and slander, as well as all types of evil behavior. Instead, be kind to each other, tender-hearted, forgiving one another, just as God through Christ has forgiven you." Forgiveness doesn't change the past but it does change the future. South African cleric Desmond Tutu said, "Forgiveness says you give another person the chance to make a new beginning." Forgiveness doesn't deny that an offense happened and it doesn't pretend you haven't been hurt. Divine forgiveness is being fully aware of the offense and making a choice to release them of their debt, refusing to punish them for their wrong, and keeping no record of what they did to hurt you. This is how God forgave you, and this is how you're to forgive others.

Forgiving someone who has hurt you and done you harm is not easy and nobody said it was. Mahatma Gandhi said, "The weak can never forgive. Forgiveness is the attitude of the strong." An Irish novelist named Laurence Sterne once said, "Only the brave know how to forgive. It's the most refined and generous element of human virtue. Cowards have done good deeds and performed kind acts. Cowards have even fought and conquered. But a coward never forgives. It is not in his nature or his heart. The power to forgive flows only from a strength and greatness of soul, conscious of its own humility and security and able to rise above all the little temptations of resenting every fruitless attempt to steal its happiness." Trust God to give you the strength to forgive for it is the most God-like thing a person can do. You are never more like God than when you forgive. The parable of the prodigal son is a story about a forgiving father. Like him, every Christian should be known for their willingness to forgive.

Love always manifests itself in forgiveness. This is why forgiving others should be the normal lifestyle for the born-again believer. It's forgiveness that prevents you from hating the person who did you wrong. 1 John 3:15 says, "Whoever hates his brother is a murderer." A lack of forgiveness is selfish and murderous in its intent. It's hostile and wishes harm and even death toward those who have harmed you in some way. Daily ask God to reveal to you any unforgiveness that may be in your heart. David wrote in Ps. 139:23.24, "Search me, O God, and know my heart; Try me, and know my anxieties; And see if there is any wicked way in me, and lead me in the way everlasting." God has given the church signs that show when people are harboring unforgiveness. The first sign is separation. Unforgiveness is a sin that separates you from God and other people. The second sign is your tongue (Matt. 12:34). Listen to the words coming out your mouth. Hateful words filled with anger and bitterness are signs of unforgiveness.

You may not feel like forgiving the person who hurt you but forgiveness has nothing to do with how you feel. It's a command of God which you must obey by faith. God says to forgive, so you forgive. Also, forgiveness doesn't always bring about reconciliation. For that to happen a transformation has to take place in the hearts of both parties. However, God calls everybody to forgive regardless if full reconciliation takes place or not. If you will genuinely receive God's command to forgive, you will begin to experience the supernatural transformation of divine forgiveness in your life. The power to forgive comes by yielding your actions to the Holy Spirit (Rom. 6:12-14). As you yield to Him, He'll give you the power to do what you can't do on your own. This is how your life and your relationships get transformed. Don't be a slave to unforgiveness. At the cross Jesus took your heart of sin and gave you His heart of love. He is willing and able to live through you but you must first choose to crucify your flesh and yield your actions to Him.

The Shepherd King

-36-

"THE SEEDS OF REBELLION"

David put Joab in his place by making Amasa commander over the army of Israel. David had expressed concern as to why the tribe of Judah has shown no interest in having him put back on the throne. Amasa rose up and decided to do something about it. "So he swayed the hearts of all the men of Judah, just as the heart of one man, so that they sent this word to the king, 'Return, you and all your servants!'" (2 Sam. 19:14). The word "swayed" means 'to bow down to.' Amasa won them over and caused all their hearts to bow down in unity as they asked David to come back and be king again. In his brokenness and humility, David does not want to be an unwelcomed king. He wants to rule by invitation only, just like Jesus. "Then the king returned and came to the Jordan. And Judah came to Gilgal, to go to meet the king, to escort the king across the Jordan" (vs. 15). As David walks back toward Jerusalem he's going to be met by several people, the first person being a former enemy of his.

David left Jerusalem as a desperate fugitive; he's coming back escorted by thousands of enthusiastic supporters. A ferryboat carries him across the Jordan River where he is met by Shimei, the man who had cursed him and thrown stones at him. A thousand men are with Shimei, as well as Ziba, the man once ordered to be the servant of Mephibosheth. The rebellion is over and Shimei wants to make peace with David. Absalom is dead and Shimei's chances of living are pretty slim. He knows his only hope is to come and fall down before David asking to be forgiven. He pleads with David, saying, "Do not let my lord impute iniquity to me, or remember what wrong your servant did on the day that my lord left Jerusalem, that the king should take it to heart. For I, your servant, know that I have sinned" (vs. 19,20). Is this sincere and true repentance or is he afraid for his life? Abishai thinks the latter and he says to David, "Shall not Shimei be put to death for this, because he cursed the Lord's anointed?" (vs. 2).

David responds, "What is it with you sons of Zeruiah? Why do you insist on being so contentious?" (vs. 22 MSG). Some people want blood no matter how much a person repents. Beware of people who make light of the grace and mercy of God, of people who want a works-based restoration. These are the people who say, "I'll forgive you but only if you do this or that." Jesus said in Matt. 5:7, "Blessed are the merciful for they shall obtain mercy." David then proclaims, "Nobody is going to be killed today. I am again king over Israel!" He turned to Shimei and gave him his word, saying, "You're not going to die." Repentance and acknowledgement of sin is crucial for restoration. Forgiveness takes place before restoration but nowhere does it say Shimei was forgiven, only that he wasn't going to die this day. In the back of his mind, David did not forget how Shimei cursed him in Bahurim. On his death bed, the last thing David says to his son Solomon before he dies is that he wants Shimei killed for what he did (1 Kings 2:8,9).

Mephibosheth also came down to meet David. He was the son of Jonathan, the person granted the divine privilege of eating continually at the king's table. "And he had not cared for his feet, nor trimmed his mustache, nor washed his clothes, from the day the king departed until the day he came back in peace" (vs. 24). His appearance shows he has been mourning David's absence. "So it was, when he had come to Jerusalem to meet the king, that the king said to him, 'Why did you not go with me, Mephibosheth?'" (vs. 25). Does David still believe what Ziba told him, that Mephibosheth was in Jerusalem waiting to be made king?

Mephibosheth answers David, "My master the king, my servant betrayed me. I told him to saddle my donkey so I could ride it and go with the king, for, as you know, I am lame. And then he lied to you about me" (vs. 26 MSG). He charged Ziba with slander and then cast his fate into David's hands. David had already spared his life and given him more than he deserved. "What more could I ever expect or ask?" (vs. 28 MSG).

Mephibosheth had said in vs. 27, "But my lord the king is like the angel of God." He knew God was going to give David wisdom and understanding in order to discern what should be done. In humility he was saying, "My life is in your hands. Do what you think is best." David had heard enough and a decision was made. He said to Mephibosheth, "You and Ziba divide the land" (vs. 29). When Ziba lied to David he was given all of Mephibosheth's land as his own. Since Ziba got this land under fraudulent circumstances, why didn't David take his land and give it all back to Mephibosheth? Did David believe Mephibosheth or did he not know who to believe? Did he make a bad decision or was this his way of rewarding Ziba for the food and supplies he brought him when he fled Jerusalem? Nobody knows why David made the decision he did. Mephibosheth responds, "Rather, let him take it all, inasmuch as my lord the king has come back in peace to his own house" (vs. 30).

Mephibosheth is saying, "Getting half my land back is not why I came to you. All I care about is that you are home safe." This is the attitude of the sinner who has been saved by grace. If Jesus is honored and glorified, worldly possessions have no meaning whatsoever. The lesson here is that relationships matter. Don't put things before people. Put nothing above your relationship with God, your family, and your friends. For Mephibosheth, David's safety and his reign as king was far more important to him than his personal enrichment. G. Campbell Morgan said, "It is a great and glorious thing when our loyalty and love make us far more concerned about the victories of our Lord than about our own unquestioned rights. Yet that should be the normal attitude of all who sit at the King's table." David had shown mercy to Shimei, at least temporarily, he gave justice to Mephibosheth, and he's now going to show kindness to an old man named Barzillai who helped him in Mahanaim during his time of crisis and distress (2 Sam. 17:27-29).

Barzillai was eighty years old, was very rich, and in Hebrew his name means "the iron man." He came down from Rogelim to help escort David across the Jordan River. David saw him and remembered the kindness and support this old man had given him. He said to Barzillai, "Come across with me, and I will provide for you while you are with me in Jerusalem" (vs. 33). He was saying, "You took care of me, now I'm going to take care of you." David wants to reward Barzillai just like God rewards those who faithfully serve Him. All the work you do for God carries with it an eternal reward. God is a loving God and He is reward-minded. 2 Cor. 5:9,10 says, "Therefore we make it our aim, whether present or absent, to be well pleasing to Him. For we must all appear before the judgment seat of Christ, that each one may receive the things done in the body, according to his own labor." The more work you do for God, the more abundance of reward you will receive.

This life will be the briefest thing you'll ever do. When compared to eternity, your life will pass by in the blink of an eye. However, that's not to say your life is insignificant for what you do in this life will surely determine what will happen to you in the next life. Rev. 11:18 says, "And that You should reward Your servants the prophets and the saints, and those who fear Your name, small and great." If you are born again, you are a saint in the kingdom of God. You don't need to be a pastor or a missionary to receive a reward in heaven, but you do need to be a witness. You need to use your time, your talents, and your treasure to benefit the kingdom. If you do, take comfort knowing that a reward is coming your way. Rev. 22:12 says, "And behold, I am coming quickly, and My reward is with Me, to give to every one according to his work." Your priorities will change once you realize your works of service determine the size and type of reward you'll receive in heaven. 2 John 8 (NLT) says, "Be diligent so that you receive your full reward."

David wants to reward Barzillai who responds back to him, "I'm old and about to die. I'd only be a burden to you. And why should the king repay me with such a reward?" Barzillai did not bring food and supplies to David for the sake of reward. He gave because he had a good heart, not for the motive of self-exaltation. Barzillai said, "Please let your servant turn back again, that I may die in my own city, and be buried by the grave of my father and mother. But here is your servant Chimham; let him cross over with my lord the king, and do for him what seems good to you" (vs. 37). Chimham is the son of Barzillai (1 Kings 2:7) and David agrees to bless and take care of him instead. He blessed Mephibosheth for Jonathan's sake; he'll now bless Chimham for Barzillai's sake. "Then all the people went over the Jordan. And when the king had crossed over, the king kissed Barzillai and blessed him, and he returned to his own place. Now the king went on to Gilgal, and Chimham went with him. And all the people of Judah escorted the king, and also half the people of Israel" (vs. 39,40).

The tribe of Judah is escorting David back to Jerusalem and everything is looking fine. But not for long. The northern tribes felt excluded in this ceremonial welcoming back of David from across the Jordan. They go to David and ask, "Why have our brothers, the men of Judah, taken over as if they owned the king, escorting the king and his family and close associates across the Jordan?" (vs. 41 MSG). These people are putting their personal wants and desires above the needs and concerns of the kingdom. David is once again king over Israel and that's all that should have mattered. The men of Judah answered their question, "Because the king is related to us, that's why! But why make a scene? You don't see us getting treated special because of it, do you?" (vs. 42 MSG). It was the idea of the ten northern tribes to bring David back and now they feel unappreciated by the tribe of Judah. The problem isn't solved and this competitive conflict between them will lead to a future civil war and the splitting of the nation.

The unity of the nation of Israel was very fragile and hanging on by a thread. The seeds of rebellion were sown when the northern tribes disapproved of the southern tribes being the ones who escorted David back to Jerusalem. Peace wasn't sought after nor did the people act in faithfulness to the Lord their God. They don't realize that unity among the brethren is priceless as evidenced by the words of Paul in 1 Cor. 1:10, "Now I plead with you, brethren, by the name of our Lord Jesus Christ, that you all speak the same thing, and that there be no division among you, but that you be perfectly joined together in the same mind and in the same judgment." David had not even made it back to Jerusalem yet when another revolt took place. Sad to say, there are people who will exploit the differences between others for their own personal advantage. 2 Sam. 20:1 tells of one such man, "And there happened to be there a rebel, whose name was Sheba the son of Bichri, a Benjamite."

Little is known of this man who took advantage of the quarrel between the tribes of Israel. The Bible calls him a "rebel" and the NIV says he was a "trouble maker." Other places in the Bible translate the word as "corrupt, perverted, and scoundrel." In Hebrew he is called "a man of Belial" or a man of the devil, a person who is lawless and godless. The people of Israel are in a weakened condition and this makes them vulnerable to the wiles of the devil. At times like this,

Satan will send a rebel to take advantage of that weakness and vulnerability. Know with certainty that where there is sin, there will always be a rebel, a person who refuses and rejects the authority God has put in place. Satan rebelled in heaven and rebellion has become the method in which he works. Sheba was insulted by the words of the men of Judah which "were fiercer than the words of the men of Israel" (2 Sam. 19:43). This riled up in Sheba a rebellious heart that wanted nothing more to do with David and the tribe of Judah.

Rebellious people are worthless people, or so the scriptures say. Paul warns in Rom. 16:17,18 (NLT), "Watch out for people who cause division and upset people's faith by teaching things contrary to what you have been taught. Stay away from them. Such people are not serving Christ our Lord; they are serving their own personal interests. By smooth talk and glowing words, they deceive innocent people." Sheba came from the tribe of Benjamin, the same tribe as Saul. Naturally he would hold a grudge against David who at this time had lost the respect of many people. Absalom rebelled first, now it's Sheba's turn. The consequences of David's sin with Bathsheba continue to come to pass as Sheba blows a trumpet and loudly proclaims, "We have no part in David, nor do we have inheritance in the son of Jesse; Every man to his tents, O Israel!" (2 Sam. 20:1). He denied the king's sovereignty and devalued David's identity. Jesse was a simple farmer and Sheba wanted to downgrade David's humble beginning.

"So every man of Israel deserted David, and followed Sheba the son of Bichri. But the men of Judah, from the Jordan as far as Jerusalem, remained loyal to their king" (vs. 2). The people of Israel no longer thought they could be fairly represented by David. They considered him a foreigner, thinking he'd favor the tribe of Judah over the other tribes. Were these people justified in their thinking? Would David favor the tribe he came from above all the others? Perhaps,

The Shepherd King

but as G. Campbell Morgan writes, "Injustice is never corrected by a yet deeper wrong." Martin Luther King Jr. once said, "Injustice anywhere is a threat to justice everywhere." Right or wrong, unity should have prevailed at this crucial time. Paul wrote in Eph. 4:3 (NLT), "Make every effort to keep yourselves united in the Spirit, binding yourselves together with peace." Sheba succeeded in drawing away the ten northern tribes and David had another civil war to deal with. But first, he had some personal business to take care of.

"Now David came to his house at Jerusalem. And the king took the ten women, his concubines whom he had left to keep the house, and put them in seclusion and supported them, but did not go in to them. So they were shut up to the day of their death, living in widowhood" (vs. 3). David is trying to establish some kind of stability in his household. Absalom publicly and openly sexually assaulted these women and David no longer had any relations with them. He supported them but still they are sentenced to a life of seclusion and solitary singleness. Why would David do this? British theologian Adam Clarke wrote, "He could not well divorce them; he could not punish them as they were not in the transgression; he could not be familiar with them because they had been defiled by his son; and to have married them to other men might have been dangerous to the state." Sin is very horrible and sometimes has long lasting effects. These women suffered permanent damage as a result of Absalom's sin as well as David's sin.

David puts away the women Absalom violated and it is now time to deal with the rebellion at hand. He knows he must act quickly. As each day goes by, Sheba is able to strengthen his position and prolong the rebellion. Time is of the essence and a delay to stop the revolt could spell disaster. "Then the king said to Amasa, 'Assemble the men of Judah for me within three days, and be present here yourself.' So Amasa went to assemble the men of Judah. But he delayed longer than the set time which David had appointed him" (vs. 4,5). Amasa was unable to do what David asked in the amount of time given him. Clearly he was not as good a leader as Joab, the person he replaced as commander of the army. Perhaps the men didn't trust him, remembering that he fought for Absalom in his rebellion against David. Perhaps also Amasa wasn't as competent and faithful as he should have been. Faithfulness and discipline is to do what you're supposed to do, when you're supposed to do it.

Where is Amasa? Did David think he defected to Sheba's side? After all, he defected once before. What is David supposed to do? Tired of waiting, he says to Abishai, "Now Sheba the son of Bichri will do us more harm than Absalom. Take your lord's servants and pursue him, lest he find for himself fortified cities, and escapes us" (vs. 6). David makes Joab's brother the commander of his own personal royal guard. Of course, if there is a battle to be fought then Joab can't be far behind. He joins the pursuit of Sheba along with all of David's mighty men. As bad and flawed as he was, Joab was a seasoned warrior, a man you'd want on your side in time of war. He's a mean man, a scoundrel, but he gets the job done. David put Abishai in charge but it's Joab who's taking over. Together with the Cherethites and the Pelethites, all these men went out of Jerusalem to hunt down Sheba the way a dog tracks down a rabbit. Six miles away at Gibeon, lo and behold, here comes Amasa. He almost made it back to Jerusalem in time. Almost, but not quite.

Joab steps forward and decides to take matters into his own hands. "Now Joab was dressed in battle armor; on it was a belt with a sword fastened in its sheath at his hips; and as he was going forward, it fell out" (vs. 8). Listen, for a man like Joab, your sword doesn't fall out unless you want it to fall out. He's deceiving Amasa into thinking he's unarmed. Joab says to Amasa, "Are you in health, my brother?" These two men are cousins and Joab then takes Amasa by the beard with his right hand to kiss him. In the culture of that time this was considered an act of friendship, an act of transparency and vulnerability. In those days it was not unusual for men to show affection for one another, in much the same way that David kissed Jonathan. Joab is cunning and deceptive and he's about to show how ruthless of a man he is. "But Amasa did not notice the sword in Joab's hand. And he struck him with it in the stomach, and his entrails poured out on the ground; and he did not strike him again. Thus he died" (vs. 10).

This is how Joab deals with any competition. He killed Abner, he killed Absalom, and here he kills Amasa. He didn't strike Amasa a second time because he wanted him to die a slow and painful death. Joab was a great fighter but he was not a godly man nor was he a man of integrity. 2 Sam. 23 lists all the names of David's mighty men and Joab is not listed among them. Having great skills and abilities does not mean you possess godly character, a life characterized by honesty, loyalty, and faithfulness. Yes, David sinned but he acknowledged it and repented of what he did wrong. At no time, however, did Saul or Joab ever deal with the sins they had committed. "But Amasa wallowed in his blood in the middle of the highway. And when the man saw that all the people stood still, he moved Amasa from the highway to the field and threw a garment over him, when he saw that everyone who came upon him halted. When he was removed from the highway, all the people went on after Joab to pursue Sheba" (vs. 12,13).

Joab takes command of the troops who remained loyal to David. He was a true leader, a man born and bred to fight, and the soldiers followed the commander who successfully led them in battle many times before. They went through the ten northern tribes looking for Sheba and found him in a fortified city on the edge of the nation's border called Abel.

This city was known for the wise people who lived there (vs. 18). Apparently, Sheba was seeking advice on what to do to save his life. Joab and his men arrive at Abel "and they cast up a siege mound against the city, and it stood by the rampart. And all the people who were with Joab battered the wall to throw it down" (vs. 15). Siege warfare was a terrible ordeal for the citizens of the besieged city. A siege mound were ramps built out of dirt, rubble, and timber. The army on the attack would push battering rams up the ramp to break through the city walls where they were the thinnest. As this was happening, a wise woman comes out to negotiate for peace.

Like Abigail who pleaded with David not to kill her fool of a husband Nabal, this woman pleads with Joab to spare the city and its inhabitants. She says to him, "We're peaceful people. Why do you attack us? Why would you swallow up the inheritance of the Lord?" Joab answers her, "Far be it from me that I should swallow up or destroy!" (vs. 20). Yeah, right. That's precisely who Joab is. He then says, "Give me Sheba and we'll leave you alone." The woman responds, "Watch, his head will be thrown to you over the wall" (vs. 21). Sheba probably thought he was safe within the walls of that city but no one is safe when they go against the will of God. People who initiate rebellion must oftentimes be dealt with dramatically and in a brutal manner. "Then the woman in her wisdom went to all the people. And they cut off the head of Sheba the son of Bichri, and threw it out to Joab. Then he blew a trumpet, and they withdrew from the city, every man to his tent. So Joab returned to the king at Jerusalem" (vs. 22).

The Shepherd King

-37-

"FAMINE IN THE LAND"

David is back on the throne but his tribulations and difficulties are far from over. From this point onward, his trials will continue to come upon him one on top of the other. A harsh reality in life is that sin always has consequences. Sad to say, sometimes those consequences affect others also, people who had nothing to do with the sin committed. It's true, you never sin in a vacuum. The sin of one individual can affect other people while the sin of a leader can affect an entire nation. Since the time David sinned with Bathsheba, he's been in one tribulation after another and it appears as if the end of his trials are nowhere in sight. Much to his chagrin, David is about to once again go through a dark valley of compounded tribulations, all because he stayed home when he should have gone to war. One thing David learned in the midst of all this hardship is that the past always catches up with you. It caught up to him concerning Bathsheba and it's about to catch up to him concerning a sin Saul committed years before.

David is nearing the end of his life but there is unfinished business that must be dealt with. God is about to awaken David and the nation concerning past injustices, about the failure to keep promises and God-honoring obligations. 2 Sam. 21:1 says, "Now there was a famine in the days of David for three years, year after year; and David inquired of the Lord." David had just survived two rebellions and now he faces three and a half years of a terrible famine in the land, the same amount of time as the famine in the days of Elijah. Famines were common in the Middle East. The Bible speaks of famines during the time of Abraham and Jacob. It was a famine that drove the children of Israel to Egypt back during the time of Joseph. The people would pass off one year of drought and famine as a bad year, and maybe even two years, but certainly not three. Something is not right here. It's not raining and the crops are not growing. As king, David has a spiritual obligation to seek God and discover what is wrong.

David sought God's face and He answered, "It is because of Saul and his bloodthirsty house, because he killed the Gibeonites" (vs. 1). Joshua 9 tells of a treaty between the people of Israel and the Gibeonites that Joshua made with them. Even though the Gibeonites tricked Joshua into making this treaty, God still expected Israel to honor their obligations to them. Somewhere along the way Saul broke this treaty as he sought to wipe out the Gibeonites. The story of Saul doing this is not recorded in the Bible and all there is to go on is what God tells David here. The Bible also doesn't say when Saul did this, only that he did it "in his zeal for the children of Israel and Judah" (vs. 2). Zeal is usually thought of as being good but Saul's misguided zeal was a sin that brought calamity on Israel. He didn't realize that good intentions are no excuse for bad behavior. Saul broke the vow Joshua made and because of that there was a famine in the land for three years. The message here is that God expects His people to keep the promises they make.

God demands that you keep your promises and honor your obligations. The divorce rate is so high because vows and promises are not kept. W. Philip Keller said, "We are to be judged in full measure by the verbal commitments we make to one another." Your promises don't have to be in writing. Just let your "yes" be "yes" and your "no" be "no" (Matt. 5:37). How good are you at keeping your word? When you say you'll do something, do you do it? If things aren't going well in your life, could it be there are promises you made that haven't been kept? Arthur Pink writes, "Troubles do not come haphazard. When the smile of God is withdrawn from us, we should at once suspect something is wrong." Job questioned his oppression by saying to God, "Do not condemn me; Show me why You contend with me" (Job 10:2). The Message Bible says, "Don't, God, bring in a verdict of guilty without letting me know the charges You're bringing." In the eyes of God, keeping your promises is a deeply felt, eagerly honored obligation.

Never let it be said that you have a history of broken promises. It has special meaning when you respond to why you did something by saying, "I gave my word." There was a time when a handshake was all you needed because giving your word was as good as gold. Always keep your word even if it's not in your best interest, even if you have to suffer for doing so. Deut. 23:21 (NLT) says, "For the Lord your God demands that you promptly fulfill all your vows, or you will be guilty of sin." People must understand that God keeps an accurate record of the things they do. When they do wrong, the judgment doesn't always come right away. If you haven't kept a promise and nothing bad happened to you yet, don't think you've dodged a bullet. Nobody gets away with anything. What you sow is what you reap. When people did wrong in the Bible, sometimes the judgment came three or four generations later. Saul broke the treaty Joshua made with the Gibeonites and scripture makes it clear that this famine was the result of that sin.

After three years of famine David knew something wasn't right so he inquired of the Lord, asking why there was no rain in the land. Why did it take David so long to do this? Probably because he didn't automatically assume this famine was caused by a spiritual problem. Not every illness or tragedy is associated with a specific sin (John 9:3) but it can be as is the case here. God said this famine was because Saul's crime consisted of breaking ancient oaths and for committing genocide against the Gibeonites. In other words, the nation didn't keep their promise to these Canaanite people. God expects everybody to keep their promises and the passing of time does not diminish one's obligations to those promises. What's happening here is that the past is catching up to the people of Israel. David knew something had to be done so he initiated a resolution with the Gideonites. He said to them, "What shall I do for you? And what shall I make atonement, that you may bless the inheritance of the Lord?" (vs. 3).

Because of what Saul did to them, David is going to let the Gibeonites define the terms of what constitutes a just and fair settlement. He went to them as a servant and not as a king. He didn't seek God about this but rather let the Gideonites decide for themselves the nature of the retribution. He does believe if the Gideonites would bless Israel then the reconciliation would be complete and God's discipline against Israel would end. David asks, "How can we repay you for what Saul did?" They answered him, "We will have no silver or gold from Saul or from his house, nor shall you kill any man in Israel for us" (vs. 4). When they made their treaty with Joshua, the Gibeonites were forced into the role of slaves and servants. You would think they'd want their freedom back, to be liberated from their life of slavery. It is interesting to note this is not what they asked for. They didn't ask for money, the slaughter of the people of Israel, or their freedom. So, what did they want?

David said to them, "Whatever you say, that I will do for you." The Gibeonites responded, "Let seven men of his descendants be delivered to us, and we will hang them before the Lord" (vs. 6). Here is a prime example of where the sin of one person can affect other people. It's like when a drunk driver crashes his car into another vehicle killing all those inside. His sin affected others. How you live makes a difference. Your actions have consequences that not only affect you but others as well. What should you do? Gal. 5:16

says, "Walk in the Spirit and you shall not fulfill the lust of the flesh." The Gibeonites wanted these seven descendants to be punished for what Saul did. David understood the validity of their request and said, "I will give them." One person who would not be turned over for execution was Mephibosheth (vs. 7). David promised to protect and bless him, the son of his best friend. He would not fulfill one promise at the expense of another. David was a man who kept his word, Saul was a man who did not.

David fulfills the agreement he made with the Gibeonites. He gave to them the two sons of Rizpah, a concubine of Saul, and the five sons of Saul's oldest daughter Merab (vs. 8). This was the same daughter who was supposed to be given to David as a reward for killing Goliath. She married Adriel instead (1 Sam. 18:19). "And he delivered them into the hands of the Gibeonites, and they hanged them on the hill before the Lord. So they fell, all seven together, and were put to death in the days of harvest" (vs. 8). These descendants of Saul were ritually executed and their bodies were exposed and unburied. They bore the curse Saul deserved and so delivered Israel from the guilt of their sin against the Gibeonites. Rizpah, the mother of Saul's sons, then holds a vigil as she keeps the vultures and wild beasts from feeding on the dead and decomposing bodies of her loved ones. She stays there until the rain began to fall which meant the famine is now over. Justice was satisfied and Israel was delivered.

The bodies of these seven men were deliberately left unburied, emphasizing the fact that they were executed as an act of judgment. However, the faithfulness of Rizpah and her vigil of love moves David to take the bodies and give them a decent burial. He gathers the bones of Saul and Jonathan from the men of Jabesh Gilead who had stolen them from the street of Beth Sham, plus the bodies of these seven men. He then buries them in the tomb of Kish, the father of Saul. They went from hanging like a criminal to being buried like royalty. "And after that God heeded the prayer for the land" (vs. 14). Reason would dictate that now would be a good time for David to step back and rest awhile. He's been through so much, more than any person should be forced to bear. This was not to be. God said the sword would not leave the house of David so who comes calling but the Philistines. "When the Philistines were at war again with Israel, David and his servants went down and fought against the Philistines and David grew faint" (vs. 15).

David's age is catching up to him for even a great man of God grows old. He is unable to fight as he once did and his life was endangered when he grew faint in battle. The NIV says he was "exhausted," revealing the inevitable slowdown that comes with age. Many men don't want to accept this fact and this is why many athletes keep playing sports well beyond their prime. Fighting for the Philistines were the four sons of Goliath. They were giants also and one of them, Ishbi-Benob, thought he could kill David. Thankfully, David's men rallied around their leader and supplied what he could not. "But Abishai the son of Zeruiah came to his aid, and struck the Philistine and killed him. Then the men of David swore to him, saying, 'You shall go out no more with us to battle, lest you quench the lamp of Israel'" (vs. 17). When David's strength failed, God protected him through the strength of others. Eccl. 4:9,10 says, "Two are better than one, because they have a good reward for their labor. For if they fall, one will lift up his companion."

In his advanced age, it was time for David to retire from the field of battle. He is old and even a little weak, but still he wants to fight. Without question, big giants will still come your way in the twilight years of life and this is why you continue to fight the good fight of faith. Yes, some of your greatest trials are kept for last, but still you are more than a conqueror through David's son, the Lord Jesus Christ. David is the lamp of Israel in the sense that he lights the way. He provides the people with leadership, guidance, and light. Adam Clarke wrote, "David is considered the lamp by which all Israel was guided, and without whom all the nation would be involved in darkness." In the temple, the lamp burned day and night and was a symbol of God's presence with the people. The men felt David symbolized this contact with God and they couldn't afford to have him die in battle. Without David they'd have no leader. They'd be in the dark without a light. For this reason, they told David his days as a fighting warrior are over.

The war with the Philistines rages on. Two battles take place in Gob and Sibbechai and Elhanon each killed a son of the giant. Three down, one to go. There was then a battle in Gath, the hometown of Goliath. His son who lived there was a man of great stature like his father. He was so big that he had six fingers on each hand and six toes on each foot. "So when he defied Israel, Jonathan the son of Shimeah, the brother of David, killed him. These four were born to the giant, and fell by the hand of David, and by the hand of his servants" (vs. 21,22). Like David, Abishai, Sibbechai, Elkanan, and Jonathan were also giant killers. After this chapter, never again are giants mentioned in the Bible. These men accomplished heroic deeds when David became too old to fight. They won the final war with the sons of Goliath. They killed the last of the giants. David killed a giant and was their example. He gave them guidance and influenced their lives. This was the legacy David left behind, and what a great legacy it was.

G. Campbell Morgan wrote, "Let those who after long service find themselves waning in strength, be content to abide with the people of God, still shining for them as a lamp, and thus enabling them to carry on the same divine enterprises. Such action in the last days of life is also great and high service." When you're old, you can still have a life of loyalty and allegiance to God. You can still show those around you the love, grace, and mercy of the King of kings and Lord of lords. Allow your victories to become a public acknowledgement to the faithfulness of God. Allow them to serve as a model for those who come after you, for your children and grandchildren. David, the sweet psalmist of Israel, had just gone through a dark, deep valley of compounded tribulations. He survived two rebellions, three years of a desperate famine, and several battles against four giants. He was still a man after God's own heart and he now writes a song of praise as he tells how God delivered him over the course of his life.

When life is tough, when you're overcome with trials and tribulations, you can always find refuge in the Lord your God. David has gone through some hard times. Like a whirlwind, fatigue, anxiety, distress, and torment have overtaken him. He is exhausted for the consequences of sin can weary even the strongest warrior. It was a time of violence and the torrents of destruction overwhelmed him. The world as he knew it was collapsing all around him yet David does not sing the blues. Instead, he sings a song of praise and adoration to his God, eternally thankful for the divine deliverance from all his enemies. Theologian James Montgomery Boice said, "The psalm appears almost as David's final words. Hence, it is a summary thanksgiving for God's many deliverances of him through his long life of service." Throughout all of 2 Sam. 22, David will thank God for His protection, His power, His provision, His perfect justice, and for His proven dependability. All these attributes of God were revealed in David's deliverance from those who opposed him.

David doesn't begin this psalm talking about his problems. No, he begins by saying who God is regardless of what he's going through. "The Lord is my rock, my fortress and my deliverer; The God of my strength, in Him I will trust, my shield and the horn of my salvation, my stronghold and my refuge; My Savior, You save me from violence" (vs. 2,3). David lists title upon title in giving praise to God. The work God did in David's life was so big and comprehensive that it couldn't be contained in one title. He was David's rock, the place of permanence, the place of fortitude and stability and certainty. He was David's fortress, in whose arms David always felt safe. God was also the power and strength of David's salvation. Each of the titles were meaningful to David because God fulfilled each one in his life. David received the Lord's deliverance over and over again in his life. God delivered him from Goliath, Saul, Absalom, the Philistines, and all of Israel's enemies. On a personal level, God delivered him from backsliding and from all his sinful passions.

What can you do to make God all of these things in your life? David tells you in vs. 4, "I will call upon the Lord, who is worthy to be praised; So shall I be saved from my enemies." David praised God for His willingness to hear and answer prayer. He calls upon the Lord for in Him there is hope. Charles Spurgeon wrote, "It is well to pray to God as to one who deserves to be praised, for then we plead in a happy and confident manner. If I feel that I can and do bless the Lord for all His past goodness, I am bold to ask great things of Him." Rom. 10:12,13 says the "Lord over all is rich to all who call upon Him. For whoever calls upon the name of the Lord shall be saved." In Greek, the words "call upon" means 'to put a name upon; to surname; to be named after someone.' It means to take upon yourself the name of Jesus, to permit yourself to be surnamed Christ. This is why you call yourself a Christian. When David says, "I will call upon the Lord," he is receiving the full nature and character of God upon his life.

When you know God as your deliverer, it is a natural thing to trust Him completely. David called upon the Lord when all the forces of the enemy was unleashed upon him. Danger surrounded David on every side and he was on the brink of ruin. The good news is that David knew God would hear him in times of trial and distress. Without reservation he cries out to God. "In my distress I called upon the Lord, and cried to my God. He heard my voice from the temple, and my cry entered His ears" (vs. 7). Everybody feels overwhelmed at times, a feeling that you're surrounded on all sides by the enemy. When that happens, call upon the Lord. With Him is a willingness to hear, a willingness to respond, and a willingness to love. God will use your trial and tribulation to show that you need a deliverer. He's been waiting since before time began for you to call upon Him, to take upon yourself all that He is, to take on His name so that He can become your deliverer. God then shakes heaven and earth in response to David's plea.

God listens to David's cry and then He responds. "Then the earth shook and trembled; The foundations of heaven moved and shook, because He was angry" (vs. 8). God gets angry when His people are at risk, when they suffer for the sake of righteousness. Vs. 9 (MSG) says, "His nostrils flared, billowing smoke; His mouth spit fire. Tongues of fire darted in and out." David pictures God coming to his rescue with glory and speed. "He rode upon a cherub, and flew; And He was seen upon the wings of the wind" (vs. 11). God doesn't keep quiet but speaks up on David's behalf. "The Lord thundered from heaven, and the Most High uttered His voice" (vs. 14). God applied all His majesty and strength to the meeting of David's need. "He delivered me from my strong enemy, from those who hated me; For they were too strong for me. They confronted me in the day of my calamity, but the Lord was my support" (vs. 18,19). David knew that the victory was due to God's hand and not his own strength and ability.

God delivers David and leads him to a place of safety. "He also brought me out into a broad place; He delivered me, because He delighted in me" (vs. 20). David was a man after God's own heart and he had a sense of God's delight in him. His plea for deliverance was rooted in relationship, not merely in a desire to survive. "The Lord rewarded me according to my righteousness; According to the cleanness of my hands He has recompensed me" (vs. 21). Yes, David sinned with Bathsheba but after repenting Nathan told him the Lord had put away his sin. David was a forgiven man and when you are forgiven, God remembers your sins no more. Jesus said in John 8:36, "Therefore if the Son makes you free, you shall be free indeed." David knew the cleanness of his hands was because God had cleansed them. Charles Spurgeon said, "Before God the man after God's own heart was a humble sinner, but before his slanders he could with unblushing face speak of the cleanness of his hands and the righteousness of his life."

"I was also blameless before Him, and I kept myself from my iniquity" (vs. 24). Paul spoke of a man cleansing himself for God's glory and for greater service. "Therefore if anyone cleanses himself from the latter, he will be a vessel for honor, sanctified and useful for the Master, prepared for every good work" (2 Tim. 2:21). When David said he was blameless before God, he was not claiming sinless perfection. Sinless and blameless are two different things. He is making reference to the position he has obtained from God. He is forgiven; thus he is blameless before God. "With the merciful You will show Yourself merciful; With a blameless man You will show Yourself blameless; With the pure You will show Yourself pure; And with the devious You will show Yourself shrewd" (vs. 26,27). G. Campbell Morgan wrote, "God is to man what man is to God." Justice is what the law of sowing and reaping is all about. God is just and He rewards the righteous and punishes the wicked. He saves the humble and brings down the haughty.

"For You are my lamp, O Lord" (vs. 29). When days are dark, God is your light. You don't need a light at the end of you tunnel, you need a light in the tunnel and that's what God is. He's your light in a dark place. Great strength and ability won't help you much if you can't see the light in the midst of your struggle. "For by You I can run against a troop; By my God I can leap over a wall" (vs. 30). God has great power that He makes available through faith. You don't have to be strong in your own might, you can be strong in His might (Eph. 6:10). David knows his ability to go on comes from God. "God is my strength and power, and He makes my way perfect. He makes my feet like the feet of deer, and sets me on my high places" (vs. 33,34). A deer can skip from place to place without losing their footing. God gave David the same skill in working through the challenges brought on by his enemies. David declares his gratitude for being given everything he needs in order to defeat his enemies (vs. 38-51). He wasn't hesitant to proclaim the victory God had given him.

-38-

"BEST OF THE BEST"

David was an amazing man. He was a songwriter, a sensitive, musically oriented person while having a warrior personality. He was a man after God's own heart and this made him great in God's eyes. He is nearing the end of his life and he records his last official words in the form of a song. Yes, he'll go on to say other things. He's not dead yet but the opening verses of 2 Sam. 23 are the final words he'll say officially. It's the last psalm he'll ever write, his final poetic composition. For sure, the final words a person speaks are most significant for they reveal what's truly important in their heart. The substance of one's final words all depend on how they lived their life. If they lived well, their final words will be full of joy and excitement. In a short while they'll be face-to-face with Jesus and their final words will express that gleeful anticipation. These are the last words of David as he begins to reflect on the circumstances of his life. You owe it to God to live in such a way that words like these will be yours also.

"Now these are the last words of David. Thus says David the son of Jesse; This says the man raised up on high, the anointed of the God of Jacob, and the sweet psalmist of Israel" (vs. 1). These are the titles David wished to be remembered by. With just a few words he gives a short but concise biography of his life. These titles reflect humility as David acknowledges that he was a nobody, a shepherd boy raised up and anointed by the God of Israel, set apart to do great things. He went from being a peasant in the fields near Bethlehem to the royal throne room in Jerusalem. Through

Jesus, the same thing happened to you. Eph. 2:6 (NLT) says, "For He raised us from the dead along with Christ and seated us with Him in the heavenly realms because we are united with Christ Jesus." Back then only priests, prophets, and kings were anointed. Today, however, 1 Peter 2:9 says, "But you are a chosen generation, a royal priesthood, a holy nation, His own special people, that you may proclaim the praises of Him who called you."

David was the sweet psalmist of Israel. He had the heart of a poet and was a person who sought deep, personal intimacy with God. While caring for his father's sheep he spent many star-filled nights singing songs to the God of heaven. No matter what he did, no matter how many mistakes he made, he always had a deep love for the Lord his God. "The Spirit of the Lord spoke by me, and His word was on my tongue" (vs. 2). David claims that he is speaking the words of God, that he was used to speak divine revelation to a world that was listening. David wasn't considered a prophet like Isaiah or Jeremiah but he did speak prophetically here and in many of the psalms. He wants it known this is not personal inspiration but a prophetic utterance. "The God of Israel said, the Rock of Israel spoke to me: 'He who rules over men must be just, ruling in the fear of God. And he shall be like the light of the morning when the sun rises, a morning without clouds, like the tender grass springing out of the earth'" (vs. 3,4).

God is called here "the Rock of Israel." In Ps. 19:14 David refers to God as the "Lord, my rock and my redeemer." God is the rock, the chief cornerstone. He is the strength people need, the shield to all who call upon His holy name. David wrote in 2 Sam. 22:47, "The Lord lives! Blessed be my Rock! Let God be exalted, the Rock of my salvation!" He saw God for who He is and he came under God's authority. Prov. 29:2 says, "When the righteous are in authority, the people rejoice; But when a wicked man rules, the people groan." This is why he who rules over men must be just. They must have personal integrity, ruling in the fear of God. Lev. 19:15 says, "You shall do no injustice in judgment." Martin Luther King Jr. said, "True peace is not merely the absence of tension, it is the presence of justice." A wise ruler is blessed when he rules with justice. French theologian Blaise Pascal wrote in the 17th century, "Justice and power must be brought together, so that whatever is just may be powerful and whatever is powerful may be just."

If you want to lead, if you want to rule over men, you must be ruled over and held accountable yourself. A person who isn't ruled over by God or other godly men is dangerous. It's what causes division in homes, churches, and nations. They're not controlled by godly fear. A good leader, on the other hand, will trust the Lord prayerfully and stand up and rule in the fear of God. This is not a superstitious fear. That's how the Canaanites saw their gods. They lived in fear of them. The fear of the Lord is not a morbid fright of God. It's a reverential awe that produces a humble submission to a loving God. All your decisions, desires, and attitudes should be filtered through the fear of God. Ask yourself, "What would God think about this?" If a person rules justly in the fear of God, his kingdom will be like a garden that blossoms and grows. God's people depend on just rulers the same way the earth depends on sunlight. Ruling in the fear of God makes one like the light of the morning when the sun rises, a morning without clouds.

"Although my house is not so with God, yet He has made with me an everlasting covenant, ordered in all things and secure. For this is all my salvation and all my desire; Will He not make it increase?" (vs. 5). David knew that a king was to be like tender grass coming up out of the earth. He also knows his reign fell short of both perfect justice and complete blessedness. He loved God with all his heart and soul but oftentimes he failed to live up to the expectations of the relationship he entered into with God. Still, God made an everlasting covenant with him in 2 Sam. 7:12-17. He gave David a kingdom that will never end. Jesus came through the bloodline of David and it is He who will reign all over the earth forever and ever. This covenant was made on the basis of God's perfect faithfulness and not on David's shortcomings as a man and king. David then says those not in the covenant will be cast away. "But the sons of rebellion shall be as thorns thrust away. And they shall be utterly burned with fire in their place" (vs. 6,7).

David was a great king but the truth remains, no man is an island to himself. Behind every successful person are several people behind the scenes doing most of the work. They don't get the credit or spend time in the spotlight but it's because of their efforts and hard work that these people are successful. Everybody has heard of Charles Lindbergh but who thinks about the mechanic who took care of his airplane? It cannot be denied that David was successful because of all the mighty men who backed him up through thick and thin, through good times and bad. These men were the best of the best, the strongest of the strong, the bravest of the brave. These were the men David trusted in under fire, men he depended on when surrounded by the enemy. Like David, they were all great in God's eyes. Charles Spurgeon wrote, "These men came to David when his fortunes were at the lowest ebb, and he himself was regarded as a rebel and an outlaw, and they remained faithful to him throughout their lives."

It cannot be denied that David was nothing without his mighty men, and they were nothing without him. They didn't come to David as great men but God used the leadership of David to transform them into the mighty men they became. G. Campbell Morgan said, "More than all his victories against outside foes, the influence of his life and character on the men nearest to him testify to his essential greatness." Perhaps your greatest legacy will not be what you did, but rather the influence you had on the people closest to you. Paul wrote in Rom. 13:7, "Render therefore to all their due." He then said to give "honor to whom honor is due." At the end of most of his epistles, Paul gives a list of names of those who helped him in ministry, people like Timothy, Titus, Barnabas, Silas, and Mark. He paid honor to them in doing so. 2 Sam. 23:8-39 does the same thing. Honor is paid to thirty-seven of David's mighty men, warriors he worked with until they became the best army in the history of Israel.

The first of David's mighty men listed here is Adino the Ezrite (vs. 8). He was the chief of the captains and all the fighting men looked up to him for leadership. He was a man of spiritual wisdom and to David was both a counselor and advisor. He was a great warrior and in one battle he killed eight hundred men at one time. He stood strong and kept fighting until God brought him the victory. Eph. 6:13 (NLT) says, "Put on every piece of God's armor so you will be able to resist the enemy in the time of evil. Then after the battle you will still be standing firm." Next was Eleazar the son of Dodo. He was from the tribe of Benjamin and vs. 10 says, "He arose and attacked the Philistines until his hand was weary, and his hand stuck to the sword. The Lord brought about a great victory that day; and the people returned after him only to plunder." Every leader knows that one's greatest ability is dependability. This man stood alone in the face of the enemy when everyone else turned and ran away. He proved he was as dependable as they come.

"And after him was Shammah the son of Agee the Hararite. The Philistines had gathered together into a troop where there was a piece of ground full of lentils. Then the people fled from the Philistines" (vs. 11). A band of Philistines attacked the food supply of the people of Israel. This shows that the enemy will always try to steal and destroy everything you've worked hard for. A bean field was a large, flat piece of ground which offered no place to hide. The vines only grew a foot or two above ground and this caused your feet to get tangled up every time you moved. Unless somebody defended this bean field, nobody was going to eat. Thankfully, Shammah knew some things were worth fighting for, even if you have to fight alone. "But he stationed himself in the middle of the field, defended it, and killed the Philistines. And the Lord brought about a great victory" (vs. 12). To win, you must stand your ground in the midst of a fallen world. Martin Luther King Jr. said, "Courage faces fear and thereby masters it."

Next is told of the exploits of three unnamed mighty men who came to David at the cave of Adullam. It was harvest time and the air was filled with dust. Farmers were threshing and winnowing their crops. David and his men were coughing and sneezing and water seemed to be the most valuable commodity in the world. David remembered how he had often quenched his thirst at the well in Bethlehem, a city now besieged by the Philistines. Thinking out loud he said, "Oh, that someone would give me a drink of the water from the well of Bethlehem" (vs. 15). Three of his men heard him and instantly decided to grant his wish. Putting their lives in jeopardy, they traveled twenty-five miles, broke through enemy lines, and came back with the water. David was honored by the self-sacrifice of these mighty men. To drink the water would belittle the brave deed these men performed. He believed the great sacrifice of these men could only be honored by pouring the water out as a drink offering to the Lord. This he did, offering his offering to theirs.

Many more warriors are listed here in the honor roll of brave men. Abishai "lifted his spear against three hundred men and killed them" (vs. 18). Benaiah "killed two lion-like heroes of Moab. He also went down and killed a lion in the midst of a pit on a snowy day. And he killed an Egyptian, a spectacular man. The Egyptian had a spear in his hand; so he went down to him with a staff, wrestled the spear out of the Egyptian's hand, and killed him with his own spear" (vs. 20,21). Other men are listed, courageous all of them, but Joab's name is not found. His two brothers are listed (vs. 18,24), as well as his armorbearer (vs. 32), but he is not. These were men of character, honorable men who could be trusted. Joab was no such man. You may be good at what you do but you won't be considered a mighty man if you're not a person of character. Bathsheba's father Eliam is listed (vs. 34), as well as her husband Uriah (vs. 39). God used all these men as a point of resistance against the enemy, thus they are all mighty.

The author of 2 Samuel chooses to end his narrative of David's life in a very peculiar and challenging way. He tells a story about another great sin David committed. For sure, it's not the most flattering way in which to end a person's biography. The good news is the chapter ends telling why David was great in God's eyes. Godly leaders, as important as their call is, are not immune from sin and the temptations that go with it. They have the same struggle with the flesh as everybody else. It cannot be denied that spiritual leaders are in the crosshairs of the enemy more than the average Christian. The reason this is true is because the devil likes the domino effect of destruction. If the leader falls, it's possible the followers will fall also. He wants to take out as many as he can with as little work as possible. David is older now, in his mid-sixties, and at this stage in his life he appears to be going through the motions of being a leader. He's cruising on auto-pilot in his relationship with God and this is when the enemy attacks him.

One thing for sure is that David is past the age of being controlled by sensual desires. No longer does he make an effort to reclaim his vanishing youth. You would think as one advances in age that things will get easier as far as temptations and sin are concerned. That's not the case at all.

As one gets older, sins of the flesh are often replaced with sins of the spirit. These sins do more harm and cause more pain than the sins of the flesh. Sin is always a tragedy. Sometimes people fall into sin like an animal in a trap (Gal. 6:1). At other times, people walk into sin with their eyes wide open. Such was the case of David in this chapter. 2 Sam. 24:1 (NASB) says, "Now again the anger of the Lord burned against Israel, and it incited David against them to say, 'Go, number Israel and Judah'" (vs. 1). Once again God's wrath has been stirred against the people of Israel. Scripture does not say what they did wrong so there is no need to guess. One thing is certain, whenever God gets angry in scripture, it is always because of sin.

Sin always opens the door for Satan to come in with schemes to steal, kill, and destroy. This is precisely what happened here. 1 Chron. 21:1 says, "Now Satan stood up against Israel, and moved David to number Israel." The name "Satan" is only mentioned a few times in the Old Testament. It's referred to in Zech. 3:1-7, Job 1,2, and here in the story of David. Alongside his sin with Bathsheba, taking this census is often referred to as the other big sin of David. Not long before this, David and his men had won several battles against the Philistine army. This shows that people can be most vulnerable after a time of victory and success. Some people have a tendency to let their guard down after winning a hard-fought battle and this opens the door for the devil to come in with his evil schemes. 2 Cor. 2:11 says, "Lest Satan should take advantage of us; for we are not ignorant of his devices." This verse can also be translated, "We are not ignorant of his ability to get into our minds and direct our thoughts."

There is nothing fundamentally wrong with taking a census. Governments do it all the time. In fact, God commanded the people to be numbered twice while in the wilderness (Num. 1; Num. 26). Doesn't a good shepherd count his sheep?

How else would he know if one is missing or not? The problem is not what David did but why he did it. He never took a census before. In the past he always trusted in the Lord and not on how big his army was. Back then numbers didn't matter but now he wants to know how big his army is. Why? In the Middle East at that time, there were three reasons for taking a census. The people were counted so the government would know how to tax them, to see how many men they could enlist to fight in battle, and so the king could magnify himself in the sight of all the people. Israel has risen to a place of prominence and has become a super power in the land. Their enemies are subdued and David is now flexing his muscles thinking how great he is. In other words, pride has engulfed his heart.

David's sin was not that he ordered a census, his sin was the reason he did it. He wanted to elevate himself to a point of glory. Anytime you start stealing glory from God, you're on dangerous ground and that's what David is doing here. Motivated by pride, which is a sin of the spirit, David wanted to know how many fighting men he had in his army so he could see the extent of his empire. He wanted to see how strong his army was so he could trust in them rather than God who said in Jer. 17:5, "Cursed is the man who trusts in man and makes flesh his strength, whose heart departs from the Lord." G. Campbell Morgan wrote, "The spirit of vainglory in numbers had taken possession of the people and the king, and there was a tendency to trust in numbers and forget God." David tells Joab to number all the soldiers in the land, from Dan in the north to Beersheba in the south (vs. 2). This is wrong! Back in 2 Sam. 22:33 he said, "God is my strength and power." Now he's is trusting in his soldiers rather than trusting God.

One thing can be said about Joab, he wasn't afraid to confront David when he thought the king was wrong. With the best interest of both David and Israel in mind, he tactfully asks David to reconsider this foolish desire to count the people. Joab said, "I hope your kingdom increases a hundredfold in your lifetime. May you live to see that day. But why would you want to do such a thing?" (vs. 3). Joab is saying it's never wise to not trust God. Ps. 33:16 says, "No king is saved by the multitude of an army; A mighty man is not delivered by great strength." Joab is saying, "You don't have to worry about how many soldiers you have. God is your strength." One of the biggest problems at this point in David's life is he was not accountable to anybody. There was nobody to counsel him against his own will and his own decisions. As good as this advice was, the king's word prevailed against Joab and the captains of the army. They then went out and spent nearly ten months counting all the soldiers in the land of Israel.

Godly leaders must be accountable to others. Godly men must be accountable to other godly men and godly women must be accountable to other godly women. This is necessary because sin is so deceiving. It looks good but it only brings pain and destruction. Other people can see what you can't see when you're blinded by fleshly desires. Once again David finds himself out of touch with God. He was given plenty of time to call off this census but he didn't do it. In pride, arrogance, and self-sufficiency he sat back and waited for the numbers to come in. Finally they did. "Then Joab gave the sum of the number of the people to the king. And there were in Israel eight hundred thousand valiant men who drew the sword, and the men of Judah were five hundred thousand men" (vs. 9). Already the country is being divided. They didn't report the total number of soldiers but instead reported the number in the northern tribes and the number in the southern tribes. This was a preview of the division that is to come.

Proud people are impressed with numbers. It matters to them how much money they make, how many cars they own, and how many people attend their church. David gets the number he asked for. Under his rule are over a million soldiers. Big deal! He could have said, "Look what God has done through me," but he didn't. Instead, he is hit with the harsh reality of what he did wrong. "And David's heart condemned him after he had numbered the people. So David said to the Lord, 'I have sinned greatly in what I have done; but now, I pray, O Lord, take away the iniquity of Your servant, for I have done very foolishly'" (vs. 10). When David laid with Bathsheba he said, "I have sinned." Here he says, "I have sinned greatly." His sin with Bathsheba was a fleshly sin, this was a sin of the spirit. The Hebrew word for "condemned" is "nakah" and it means 'to be attacked or assaulted.' It was a word used to describe a city that has been burned down and destroyed. It carries the idea of being wounded or crippled, of being in deep anguish.

God sends Gad the prophet to David and does something not seen anywhere else in scripture. He gives David a set of alternate judgments to choose from. The first choice was three years of famine which meant there would be no food and with it would come an economic meltdown. The second choice is he could spend three months being pursued by his enemies. His army would lose battle after battle and many soldiers would be killed. The third option was three days of plague where many people would get sick and die. When David sinned with Bathsheba, Nathan showed him the consequences of his sin and then he repented. Here, David confesses his sin first and then he's shown the consequences of his sin. God is not into punishing people, He's into correcting them. A big correction needs to take place as God sets out to remove the idols from David's heart, the idols of power and control. All three of these options are very bad. No matter what David chooses, the consequences are going to be horrible and devastating.

The Shepherd King

-39-

"THE NEXT IN LINE"

Pride is a horrible, horrible sin and it does two things to you. It will blind you to the source of real strength and it will deafen you to the godly counsel of good people. At this point in his life, David became a man of pride, a man who trusted in his own ability as a leader. Didn't he realize that when you serve your own sin nature, whether it be through lust or pride, that those around you will suffer also? The sins of a leader can affect an entire nation as was the case of the famine that came because Saul broke the treaty with the Gibeonites. As unfair as it may appear to be, sin often brings consequences to innocent people. The problem is most people don't realize this until it's too late. David sinned and God said to him, "Choose your own punishment." David has a choice to make but he can't do it. He knew God was merciful while also being holy and just so he says to Gad the prophet, "I am in great distress. Please let us fall into the hand of the Lord, for His mercies are great; but do not let me fall into the hand of man" (vs. 14).

David heard the judgment against him and could barely handle his feelings of overwhelming guilt and despair. The Hebrew word for "distress" means 'tied up, cramped, restricted.' What he's going through is so severe and traumatic that it feels like he's been kicked in the stomach.

David feels tied up in knots so he falls on the mercy of God for he believes God's discipline is better than man's judgment. Micah 7:18 says, "Who is a God like You, who pardons sins and forgives the transgressions of the remnant of His inheritance? You do not stay angry forever but delight to show mercy." David wants God to make the choice for him but, when he said he didn't want to fall into the hand of man, he was in fact making the choice himself. The first two choices meant he'd have to rely on the mercy of man, and he knew men were cruel. A famine meant he'd have to get food from other nations, and being pursued by his enemies meant he'd be at the mercy of those who hated him most. This meant he chose the three days of plague.

Adam Clarke wrote, "Had he chosen war, his own personal safety was in no danger because there was already an ordinance preventing him from going to battle. Had he chosen famine, his own wealth would have secured his and his own family's support. But he showed the greatness of his mind in choosing the pestilence, to the savages of which himself and his household were exposed equally with the meanest of his subjects." Sin always has consequences and as merciful as God is, the wages of sin remain death. 1 Chron. 21:7 says, "And God was displeased with this thing; therefore He struck Israel." David was their leader but God struck the entire nation. "So the Lord sent a plague upon Israel from the morning till the appointed time. From Dan to Beersheba seventy thousand men of the people died. And when the angel stretched out his hand over Jerusalem to destroy it, the Lord relented from the destruction, and said to the angel who was destroying the people, 'It is enough; now restrain your hand'" (vs. 15,16).

"And the angel of the Lord was by the threshing floor of Araunah the Jebusite" (vs. 16). For sure, angels are very powerful. One angel killed almost two hundred thousand Assyrian soldiers in 2 Kings 19:35. What happened here was like the death angel who swept through the land killing the firstborn in every Egyptian household. Seventy thousand men died because of one man's pride. David is a broken man as he sees the consequences of his arrogance and wrong decisions. Indeed, the plague accomplished its task. David assumes full responsibility for his sin. He is moved to cry out to God, begging him to remove the hand of discipline and judgment. He pleads with God, saying, "Surely I have sinned, and I have done wickedly; but these sheep, what have they done? Let Your hand, I pray, be against me and against my father's house" (vs. 17). Getting right with God comes with a price so the prophet Gad says to David, "Go up, erect an altar to the Lord on the threshing floor of Araunah the Jebusite" (vs. 18). God commands the altar of sacrifice to be built on the very spot where the plague would be halted.

God's plan is to save David from the pit of sin he's fallen into. Gad tells him to go offer a sacrifice to God and the plague will stop. The threshing floor of Araunah was up high on Mt. Moriah where the wind blows. Jerusalem is built on Mt. Moriah and this is the same place where Solomon will one day build a temple for God, the same mountain where Jesus died on the cross. David obeys and went up to the threshing floor as the Lord commanded. "Now Araunah looked, and saw the king and his servants coming toward him. So Araunah went out and bowed before the king with his face to the ground" (vs. 20). Araunah wasn't a Jew, he's a Jebusite living in Jerusalem but still he comes under David's authority. Jerusalem used to be called "Jebus" and then it was called "Salem." It later became "Jerusalem." The word "Jeru" means 'Jehovah' and "Salem" means 'peace,' thus the name of the city means "Jehovah's Peace." David tells Araunah why he has come. Araunah has a generous heart and offers to give the land and animals to David for free.

David responds, "No, but I will surely buy it from you for a price; nor will I offer burnt offerings to the Lord my God with that which costs me nothing" (vs. 24). David knows his sacrifice must cost him something. If it didn't, it wouldn't be a sacrifice. "So David bought the threshing floor and the oxen for fifty shekels of silver." Adam Clarke wrote, "Had Araunah's noble offer been accepted, it would have been Araunah's sacrifice, not David's; nor would it have answered the end of turning away the displeasure of the Most High." David didn't look for the cheapest way possible to please God. Real worship costs something. People today have replaced sacrifice with convenience. If it's not convenient, they don't worship. Adam Clarke also said, "He who has a religion that costs him nothing, has a religion that is worth nothing." David built the altar and offered burnt offerings and peace offerings. He turned his sin into an opportunity to worship God. "So the Lord heeded the prayers for the land, and the plague was withdrawn from Israel" (vs. 25).

The pages of David's final days are turning rapidly. He is old and frail and coming to the end of his life. 1 Kings 1:1 says, "Now King David was old, advanced in years; and they put covers on him, but he could not get warm." This is a sad sight. This one-time prominent warrior had fought lions and bears and giants. On the battlefield he killed his tens of thousands and not once lost a military campaign. Now here he is shivering because he can't get warm. He's only seventy years old but he had a lot of mileage on his life, a life lived with the throttle wide open. He never slowed down and his experiences have caused him to age faster than the normal person. All this is now taking its toll on him. His body is beat up and worn down as he's now confined to his bed in his sleeping quarters. David is about to die but there is still much work to be done before he does. 2 Kings 20:1 says, "Thus says the Lord: 'Set your house in order, for you shall die and not live.'" A new king had to be selected and preparations for the temple had to be made.

The fountain of life has been sapped out of David. He can't even keep himself warm let alone rule an entire nation. His declining health creates a political vacuum in the land and gives people with an agenda of their own an opportunity to rise up and seek to take the throne. David had many servants and their only concern was helping him get warm. They sought for a lovely young woman to care for him, a virgin who could lay with him so her body heat could keep David warm. Why a lovely young woman? Theologian William Poole said, "Her beauty might engage his affections, and refresh his spirits, and incite him to those embraces which might communicate some of her natural heat to him, as was designed." There was no sexual relations involved here. This was a normal, accepted procedure practiced often in Israel and Greece up to the Middle Ages. Even Eccl. 4:11 says, "If two lie down together, they will keep warm; But how can one be warm alone?'

David's servants "found Abishag the Shunammite, and brought her to the king. And the young woman was very lovely; and she cared for the king, and served him; but the king did not know her" (vs. 3,4). David's strength was impaired and his diminished ability to rule reveal the need for a successor to the throne to be found. The question is, who is the next in line to be king? Absalom's younger brother Adonijah thinks it's him so he takes it upon himself to make it happen. He exalts himself saying, "I will be king," and he prepared for himself chariots and horsemen, and fifty men to run before him (vs. 5). Absalom did the same thing. A long motorcade makes a politician look important and Adonijah is putting forth the image of being a leader, an image the people are going to like. David's three oldest sons are dead and Adonijah considers himself the next in line for the throne. Like Absalom, he also was a very good-looking man and in the eyes of the people he's next in line to be king.

Unfortunately, Joab and Abiathar the priest followed him (vs. 7).

It seems like everybody is trying to take David off the throne. Why is Adonijah doing this now? A clue is given in vs. 6 where it says David had not rebuked him one time as he was growing up. David was too busy running the nation to train his children. Boundaries were never set and David allowed them to do whatever they wanted to do. This set the stage for the rebellion that is now taking place. Adonijah has never been restrained and this created a prideful selfishness that says, "It's all about me." He now thinks he can become king because David never stopped him from doing anything in the past. He's proclaiming himself to be the new king not realizing that God had already determined who the next king will be. Ps. 75:6,7 says, "For exaltation comes neither from the east nor the west nor from the south. But God is the Judge: He puts down one, and exalts another." David also knows who the next king will be but there's confusion and conflict in the kingdom because he hasn't made known who's going to rule after him.

David is sick and he's dying but he still must take the lead and give direction as to who the next king will be. Is it going to be Solomon who God said will be the next king, or will it be Adonijah who has picked himself to be king? David must be clear about the plan and direction God has for the nation. Prov. 29:18 says, "Where there is no revelation, the people cast off restraint." Without godly leadership and direction there will be confusion, discord, and conflict. As David is preoccupied trying to keep warm, Adonijah proclaims himself the new king and throws a banquet in celebration of his conquest. Invited to the feast were all the king's sons, all the men of Judah, and all the king's servants (vs. 9). It is sad to see these once trusted associates of David turning against him late in his life. The truth is, they were doing what was best for themselves without seeking the will of God.

Thankfully, some prominent people remained loyal to David. Among them were Nathan the prophet, Benaiah the warrior, the mighty men, and his son Solomon.

Nathan, the same man who confronted David over his sin with Bathsheba, has seen enough. David doesn't know what's happening so Nathan informs Bathsheba of what Adonijah is doing. He says to her, "Come, please, let me now give you counsel, that you may save your own life and the life of your son Solomon" (vs. 12). What he's saying is that in order for Adonijah's throne to be established, he must eliminate all those who would oppose him. Nathan understands this so he goes and tells Bathsheba to do something about what Adonijah is doing. If she doesn't, both she and her son Solomon will be killed. He tells her to immediately go to King David and then tells her what to say. He will come in afterward and confirm everything Bathsheba said. Nathan was fully aware of the law of witnesses as stated in Deut. 29:15, "One witness shall not rise against a man concerning any iniquity or any sin that he commits; by the mouth of two or three witnesses the matter shall be established."

As David is being ministered to by Abishag the Shunammite, Bathsheba comes in and bows down and pays homage to the king. She knew he was worthy of special honor and respect and she gives it to him openly and willingly. David said to her, "What is your wish?" (vs. 16). He knew she wanted something. Why else would she be there? She then reminds David of an oath he made a long time ago. "My lord, you swore by the Lord your God to your maidservant, saying, 'Assuredly Solomon your son shall reign after me, and he shall sit on my throne'" (vs. 17). David making this specific promise to Bathsheba is not recorded in scripture but 1 Chron. 22:5-9 shows that David intended for Solomon to succeed him as king. She continues, "So now, look! Adonijah has become king; and now, my lord the king, you do not know about it" (vs. 18). This shows how far from reality David was. He didn't know what was going on in his kingdom. Adonijah has not been anointed to be king, but he publicly claims he is the new king.

Bathsheba has David's full attention as she frantically says to him, "Don't you realize what's happening out there? While you're laying in bed dying, Adonijah has made himself king! You've got to do something about this! You must communicate clearly what God's will is." She then tells of Adonijah's feast that is going on even as she speaks. "He has sacrificed oxen and fattened cattle and sheep in abundance, and has invited all the sons of the king, Abiathar the priest, and Joab the commander of the army; but Solomon your servant he has not invited" (vs. 19). The reason Adonijah was very selective about who he invited to the feast is because he knows he's doing something he shouldn't be doing. He's acting spiritual by sacrificing all these animals in an effort to make the people think his authority to be king came from God. Bathsheba tells David that all of Israel is looking to him to tell them who the next in line to the throne will be (vs. 20). What's needed now is for David to step up and take charge over this situation.

The people are in confusion and everyone is looking to David for direction. If he doesn't do something right now, Bathsheba says to him, "Otherwise it will happen, when my lord the king rests with his fathers, that I and my son Solomon will be counted as offenders" (vs. 21). In other words, they'll both be killed. It was at this moment that Nathan the prophet comes in. As Bathsheba leaves the room, Nathan bowed down before the king with his face to the ground. He then asks David, "My lord, O king, have you said, 'Adonijah shall reign after me, and he shall sit on the throne'?" (vs. 24). Nathan knew it was God's will for Solomon to be the next king (2 Sam. 12:24,25). He's saying to David, "I'm confused. Did you say Adonijah will be the next king?

Did you change your mind?" He repeats the words of Bathsheba by telling of the feast that is going on. He tells David, "They are eating and drinking before him; and they say, 'Long live King Adonijah!'" (vs. 25). He then tells how those loyal to David were not invited to this feast.

Nathan asks a second time, "Has this thing been done by my lord the king, and you have not told your servant who should sit on the throne of my lord the king after him?" (vs. 27). David is old and he's sick. Nathan asks him, "Did you do this, David? Is it possible you have chosen Adonijah to be king? Did you do this without telling me?" David has heard enough. He now has to make a decision that will affect the entire nation, both now and forevermore. Thankfully, he did not run away this time like he did with Absalom. He calls for Bathsheba and assures her that Solomon will be the next king. Taking an oath, he says to her, "As the Lord lives, who has redeemed my life from every distress, just as I swore to you by the Lord God of Israel, saying, 'Assuredly Solomon your son shall be king after me, and he shall sit on my throne in my place,' so I certainly will do this day" (vs. 30). This was music to the ears of Bathsheba. She bowed her face to the earth and paid homage to the king saying, "Let my lord King David live forever" (vs. 31).

What David told Bathsheba was unprecedented, saying Solomon will be made king today. Normally you wait for the king to die and then somebody else becomes king. Not this time. David is in bed sick but still he's going to communicate clearly to the people the will of God. He calls for Zadok the priest, Nathan the prophet, and Benaiah the son of Jehoiada, telling them that Solomon is to be anointed as the new king. Here is a rare glimpse of all three spiritual offices working together. The king ruled over the nation, the priest represented the people to God, and the prophet represented God to the people. Added to this threesome was Benaiah, a fighting warrior who replaced Joab as commander of the king's army. These three men came before David and he says to them, "Take with you the servants of your lord, and have Solomon my son ride on my own mule, and take him down to Gihon" (vs. 33). This is a big deal. Mules were imported and were very expensive. Common people rode donkeys while mules were reserved for royalty. To sit on the king's mule is to say, "I'm the king."

David wants Solomon to be taken to Gihon, a spring just outside the city in the Kidron Valley. It was Jerusalem's major source of water and was a place where many people were gathered. David continues his instructions, "There let Zadok the priest and Nathan the prophet anoint him king over Israel; and blow the horn, and say, 'Long live King Solomon!' Then you shall come up after him, and he shall come and sit on my throne. and he shall be king in my place. For I have appointed him to be ruler over Israel and Judah" (vs. 34,35). Clearly, David wants the matter settled now. He takes away any chance that Adonijah might have to be king. The warrior Benaiah rises up and says, "Amen! May the Lord God of my lord the king say so too" (vs. 36). The word "Amen" means 'truth.' Benaiah is saying, "This is truth! So be it." He continues, "As the Lord has been with my lord the king, even so may he be with Solomon, and make his throne greater than the throne of my lord King David" (vs. 37). Solomon was then taken to Gihon.

History will now be made. "Then Zadok the priest took a horn of oil from the tabernacle and anointed Solomon. And they blew the horn, and all the people said, 'Long live King Solomon!'" (vs. 39). The anointing oil was symbolic of the Holy Spirit coming upon a person. Solomon is in his early twenties and, as the oil drips off his head, he becomes the new king of Israel. "And all the people went up after him; and the people played the flutes and rejoiced with great joy, so that the earth split with their sound" (vs. 39,40). The Message Bible says, "Everyone joined the fanfare, the band playing and the people singing, the very earth reverberating to the sound." Half a mile away, Adonijah and his guests were nearly finished eating their banquet meal. They were too consumed with themselves to realize that the will of God was being fulfilled just a short distance away. Joab heard the horn being blown and asked, "Why is the city in such a noisy uproar?" (vs. 41).

Jonathan, the son of Abiathar the priest, comes in and tells everybody what happened. He says the city is in an uproar because David just made Solomon king. It is he who sits on the throne of the kingdom, not Adonijah. He also tells of David's response to his wishes being carried out. "Then the king bowed himself on the bed. Also the king said thus, 'Blessed be the Lord God of Israel, who has given one to sit on my throne this day, while my eyes see it!'" (vs. 47,48). In other words, Adonijah, the party is over. He made himself king but David made Solomon king. That's a big difference. There is panic at the feast of Adonijah. His guests are no longer loyal to him for they know they'll be in danger if they continue to support him as king. "Then all the guests who were with Adonijah were afraid and arose, and each one went their way" (vs. 49). These men were traitors. They only had one fate and that was death. These guests were not the only ones who felt this way. Adonijah was also afraid.

"Now Adonijah was afraid of Solomon; so he arose, and went and took hold of the horns of the altar, saying, 'Let King Solomon swear to me today that he will not put his servant to death with the sword'" (vs. 50,51). Adonijah is pleading for mercy. There were horn-like projections at the four corners of the brazen altar of burnt offerings (Ex. 27:2). This was a place of refuge for fugitives. Those who caught hold of the horns of the altar were granted asylum. However, in Ex. 21:14 people were pulled from the altar because they sinned and were killed. This was not as safe a place as Adonijah thought it was. Solomon gives his response to Adonijah's plea, "If he proves himself a worthy man, not one hair of his shall fall to the earth; but if wickedness is found in him, he shall die" (vs. 52). Solomon doesn't promise him anything but vows that the law of sowing and reaping would rule supreme. Adonijah is brought before Solomon and bows before him. Solomon says, "Go to your house" (vs. 53). In other words, "I'll deal with you another day."

Randall J. Brewer

-40-

"GOING OUT IN STYLE"

David knows his days are numbered as he gathers all the leaders of Israel together at Jerusalem so he can give them his last will and testament. Through an end-of-life perspective, David looks back on his life as he delivers a message about priorities, a message about putting God's will above their own. Imagine David as he rose to his feet. Before him are thousands of faithful friends and supporters, among them Solomon and all the mighty men of valor. They are shocked at how weak and frail he looks. They realize he won't be with them much longer. They ask themselves, "What's he going to say? What's going to happen?" They look at the young and inexperienced Solomon standing by his side and wonder, "Does he have what it takes to be king?" They watch as David reaches inside for all the strength he can muster up as he stands in dignity before them one last time. He begins to share with the people as he points them to the future and seeks to direct their thoughts to God and His plan for their lives.

David begins by telling the people of the greatest disappointment of his life, a dream that went unfulfilled. "Hear me, my brethren and my people: I had it in my heart to build a house of rest for the ark of the covenant of the Lord, and for the footstool of our God, and had made preparations to build it. But God said to me, 'You shall not build a house for My name, because you have been a man of war and have shed blood'" (1 Chron. 28:2,3). In order to fulfill God's will for your life, you must first be willing to crucify your own will. You must be willing to say to God, "Not my will but Your will be done." It is crucial that you do this because it's your will that drives and controls your flesh. It's your flesh that takes you out of God's plan for your life. It's when you want what you want more than what God wants. Prov. 19:21 (NIV) says, "Many are the plans in a person's heart, but it is the Lord's purpose that prevails." The Message Bible says, "We humans keep brainstorming options and plans, but God's purpose prevails."

God's not here to support your plan, you're here to fulfill His plan. Ignore the song that says "I did it my way" for that is pride in full manifestation. Instead, live in such a way so that at the end of your life you can say, "Lord, I did what You told me to do." David couldn't build the temple but God still had a plan for his life. He made David king over all of Israel. He was God's representative who ruled the people as a servant of the Lord. David's reign as king is now over and he knows it is God's will for Solomon to be the new king. So doubt would not prevail, David tells the people what the will of God is for their new king. "Now He said to me, 'It is your son Solomon who shall build My house and My courts; for I have chosen him to be My son, and I will be his Father'" (vs. 6). David wanted to build God a temple but God said Solomon would build it instead. Knowing this, David turned to Solomon and says to him, "I go the way of all the earth; be strong, therefore, and prove yourself a man" (1 Kings 2:2).

David knew he was dying so he "charged" his son to be a man of great character (1 Kings 2:1). The word "charged" is a military word and means 'commanded.' In the military you do what you're told, no questions asked. David had been a warrior all his life and this was not a casual chat between father and son. No, this is an order from a man who's been king for forty years. Great responsibilities require great strength and courage. This is why you must live by God's Word and God's power. Eph. 6:10 says, "Be strong in the Lord and in the power of His might." How do you prove yourself a man? Become like Jesus and be willing to stand up for truth and what is right. You must defend the faith at all times. David knew Solomon would face some difficult times so he needed to be a strong, mature man of God. Solomon was never described as a tough guy. His name means "peace" and David is saying, "I know you're a man of peace but you're going to have to be tough." The Message Bible says, "Show what you're made of."

David is telling Solomon what he needs to do in order to be a successful king. Most leaders don't think about what's going to happen once they're gone, the day they're no longer here. It's no secret that people are like flowers in the wind who are quickly fading away. They're here today, gone tomorrow. It will do you well to get on your knees and say, "Lord, teach me the brevity of human life. Teach me to live for eternity." Whether you realize it or not, you always leave something behind when you pass on to the other side. It's called a legacy. David's legacy is represented by Solomon who was a man of peace. God needs warriors but it's the peacemakers who build the temple. David calls on Solomon to continue the legacy God called him to. He says in 1 Chron. 28:9, "As for you, my son Solomon, know the God of your father, and serve Him with a loyal heart, and with a willing mind; for the Lord searches all hearts and understands all the intent of the thoughts. If you seek Him, he will be found by you; but if you forsake Him, He will cut you off forever."

David was a man after God's own heart and he wants Solomon to be the same way. This is why he doesn't give him any practical advice about how to rule the nation. Instead, he tells him to know God, serve God, and seek God. Get personal and intimate with Him, experience His grace and mercy. Seek His face and not His hand. David next gives his son a great exhortation, "Consider now, for the Lord has chosen you to build a house for the sanctuary; be strong and do it" (vs. 9). He's saying, "Son, God has a specific call on your life for which there can be no retreat and no surrender. Be strong and fulfill your call! Do it!" David had already defeated all the nation's enemies and there is peace in the land so Solomon can build the temple. He gives his final charge to Solomon in vs. 20, "Be strong and of good courage, and do it; do not fear nor be dismayed, for the Lord God - my God - will be with you. He will not leave you nor forsake you until you have finished all the work for the service of the house of the Lord."

David knew there was nothing more important than the building of the temple for God. He couldn't build it but he did have the plans drawn up for it, plus he provided all the material needed for the temple to be built. He also knew that in order for Solomon to fulfill his calling, his kingdom would have to be established by eliminating all his enemies. David then tells Solomon about some unfinished business from the past that needs to be dealt with. He begins by talking about that bloody scoundrel Joab who had been a thorn in David's side for a long time. At times he was fiercely loyal to David but he was not an obedient and godly man. He was a skilled warrior but was very evil, having killed two innocent men in peacetime. David tells Solomon, "Therefore, do according to your wisdom, and do not let his gray hair go down to the grave in peace" (1 Kings 2:6). David next tells Solomon to bless the sons of Barzillai and allow them to eat at the king's table just like Mephibosheth ate at his (vs. 7).

The third person David talks to Solomon about is Shimei, the rebellious, loud-mouthed man who cursed David and threw stones at him. David had spared his life but the man did not inwardly change. He said he was sorry but did he really mean it? Some people you're not sure about and you'll need wisdom and discernment to deal with them. David tells Solomon, "Now therefore, do not hold him guiltless, for you are a wise man and know what you ought to do to him; but bring his gray hair down to the grave with blood" (vs. 9). Confident that Solomon would obey the commands given him, David knew his son's kingdom would be firmly established and the temple would indeed be built. He turns to the people and says to all the congregation, "My son Solomon, whom alone God has chosen, is young and inexperienced; and the work is great, because the temple is not for man but for the Lord God" (1 Chron. 29:1). The work is great because before a great God there are no small works. Everything should be done for the glory of God.

Everybody has a purpose to fulfill. What a tragedy it is to live your life and never discover the reason you are here. Mark Twain once said, "The two most important days in a person's life are the day they are born and the day they discover why." David figured out why he was born and said in vs. 3, "Moreover, because I have set my affections on the house of my God, I have given to the house of my God, over and above all that I have prepared for the holy house, my own personal treasure of gold and silver." David understood and fulfilled his destiny. Truly, there's never been a man like David who was unlike any king in history. As king, one of the first things David did was bring the ark to Jerusalem. This was not a religious relic; it represented the power and presence of God. Being in the presence of God must be the top priority of your life for He is looking for people who are hungry and thirsty for Him. This is why Paul said in Col. 3:2, "Set your mind on things above, not on things on the earth."

David asks the people in vs. 5, "Who then is willing to consecrate himself this day to the Lord?" David gave a massive amount toward the building of the temple and he asks the people if they'll give also. He's saying don't give God a part of yourself, give Him all of you. Give Him all your heart, your soul, your strength, and your resources. "For where your treasure is, there your heart will be also" (Matt. 6:21). In the kingdom of God there is always a part you have to play. God makes the wind blow but you have to raise your sails. He makes the plants grow but you need to plant the seeds in the ground. The people responded to David's invitation and freely gave also. "Then the people rejoiced, for they had offered willingly to the Lord; and King David also rejoiced greatly" (vs. 9). The generous giving of the people showed David that they also had a heart for God. He knew you can give money to God without giving of yourself, but you can never give of yourself without giving your money also.

David is so joyful that he blessed the Lord before all the congregation. "Blessed are You, Lord God of Israel, our Father, forever and ever" (vs. 10). This is the first time in scripture that God is addressed as a Father over the people. "Yours, O Lord, is the greatness, the power and the glory, the victory and the majesty; For all that is in heaven and in earth is Yours; Yours is the kingdom, O Lord, and You are exalted as head over all" (vs. 11). It is very possible that Jesus had these words in mind when He taught the disciples how to pray. He told them to begin by saying, "Our Father" (Matt. 6:9) and He concludes the Lord's Prayer saying, "For thine is the kingdom" (Matt. 6:13). David is at the end of his life and he's going out in style. He's finishing his life the same way he started it, with a heart for God. He gives all the glory and honor to Him and then acknowledges that all things come from God. "O Lord our God, all this abundance that we have prepared to build You a house for Your holy name is from Your hand, and all is Your own" (vs. 16).

David commits the offering received from the people unto God and then prays that the hearts of the people would forever seek after God. He concludes his prayer of thanksgiving praying for his son Solomon. "And give my son Solomon a loyal heart to keep Your commandments and Your testimonies and Your statutes, to do all these things, and to build the temple for which I have made provision" (vs.

19). David is doing everything he can to ensure that the next generation seeks and follows after God. The youth of today represent a portion of the population but they represent one hundred percent of the future. This is why 3 John 4 says, "I have no greater joy than to hear that my children walk in truth." David then leads all the people in praise to God. "So all the congregation blessed the Lord God of their fathers, and bowed their heads and prostrated themselves before the Lord and the king" (vs. 20). What a glorious sight this must have been. It very well could have been the greatest day in David's life.

The next day thousands of animals were sacrificed to the Lord in abundance for all Israel. The people then rejoiced exceedingly as Solomon is enthroned as king. "So they ate and drank before the Lord with great gladness on that day. And they made Solomon the son of David king the second time, and anointed him before the Lord to be the leader, and Zadok to be priest" (vs. 22). The first time it was done suddenly and hastily because of Adonijah's claim that he was the new king. This time it was done earnestly in an impressive ceremony as the people gave Solomon his just due, the respect and honor befitting a new king. "Then Solomon sat on the throne of the Lord as king instead of David his father, and prospered; and all Israel obeyed him. All the leaders and the mighty men, and also all the sons of King David, submitted themselves to King Solomon. So the Lord exalted Solomon exceedingly in the sight of all Israel, and bestowed on him such royal majesty as had not been on any king before him in Israel" (vs. 23-25).

There was nothing left for David to do but go home to the God he so deeply loved. "So he died in a good old age, full of days and riches and honor; and Solomon his son reigned in his place" (vs. 28). So ended the earthly life of one of the greatest men to ever walk the planet. Adam Clarke wrote, "He has had few equals, and no superior, from his own time to the present day." 1 Kings 2:10 says, "So David rested with his fathers, and was buried in the City of David." It cannot be denied that David failed God probably more than anybody else. However, the legacy he left behind is that he loved God more than anybody else. He was a man after God's own heart and this made him a very great man. Yes, he got knocked down many times but he always got back up. He always responded to the grace of God as he continually sought to be in His presence. Bible commentator John Trapp wrote, "He swam to the throne through a sea of sorrows; and so must all saints to the kingdom of heaven."

The story of David would not be complete unless one sees what Solomon did after his father passed on to the other side. Thankfully, Solomon had something David never had, a father who believed in him. David's father sent him into the fields to attend sheep and then forgot about him. Not David. He counseled his son and made it very clear what Solomon was to do. He had to first establish his kingdom by eliminating all his enemies. Because of what David told him, Solomon knew who those enemies were. The first person to be dealt with is his half-brother Adonijah who still wants to weasel his way past Solomon to the throne. He is suffering from delusions of grandeur, thinking he has widespread support from the people. In reality, only a handful of malcontents supported him who, by the way, quickly deserted him when it was made known that David favored Solomon. He thinks he's more popular than Solomon so he goes to Bathsheba and requests that she ask Solomon if he can marry Abishag, the nurse assigned to David to keep him warm.

In all likelihood, Abishag became one of David's concubines even though they never had physical relations with one another. All that belonged to David went to Solomon who is the new king. Abishag now belongs to Solomon and Adonijah wants her. By asking for her, Adonijah is asking for the king's property which will give him the right to be king. Solomon is a wise person and he sees right through what Adonijah is trying to do so he acts quickly. "So King Solomon sent by the hand of Benaiah the son of Jehoiada: and he struck him down, and he died" (1 Kings 2:25). Next to be dealt with is Abiathar, the priest who followed Adonijah in his quest to be king. Solomon tells him he is worthy of death for committing treason against both God and David. He gives him mercy instead because of his past standing as a high priest and his one-time support of David. Solomon tells him he can no longer be a priest and he must now work in his own fields to support himself. Not being able to serve the Lord is a punishment worse than death.

Next in line to be dealt with is Joab. Solomon is cleaning house and Joab knows it. He imitates Adonijah's attempt to find refuge by taking hold of the horns of the altar. Charles Spurgeon wrote, "He was a rough man of war, and cared little enough about God, or the tabernacle, or the priests, or the altar, but when he was in danger, he fled to that which he had avoided, and sought to make a refuge of that which he had neglected." Joab is told to come out away from the altar and he answers, "No, I will die here" (1 Kings 2:30). Since Joab refused to leave, Solomon had him executed right there at the altar (vs. 34). Finally, Shimei is dealt with. He was shown mercy and was told he was being confined to Jerusalem. Solomon said, "If you leave the city, I will kill you." Three years later he did leave the city in search of some runaway slaves. When he returned to the city, judgment was waiting for him. At the king's command, Benaiah "went out and struck him down, and he died" (vs. 46).

An old proverb says a tree is best measured when it is down. Not until a person passes on can one adequately measure the length of their significance on the earth, the breadth of their impact on the lives of others, and the depth of their character before God and man. Without a doubt, the legacy of David will live on forever. Left behind in his wake is a spiritual inheritance that all people can use to experience the grace of God on a daily basis. The lasting influence of David's life began as a shepherd boy in the fields outside Bethlehem. He was faithful over little things and God made him ruler over an entire nation. Since the moment when Samuel poured the anointing oil on his head, David had a sense of clarity about what God was going to do in his life. He was just a humble shepherd boy but he had a heart that was right toward God. And it was his heart that made him the perfect candidate to be the next king of Israel. You learn from David's early days that God doesn't call the qualified, He qualifies those He calls.

In his younger days, whoever looked at David saw a smooth-skinned shepherd boy. What they didn't see was his war-like confidence in God that caused him to step out and do things other people were not willing to do. He was willing to face a lion and a bear who attacked his father's sheep and he refused to back down from Goliath. He had confidence in God because God had always been faithful to him in the past. It's those past experiences that God uses to promote you into your divine purpose. David was also a worshiper of God. He was a singer, the sweet psalmist of Israel, and he wrote many songs of praise and worship to his God. He was also a statesman, a leader among the people who unified the divided nation. He gave Israel its capital city of Jerusalem and there he brought the Ark of the Covenant. He built a massive military force with which they subdued all their enemies. He expanded their borders, established a flourishing economy and, most of all, turned the hearts of the people to the Lord their God.

David was many things in his life. He was a shepherd, a soldier, an outlaw, a king, a fugitive, a sinner, a saint, a poet. In all these roles are lessons one can learn to live a godly life. First and foremost, one learns from the life of David the importance of seeking to know God and to follow His will. Ps. 112:1 (NLT) says, "Praise the Lord! How joyful are those who fear the Lord and delight in obeying His commands." David wasn't perfect but he was quick to repent when he fell. Don't be too prideful to admit that you've failed, that you missed the mark. At the same time, be quick to give grace to others when they fall. Forgive quickly and hold no grudges. Don't die with bitterness in your heart and don't pass on a legacy of hate. Walk in love instead and be compassionate. Ps. 112:4,6 (NLT) says, "Light shines in the darkness for the godly. They are generous, compassionate, and righteous. Such people will not be overcome by evil. Those who are righteous are long remembered."

Another lesson to learn from David's life is that you need to surround yourself with godly people. Your crew determines your view so be careful who you let into your inner circle. 1 Cor. 15:33 says, "Do not be deceived. Evil company corrupts good habits." The NLT says, "Bad company corrupts good character." Who you hang around with can and will affect your destiny. David left a lasting legacy and you can too. Realize that your legacy don't start the day you die, it starts today. If you're not dead, you're not done so pour all you know and have into others. Become a mentor to someone. Somebody needs what you have so give it to them. There's a leadership vacuum in the world today so allow God to use you to fill that void. You've only got one life to live so give it all you've got. Stop living in your easy chair watching television all day. Wake up! Do something! Don't put it off until tomorrow. So what if you've had a rough life. Who on this planet hasn't? You can't change the past but you can definitely change the future.

Randall J. Brewer

The Shepherd King